WE CARE

WE CARE

A Preschool Curriculum
for Children Ages 2–5

Bertie W. Kingore & Glenda M. Higbee

Scott, Foresman and Company
Glenview, Illinois   London

 Good Year Books

are available for preschool through grade 12 and
for every basic curriculum subject plus many
enrichment areas. For more Good Year Books,
contact your local bookseller or educational dealer.
For a complete catalog with information about other
Good Year Books, please write:

Good Year Books
Department GYB
1900 East Lake Avenue
Glenview, Illinois 60025

DEDICATED TO:

Wonderful husbands who help us to be all we can be;
Enthusiastic sons and daughter who knew we could do it;

Caring parents who nurtured us as children and adults;
All the teachers and children at Pioneer Drive Child Development Center;
Rewarding feelings which result from creating;
Educators of young children everywhere.

Preface

WHY WE CARE

Parents entrust to us for caring and nurturing a most cherished part of themselves—their children. But children of preschool age are capable of more than mere playtime and naptime. Children two through five *can* learn and begin to function in group situations. This book is dedicated to helping the teacher create a delightful learning environment for preschool children.

WE CARE provides a well-balanced curriculum in an easy-to-follow organizational format. Written in a simple, clear style, the text allows teachers to readily use the *hundreds* of monthly ideas and activities.

All of the fingerplays and songs are adaptations created by the authors. You are encouraged to take these and other traditional fingerplays and songs and adapt them to meet the unique needs of the children in your group.

There are many curriculum books for young children on the market. But since most of those books are really targeted at kindergartens, teachers of two, three, four and five-year olds find those activities inappropriate and ineffective for their classes. WE CARE has been proven to have effective content for two through five-year olds. As one teacher of two-year olds told us: ''I was so surprised! My kids could really do those activities!''

We encourage teachers to be creative. Adapt the activities and add your personal touch to our suggested methods. In your hands, this book can be a tool to enrich each child's educational opportunities. And WE CARE may become the most often-used book in your school's collection!

For their helpful comments during various stages of the book's development, the authors would like to thank Susan B. Cruickshank and Barbara P. Owens.

Table of Contents

INTRODUCTION   1

Organization of the Book   1

Beliefs Incorporated Throughout the Book   2

A Calendar for Communication and Organization   3
    Sample Calendar   4
    Blank Calendar for Duplicating   5

Art Recipes   6
    Art Bread Dough   6
    Ceramic Dough   6
    Egg Dye   6
    Finger Paint   6
    Glistening Squeeze Bottle Painting   7
    Hanging Soap Balls   7
    Modeling Goop   7
    Play Dough   7
    Sparkle Paint Recipe   8
    Transfer Art Mixture   8
    Whipped Snow Recipe   8

SEPTEMBER CURRICULUM   9

Discovering Me   10

    CONCEPTS   10
    ART   10
    BLOCKS   13
    BULLETIN BOARD   13
    COOKING   14
    LANGUAGE ARTS   15
    MATH   17
      Number Concepts   17
      Math Vocabulary   18
    MOVEMENT   18
    MUSIC   19
    ROLE PLAY   20
    SCIENCE   20

Families   23

CONCEPTS   23
ART   23
BLOCKS   25
BULLETIN BOARD   25
COOKING   26
LANGUAGE ARTS   26
MATH   29
  Number Concepts   29
  Math Vocabulary   30
MOVEMENT   30
MUSIC   30
ROLE PLAY   31
SCIENCE   31

Where I Live   33

CONCEPTS   33
ART   33
BLOCKS   36
BULLETIN BOARD   36
COOKING   36
LANGUAGE ARTS   37
MATH   41
  Number Concepts   41
  Math Vocabulary   42
MOVEMENT   42
MUSIC   43
ROLE PLAY   43
SCIENCE   44

OCTOBER CURRICULUM   47

Fire Prevention and Safety at Home and School   48

CONCEPTS   48
ART   48
BLOCKS   50
BULLETIN BOARD   50
COOKING   51
LANGUAGE ARTS   51
MATH   54
  Number Concepts   54
  Math Vocabulary   54
MOVEMENT   54
MUSIC   55

ROLE PLAY   55
SCIENCE   56

People Who Work   57

CONCEPTS   57
ART   57
BLOCKS   61
BULLETIN BOARD   61
COOKING   62
LANGUAGE ARTS   63
MATH   65
  Number Concepts   65
  Math Vocabulary   66
MOVEMENT   67
MUSIC   67
ROLE PLAY   68
SCIENCE   69

Fall Changes   73

CONCEPTS   73
ART   73
BLOCKS   76
BULLETIN BOARD   76
COOKING   76
LANGUAGE ARTS   77
MATH   80
  Number Concepts   80
  Size Relationships   80
  Math Vocabulary   81
MOVEMENT   81
MUSIC   82
ROLE PLAY   82
SCIENCE   82

Fun and Safety At Halloween   85

CONCEPTS   85
ART   85
BLOCKS   89
BULLETIN BOARD   89
COOKING   91
LANGUAGE ARTS   92
MATH   95
  Counting and Numeral Recognition   95
  Math Vocabulary   97

MOVEMENT   97
MUSIC   98
ROLE PLAY   99
SCIENCE   100

NOVEMBER CURRICULUM   103

Shapes and Sizes   104

CONCEPTS   104
ART   104
BLOCKS   108
BULLETIN BOARD   108
COOKING   109
LANGUAGE ARTS   110
MATH   115
  Number Concepts   115
  Math Vocabulary   118
MOVEMENT   118
MUSIC   119
SCIENCE   120

Shopping   121

CONCEPTS   121
ART   121
BLOCKS   123
BULLETIN BOARD   123
COOKING   124
LANGUAGE ARTS   125
MATH   128
  Number Concepts   128
  Math Vocabulary   128
  Size Relationships   128
MOVEMENT   129
MUSIC   129
ROLE PLAY   130
SCIENCE   131

Thanksgiving and Life in Early America   132

CONCEPTS   132
ART   132
BLOCKS   136
BULLETIN BOARD   136
COOKING   137
LANGUAGE ARTS   138

MATH   142
  Number Concepts   142
  Shape Concepts   143
MOVEMENT   143
MUSIC   145
ROLE PLAY   145
SCIENCE   146

DECEMBER CURRICULUM   149

Celebrations Around the World   150

CONCEPTS   150
ART   150
BLOCKS   153
BULLETIN BOARD   153
COOKING   154
LANGUAGE ARTS   156
MATH   159
  Number Concepts   159
  Math Vocabulary   160
MOVEMENT   160
MUSIC   162
ROLE PLAY   162
SCIENCE   163

Christmas   168

CONCEPTS   168
ART   168
BLOCKS   173
BULLETIN BOARD   173
COOKING   174
LANGUAGE ARTS   175
MATH   179
  Number Concepts   179
  Math Vocabulary   179
MOVEMENT   181
MUSIC   182
ROLE PLAY   183
SCIENCE   184

Toys   185

CONCEPTS   185
ART   185
BLOCKS   188

BULLETIN BOARD   188
COOKING   189
LANGUAGE ARTS   189
MATH   193
  Number Concepts   193
  Math Vocabulary   193
MOVEMENT   194
MUSIC   195
ROLE PLAY   196
SCIENCE   196

JANUARY CURRICULUM   197

Life in Winter   198

CONCEPTS   198
ART   198
BLOCKS   203
BULLETIN BOARD   203
COOKING   203
LANGUAGE ARTS   204
MATH   207
  Number Concepts   207
  Math Vocabulary   207
MOVEMENT   208
MUSIC   209
ROLE PLAY   209
SCIENCE   209

Dinosaurs   215

CONCEPTS   215
ART   215
BLOCKS   218
BULLETIN BOARD   218
COOKING   218
LANGUAGE ARTS   220
MATH   223
  Number Concepts   223
  Math Vocabulary   223
MOVEMENT   224
MUSIC   224
ROLE PLAY   225
SCIENCE   225

Five Senses 230

CONCEPTS 230
ART 230
BLOCKS 234
BULLETIN BOARD 234
COOKING 234
LANGUAGE ARTS 235
MATH 239
  Number Concepts 239
  Math Vocabulary 240
MOVEMENT 240
MUSIC 241
ROLE PLAY 242
SCIENCE 243

FEBRUARY CURRICULUM 245

Health and Nutrition 246

CONCEPTS 246
ART 246
BLOCKS 249
BULLETIN BOARD 249
COOKING 250
LANGUAGE ARTS 251
MATH 255
  Number Concepts 255
  Math Vocabulary 256
MOVEMENT 257
MUSIC 258
ROLE PLAY 258
SCIENCE 259

Valentines 260

CONCEPTS 260
ART 260
BLOCKS 263
BULLETIN BOARD 263
COOKING 264
LANGUAGE ARTS 265
MATH 268
  Number Concepts 268
  Math Vocabulary 269
MOVEMENT 269
MUSIC 269

ROLE PLAY   270
SCIENCE   271

Famous People and Birthdays   272

CONCEPTS   272
ART   272
BLOCKS   275
BULLETIN BOARD   275
COOKING   276
LANGUAGE ARTS   277
MATH   280
  Number Concepts   280
  Math Vocabulary   280
MOVEMENT   281
MUSIC   281
ROLE PLAY   282
SCIENCE   282

Care of Pets   285

CONCEPTS   285
ART   285
BLOCKS   290
BULLETIN BOARD   290
COOKING   290
LANGUAGE ARTS   291
MATH   294
  Number Concepts   294
  Measurement   294
  Counting   295
  Math Vocabulary   295
MOVEMENT   295
MUSIC   296
ROLE PLAY   297
SCIENCE   297

MARCH CURRICULUM   299

Ways We Travel   300

CONCEPTS   300
ART   300
BLOCKS   304
BULLETIN BOARD   305
COOKING   305
LANGUAGE ARTS   307

MATH   312
   Number Concepts   312
   Math Vocabulary   313
MOVEMENT   313
MUSIC   314
ROLE PLAY   315
SCIENCE   316

Communication   318

CONCEPTS   318
ART   318
BLOCKS   320
BULLETIN BOARD   320
COOKING   321
LANGUAGE ARTS   321
MATH   325
   Number Concepts   325
   Math Vocabulary   326
MOVEMENT   326
MUSIC   327
ROLE PLAY   327
SCIENCE   328

Feet   329

CONCEPTS   329
ART   329
BLOCKS   332
BULLETIN BOARD   332
COOKING   333
LANGUAGE ARTS   333
MATH   336
   Number Concepts   336
   Measurement   337
   Math Vocabulary   337
MOVEMENT   337
MUSIC   338
ROLE PLAY   339
SCIENCE   339

APRIL CURRICULUM   341

Easter   342

CONCEPTS   342
ART   342

BLOCKS   346
BULLETIN BOARD   346
COOKING   346
LANGUAGE ARTS   347
MATH   351
  Number Concepts   351
  Math Vocabulary   351
MOVEMENT   352
MUSIC   352
ROLE PLAY   353
SCIENCE   354

Color   355

CONCEPTS   355
ART   355
BLOCKS   358
BULLETIN BOARD   358
COOKING   358
LANGUAGE ARTS   359
MATH   362
  Number Concepts   362
  Math Vocabulary   363
MOVEMENT   363
MUSIC   364
SCIENCE   365

Spring and Growing Things   367

CONCEPTS   367
ART   367
BLOCKS   371
BULLETIN BOARD   372
COOKING   372
LANGUAGE ARTS   373
MATH   376
  Number Concepts   376
MOVEMENT   377
MUSIC   377
ROLE PLAY   378
SCIENCE   379

Wild West   385

CONCEPTS   385
ART   385
BLOCKS   388

BULLETIN BOARD   388
COOKING   389
LANGUAGE ARTS   389
MATH   393
   Number Concepts   393
   Math Vocabulary   393
MOVEMENT   394
MUSIC   394
ROLE PLAY   396
SCIENCE   396

MAY CURRICULUM   399

Mothers and Mother's Day   400

CONCEPTS   400
ART   400
BLOCKS   404
BULLETIN BOARD   404
COOKING   404
LANGUAGE ARTS   405
MATH   408
   Number Concepts   408
   Math Vocabulary   409
MOVEMENT   409
MUSIC   410
ROLE PLAY   410
SCIENCE   411

Farm Animals   412

CONCEPTS   412
ART   412
BLOCKS   416
BULLETIN BOARD   416
COOKING   417
LANGUAGE ARTS   418
MATH   423
   Number Concepts   423
   Math Vocabulary   424
MOVEMENT   424
MUSIC   425
ROLE PLAY   426
SCIENCE   426

Nursery Rhymes   428

   CONCEPTS   428
   ART   428
   BLOCKS   431
   BULLETIN BOARD   431
   COOKING   432
   LANGUAGE ARTS   432
   MATH   436
     Number Concepts   436
   MOVEMENT   437
   MUSIC   438
   ROLE PLAY   438
   SCIENCE   439

Introduction

ORGANIZATION OF THE BOOK

WE CARE contains thirty units of study organized into nine monthly sections for two- through five-year-olds. Each unit includes hundreds of activities in multiple curriculum areas. They are divided into suggested age groups because teachers have told us they need help knowing which art activities their youngest children could do successfully. You are encouraged to select and adapt the various activities to fit the needs and readiness of your group. The activities are clearly marked with Block symbols to indicate age appropriateness.

KEY

[2 3 4 5]	Two- through five-year-olds
[4 5]	Four- to five-year-olds
[4]	Four-year-olds
[3 4 5]	Three- through five-year-olds
[3 4]	Three- to four-year-olds
[3]	Three-year-olds
[2 3]	Two- to three-year-olds
[2]	Two-year-olds

Some units are intended for one week of instruction. Other units, with more complex concepts to develop and expand upon, are planned for two weeks of instruction. Still, all units contain completely developed ideas and activities, rather than mere sketches and suggestions. And all units have been classroom tested. Before publication, this curriculum was used for over two years in multiple day care and public kindergarten classrooms that provided extensive feedback for elaboration and revision of these units. Indeed, hundreds of young children have proven these activities work!

Every unit has several important and useful features.

- Activities and teaching ideas in art, block play, cooking, language arts, math, movement, music, role play, and science.

- One or more bulletin board ideas appropriate to that content. Often the finished board presents still another manipulative learning task to challenge your children's problem-solving skills.
- Activities identified as appropriate for two-year-olds, three-year-olds, and four-five-year-olds.
- Multiple ideas and activities easily adaptable to large group, small group, or individual instruction.
- Topics related to a specific time of the year but also useable at other times.
- A bibliography of delightful and effective books which relate to the unit. Some of the books are classics and favorites; many of the books are new publications to expand your choices.
- Patterns needed for art activities are included on separate pages within each unit.

Every month includes four unit-related sketches that are useful for calendar, math, and language arts activities. It is also helpful to use the blank calendar (see A CALENDAR FOR COMMUNICATION AND ORGANIZATION) to fill in monthly plans and then to post it so parents may know what is being learned by their children.

BELIEFS INCORPORATED THROUGHOUT THE BOOK

All of the activities are based on the following important beliefs.

- **Process is more important than product.**
  With young children, the ulitmate value of an activity is the experience of doing the activity, rather than the quality of the product produced.
- **Children learn by doing.**
  Avoid doing for children anything which they might do for themselves. As much as possible, allow children to do their own drawing, cutting, experimenting, buttoning, etc.
- **The creativity of each child must be encouraged.**
  The end result of an activity should not be a group of products which all look the same. Ask children: "What else could you do?" "What do you think?" "How can you make yours different?"
  The majority of the activities in the ART section of each unit are creative experiences that invite children to experiment and explore through art. Other experiences that may involve such typical art and crafts activities as cutting and pasting but do not encourage the creativity of children are considered to be skill developers and are included in the most appropriate curriculum areas for that skill. Examples of these activities are often included in the LANGUAGE ARTS section of each unit. Children enjoy crafts and patterns. We just want to emphasize that such activities should be in *addition* to creative experiences, not in substitution of creative experiences.
- **All activities are also opportunities to help each child develop responsibility**.
  Cleanup should be organized so children can do it themselves. Prevent unnecessary messes by having children cover work areas. Plan ahead and provide needed guidance so children can clean up during and after activities.

■ **Activities do not have to be expensive.**

A myriad of learning experiences can be done using readily available and free or inexpensive materials. The equipment and materials needed to implement the WE CARE curriculum are minimal because excellent facilities frequently operate on limited budgets.

A CALENDAR FOR COMMUNICATION AND ORGANIZATION

Mother: "What did you do in school today?"

Young child: "Nothing."

The above response is typical! It's not that children don't want to verbally share their day. They just need more concrete probes to help them remember what they would like to discuss. So use the blank calendar to fill in and highlight some of your main activities and plans for each month, similar to the sample included from one teacher's room. Post the completed calendar by your door (or provide a copy for each family). As the child is picked up the adult can look at the calendar and say: "What's this about making _____ today?" The child then has something concrete to remember, and responds with: "Oh, it was great! We...."

Thus the calendar subtly encourages more parent-child communication and better teacher organization. It is also an effective tool for teacher-parent communication as the teacher can note on the calendar any special help needed from the parents, such as some throwaway items to be saved to use for an art project or some props needed for role play.

Each month's calendar may be decorated with symbols appropriate for that time of year or even surrounded with the children's artwork. But either plain or fancy, the calendar works! It provides teachers, parents, and children with important information and an overview of the exciting plans for the month.

February

Miss Wilhelm's 3 year olds

Monday	Tuesday	Wednesday	Thursday	Friday
3 Health and Nutrition Art: 3-D Circles ✴Doctor's Office New Song: "Healthy Way"	**4** Floor Puzzle Visit from Dr. Brewster 	**5** Art: Fruit Folks Puppet – Dentist What's for Lunch-Carle	**6** Tempera Painting Cooking: Applesauce – Nutrition Graph (Math) –	**7** Art: Pizza Pan Prints Food Group riddles Gregory the Terrible Eater - Sharmat
10 Valentines Art: Valentine Bags ⟶ ⊕Keith's birthday⊕ Valentine Hearts–Fingerplay	**11** Cooking: Cinnamon Hearts	**12** Stencil Painting Hidden Messages Good Morning to You, Valentine – Hopkins	**13** Dictating letters Whole–Half (Math)	**14** Art: Doily Prints The heart (Science) The Post Office Book - Gibbons
17 Famous People and Birthdays Finger Painting Silhouettes Size discrimination (Math) The Surprize - Shannon	**18** Un-birthday Tree Shadows (Science) "The Un-birthday Song"	**19** Cooking: Washington Cherry Tarts VIP Awards	**20** ⊕Sarah's birthday⊕ Quill Pen Writing	**21** Un-birthday Party Un-birthday Cake Cones Happy Birthday, Sam - Hutchins
24 Care of Pets Measurement (Math) Art: Styrofoam Pets "Dog's Day"- Silverstein Class bean bag pillow–	**25** Pet Show– Keats Stuffed animal day! make, stuff, enjoy!	**26** Art: Pet Graffiti Cooking: Peanut Butter S'Mores Pet Rhymes Harry the Dirty Dog-Zion	**27** Comic Pets "There Was a Little Turtle"– Fingerplay Hi Cat! - Keats	**28** Group Pet Book Dictate sentences Field Trip- Pet Store Kid's Cat Book - DePaola

✴ Needed for doctor's office for role play: fold-up cot; stethoscope; old white sheets to tear into bandages

	Monday	Tuesday	Wednesday	Thursday	Friday

Art Bread Dough

For each child:

3 slices of white bread—remove crusts
3 tablespoons of white glue
1 teaspoon of lemon juice

Let children break the bread into the small pieces and use a popsicle stick or their hands to mix together all the ingredients in a plastic bowl. Encourage them to mix well.

Ceramic Dough

2 cups salt
2/3 cup water

Mix together in a pan. Stir until mixture is well heated (3-4 minutes). Remove from heat.

1 cup cornstarch
½ cup cold water

Mix together. Stir quickly into first mixture. Mixture should be stiff dough. (If it does not thicken, reheat and stir for one more minute.)

Egg Dye

Mix in plastic bowls:

1 cup hot tap water
1 cup vinegar
2 or more drops of food coloring

Finger Paint

Liquid starch
Dry tempera powder
Large pieces of white shelf paper or finger painting paper

Wetting the shelf paper with a sponge of clear water lets the paint move more easily.

Place a 1-2 inch size drop of starch on each piece of wet shelf paper. Sprinkle on dry tempera powder. Each child uses one hand to mix the tempera in the starch.

After the tempera is well mixed, let the children spread the color over all of the paper. They are now ready to finger paint.

With young children it is sometimes most effective to have them finger paint with only one hand and to keep the other hand behind their back. This keeps one hand clean to scratch noses, open doorknobs, and to hug the teacher without a mess!

Glistening Squeeze Bottle Painting

½ cup flour
½ cup salt
½ cup water
1 teaspoon powdered tempera paint

Mix and pour into plastic squeeze bottles such as old liquid detergent bottles. Let children squeeze the mixture onto tagboard or cardboard pieces. The salt makes the mixture have a glistening effect after it dries. Provide several different colors of the mixture so children may experiment with color blending as they make designs.

Hanging Soap Balls

3 cups Ivory Snow soap powder
4 tablespoons warm water
Waxed paper
24-inch pieces of wide yarn, any color

Knot together the two ends of each piece of yarn. Let the children help measure the ingredients into a large mixing bowl. Beat with an electric mixer at high speed until the mixture has a claylike, thick consistency. Makes about four cups of mixture.

Give each child a knotted piece of yarn and about one-half cup of the mixture. Let them quickly mold the mixture around the yarn knot to make a ball with a hanging string.

Modeling Goop

2 cups salt
2/3 cups water
1 cup cornstarch
½ cup cold water

Mix salt and water. Heat 3-4 minutes. Remove from heat and add the cornstarch which has been dissolved in the cold water. Stir quickly. If the mixture does not thicken into a stiff dough, place over low heat and stir for about 1 minute until it forms a smooth lump. It may be stored in plastic.

Play Dough

1 cup flour
½ cup salt
1 cup water
1 tablespoon oil
2 teaspoons cream of tartar
Food coloring

Mix together all of the ingredients. Cook over medium heat until it forms a ball. Pour out and knead a few minutes to increase smoothness. Keep in a plastic bag or a tightly covered container.

Sparkle Paint Recipe

1/3 cup salt
1/3 cup flour
Approximately 1/3 cup water

Mix the ingredients together. Add more or less water to get a paint thickness.

Transfer Art Mixture

2 tablespoons of Ivory Snow soap powder
½ cup hot water
1 tablespoon turpentine

Dissolve the soap powder in hot water and stir in the turpentine. When the mixture cools, pour it into a bottle with a tight fitting lid. Makes about 3/4 cup.

How to use: Brush over a comic picture from the newspaper. Let it set for about 10 seconds. Place a piece of paper over the picture, rub all over the paper with the back of a spoon, and the picture will transfer to the paper. One picture can usually be used more than once.

Use the Transfer Mixture to make greeting cards, collages, scenes, stationery, and even to decorate T-shirts. The mixture may be stored indefinitely without refrigeration. (If it solidifies, set the bottle in a pan of warm water.) Shake or stir well before using.

Whipped Snow Recipe

1 tablespoon Ivory Snow soap powder
1 tablespoon water

Let children work in pairs taking turns measuring and mixing their own amount of whipped snow. One child firmly holds the bowl as the second child beats the mix with an eggbeater until very stiff. The child then spoons it from the bowl and uses fingers, or the back of the spoon, to spread it onto a cardboard pattern.

September Curriculum

1. Discovering Me
2. Families
3. Where I Live

Discovering Me

CONCEPTS

- Every person is unique and special.
- Everyone can do some things well. There are many new things to learn to do.
- Everyone has feelings: happy, sad, scared, angry, tired, and surprised.
- Everyone has a body with many parts. Children's bodies grow bigger until they are adults.
- Everyone can be a friend and have a friend.

ART

Friendship Tree

Tree branch; plaster of paris or cement; construction paper.

"Plant" a real tree branch in a coffee can and fill it with cement or plaster of paris. Let the children (or teacher) trace around each child's hand on a piece of construction paper and cut it out. Print the child's name on the hand. Use a hole punch to punch a hole in the hand and hang the hands on the tree with an 8 inch piece of yarn.

Place the caption "Friendship Tree" on the coffee can or above the tree.

Variation: Let the tree become a "Magic Tree." Cut out construction paper stars and print the children's names on them. Stick a candy lollypop through the star and hang one star on the tree for each child. Watch the children's surprise when they see the Magic Tree the next morning!

Dough Frames

Ceramic play dough (see Art Recipes); waxed paper; construction paper or posterboard; glue.

Take a photograph of each child or ask each to bring a picture from home. Glue the photo on a piece of construction paper or posterboard slightly larger than the photo.

Let the children have a ball of play dough to work on a piece of waxed paper. Let each child make a play dough frame for the photo. The frame could be made by rolling long "snakes" of dough to outline the photo, by braiding play dough, or by rolling small balls of dough and placing them around the photo.

After the dough has dried it may be painted. Then use several spots of white glue to hold it securely in place on the construction paper and photo. Glue or tape a 2 inch piece of string or yarn in a ——shape on the back, so the photo may be hung.

"Handy Me" Booklet

Construction paper; tempera paint.

Trace a child's hand on a piece of folded construction paper. Cut out the hand, leaving the fold uncut, so you end up with a hand-shaped booklet that will open, as shown.

Provide small amounts of tempera paint in meat trays or paper plates. Let the children decorate their hand booklet by touching one thumb in the paint or by painting their thumb with a paintbrush, then dotting thumb prints all over the outside of the booklet.

Print each child's name in large letters on the outside. Weigh and measure the height of each of the children. Then print each child's height and weight on the inside of his/her booklet.

"Celebration of Me" Placemats and Cups

Construction paper; styrofoam cups; crayons or markers.

Placemats: Provide a 12 × 18 inch piece of construction paper for each child. Let them fringe the edges of the paper by cutting 1 inch cuts all around the outside. Then have them draw a picture in the center of the paper. Print the child's name in large letters under the picture. This will be the child's special placemat for the Celebration of Me party.

Cups: Provide a white styrofoam cup for each child. Use a marker to print their name near the top edge of the cup. Let the children decorate each cup with their favorite colors of crayons or markers. Let them use this cup for their drink during the Celebration of Me party.

Shaving Cream Faces

Shaving cream.

Put a small amount of shaving cream on a tabletop. Show the children how you can spread out the cream to make a smooth area. Draw a circle in the cream. Add eyes, nose, ears, hair, and other details as children suggest them. Lightly rub over the area to "erase" the picture and then draw it again.

Put a small amount of shaving cream on the tabletop for each child. Let the children spread the cream and draw faces.

For added pleasure, take a picture of each child standing by his/her shaving cream face. Display the pictures on the wall or door, at the children's eye levels, with their names under the pictures.

Light-Up Pictures

Q-Tips; tempera paint; manila paper; salad oil.

Provide Q-Tips and small amounts of tempera paint in meat trays. Let the children use the Q-Tips to paint designs on 9 × 12 inch manila paper. After the paint is dry, let the children use a paintbrush or basting brush to quickly spread salad oil over the entire picture. Light will show through and light up the picture when it is hung in a window.

Plate Faces

Paper plates; construction paper scraps; mirror; glue; yarn pieces.

Provide inexpensive paper plates and assorted construction paper cutouts of eyes, noses, mouths, and ears. Discuss the parts of our face. Have children touch and feel each part of their face as you discuss it. Provide a mirror for children to look into.

Let children experiment making several different faces by showing them how to choose different eyes, noses, etc., and lay them in the appropriate place on a paper plate to look like a face.

Later, provide glue and let the children glue their favorite face on a plate. Provide yarn for the children to cut in short pieces for hair, if desired.

Feeling Collage
(Whole Class Project)

Magazines; 24 × 24 inch butcher paper.

Provide pages torn out of magazines and newspapers showing pictures of people's faces. (The children can handle the pictures best if they have already been torn from the magazine.) Use a marker to divide the butcher paper into sections. Label each section with a common emotion word such as happy, sad, surprised, etc.

Let children cut out the faces and glue them in the appropriate section.

Burlap Sewing

8 or 10 inch squares of burlap; yarn; plastic darning needles; glue or tape.

Use plastic darning needles or, for an inexpensive and easily found "needle," use bobby pins. Thread brightly colored 12 inch pieces of yarn through the "needles." Tie a large knot in one end. Let the children freely sew a design of their choice by weaving in and out of the burlap. Have several colors of yarn available. Encourage children to try several colors and overlap the colors on their design. The ends may be left loose, or glued or taped down to prevent accidental pull-outs.

Mural of Friends
(Whole Class Project)

24 × 36 inch butcher paper; 8 inch circles of cardboard or posterboard; yarn; buttons; construction paper scraps; macaroni; glue.

Let the children take turns tracing around a circle to make a face shape on the butcher paper. Each child then completes a face by gluing on: yarn or construction paper strips for hair; buttons, construction paper shapes, or small pebbles for eyes and a nose; construction paper mouths; macaroni or construction paper eyebrows; ear shapes.

Print each child's name under his/her face creation. Place a caption above the mural: "Friends" or "Friendly Faces."

DISCOVERING ME

Dancing Puppet

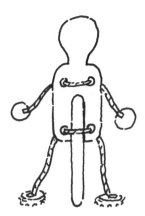

Two 2 inch pieces of yarn, a popsicle stick, and two bottle caps for each child; three or more puppet body patterns cut from cardboard or posterboard; markers or crayons; string; glue.

Show the children how to hold the pattern with one hand while they use the other hand to trace around the pattern on a piece of paper. Let the children cut out the puppet body. Use a hole punch to make the four holes shown.

Let the children decorate their puppet head and body with markers or crayons. Then let them string one piece of yarn in and out of the top holes and leave the ends dangling for arms. Glue one circle at each end of the yarn for a hand. Then string the second piece of yarn in and out of the bottom holes for legs. Glue a bottle cap at each end of the yarn for feet that will tap and click when moved. Glue a popsicle stick toward the bottom of the back to be used as a handle. When dry, the children can hold onto the stick and make the puppet dance. Great fun because the arms and legs move so freely!

Traceable Me

White butcher paper; crayons or markers.

Let children take turns lying on a large sheet of paper while the teacher or another child draws around their body shape. Before coloring, discuss and name the different parts of the body: "What parts do we have on our faces?" "What could we draw or color on your body shape drawing to make it look more like you?" Discuss the individual features of each child. Provide mirrors (especially a full-length mirror) so children may study their own features.

Encourage the children to color their Traceable Me so it shows the clothes they are wearing. Some children will do best on this activity if only part of it is completed each day to prevent fatigue in coloring.

BLOCKS

During the week, introduce the block area. Establish any rules that you might have concerning time to be in the block area, how many may participate at one time, blocks are for building not hitting, etc. Let the children demonstrate their abilities in block building. Try building a group block structure. Encourage language among the children in asking for a needed block, helping each other find just the "right" block needed. Stress that the block area is a place for sharing. Help children learn to resolve a conflict over a block by talking.

BULLETIN BOARD

There Was an Old Woman Who Lived in a Shoe

Draw an old fashioned high-top shoe. Cut flaps to open like windows all over the shoe—one for each child in the class. Print a child's name under each flap. Glue a picture of each child behind each flap so others may open the window to see each child. Recite the nursery rhyme "There Was an Old Woman Who Lived in a Shoe."

Cinnamon Me's

Refrigerated biscuits
Cinnamon sugar (½ cup sugar + ½ teaspoon cinnamon)
Melted butter or soft butter

Wash hands. Provide a piece of waxed paper for each child to use as a clean work area on a tabletop.

Let the children roll one or two biscuits into long snakes and then shape them into their first name initial. (Give each child a card with their initial on it so they have an accurate model to follow.)

Lay the initials on a cookie sheet for baking. Then let each child brush the initial with melted or soft butter and sprinkle cinnamon sugar generously over it. Bake as directed on biscuit can.

Milky Me's

Chocolate syrup
Milk

Wash hands. Fill cups 2/3 full of milk. Let each child add one or two teaspoons of chocolate syrup and stir up a yummy drink.

Cracker Faces

Ritz crackers or any round crackers
Peanut butter
Raisins
Miniature marshmallows

Wash hands. Let children use table knives to spread peanut butter on the crackers. Then let them use raisins and the miniature marshmallows to make a face on each cracker before eating it.

Thumb Print Cookies

2 cups flour
1 teaspoon salt
½ cup margarine
⅓ cup water

Wash hands. Let the class watch and help as all of the ingredients are mixed together into a stiff dough.

Give each child a small amount of the dough. Working on waxed paper, let them roll the dough into a ball. Then have each child put a dough ball on a cookie sheet and press a thumb print into the ball.

Bake at 350 degrees for 8-10 minutes. Fill the warm, cooked thumb prints with jelly before eating.

LANGUAGE ARTS

Books

Ahlberg, Janet and Allan. *The Baby's Catalogue*. Little, Brown, and Co., 1982.
Albert, Burton. *Mine, Yours, Ours*. A. Whitman, 1977.
Aruego, Jose. *Look What I Can Do*. Scribner, 1971.
Carle, Eric. *Do You Want to Be My Friend?* Crowell, 1971.
DePaola, Tomie. *Andy (That's My Name)*. Prentice-Hall, 1973.
Doney, Meryl. *Now I Am Big*. Winston Press, 1983.
Kahn, Peggy. *The Care Bears' Book of Feelings*. Random House, 1984.
Kraus, Robert. *Leo the Late Bloomer*. Crowell, 1971.
Mayer, Mercer. *All By Myself*. Western Publishing, 1983.
Mayer, Mercer. *I Was So Mad*. Western Publishing, 1983.
Mayer, Mercer. *When I Get Bigger*. Western Publishing, 1983.
McGovern, Ann. *Feeling Mad, Sad, Bad, Glad*. Walker and Co., 1978.
Moncure, Jane Belk. *About Me*. Children's Press, 1976.
Moncure, Jane Belk. *Now I Am Two!* Children's Press, 1984.
Moncure, Jane Belk. *Now I Am Three!* Children's Press, 1984.
Moncure, Jane Belk. *Now I Am Four!* Children's Press, 1984.
Moncure, Jane Belk. *Now I Am Five!* Children's Press, 1984.
Ourth, John and Kelly Liedtke. *Show You Care*. Good Apple, 1980.
Piper, Walter. *The Little Engine that Could*. Platt and Munk, 1961.
Riley, Sue. *Sharing*. Child's World, 1978.
Seuss, Dr. *My Book about Me*. Beginner Books, 1969.
Steptoe, John. *The Story of Jumping Mouse*. Lothrop, Lee, and Shepard, 1984.
Timmons, Christina. *The Me and You Book*. Encyclopaedia Brittanica, 1974.
Udry, Janice May. *Let's Be Enemies*. Harper and Row, 1961.
Viorst, Judith. *Alexander and the Terrible, Horrible, No Good, Very Bad Day*. Atheneum, 1981.
Zolotow, Charlotte. *William's Doll*. Harper and Row, 1972.

Fingerplays

I have two little hands.	(Hold up both hands.)
They both belong to me.	(Point to self.)
And they can help me do things.	
Would you like to see?	(Hold out hands.)
They can pat you on the back.	(Add appropriate actions for each line.)
They can pet a kitten.	
They can wave up in the air.	
They can wear a mitten.	
They can help me work and work.	
They help me have some fun.	
Then I can fold them together	
To rest when their job's done.	(Quietly fold hands and place in lap.)

Most Special Person Box

Put a small mirror inside a little box with a lid. Tell the children to take turns opening the box and looking inside to see who is *a most special person*!

Feelings

Read Judith Viorst's *Alexander and the Terrible, Horrible, No Good, Very Bad Day.* Talk about feeling happy, sad, angry, surprised, etc. Help children know that *everyone* has those feelings sometimes.

Celebration of Me!

Provide a party atmosphere to celebrate the special uniqueness of each child and encourage positive self concepts. Make the placemats and cups suggested in the ART section. Talk about each child's favorite colors, as displayed on his/her decorated cup.

Serve Cinnamon Me's and Milky Me's. Or, serve Thumb Print Cookies and talk about how each child's thumb print is different: "No one is exactly like you. You are special."

Sing the "I Am Special" song from the MUSIC section. Ask children to tell something they like about themselves.

Me Page

Working with one child at a time, complete a Me Page. Help them trace around one hand. Help them color and measure to complete the page. This activity provides an important time to show how each child is truly special to *you* by interacting with just him/her.

Cutting Center

Provide a molded wading pool or a folded sheet. Let two children at a time sit in the pool or on the sheet to practice cutting with scissors. This insures easy clean up!

Recorded Interviews

Tape record an interview with each child. Ask each child two or three questions. Last of all, ask each child: "What is your name?"

After all the children have been recorded, play back the tape during snack time or group time for fun listening. Stop the recorder each time just before the child says his/her name so the class can guess who it is.

Some questions might include: "Are you a boy or a girl?" "What color hair do you have?" "Who is in your family?" "What do you like to do after school?"

My Name Is Important to Me!

Laminate 3 × 6 inch cards carefully printed with the first name of each child. Each card will last a long time and provide a correct model for the child to look at and perhaps try to copy.

DISCOVERING ME

Games

1. *Play Dough*

   Let children roll play dough snakes and lay over the letters on the laminated card to make their names.

2. *Name Hunt*

   Place the name cards all around the room on chalkboard rails, on chairs, along baseboards, etc. Let the children tiptoe around the room to find their own name. Later, hold up one child's duplicate name card and let others tiptoe around to silently find the name card to match the one held by the teacher.

3. *Fishing*

   Put a paper clip or two on each name card. Lay the names on the floor. Let children take turns using a pole and a string with a magnet to catch their own name.

4. *Silent Line-Up*

   After much practice with the name cards, call children to line up by silently standing in front of the class and holding up each child's name. Children walk to the line as they see their name.

"I Can" Classification

Staple three pockets on a trifolded sheet as shown. Make a set of cards which will fit in the pocket. Glue on the cards some pictures of common tasks children

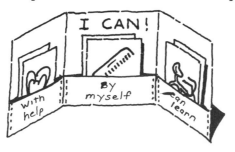

learn to do around age 4-5. Let children take turns classifying each card as a task they can do with help, alone, or can learn to do in the future.

MATH

NUMBER CONCEPTS

Geometry Boards

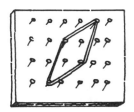

Nail evenly-spaced nails in a 6 or 9 inch square piece of wood as shown. Be sure not to pound the nail all the way in. Leave some space between the head of the nail and the board.

Provide rubber bands and let children explore learning what shapes they can make. Later, make some shapes, letters, or numerals on index cards. Let the children choose a card and then make that shape on the geometry board.

Height and Weight

Weigh and measure the height of each child. Display the measurements on a wall chart, poster, or door decoration. Children enjoy seeing their name and measurements and "reading" each other's. (Try the Friendship Tree or Handy Me Booklets in the ART section.) A dachshund standing on his hind legs or a giraffe with a very long neck make attractive ways to mark heights and display at the proper height.

Natural Counting Opportunities

As a group, look for natural opportunities to count real things in the room. For example, count the number of shoes with shoelaces or velcro or buckles; count the number of buttons on one of the children's clothes.

MATH VOCABULARY

Big—Little

1. Provide different sizes and kinds of balls from golf balls to basketballs. Hold up two of the balls. Let the children take turns selecting the one that is the big or little, as you instruct. Let the children lead the game after a while.
2. Let children arrange the balls in ascending and descending order as they gain expertise in this concept.

MOVEMENT

Name Game

The class sits in a circle. The teacher says one child's name and rolls a large, soft ball to that child. (An inflatable beach ball works especially well.) The child catches the ball, says another child's name, and rolls it to that child. Continue the game until all children have had a turn.

Simon Says

Play Simon Says using body parts: "Simon Says touch your knee." "Simon says wiggle your arm."

Tangle Up

Begin by saying one simple body movement for the children to follow. The class must continue to do that movement as each new direction is added. Continue adding one more movement until someone becomes too "tangled up." Then say "Tangle Up" and everyone falls down! The children laugh and really love to do this game. Begin again, and repeat the game several times using different directions: "Put one hand on one knee. Now put your elbow on your hip. Also stand on one foot. Now touch your nose, etc."

Look What I Can Do

Read to the children Jose Aruego's book, *Look What I Can Do*. Reread the book, stopping on each page for the children to try to stand in place and do the movement suggested by each character in the story.

MUSIC

Record

Use Mr. Rogers' album, "You Are Special."

Dancing Puppets

Make Dancing Puppets (see ART, three-year-olds) and let children dance the puppets in rhythm to a record.

There's No One in the World Like Me

(Tune: "Row, Row, Row Your Boat")

There's no one in the world like me,
Me, me, me.
Ever was or ever will be,
Like me, me, me.

Look at me, oh, look at me,
I'm glad that I am me!
I'll be the best I ever can be,
Me, me, me.

Going to School

(Tune: "Mulberry Bush")

This is the way we go to school,
Go to school, go to school.
This is the way we go to school
Early in the morning.

Let the children suggest ways they can get to school, such as walking, in a car, or in a bus. As the verse is repeated, have the children act out a different way to get to school.

"I Am Special"

(Tune: "Are You Sleeping")

I am special, I am special.
So are you, so are you.
We can play together. We can work together.
While we're at school. While we're at school.

ROLE PLAY

Interview

Children interview each other. Provide a cylinder block or an empty toilet paper roll for a microphone. A real microphone and cassette tape player may be used if preferred. Provide dress-up clothes so children can choose to dress like adult reporters.

Getting Ready for School

Provide dolls and health care items. Let the children role play getting the dolls all clean and ready for school.

I Used to Be a Baby

Provide dolls and a plastic tub with 1-2 inches of water. Let the children add a little soap and bathe the babies. Have lots of towels available. A little baby powder adds to the fun.

SCIENCE

Me

Look at skin, hair, fingernails, etc., with a magnifying glass.

Fingerprints

Examine fingerprints. Let children make fingerprints with a stamp pad and paper. Talk about how the prints look with a magnifying glass.

Discover About Air

Glass; paper towels; tub of water.

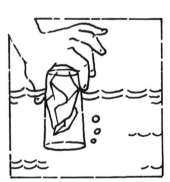

Let the children dip a paper towel into the water. Then talk about how wet the towel gets. Lay the towel aside.

Let the children stuff a paper towel into the glass. Turn the glass upside down and lower it into the water. Then lift out the glass and let the children feel the paper to see that it is still dry. Talk about the air still in the glass. The air takes up all the room so the water can't get into the towel.

Lower the glass into the water again with the towel inside. Now tilt the glass. Have the children watch the air bubble move. The air goes out and the water has room to go in. Lift out the glass and let the children feel the wet towel.

Repeat the whole experiment, if possible. Ask the children to say what will happen during each step and why.

Dancing Puppet Pattern

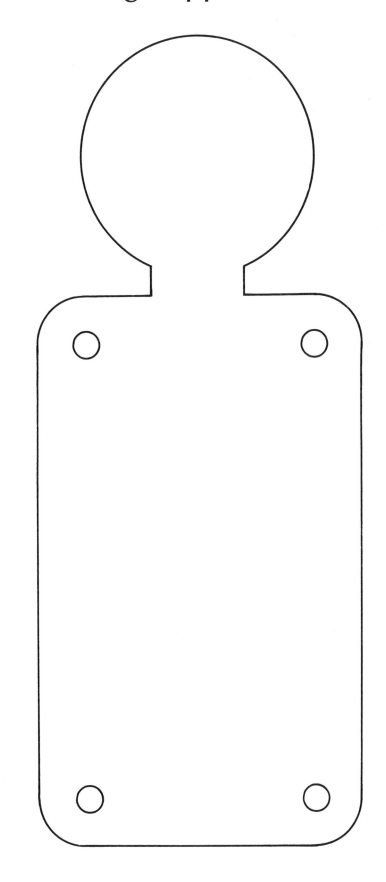

Me Page

This hand print belongs to _____

My eyes are this color. _____

My hair is this color. _____

My finger is this long. _____

My big toe looks like this.

Families

CONCEPTS

- A family is generally made up of adults and children who live together and care for each other.
- Each member in a family is important and special.
- Family members are alike in some ways, different in some ways.
- Children are sometimes adopted into a family; some children are born into a family.
- Some families are single parent families.
- Families can have other people living in the home.
- Some families are large, some are small.
- Families do many things together.
- Every member of a family has responsibilities which help that family function successfully.

ART

Family Collage

Magazine pictures of families; glue; butcher paper.

Cut out the pictures of families. Glue them on a large piece of butcher paper as a group project. Display the collage on the wall low enough for the children to see and talk about the family members. Add the caption: ''Everyone in a family is important.''

Paper Cup Family

Styrofoam cups in different sizes; styrofoam craft balls; sewing notions; markers or crayons.

Provide two or three sizes of cups to make the appropriate family members. Provide assorted sizes of craft balls to glue to the bottoms of the cups to represent the heads. Let the children use markers to add features to the head and draw clothes on the cup. Sewing notions such as sequins, yarn, ric rac, small buttons, glass beads, etc., may also be used to increase the fun and total effect. Cut out feet or shoe shapes from one scrap piece of tagboard, then glue them just under the edge of the cup to make the feet.

Have the children role play conversations among the family members. Encourage them to talk about the jobs each family member does to help the family.

Happy Family

Manila paper; Q-Tips; tempera paint.

Let the children use Q-Tips on manila paper to paint their family or some family members. Encourage the children to talk about who they are painting and/or what the family is doing together. Some older children may like to have a caption written at the bottom of the painting as they talk about their painting. Some children may just want to have a name or label under each person's painting in the picture.

Marble Painting

Shallow box; manila paper; tempera paint; marbles; golf ball.

Cut the manila paper to fit in the bottom of the box. Pour two to six colors of tempera into several bowls. Put a marble into each color. Using a plastic spoon, remove each marble and place it into the box. Tip the box first one way, then the other, so the marble rolls over the paper. Dip the marble in the paint as necessary. Use several colors to produce a rainbow of designs.

Variation: Use a golf ball in the paints to obtain a different effect. After the paintings are dry, let the children identify which lines were made by the marbles and which were made by the golf ball.

Paper Plate Mask

Small paper plates; construction paper cutouts of noses, mouths, and ears; yarn; popsicle sticks.

Provide each child with enough paper plates for each family member. Have an adult cut out eye shapes from the plates so children will be able to see out of their masks. Let the children use cutouts of noses, mouths, and ears to glue on their plates. Provide cut lengths of yarn to glue on for the hair. Attach a popsicle stick at the bottom for the child to hold. Children can use these masks to role play different family members.

Heart Necklaces

Ceramic play dough (see Art Recipes); red tempera paint; brushes; yarn or string.

Give each child a 1½ inch sized ball of play dough. Let the children roll the play dough and experiment with it for a time. Then show them how to mold the dough into a heart shape. Scratch the child's initials on each heart and poke a hole in the top of the heart with a pencil. Let the heart shapes dry for 1-2 days.

Next, have the children paint their hearts using tempera and brushes. Once dried, pull a piece of yarn or string through the heart to make a necklace.

If possible, let the children make more than one heart necklace each and encourage them to give one heart to a family member.

Variation: Let the children use heart-shaped cookie cutters to mold the heart shapes. Though less creative for the children, it does work well, if desired.

Paper Doll Family

Paper doll patterns cut out of posterboard; manila paper; scissors; construction paper; scraps; crayons or markers; glue.

Let the children trace around a doll pattern to represent each member of the family. Then let them cut out each family doll and decorate it with construction paper scraps, crayons, or markers—to look like the people in their families. Glue the hands together for each family chain.

Helping Hands

Construction paper; scissors; glue; old catalogues and magazines; stapler.

Each child traces around one of their hands, then uses that as a pattern to cut out several copies of that hand. The children then cut out small pictures in magazines and catalogues to represent ways they can help their family. Next, they glue one helping picture on each hand. Then write a sentence for the children by each picture to explain what that helping hand can do. For example: picture of silverware + ''I can put away the silverware''; picture of grass or flowers + ''I can help in the yard''; picture of toys + ''I can put my toys away''; or picture of socks + ''I can fold and put away the washed socks.''

Staple the hands together like a booklet for each child. Print ''Helping Hands'' for a caption and display the hands on a bulletin board, if desired.

BLOCKS

Let the children choose a ''block family'' and build a house for them. They might choose a father-sized block, mother-sized block, children-sized blocks, and grandparent-sized blocks. Encourage role play between children in the classroom and their block families.

BULLETIN BOARD

Families

Caption: FUN FAMILY VACATIONS; FUN FAMILY TRIPS; or FAMILIES DO THINGS TOGETHER. Send a note home to parents requesting family snapshots or any brochures obtained while on an outing. Encourage all of the children to participate. The teacher may also contribute items from a vacation for the bulletin board.

Variation: If a large board is available in the hall, this could easily become a school-wide activity.

FAMILIES

25

COOKING

Uncooked Oatmeal Cookies

3/4 *cup sugar*
2/3 *cup margarine, soft*
3 *tablespoons cocoa*
1 *tablespoon water*
½ *teaspoon vanilla*
2 *cups oatmeal, dry*

Wash hands. In a large mixing bowl, cream the sugar and margarine. Add all other ingredients except oatmeal. Mix well. Blend in the oatmeal with a wooden spoon.

Let the children form dough into balls. Roll the balls in powdered sugar if desired. Eat and enjoy!

Purple-Urple Juice

1 *6-oz. can of frozen grape juice*
1 *6-oz. can of frozen orange juice*
6 *cans of water*

Mix both kinds of juice in the same large pitcher. Let the children take turns pouring in the water. Makes 48 ounces.

Family Favorite Fruit Salad

Whipped cream
Variety of fresh fruits
Plastic serrated knives

Each child brings one or two pieces of their family's favorite fruit (or simply provide a variety of fresh fruits for the whole class). Wash hands. Let the children help wash the fruit. Cut the fruits in half; show and talk about the seeds inside of each.

Children can use the plastic knives to cut the halves into bite-sized pieces. Mix all the fruit in a large bowl. Stir in the whipped cream. Serve.

LANGUAGE ARTS

Books

Alex, Marlee and Benny Alex. *You and Me and Our New Baby*. Zondervan, 1982.
Berenstein, Stan and Jan. *Go to School*. Random House, 1978.
Berenstein, Stan and Jan. *In the Dark*. Random House, 1982.
Berenstein, Stan and Jan. *Moving Day*. Random House, 1981.
Berenstein, Stan and Jan. *The Truth*. Random House, 1983.
  (Any of the Berenstein bears books will show the family doing things together. Children love the humor.)
Charlip, Benny and Lilian Moore. *Hooray for Me*. Scholastic, 1980.
De Paula, Tomie. *Nana Upstairs and Nana Downstairs*. Puffin, 1981.
Eastman, P.D. *Are You My Mother?* Random House, 1960.
Fassler, Joan. *My Grandpa Died Today*. Behavioral Publications, 1971.

Fehr, Howard. *This Is My Family*. Holt, Rinehart, and Winston, Inc., 1963.

Hoban, Russell. *A Baby Sitter For Francis*. Harper and Row, 1964.

Lorian, Nicole. *A Birthday Present for Mama*. Random House, 1984.

Ormerod, Jan. *101 Things to Do With a Baby*. Lothrop, Lee & Shepard, 1984.

Pendergast, Kathleen. *Say Another One About My Family*. Madison Park Press, 1982.

Polushkin, Maria. *Mother, Mother, I Want Another*. Crown, 1978.

Sharmat, Marjorie Weiman. *What Are We Going to Do About Andrew?* Macmillan, 1980.

Showers, Paul. *Me and My Family Tree*. Harper and Row, 1982.

Simon, Norma. *All Kinds of Families*. Whitman and Co., 1976.

Tester, Sylvia R. *Family*. Children's Press, 1980.

Thaler, Mike. *Owly*. Harper and Row, 1982.

Williams, Vera B. *A Chair for My Mother*. Greenwillow Books, 1982.

Zolotow, Charlotte. *Mr. Rabbit & the Lonely Present*. Harper and Row, 1962.

Fingerplays

Where Is Mother?

Adapt the popular fingerplay "Where Is Thumbkin?" by using different family members such as mother, father, brother, sister, baby, grandma, grandpa, aunts, uncles, etc., for each verse. Try to use different voice inflections to add to the fun. Encourage the children to act out the play along with you. Let the children suggest which family member to name next.

Special Family

(Hold up one hand; wiggle each finger in turn.)

Loving mother, how do you do?
My dear daddy, glad to see you.
Hi tall brother, pleased you are here.
Hello sister, you need not fear.
We work and play together too.
Special family, I love you.   (Hug arms around self.)

Family Talk

Allow the children to tell what their family does for fun and to be together.

Have the children tell what jobs and/or chores each family member does to keep the household running smoothly.

Some children will like to make up one sentence about their family. Print their sentences on chart paper with the child's name beside it.

Family Booklet

Manila paper; crayons or markers.

Provide one half sheet of manila paper for each family member per child in the classroom. (The child may want to include pets.) Encourage the children to draw one family member on each page. You print the caption that the child dictates on the bottom of each page. Provide paper for a cover, then let the child staple the book together. Some children will want to "read" their books to the class before taking them home.

Picture Security

It helps some children to have a picture of mom, dad, or family with them to look at sometimes. It helps them relate the familiarity of home with the newness of school. It also gives them something to show others and to talk about with the other children.

Are You My Mother?

Adapt this popular book as a flannel board story. Make characters from non-fabric interfacing by tracing the book's illustrations onto the interfacing and then coloring them. Let the children take turns putting up characters as the story progresses.

Perhaps a special sound effect could be added to each event in the story. For example, when the car appears in the story, all the children could make a car sound as one child puts the illustration on the flannel board. Adding sound effects may increase the children's involvement and enjoyment.

Feel Box

(To make a feel box, see two-year-olds, LANGUAGE ARTS, in the Spring and Growing Things section of the April Curriculum guide.)

Put a piece of fruit in the feel box and let the children take turns deciding, by feeling, what is inside the box.

Which One Is Missing?

Provide a group of pictures of different family members cut from magazines or real photographs. Include a good variety of ages, cultures, and clothing styles. Show each picture to the children and discuss who it might be and what that person might do in a family.

Place three or more of the pictures in a row on the table or floor where all the children can see them. (Vary the number according to the ability of the children.) Ask the children to close their eyes while you take away one picture. As a group or by taking turns, let the children tell you which picture is missing.

Chart of Family Favorites

	🍌	🍎	🍇
JEFF	X		X
MIKE		X	
SUE		X	X
HOLLY	X		

Make a chart listing the children's names down the left-hand side. Put pictures of fruits across the top.

Let each child make an "X" to show which fruit is their family's favorite.

After every child has had a chance to mark on the charts discuss which fruit got the most votes, least votes, etc.

Typewriter

Provide an old but functional typewriter. Have available a paper which lists the printed names for people in a family (such as mom, dad, aunt, etc.) with a picture beside each name to help children identify the word.

Provide blank typing or scrap paper. Let the children type the names for the people in their family.

MATH   NUMBER CONCEPTS

Stand and Count

Ask the children wearing anything red to stand up. One class member or the whole group counts the people standing. Then people with white tennis shoes stand up. Another person counts those children. Continue with other categories until the class tires of the activity.

Flannel Board Counting

Using a catalogue, cut out pictures of items associated with fathers, mothers, children, babies, and pets. Laminate them if desired, and glue a small piece of sandpaper to the back so that each will stay on a flannel board.

Put a set of father items on the flannel board. The children take turns identifying the items, then everyone counts the items as you point to or remove the items. This activity is easily adapted to fit the needs of the individual children.

Family Puzzles

Find pictures which show family groups of two, three, four, five, or more people. If desired, glue each picture on construction paper or tagboard to make it more sturdy. Cut each picture into the same number of pieces as the number of people in the picture. Provide cards with numerals written on them. Let the children put together each family puzzle and then place it by the card with the appropriate numeral on it.

Kerplunk

Tin can; buttons or pop-bottle lids.

Let each child take a turn telling the names of everyone in his/her family. As each name is said, the child is given a button to hold. Then the child drops a button into the tin can for each person in his family. As the buttons drop, the rest of the children count the "kerplunks."

Variation: Let two children stand together. "Let's see how many people are in _____ 's and _____ 's families if we count them together."

Big—Little

Talk about making your bodies as big as you can and as small as you can. Then everyone stretches arms high above heads to become as big as possible. Next, huddle in a ball position on the floor to become as little as possible. Do this activity several times as you say "big" and "little."

Big and Little Animals

Have pictures of animals of different sizes available to stand up on the chalk tray, flannel board, etc. Call out "big" and let one child choose a big animal to display. Say "little" and let another child choose a little animal to display. Sometimes reverse the order, choosing the little animal first and then the big.

MOVEMENT

Farmer

Play the circle game and sing the song, "The Farmer in the Dell." Accent the family members named in the song. Let the children suggest other family members to add to the song.

Family Fitness

Sit ups; jog in place; log roll by lying on the floor with arms stretched over head and then roll over and over; open-close (one-half of jumping jacks movement); twist at the waist, side to side with arms extended.

Walk the Line

Put an 8 to 10 foot strip of masking tape on the floor. Let the children walk the line in suggested ways. Walk like dad; walk the line like an old grandfather; walk the line like a child going to school; walk the line like a little baby; crawl the line like an infant.

Rock-a-Bye Baby

Sing the song through once to remind everyone of the familiar song. Let everyone sit and rock side to side while they sing. Roll side to side on stomachs while singing. Lay on backs and hold knees; rock and sing.

MUSIC

Coming Round the Mountain

Using "She'll Be Coming Round the Mountain," make up verses about families going places. For example, shopping, picnicking, movies, camping, etc. Sample verses could include: We will all be going shopping at the mall.... We will all have a picnic at the lake.... We will all go swing and sliding at the park.

It's Fun to Be a Family

(Tune: "The More We Get Together")

It's fun to be a family, a family, a family,
It's fun to be a family and here's what we do.
   (Get the children to tell different things the family can do together. Use each
   idea in the song and add an action whenever possible.)
We eat and we play and we work and we travel.
It's fun to be a family and care for everyone.

ROLE PLAY

Family Activities

Encourage the children to role play going to the store or out to eat with their families. Props from the home living center could be used.

Role play going on vacation. Use the chairs to make the bus, train, or airplane. Make a family car. Decide which family member will drive, read the map, describe the scenery, etc.

Role play going to work, day care, school, taking brothers or sisters shopping, reading a bedtime story, etc.

Pretending Game

Ask the children one or both of the following questions. The children take turns answering and exercise thinking skills.

What would you do... or what would you wear... if you were a dad going to work? if you were a mom going to work? if you were a mom or dad going on an errand? if you were a grandfather going fishing?

Grocery Store

Set up a grocery store with shelves, a play cash register, paper money, etc. Let the children "buy" the fruit provided for making the fruit salad (see COOKING).

SCIENCE

Classification

Use the seeds from the fruits used in making the fruit salad. Have pictures of each of the fruits and let the children match the seeds to the appropriate picture.

Nature Observation

Go for a science walk outside. Collect interesting items to display on a low table. Provide a good magnifying glass for the children to examine the treasures. A few of the items might include: leaves, bark, twigs, rocks, insects, nests, etc.

Pull a weed from the ground with the root system still intact. Break off the excess soil to expose all of the roots. Put the weed on the science table with the magnifying glass. Encourage the children to examine the root structure closely.

Invite the children to bring items for the science table that they might collect while on a family outing. Pine cones from a camping trip or shells from the beach are great to share.

Where I Live

CONCEPTS

- A home is a place where a family lives together.
- People live in different kinds of homes such as single houses of one, two, or three stories; mobile homes; apartments and condominiums; houseboats; etc.
- Some people live in the city; others live in the suburbs; still other people live in rural areas.
- Each house or apartment has an address.
- In the past, some people lived in homes which differ from today's home styles.

ART

Paper Cup Village

Large paper cups; empty thread spools; small beads; dowel rods or pencil stubs; shoe boxes.

An adult may cut doors and windows in the paper cups. Poke a piece of dowel rod or pencil stub in the bottom of the cup to represent a chimney.

"People" may be made using the spools and beads. Paint the spools with tempera if desired. Allow to dry. Glue a bead on the top of the spool to represent the head. Dry thoroughly.

Other stores in the village may be added by decorating shoe boxes or other small boxes. Let an adult carefully cut out any needed doors or windows.

Class Mural

Large piece of butcher paper; construction paper; tempera paint; glue; house, car, and bus cutouts of posterboard to trace around.

Attach the butcher paper to a wall. Protect the floor and wall with newspapers and/or plastic drop cloths. The children take turns painting the sky, ground, trees, a pond, roads, sun, etc.

When the mural background colors are dry, the children glue on houses or places to live which they have traced from a pattern and cut from construction paper. They may also draw and cut out cars, trucks, or buses to glue on the mural. For added enrichment, the address of the child cutting out a house may be printed on the paper.

Variation: Fold the paper in half lengthwise and attach it to the wall. Let the children paint the top half all blue for the sky. When dry, reverse to the other half of the paper for the ground color. Let the two-year-olds glue cutouts of trees, sun, pond, etc., to the mural when the paint is dry.

Places to Live (Group Collage)

Cutouts of different places to live; glue; 24 x 36 inch piece of butcher paper (in a bright, attractive color, if possible).

The teacher may provide the cutouts, or let the children bring from home cutouts from newspapers and magazines of tents, trailers, houses of all sizes and styles, houseboats, etc. The children all help glue the cutouts on the butcher paper to make a colorful collage. Add the caption: ''Places to Live.''

Stand-Up City

Construction paper; house cutouts; roof cutouts; large piece of cardboard; glue; tempera paints; tape.

Provide several different varieties of cutout construction paper house shapes and roof shapes such as single-story, two-story, apartment building, etc. Let the child choose the house and the roof shape which are most like his/her own.

Let the children glue the roof to the house. Then they can add doors and windows to the house with markers or construction paper shapes.

Print the child's real address on the roof.

Let the children paint the cardboard with green tempera. When dry, they can add roads and sidewalks with brown or gray paint or with construction paper strips. To display the house free-standing along the road, make a half inch cut at the center bottom edge of each house. Fold one half forward and the other half back. Tape the folded edge to the cardboard along the roads.

String Painting

9 × 12 inch manila paper; string or yarn; tempera paint.

Cut a simple house shape for each child out of the manila paper. Cut the string into 12 inch lengths.

Cover tabletops with newspapers. Let the children dip a string into the tempera paint and gently wiggle the string around on a house shape to create an interesting design. Encourage them to use different colors each time, so the colors of the design blend and mix.

Helpful hint: Tie a button to the end of each string to make it easier to hold.

Apartment Buildings

12 × 18 inch construction paper; 1 inch yellow squares; glue.

Each child glues 1 inch squares on a 12 × 18 inch piece of construction paper to make rows and rows of windows on an apartment house. Glue the squares together to make a door, or make a 3 inch cut in the shape of a "T" at the bottom of the paper to be double doors that really fold back to open and close.

For added enjoyment, provide old magazines and let the children cut out a picture of a person or two. Glue the picture behind the apartment door such that when the door opens we see who lives inside.

House Painting

Large sheets of newsprint; tempera paint; brushes.

Provide large sheets of paper at the easel or on tabletops covered with newspapers. The children paint a large picture of their own house or a house they like. To encourage more details in the paintings, talk about doors, doorknobs, windows, sidewalks, steps, chimneys, etc. Urge the children to include a picture of who lives in the house, as well.

Pretend City

5 to 8 foot long piece of butcher paper; small boxes; pint-sized drink boxes; tempera paint; markers.

Draw two lines for a street down the middle of the paper. Ask the children to paint the street with gray tempera and paint the area on either side of the street to look like grass.

Let the children use tempera or markers to decorate the small boxes and the drink containers to look like places to live. An adult may cut doors and/or windows in the box houses, if desired.

The children then place their houses along the painted paper street to build a pretend city. The houses may be glued in place or left unglued, so children can move them around and rearrange the city. If you choose to, add a building for the school.

The children may drive small matchbox-sized cars and trucks in the pretend city. Also, use thread-spool people (ART, two- to five-year-olds) for creative play.

House Book

Wallpaper book; magazine or catalogue.

As shown, cut simple house shapes as large as possible from pages of the wallpaper book. Provide several of these cutouts for each child. Let the children assemble their pages in book fashion by stapling several house-shaped pages together. Then let the children cut out pictures from the catalogue of objects which belong in the different rooms of the house. The children glue the pictures belonging in one kind of room on each page. Make a kitchen page, a living room page, a bathroom page, and bedroom pages.

BLOCKS

Encourage the children to build a block neighborhood similar to their own neighborhood. For example, put the blocks side by side as if they were attached row houses, apart as if single family houses in the suburbs, or place in rows as if representing a mobile home park. Provide small cars and other props to enhance their play. Ask the children to tell you about where they live, where they play or buy groceries, etc.

BULLETIN BOARD

This Is Where We Live

Using a house pattern like the one below or the one on the front of the unit, cut from construction paper a house for each child and the teacher. Cut an oval shape out of each house front. Request a picture of each child from the parents. Glue a child's picture on the back of each house so it shows through the oval. Then print their name, address, and phone number under their picture.

Staple strips of construction paper or butcher paper in a pattern to resemble streets. Tape the houses along the streets.

The children may contribute trees, a sun, clouds, flowers, cars, and other details made from construction paper or other craft items.

COOKING

S'mores

Individual recipe:

> *2 graham crackers*
> *2 teaspoons chocolate frosting*
> *2 teaspoons marshmallow cream*

Wash hands. Let the children use table knives to spread the frosting on one cracker. Spread the marshmallow creme in the other cracker. Put the crackers together. Eat!

House Sandwiches

House-shaped cookie cutter
Slices of bread
Cream cheese—softened
Jelly

Wash hands. Let the children use the cookie cutter to cut two houses out of bread slices for each sandwich. Then the children use table knives to spread the cream cheese on one piece of bread and the jelly on the other. Put the two pieces together to complete the house sandwich.

Shake-Shake Bars

1 cup flour
1½ teaspoons baking powder
½ teaspoons salt
2 eggs
½ cup sugar
½ cup oil
½ cup orange juice

Wash hands. Let the children help measure and stir together flour, baking powder, and salt. Set aside.

Break the eggs one at a time, into a small jar or plastic bowl with a *tight-fitting* lid. Cover and ask the children to take turns shaking each egg about ten times. Add sugar, oil, and orange juice. Shake again about twenty times. Add flour mixture and shake until smooth. Pour batter into greased 7 × 11 pan. Bake 20-25 minutes at 375°. Cut into twelve bars.

To add to the fun and keep the children more actively involved, sing a song while mixing the ingredients.

''Shake Bars Song''

(Tune: ''Ten Little Indians'')

One little, two little, three little shake-shakes,
four little, five little, six little shake-shakes,
seven little, eight little, nine little shake-shakes,
Making Shake-Shake Bars.

LANGUAGE ARTS

Books

Barkin, Carol & Elizabeth James. *I'd Rather Stay Home*. Raintree Children's Books, 1975.
Barnett, Judith. *Old MacDonald Had an Apartment House*. Atheneum, 1969.
Duvoisin, Roger. *House of Four Seasons*. Lothrop, 1956.
Heilbroner, Joan. *This Is the House Where Jack Lives*. Harper and Row, 1962.
Hoberman, Mary Ann. *A House Is a House for Me*. Viking Press, 1978.

Jameson, Cynthia. *The House of Five Bears*. Putnam, 1978.
Miles, Betty. *A House for Everyone*. Random House, 1958.
Milne, A.A. *The House at Pooh Corner*. Dell, 1971.
Oechsli, Kelly. *Home Sweet Home*. Raintree Children's Books, 1983.
Shapp, Martha. *Let's Find Out About Houses*. Watts, 1975.
Spier, Peter. *Oh, Were They Ever Happy!* Doubleday & Co, 1978.
Stevens, Janet. *The House that Jack Built*. Holiday House, 1985.
Watson, Carol. *The House*. Hayes Books, 1980.

Teacher Resource Books

Bowyer, Carol. *The Children's Book of Houses and Homes*. Usborne, 1978.
Devlin, Harry. *To Grandfather's House We Go: A Roadside Tour of American Homes*. Parent's Magazine Press, 1967.
Huntington, Lee Pennock. *Americans at Home*. Coward, McCann and Geoghegan, 1981.

Fingerplays

Where I Live

Some people live in big houses
    (Stretch arms out as wide as possible.)
But some people's houses are small.
    (Bring arms in close together.)
People live in mobile homes
    (Arms move in round wheel motions.)
Or in apartments so tall!
    (Stretch up on tip toes.)
But I think the place where I live
    (Point to self.)
Is the very best place of all!
    (Smile broadly, thumbs pointed up confidently.)

Living in Different Places

Show pictures and talk about living in different places such as city apartments, farms, houseboats, on a mountain, etc.

Check your local library for films appropriate for this discussion and your age group. Encourage parents to speak and bring pictures, slides, or films if they have lived in other places in the country or world.

Match-Ups

Assemble an assortment of pairs of real objects often used together in or around the house. Some examples: broom and dust pan, paper and pencil, spoon and fork, cup and saucer, shoe and sock, salt and pepper.

Discuss how and why each object may be used where we live. Let the children handle the objects. Then mix up all of the objects. Ask the children to find two objects that go together.

Living in the Country/ in the City (Folder Game)

Show several pictures (or a film) that portray living in the country and living in the city. Talk about which things are in the country, which in the city.

Tape a piece of paper to make a pocket on each side of the folder. Label one side of the folder ''Country'' and the other side ''City.'' Provide several small pictures of obvious things found where people live in the country or in the city, such as a tractor, fire hydrant, barn, store, apartment building, etc. Let the children place each picture in the pocket on the appropriate side of the folder. If possible, ask them to explain why they think the pictures belong on one side or the other.

Variation: For more able children, provide some pictures that could belong in either one of the pockets. Discuss how some things are different in the different places we live, but that other things remain the same.

House Match

Using the house pattern in the front of the unit, make a house card for each child in the classroom. For the two- and three-year-olds, print the child's name on the card. For the four- and five-year-olds, print both their name and address. (Laminate, if desired.)

Display the cards on the chalkboard tray or a table. Give each child another card with his/her name (and address) on it. Let the children take turns trying to match the two cards. If the *This Is Where We Live* bulletin board is being used, let the children take turns matching their cards with their houses on the bulletin board.

Talking About Where I Live

Encourage the children to make up sentences using words such as: house, home, parents, family, street, road, name of city, etc. Print the sentences on chart paper or the chalkboard to ''read'' during the day. If one or two children are very able and interested, print their sentence on tagboard also. Then cut the sentences in half for the child to arrange the words again in a sentence by matching to the sentence on the chalkboard.

Home Matching Game

Read aloud the book ''A House is a House for Me.'' Provide pictures of different animals and places where those animals live. Have pictures of children and different kinds of houses. Match each picture with the appropriate home. If desired, you may laminate pictures and glue sandpaper squares on the back so they may also be used on the flannel board. Begin by providing four or five pictures to match. Add more pictures to the game as children are able to do more.

Ant—ant hill	Child—apartment	Beaver—dam
Bee—bee hive	Child—mobile home	Lion—jungle
Bird—nest	Child—tent	Cow—barn
Squirrel—tree	Child—farm	Dog—dog house
Eskimo—igloo	Fish—aquarium	Crab or snail—shell
Child—house	Shark—ocean	

Lacing Cards

Posterboard or cardboard; hole punch; yarn or shoelace.

Draw a simple line drawing of several different house shapes on pieces of posterboard or cardboard. Use a hole punch to punch holes all along each shape. Tape a long piece of yarn or a colorful shoelace by the top hole on the left of each shape (to reinforce working from top to bottom and left to right). Let the children practice lacing in and out of the holes. Later you might want to number the holes so the children follow a particular pattern.

Hint: Stiffen the end of the yarn by wrapping tape around it or by dipping the end in glue and letting it dry overnight.

Different Kinds of Homes
(Graph Making)

Talk with each child to learn in what kind of home each lives. Find or draw a simple picture of each kind of home mentioned. Make a chart, as shown, with the pictures of the different categories of homes along the left margin. By each type of home, put the names and/or photographs of the children in the class who live in that home style. Talk with the children about the ways in which the homes are different and the ways in which they are the same.

The House That Jack Built

Read the book *The House That Jack Built* aloud to the class. Read it again, letting the children help ''read'' the story by saying out loud with you the repeating lines as they occur.

The Three Little Pigs

Piece of straw; stick; brick.

Read or tell the story of ''The Three Little Pigs.'' Talk about why the house built of bricks was the strongest. Let the children try to break in half a piece of straw, a stick, and a brick.

Ask the children to think of all the things with which today's houses might be built. Do we build houses of straw or sticks or bricks in most cities today? If possible, take a field trip to a construction site where a house is being built.

Three Little Pigs— Sets of Three

Make sets of three: three pigs, three squares, three windows, three people, three chairs, etc. Let the children take turns finding or creating sets of three in the room such as three crayons, three books, etc.

Puzzles of Three

Provide cardboard or posterboard cutouts of a 6 inch or larger numeral 3. Let the children trace around the pattern. They then cut their numeral 3 into three pieces to make a puzzle to put together again and again.

Different Kinds of Houses

Use the graph discussed in the LANGUAGE ARTS section. Count together the number of: 1) different kinds of homes; 2) children living in each category of home; and 3) girls (or boys) living in each style of home.

Number Houses

Opened cans; black marker; masking tape or folio.

Use three to five clean, opened cans. Use a black marker to print a numeral on each can (like a house number). Make a small ball about the size of a large walnut by wadding up pieces of masking tape or foil.

Set the number houses on the floor against the wall and out of the traffic area. The children play the game by tossing the tape ball into a can. They then read the numeral on the can and do an action as suggested by the teacher: hop on one foot that many times, clap hands that many times, count to that number, etc.

Math Mother Says

Math Mother says hold up three fingers.
Math Mother says wave elbow two times.
Math Mother says walk in a circle.
Hold up five fingers.
Math Mother says hop on one foot three times.

Continue the game, varying the actions called for, until the children tire of the activity. (Played like Simon Says.)

Counting and Sorting

Laminated house shapes may be made using construction paper of various colors and the pattern in the front of the unit. Make enough so that the children will each have five or six to count or to sort by color.

Big and Little Riddles

Play the following game where children complete the riddle sentence.
Moms and dads are big; children are _____ .
Babies are little; children are _____ .
Elephants are big; kittens are _____ .
Dogs are little; cows are _____ .

Big and Little With Play Dough

Let the children use play dough to make big and little sizes to compare. Roll out shapes for big streets and little streets. Make big balls and little balls. Pat out big house shapes and little house shapes.

MOVEMENT

Hopping Home

Label a table or corner "home." Lay carpet squares on the floor in a zigzag pattern ending at "home." In a small box put small squares of paper with a numeral 1 through 4 on the pieces. Include one red piece of the same size with no numeral on it. Start the game farthest away from the "home" area. The children take turns drawing a piece of paper from the box, then hopping that many carpet squares. If the child draws the red piece he/she loses a turn. Three children playing at a time works well as they take turns drawing numbers and trying to move to "home." Put down as many squares as possible to make the game more fun.

Where Do I Live?

Where are you going Mr. Bird, Mr. Bird?
I'm flying to my home in the tree.   (Fly like a bird.)

Where are you going Mr. Horse, Mr. Horse?
I'm trotting to the barn don't you see?   (Trot in place or around the
                                               room.)

Where are you going Mr. Fish, Mr. Fish?
I'm swimming in the pond let me be.   (Lie on the floor; move arms and
                                               legs in swimming motions.)

Where are you going little boy, little boy?
I'm skipping to my house come with me!   (Skip around the room.)

MUSIC

At Our Home

(Tune: ''London Bridge'')

Let the children suggest different actions and verses to show the things they do at their home.

This is how we play with our pets, play with our pets, play with our pets, this is how we play with our pets, at our home.
This is how we read a story. . . .
This is how we make our beds. . . .

ROLE PLAY

Family Dollhouse

Sturdy cardboard box with four or six dividers; carpet pieces; wallpaper sample book; tagboard; glue; catalogue.

An adult cuts openings in the box for doors and windows. Take the dividers out of the box. Cut a piece of carpet or vinyl flooring to fit in the bottom of the box. Let the children choose wallpaper to cut to size to glue on the dividers. Put the dividers back in the box. Cut out figures from a catalogue to be the mom, dad, baby, children, grandparents. Glue these figures to tagboard and laminate if desired. (Instructions for another more involved doll figure follow this description.) The children thrill over this type of family house because they helped to create it.

Dollhouse Figures

Cardboard or posterboard; catalogue; fabric scraps; pinking shears; coarse sandpaper; glue.

Cut out simple cardboard figures from a box or posterboard. Cut enough to make several different family members such as mother, father, children, baby, grandparents, and one or two extra people for others who may live with the family. Find heads in the catalogue to glue on the figures.

Cut out a variety of clothes from scrap fabric. Use pinking shears so fabric will not ravel easily. Glue pieces of coarse sandpaper at the shoulder area and the waist area to hold the clothes to the body.

This activity is almost entirely teacher made and extra effort is involved, but the children will love to role play with these figures, especially if a box dollhouse, as described above, is also created.

Three Little Pigs

Let the children act out ''The Three Little Pigs.'' Let them devise their own props and use their own spontaneous dialogue between the characters. Talk about where each pig lived. Perhaps use small chairs to create the area for each of the three houses.

Keeping Where I Live Clean

Provide simple cleaning props such as broom and dust pan, rag, soapy water, sponge, etc. Let the children clean and organize the home living area of the room.

SCIENCE

Treasures from Where I Live

Styrofoam meat trays; plaster of paris.

Encourage the children to go on a treasure hunt outside their homes. (A note home to parents might insure the success of this activity.) Ask them to bring their treasures to school in a sack marked with their name.

Using small styrofoam meat trays, pour plaster of paris. Allow it to begin to set, then have the children put their treasures from home into their individual meat tray of plaster. Allow the mixture to dry completely before removing the meat tray. Display for a few days on a table with the sign: "Treasures from Where I Live." Talk about which things are the same/different among the children's treasures. Talk about which things are natural and which are man-made.

Straw, Sticks, Bricks

Straw; sticks; bricks.

After retelling "The Three Little Pigs," have samples of straw, sticks, and bricks available to feel and discuss. Place one of each of the materials on a tabletop. Let the children try to blow each one to make it move. Observe and discuss what happens. Ask if anyone would like to live for a long time in a house made of sticks or straw.

Cut and Paste

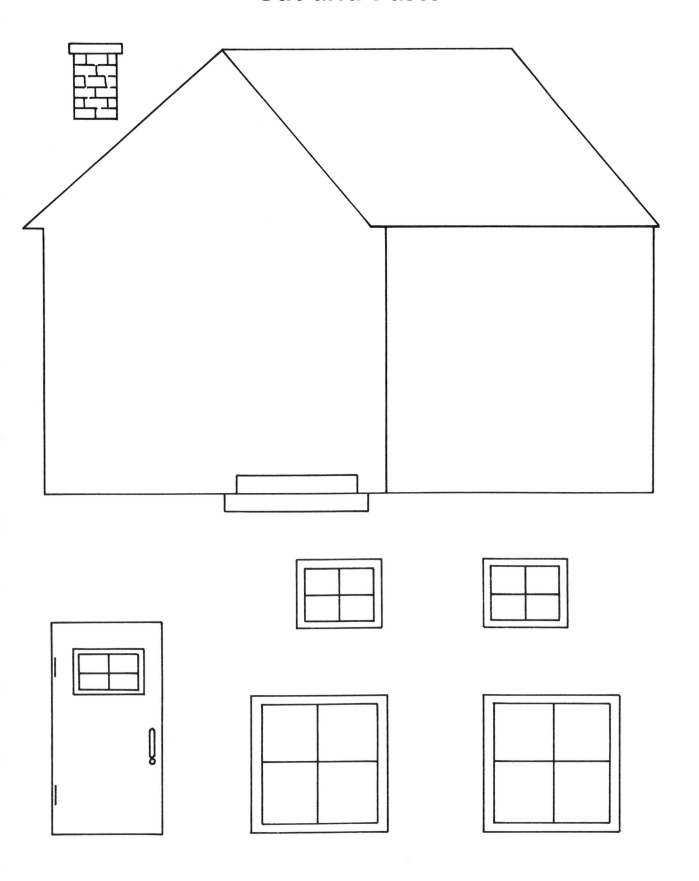

October Curriculum

1. Fire Prevention and Safety at Home and School

2. People Who Work

3. Fall Changes

4. Fun and Safety at Halloween

Fire Prevention and Safety at Home and School

CONCEPTS

- Fire is useful for warmth, cooking, and as an energy source for power.
- Three components (fuel, heat, and oxygen) must be present for fire to exist.
- Certain procedures can be learned as safe procedures in fire prevention.
- Certain procedures can be learned as methods of reporting fires.

ART

Firefighter Hats

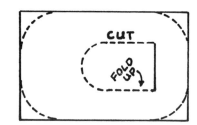

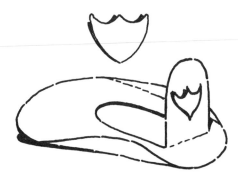

12 × 18 inch red construction paper; gold foil wrapping paper or yellow construction paper; glue.

Cut the outside shape of a firefighter's hat by rounding off the corners of red construction paper. Cut an oval hole large enough for the child's head to fit through. Fold up the cutout so it will stand up to make the top shape of the hat.

Cut badge shapes out of gold foil or yellow construction paper. Let the children decorate them, perhaps print a number on them, and glue them on the hats.

Finally, show the children how to roll up the sides of the hat brim slightly. Discuss with the children how this rolled brim helps to make the water drip back down the brim and helps keep the firefighter dry.

Book of Matches

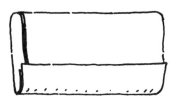

Cut 9 × 12 inch construction paper in half. Each half paper will make one book of matches.

Fold up the bottom 1½ inches; fold the top down, then tuck into the first fold to look like a book of matches. Let each child decorate their book of matches. On the inside, print for them: ''_____ (child's name) does *not* play with matches!''

**Fire Engines—
Easel or Tabletop
Painting**

Tempera paints; brushes; large cutouts of a simple fire engine.

Let the children use red or yellow tempera and brushes to paint their fire engines. Provide black paint so children may add wheels and other details.

Variation: After the fire engines are painted and dry, provide black circles to be used for wheels. Attach the wheels using brads, so the wheels may rotate.

Fire Masks

White construction paper; red tempera paint, crayons, or markers; popsicle sticks; glue.

Cut the white construction paper into mask shapes with flame-like points for hair. Cut out two holes for the eyes.

The children—using red tempera, crayons, or markers—color the masks. Let them glue on a popsicle stick for a mask handle.

Talk with the children about making their mask a happy fire mask by always helping adults to be very careful with fires.

**Flame Paints with
Marbles**

Yellow and red tempera paint in small cups or bowls; marbles; box lid; manila paper.

Let children lay a piece of manila paper in the box lid. They then spoon out one to three small blobs of paint on the paper and place one or more marbles in the lid. By tilting the lid slightly the marbles will roll around through the paint and make "flame" designs. Add more spoonfuls of paint as desired to increase the color blending. Children usually want to do this activity again and again.

**Collage
(Group Project)**

24 × 24 inch paper; magazines; glue.

Divide the paper in half and label one half: "Things We Play With", and the other half, "Things We Don't Play With." Provide pages from magazines showing appliances, camping cooking equipment, and toys. Let the children tear or cut around the pictures and glue them on the appropriate half of the paper.

**Straw Blowing—
Flaming Paints**

Straws; manila paper; cups of yellow and red tempera paint.

Working on a tabletop covered with newspapers, children put a spoonful of paint on a piece of paper and create designs by blowing through a straw to make the paint move. Using both yellow and red paint will produce flame designs. Children may add more spoonfuls of paint to blend colors and extend the design.

We Prevent Fires!

Crayons and/or markers; manila paper.

Using crayons or markers, the children draw pictures of firefighters, trucks, and other fire-fighting equipment. Display the pictures under the caption: ''We Prevent Fires!''

BLOCKS

Build a fire station for the fire trucks. Use tape or blocks to construct roads for the trucks to travel. Build an office building or house and pretend it is on fire. Role play getting the people out safely and putting out the fire. A length of tubing or hose will add to the fun.

BULLETIN BOARD

**Things We Play With/
Things We Don't Play
With**

Use the collage group project suggested in ART for three-year-olds and make it a child-produced bulletin board. Divide the bulletin board in half using a piece of thick yarn, rope, or construction paper strips. On one half of the board put the caption ''Things We Play With.'' On the other half of the board put ''Things We Don't Play With.'' Discuss ideas for each category with the children. Provide pages from magazines displaying appliances, camping cooking equipment, and toys. Let the children tear or cut out pictures to classify in each category. Provide push pins so the children can pin up each picture on the appropriate side of the bulletin board. Several small real objects such as matchbooks and puppets may also be pinned on the board. Frequently talk about the choices children find to display on each part of the board: ''Why is that a good choice for play?'' ''Why is that not a safe choice for children?''

FIRE PREVENTION AND SAFETY AT HOME AND SCHOOL

COOKING

Flame Cups

Lemon jello cubes
Strawberry jello cubes
Whipped topping

The children place yellow and red jello cubes in small cups. Then let them top their jello with a spoonful of whipped topping.

Energy Chews

Let each child mix in a cup:

1 tablespoon peanut butter
½ teaspoon honey
1 tablespoon raisins
1 teaspoon chopped apple
1 tablespoon raw oatmeal

Wash hands. Then each child stirs the mixture and rolls it into balls. The mixture may be chilled for a while or eaten immediately. Firefighters need to have high energy!

Candle Salad

Individual recipe:

1 maraschino cherry
One-half banana
1 pineapple ring
Small paper plate
1 toothpick

Wash hands. Place the pineapple ring on the plate. Stand the banana half in the hole of the pineapple ring. For the candle flame, put a cherry on a toothpick and push it onto the top of the banana.

LANGUAGE ARTS

Books

Arnold, Caroline. *Who Keeps Us Safe?* Watts, 1982.
Bester, Roger. *Fireman Jim*. Crown, 1981.
Bundt, Nancy. *The Fire Station Book*. Carolrhoda Books, 1981.
Elliot, Dan. *A Visit to the Sesame Street Firehouse*. Random House, 1983.
Fisher, Keonard Everett. *Pumpers, Boilers, Hooks and Ladders: A Book of Fire Engines*. Dial Press, 1961.
Gibbons, Gail. *Fire! Fire!* Harper and Row, 1984.
Keeping, Charles. *Willie's Fire Engine*. University Press, 1980.
Peterson, Barby. *Let's Visit the Fire Department*. Golden Press, 1974.

Teacher Resource Books

Landers, Eugene. *Fire Prevention and Safety Handbook for Texas Public Schools*. Board of Insurance Commissioners, Fire Insurance Division, 1954.

Seder, Susan. *Teaching About Safety, Vol. 1: Fire*. National Safety Council, 1972.

Sesame Street Fire Safety Resource Book. Children's Television Workshop, 1981.

Fingerplays

Five Firefighters

Five strong firefighters waiting at the station.	(Hold up five fingers.)
Then comes the signal to go into action.	
The first one puts on a firefighter's hat.	(Wiggle or bend down each finger as discussed in rhyme.)
The second does boots just like that.	
The third one slides down the pole just right.	
The fourth jumps on the back and holds tight.	
The fifth one drives the truck to the fire	
Before the flames go higher.	
Listen to the fire engine say,	(Imitate siren.)
"Cars and trucks—out of my way."	
Whoosh! Comes the water from the hose spout.	(Put fists on top of each other. Move side to side and squirt water on the fire.)
Before you know it, the flames are out.	(Clap hands.)

Sesame Street Fire Safety

Bert, Ernie, and other Sesame Street characters appear on their regular television show in segments which teach preschool children about fire safety. They have also developed the *Fire Safety Resource Book* for adults to use with young children. The book contains activities which stress that matches are for grown-ups and also instruct children about what they should do in case of a fire. Songs, fingerplays, and poems are included in the book.

Firefighter Visit

Plan to visit a fire station or invite a firefighter to come to the classroom. The day before, write out the questions the children dictate to you about firefighters and fire prevention. This chart of questions can be talked about again the day after seeing the firefighter, to serve as a reminder of what they learned.

Letter Writing

After the field trip or visit from the firefighters, let children dictate a letter to the firefighters thanking them and telling what the children have learned. Let the children draw pictures to send to the firefighters with the letter, if they choose.

Free Materials

Ask for fire prevention materials from your local fire department. They frequently have coloring booklets aimed at young children.

Danger of Matches

Talk with the children about the dangers of playing with matches. (Seventy thousand fires every year are started by young children playing with matches.) "Why are matches dangerous for children? What could you do if you saw someone playing with matches?"

Fire Drills

Make a special effort to practice the things to do if there were a fire in the building. Take a special tour of your building with the children, pointing out fire prevention equipment (smoke alarms, extinguishers, etc.) so the children see how the school protects them.

The Child Who Cried Fire

Tell the story of "The Boy Who Cried Wolf." Then tape record the children as they make up a similar story about a child who keeps crying "Fire" when there really is no fire. The teacher should act as the narrator to keep the story progressing. Later replay the tape for the group or let the children take turns listening to it with ear phones.

Fire Prevention Rules

Make a chart of fire prevention rules dictated by the children. One effective method is to write out all the children's names, leaving two or three blank lines between each. Ask each child to offer a fire safety or fire prevention rule, then print it on the chart by the child's name. Children will come to the chart many times to find their name and "read" their rule!

Some examples of rules to discuss with children are:

Don't play with matches.
Keep away from things that are hot.
Don't play with electric sockets or plugs.
Don't play with fireworks.
Keep things that can burn away from hot things.

"Jack Be Nimble"

Repeat the nursery rhyme, "Jack Be Nimble." Ask the children if Jack is being very smart to jump over a fire. "What might happen?" "What do you think Jack should do?"

Let the children work together to make up a new rhyme, such as:

"Jack be safe, Jack be smart.
Don't play with candles.
Don't let a fire start!"

Safe Scenes

Discuss how families need to have a place to meet outside their home after a fire drill or real alarm so everyone knows everyone is safe. Talk about where these meeting places should be.

For each child, print a sentence on a strip of paper as the child describes his/her safe place. Ask them to talk about this safe place with their family.

MATH
NUMBER CONCEPTS

Counting

1. Count the number of exits, smoke alarms, fire alarms, and fire extinguishers in the entire school.
2. Have the children count the number of door exits in their homes and tell the class the next school day.

Number Sequence

Make five or more copies of the firefighter on the front page of the October Curriculum guide. Print a numeral from 1 to 5 or more on each badge on the hats. Let children put the firefighters in the correct sequence.

Firefighter Equipment Counter

2 × 4 board; finishing nails; small wooden beads or large buttons.

Pound finishing nails (headless) into a 2 × 4 piece of board. Number each nail on the board from 1 to 5 or more. Let the children help the firefighters organize their equipment by putting the correct number of small wooden beads on each nail. (Large buttons will also work as well as beads.)

MATH VOCABULARY

Large—Small

Divide the flannel board into two sections with yarn. Put the word LARGE in one section, the word SMALL in the other. Put an example under each word as a clue. Use construction paper figures or actual pictures, laminated to preserve. Prepare the pictures for use on the flannel board by letting the children take turns categorizing each picture as large or small. Use pictures associated with firefighters, fire prevention, safety, etc.

MOVEMENT

Stop, Drop, and Roll

Tell children that if their clothes ever catch on fire they are supposed to stop, drop, and roll. Let the class jog in place for a few seconds. Then have them stop, drop to the floor, and roll gently back and forth as if putting out flames. Repeat the action several times.

Crawl Under Smoke

Pretend the room is filled with smoke. Let the children crawl on their hands and knees across the room to the door. Later, have the children lay on their stomachs and pull themselves with their arms across the room to the door.

Fire Engine Run

Use two strips of masking tape to mark a place on the floor for the fire station and a second place, some distance away, for a burning house. Have a bell or mimic a bell by tapping on a glass. When the bell sounds, let children take turns (one to three children at a time) running from the fire station to the burning house, pretending to hold a hose to put water on the fire, then running back. Let the children make a siren sound as they go toward the house, but not when they come back. Explain why.

Keep the activity moving quickly to increase fun and lessen children's time waiting. The activity is also effective if done outside.

MUSIC

Did You Ever See a Firefighter?

(Tune: "Did You Ever See a Lassie?")

Did you ever see a firefighter, a firefighter, a firefighter,
Did you ever see a firefighter slide down the pole?
Slide this way and that way and that way and this way?
Did you ever see a firefighter slide down the pole?

Other verses:

1. Ride on the truck
2. Hook up the hose
3. Put out the fire
4. Go back to the station

Let the children suggest different actions to act out as the verse is repeated several times.

ROLE PLAY

Calling the Fire Department

Provide play phones and a card with the 911 emergency number or the phone number for the local fire department. Let children act out calling the fire department to report a fire.

Stress that they should only call if there is a real fire. Calling the fire department as a trick is a very dangerous and foolish thing.

Firefighters

Provide several props for children to use to act out fire prevention and safety. Props may include: hats, shirts, boots, a garden hose or vacuum cleaner hose, and a small ladder. (A toy ax is also a possible prop, but it may encourage negative behavior and is not recommended.)

Box House

Get a large box. Cut out windows. Then cut out a door—cutting out only three sides so the fourth side acts as a hinge allowing the door of the house to be opened and closed.

Let the children act out touching the door to see if it is hot before opening it to escape outside. Use the firefighter props to pretend to put out fires in the house.

SCIENCE

Fire Safety

For fire safety with young children, it is recommended that you talk about fire and use pictures to help the children understand. Using real matches and candles to demonstrate is discouraged.

Simple Machines

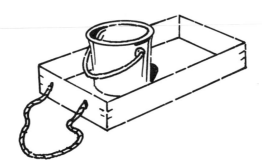

Explore with the children how simple machines help make work easier. Provide one to three buckets with handles. Have the buckets 1/2 to 3/4 full of sand so they are heavy to lift. (If sand is unavailable, consider using gallon milk jugs with tight fitting, screw-on lids. Fill the jugs 3/4 full of water.)

1. Use a strong, shallow box such as a beverage can box. Punch two holes in one end and tie on a rope for a pulling handle. Ask the children to lift the sand buckets and carry them to a place several feet away. Talk about how heavy they feel. Then place the sand buckets in the box and let children pull the box to the same place. Explore with the children to see how the sleigh helps make the work easier. The children see how much one child can carry with and without the sleigh.

2. Tell the children how, in earlier days, water to put out a fire was carried in buckets by hand. Help them understand that fire trucks are also machines that help make the firefighters' job easier.

People Who Work

CONCEPTS

- There are many kinds of work that people do.
- People work to earn money to buy the things they need to live.
- People use different kinds of tools or machines to perform their jobs.
- Some people wear uniforms or special clothing to do their jobs.
- Different skill levels are involved in doing every job.
- Every kind of job and every worker is important.
- Most jobs may be done by either a woman or a man who wants to do that kind of work and who is trained to do that kind of work.

ART

Worker of the Day
(Group Collage)

12 × 18 inch or 24 × 24 inch manila paper or newsprint.

Choose a different occupation to talk about each day. Try especially to discuss the types of work done by the parents of the children in the class.

Have the children bring cutouts from magazines, catalogues, and newspapers of pictures of the things that are used by that worker each day. Provide several cutouts of things not used by that worker. Let the children decide which cutouts to glue on the group collage.

Label each collage with a word or two to name the type of work. Display all of the Workers of the Day along the wall. Suggestions for the daily worker: repair person, bank worker, teacher, doctor and nurse, lawyer, police officer, firefighter, librarian, veterinarian, dentist, post office worker, store worker, vehicle driver, and artist.

Avoid male and/or female stereotypes in the word choices for each occupation. For example, use *firefighter* instead of *fireman*.

Worker Shape-Ups

Construction paper triangles, squares, circles, and rectangles in several different sizes and colors; 9 × 12 inch manila or construction paper; glue.

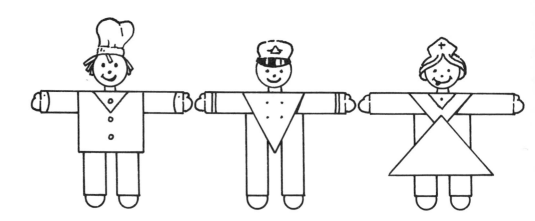

Let the children experiment using the shape cutouts to make the shapes of people who work. Show them different shapes to use for heads, bodies, etc. After the children have made the worker-shape they like, give them a piece of paper and let them glue the shapes on the paper. Use small geometric shapes or crayons to add facial details to the worker.

Fire Finger Painting

Finger paint with red and yellow paint to create a "fire picture." Display on a bulletin board or wall beside a picture of a firefighter with a hose in hand.

Trash Mural (Class Project)

Go for a walk, picking up litter along the way. Return to the classroom and glue the litter on a large piece of paper cut in the shape of a trash can. The mural could be titled "Helping the Trashperson."

Wood Shaving Collage

Wood shavings (collected from construction sites); glue; 9 × 12 inch construction paper.

The children create a collage by gluing the thin wood curls and pieces made from using a wood plane to smooth a board. If possible, show a real wood plane. Talk about who uses wood planes and why.

Yarn Prints

Several 4-6 inch squares of cardboard or posterboard with worker faces made from glued-on yarn; construction paper hats for various jobs; tempera paints; brushes; 9 × 12 inch manila paper.

The children lightly brush paint over the yarn outline, then press it on a paper to make a print. Encourage them to repeat the process several times using different faces and colors. Encourage them to overlap the prints for a more interesting effect. After the paint is dry, let the children glue hats on several of the prints on each paper.

Crayon Resist Picture

Crayons; manila paper; black or blue tempera paint.

Using heavy pressure on crayons, let the children use bright colors to color a picture on manila paper. Then paint over all paper with a thin wash of black or blue tempera paint.

Walnut Finger Construction Puppets

Walnut shell halves; cardboard egg cartons; yarn scraps; glue; markers.

Cut out the tall dividers from a cardboard egg carton so that each child can have one or more. Children may use pointed markers to make the face, pieces of yarn glued for hair, and walnut shell halves glued on top to make a construction worker with a "hard hat."

Trashy Snake

3 foot length of butcher paper; markers or tempera paints; scissors; stapler; newspaper.

Fold a 3 foot length of butcher paper in half lengthwise. Draw two parallel snake-like lines as wide as possible. The children may take turns cutting the snake out. Staple the two pieces together, leaving an opening for stuffing. The children should draw the eyes and mouth, then color or paint the body. Stuff newspaper wads inside and staple shut. Go for a "litter walk" as a class outing. Glue or staple litter to the snake. Display on a table with a sign "Litter Monster Helpers."

People Pop-Ups

Styrofoam or paper cups; popsicle sticks; construction paper scraps; posterboard, 2 inch circles; yarn scraps; markers; glue.

Let the children glue a stick to a circle. They then use markers, yarn, and/or construction paper to add hair and facial features. They may also add a hat to show what kind of work their person does.

Push the stick gently through the bottom of the cup. Pull the stick down to hide the person. Push the stick up to make the person pop-up.

Tool People

Tool stencils; markers or crayons; manila paper.

Provide cardboard or posterboard stencils of tools for children to trace around. The stencils should be tools useful to workers in their jobs. Let the children make the tool into a person by adding eyes, arms, legs, and other features.

Worker Stick Puppets

Hat stencils; markers; scissors; glue; popsicle sticks.

Using the hat stencils from the Hat Mirage Collage, let the children trace and cut out the hat of their choice. Then let them cut out a circle for the face and glue on the hat. They may add facial features with markers or glue pieces of construction paper for eyes, nose, and mouth. Glue or staple the face to a tongue depressor or popsicle stick. The children could then put on a puppet show for a younger class.

Trash Monsters

Grocery sacks or butcher paper; scissors; stapler; markers or tempera paints; newspapers.

Cut out two giant head shapes from a grocery sack or from two 24 inch pieces of butcher paper. (Three or four per class may be used.) Let the children draw or paint on one piece for the front (face) of the head and one piece for the back of the head. Staple the head shut, leaving an opening for stuffing. Let the children stuff the head with wadded-up newspaper. Then the children may stuff an old shirt and pants with newspaper wads, tie the ends of arms and legs with yarn, and staple the shirt body to the pants body. Finally, attach the head to the shirt with the stapler. The children bring back trash from a "litter walk." Children may staple, glue, or tape litter all over the monster's body. Display the trash monster sitting in a corner or tied in a chair with the label, "Trash Monster."

Hat Mirage Collage

Hat stencils; markers or crayons; manila paper.

Provide a variety of hat stencils, approximately 5 × 5 inches in size. Using a marker or crayon, let the children trace around the inside of each stencil randomly on a 12 × 18 inch piece of manila paper. Encourage them to overlap for interesting effects and to experiment with different colors.

Helicopter Pilots

Markers or crayons; scissors; tape.

Duplicate the pattern below. Let the children decorate the patterns with markers or crayons, then cut them out. The children may help each other fold and tape their patterns. The helicopters may then be flown inside or outside the room by simply dropping them gently from a raised hand.

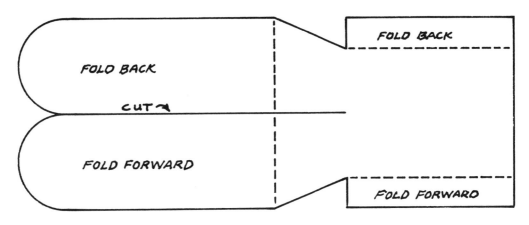

BLOCKS

Provide some props and suggestions to encourage the children to create an environment for a different occupation each day. Some possibilities include construction site, doctor's office, fire station, delivery truck roads, and office buildings.

BULLETIN BOARD

What Do People Do?

Ask the children to bring in pictures of people working. Glue each on 9 × 12 construction paper. Print on each paper a sentence the child dictates telling what job each person in the picture is doing. Some children may also tell why the job is important and/or how it helps us.

Classification

1. *Inside—Outside*
   Divide a bulletin board in half with yarn. Cover one half with outside scenery—blue sky, sun, birds flying, etc. Cover the other half to resemble the inside of a building. Provide several pictures of different workers at their jobs, both inside and outside. Children may use push pins to pin pictures to the outside or inside half.
2. *Heavy—Not Heavy*
   Provide pictures of tools needed by different workers: cement mixer, tractor, ruler, typewriter, pencil, fire ax, whistle, etc. Classify the pictures as heavy or not heavy. This activity may be done individually or as a class.

COOKING

"Worker Day" Lunch

Everyone brings a small sack from home on "Worker Day." Let the children decorate their sack. Put the child's name on each sack.

Wash hands. Let each child pack a lunch for "Worker Day." Provide the ingredients for the children to spread "Secretary Sandwiches": tuna or peanut butter and bread. Also add to the sack lunch an apple, carrot sticks, chips, and maybe a cookie. Prepare the menu early in the day and save until lunch. Eat outside if weather permits or in some unusual place to add to the fun of the day.

Energy Cereal

4 cups old-fashioned oats, uncooked
2 cups milk
1 cup raisins
1 cup orange juice
½ cup honey
1 teaspoon cinnamon

First Day: Mix all of the ingredients together. Cover with a tight-fitting lid. Refrigerate overnight.

Second Day: Serve like a cereal with milk. No sugar is needed.

Banana Shake

3 cups milk
2 ripe bananas
1 teaspoon vanilla
1 tablespoon honey
Blender

Put the bananas in the blender and mash them. Add the other ingredients. Mix until slightly frothy. Makes eight ½-cup delicious servings.

Books

Broekel, Ray. *Fire Fighters*. Children's Press, 1981.

Broekel, Ray. *Police*. Children's Press, 1981.

Discover the World of Work. U.S. Gov. Printing Office, 1976.

Francoise. *What Do You Want to Be?* Scribner's, 1957.

Gibbons, Gail. *The Post Office Book*. Harper and Row, 1982.

Goldreich, Gloria and Esther Goldreich. *What Can She Be? A Police Officer*. Lothrop, 1975.

Greene, Carol. *Astronauts*. Children's Press, 1984.

Junior Occupational Briefs. Science Research Assoc., 1964.

Kaufman, Bill and Alan H. Zwiebel. *Be a Police Officer!* Random House, 1984.

Medsger, Betty. *People on the Job*. Mind Openers, 1977.

Merriman, Eve. *Mommies at Work*. Alfred A. Knopf, 1961.

Mitchell, Joyce Slayton. *My Mommy Makes Money*. Little, Brown, 1984.

Nau, Pat. *State Patrol*. Carolrhoda Books, 1984.

Pellett, Elizabeth, Deborah K. Ose, and Marguerite May. *A Woman Is*. Aardvark Media, 1974.

Pellett, Elizabeth, Deborah K. Ose, and Marguerite May. *A Man Is*. Aardvark Media, 1974.

Puner, Helen. *Daddies, What They Do All Day*. Lothrop, Lee and Shepard, 1969.

Reif, Patricia. *Big Work Machines*. Western Publishing, 1984.

Shanks, Ann Z. *About Garbage and Stuff*. Viking Press, 1973.

Showers, Paul. *Where Does the Garbage Go?* Harper and Row, 1974.

Fingerplays

If I Were

If I were a baker	(Pretend to put on hat and apron.)
What would I do?	
Bake lots of cookies	(Make a circle with thumb and forefinger.)
For me and for you.	(Point to self and a friend.)
If I were a secretary,	(Pretend to type and write on a notepad.)
What would I do?	
Answer the phone,	(Hold pretend phone to ear.)
"How do you do?"	
If I were a veterinarian,	(Pretend to put stethoscope in ears.)
What would I do?	
Care for your pet	(Pretend to examine a cat or dog.)
It's special to you.	
If I were a dentist,	(Look in mouth of a friend.)
What would I do?	
Check those teeth	(Pretend to drill or x-ray friend's teeth.)
That's good for you!	

Field Trips

Possible field trips for each age group might include: the hospital, post office, construction site, veterinarian's office, fast food restaurant, car repair shop, etc.

Worker Day

The last day of the unit, let the children come to school dressed as the worker of their choice. Encourage the use of hats, badges, shoes, etc. A large note posted at the door for parents will help make this activity a success.

Riddle Time

The teacher makes up riddles about a job or worker and the children guess about whom the teacher is thinking. ''I'm thinking of someone who wears a protective coat and boots and hat. Sometimes this person rides standing up on a big red or yellow truck. A large hose is one piece of equipment that this person uses on the job.''

Game: ''Good Morning Worker''

One child is the worker and stands with back to rest of group. A second child is chosen to tiptoe up to the first child and say: ''Good Morning, _____ .'' Take turns using different types of jobs, such as dentist, judge, teacher, doctor, cook, bus driver, etc. The first child tries to guess the name of the child who says good morning.

Job Scene

Butcher paper; glue; scissors.

The class may cut or tear out pictures of people working different jobs. You may assist in finding as large a variety as possible. Glue the pictures on a large piece of butcher paper.

What's Your Job?

Walk around the school and talk to the different people that work there. Let the children ask questions about the job and the tools used to perform the task.

Famous Workers

You ''interview'' each child with the aid of a tape recorder. The children pretend to have the job of a famous character: Santa Claus, Easter Bunny, Ernie, Big Bird, Frosty the Snowman, etc. Play the tape back as the children listen and try to guess who is talking.

Guess-a-Job

You hold up pictures of objects used in more than one type of job: hammer, typewriter, stethoscope, shovel, etc. The children try to name as many occupations as possible that use that tool.

Worker Equipment

You hold up either an actual hat, or else a stencil or picture of a hat. The children take turns naming the kind of hat, the job, other equipment needed to perform that job, and whether it is an inside or outside job.

PEOPLE WHO WORK

Chart Story: Working

Write on a large chart paper: "What job would you like to have?" List the children's names with room to print their replies. Jeff said, "_____ ." Karen said, "_____ ."

What Shall I Be?

Conduct "interviews" with each child. Some questions might be about the parents' jobs, what the child wishes to be when grown up, and what the child thinks a teacher's job entails.

Masks and Protective Glasses

Plastic drink can holders; hole punch; pipe cleaners.

Some workers use a type of mask or protective glasses when they work. Display real masks or have pictures of a surgery mask, football helmet with face guard, oxygen mask, welder or sander goggles, safety glasses, and dark sunglasses. Let the children try on the masks or glasses and guess who wears them. Talk about why workers need to wear each kind of mask or glasses.

Make glasses using the plastic rings from a six-pack drink-can holder. Cut the rings apart in twos. Punch a hole in the outside edge of each ring. Insert pipe cleaners and twist to stay. Bend back part to fit over child's ear.

Worker of the Day

Invite a different worker to visit the class for a few minutes each day. Parents who work may be able to visit for ten minutes on their way to work or during their lunch hour. Workers in the building may also be used.

Let the children interview the workers about their jobs. Plan some questions for the children to ask: "Where do you work?" "What do you do at work?" "What do you have to wear?" "What tools or things do you use to do your work?"

Make a worker-of-the-day collage for each visitor (see ART, two- to five-year-olds). If possible, take a photograph of each visitor to display by the collage.

MATH   NUMBER CONCEPTS

Matching Sizes

Buttons or circle cutouts; glue.

Duplicate the handout with the circles on it at the end of this section. Give each child the required number of buttons or circle cutouts. The child glues the buttons or circles in place by matching the sizes.

A Teacher at Work

Catalogue; pieces of flannel; glue.

Cut out a picture of a teacher from a catalogue. Glue a piece of flannel to the back. Cut out pictures of children, also, and apply flannel to those pictures. The children may then put the pictures of teacher and class on the flannel board, counting the children as they are added to the board.

Sewing Strings

Blunt needles; thread or string; buttons.

Pretend to be a seamstress by using a blunt needle and thread or string. String buttons on the string and count as each one is added.

Give each child a needle and thread. Call out different amounts of buttons for them to add to their threads each time. Continue for several different amounts.

Variation: Older children might actually sew on a piece of felt. Use a marker to write one numeral on one side and another numeral on the other side of the felt. The children look at the numeral, then sew the required number of buttons on each side of the felt. A large crewel needle works well.

Matching Shapes

Duplicate the Matching Shapes handout at the end of this section. Provide construction paper cutouts of the shapes. Let the children match the shapes to the outline on the handout to complete each worker.

MATH VOCABULARY

Long—Short

1. Refer to things as being long or short as often as possible in natural conversation throughout the day.
2. Cut long and short lengths of yarn; one size for each child. Ask each child to hold the yarn by both ends and pull taut. Decide as a class if it is long or short.
   Variation: As the children become proficient at deciding correctly, have them close their eyes or blindfold them, then give them a piece of yarn to feel and determine if it is long or short.
3. The children fold a piece of manila paper in half. With markers or red crayon, draw a long fire-fighting ladder on one side and a short ladder on the other side. Print *long* and *short* on each appropriate side.

Disappearing Game

Suggestions for object pairs: long and short envelopes, long and short wooden spoons from the kitchen, long and short pencils or pens, long and short brooms or mops.

Use a selection of several objects. The number should be determined by the ability of the group. Show and discuss the objects to be used in the game. Cover and remove one or more. Individual children (or the class as a whole) take turns deciding which are missing—the long or short object from each pair.

MOVEMENT

Worker Pantomime

Stand in a circle and pretend to be workers doing different jobs. Children may take turns suggesting occupations: a secretary typing, a construction worker building a house, a chef preparing a cake, a janitor cleaning the school, etc.

The Police Say

The children take turns using the police props to play the game Simon Says.

Telephone Repair (Played Like a Bear Hunt)

Give directions and let the children use motions to silently act out each step of a telephone repair person fixing the broken wire on the telephone line.
1. Get in our truck.
2. Drive the truck to the place needing repair.
3. Haul out all the equipment we will need.
4. Put it on our back.
5. Climb the tall telephone pole.
6. Fix the wires.
7. Climb down the pole.
8. Ooops. We forgot our tools. Climb back up the pole.
9. Get our tools.
10. Climb down the pole.
11. Dial a repair phone to check that the wire is working well now.
12. Get in the truck and drive away.

Add additional actions as desired. Use exaggerated movements to increase the fun and exercise value of the activity.

Jumpers

Follow the carpet square path. Arrange carpet squares in a path around the room. Leave a distance between them. Let the children jump from one to the other. (Avoid using carpet squares which slide when jumped on.)

MUSIC

Workers Work

(Tune: "Mulberry Bush")

The children suggest different occupations, then plan how to act each one out as the song is sung together.

This is the way the baker bakes...
This is the way the doctor helps us...
This is the way the teacher teaches...
This is the way the bus driver drives...
This is the way the children work...

Mailperson

(Tune: "Happy Birthday")

Who delivers mail to you?
Who delivers mail to you?
Your friendly mailperson that's who-oo,
Delivers mail to you.

Teachers

(Tune: "Mary Had a Little Lamb")

Our teacher comes to school each day,
School each day, school each day.
Our teacher comes to school each day,
To help us learn and grow.
She smiles and helps us learn all day,
Learn all day, learn all day.
She smiles and helps us learn all day,
We're glad we come to school.

ROLE PLAY

People Who Work
(Props)

Doctor:

Stethoscope	Cotton balls
Bathroom scale	Nurse puppets
Bandaids, bandages	White coat
Tongue depressors or	Doctors bag
popsicle sticks	Paper for prescriptions

Librarian:

Books	Ink pad
Magazines	Date stamp

Index cards or paper rectangles to use as checking out cards

Farmer:

Wood or play barn	Straw hat
Toy farm amimals	Neckerchief
Tractor	Fences
Truck	

Firefighter:

Firefighters' hats	Child's rubber raincoat
Flashlight	Child's rubber boots
Small bucket	Toy fire truck
Rope	Hose

"Fire extinguisher" (potato chip can, covered with foil and a small plastic tube inserted in the side)

Dentist:

> Cardboard toothbrushes
> White coat
> Mirror

Large teeth (to pretend to brush with the cardboard toothbrushes)
Appointment book

Teacher:

> Desks or table and chairs
> Ruler
> Chalkboard
> Paper

Pencil
Crayons
Books

I Want to Be

Provide clothing, props, and opportunity for the children to role play as many varieties of jobs as possible. Suggestions: secretary, firefighter, doctor, nurse, fast-food worker, construction worker, police officer, postal worker, janitor, teacher, etc.

Variation: You may suggest a fictional character, then the class pretends to do the job of the character.

Hats

Use large sheets of paper and cut hats as shown at the end of this section. With a little variation, you can create hats for several other occupations.

SCIENCE

Machines

Walk around the school, searching for as many different kinds of machines as you can find. Talk about a typewriter, record player, pencil sharpener, film projector, vacuum cleaner, and other machines used to help run the school.

Discuss simple machines such as a hole punch, pair of scissors, and tweezers. Let the children show you how these simple machines work.

Provide a pair of kitchen tongs, a pincher-type clothespin, and some tweezers. Let the children experiment with picking up paper, crayons, paper clips, and small blocks using these simple tools. "Which works best for each object?" "How are these the same?" "How are these different?"

Repair Discovery

Provide an unusable clock, hair dryer, watch, radio, etc. Talk with the children about how these items are unusable, ready to be thrown away. Explain that, since the items are unusable, the class may experiment with them. Provide safe tools and let the children help take each item apart. Observe and talk about what is inside. Remind the children that they would always need adult permission to use tools and to take things apart.

Button, Button...

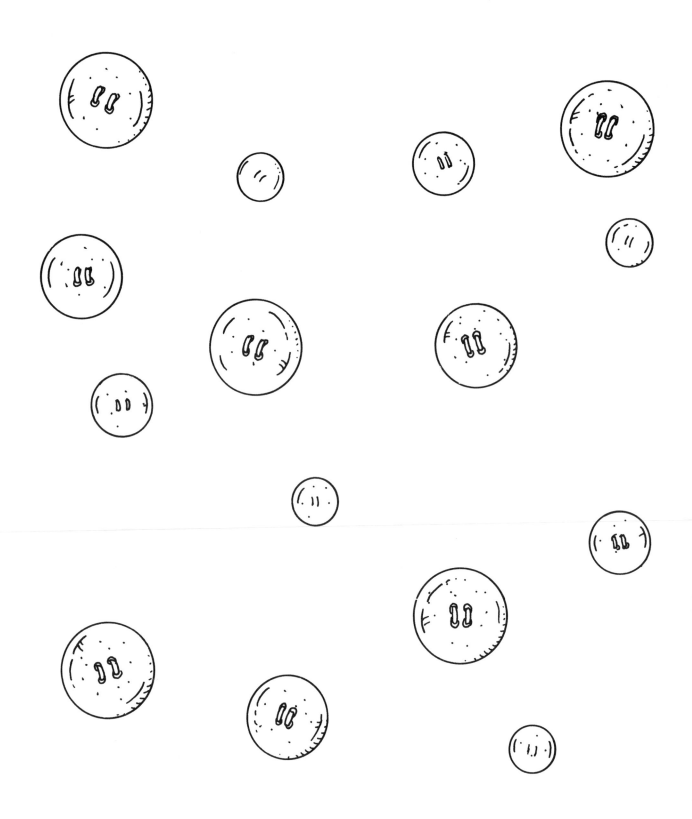

Matching Shapes

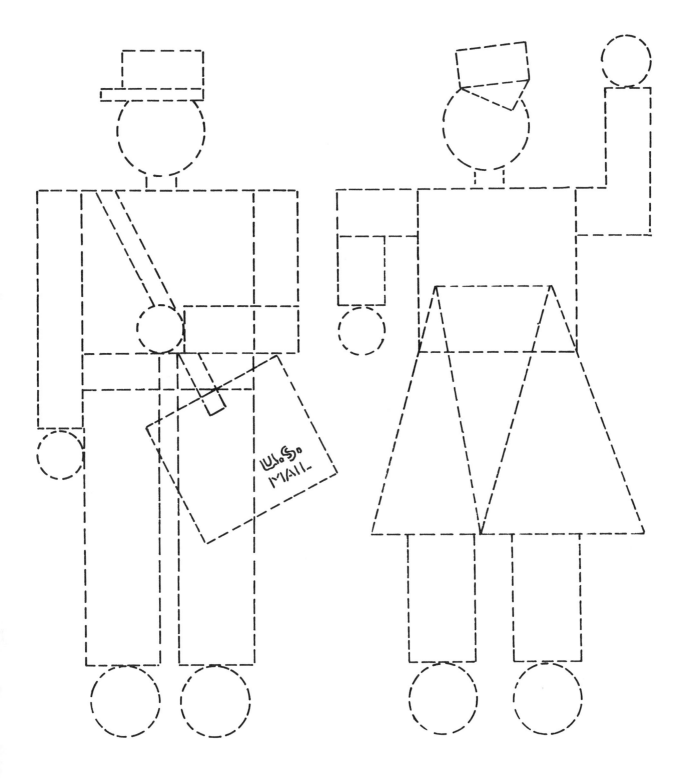

Post Office Worker

Police Officer

From *We Care*, Copyright © 1988 Scott, Foresman and Company.

Hats

Fall Changes

CONCEPTS

- Fall is a season that comes after summer and before winter.
- Autumn is another name for fall.
- Leaves on most of the trees change color and later die. Many leaves fall to the ground.
- Many foods ripen and are harvested in the fall. Some of these foods are: apples, pumpkins, nuts, and potatoes.
- The weather becomes cooler in the fall, and people begin wearing sweaters and jackets.
- Days become shorter and nights become longer.

ART

Fall Tree Door or Wall Decoration

Real tree branch; large container; small rocks or dirt; brown butcher paper; tempera paint in fall colors, tissue paper in fall colors, or real leaves.

Put up a bare tree by using either a real tree branch "planted" in a large container *or* by cutting a tree shape from brown butcher paper. Choose one of the following ways for the children to make fall leaves for the tree.
1. Make children's handprints with tempera and cut out.
2. Cut tissue paper in squares. Twist each square and glue it on the tree.
3. Have the children find real leaves. Dry the leaves by pressing in heavy books between sheets of waxed paper.
4. Make feet prints with tempera and cut out.

Nature Collages

Nature items gathered from taking a Nature Walk; construction paper; glue.

The children make collages using the items they collected on a Nature Walk. Talk about the colors of fall. Encourage the children to talk about how each item feels to their touch as they finish their collages.

Leaf and Twig People

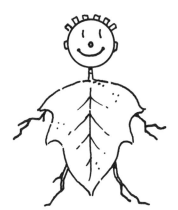

Real leaves and twigs; construction paper; markers; buttons; cotton balls; bark; glue.

The children collect leaves and twigs on a Nature Walk. Then they glue a leaf to the middle of a piece of construction or manila paper, to serve as the body of a leaf person. Let the children glue on small twigs to make arms, legs, hands, and feet on the leaf person. Finally, draw a head and add facial features with markers, construction paper scraps, buttons, cotton balls, broken pieces of twigs or bark, etc.

Leaf Mobile

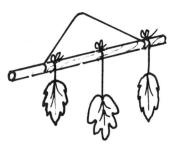

Real leaves; clear contact paper; string or yarn; small piece of tree branch.

Cut squares of clear contact paper. Stick one square of contact paper to each side of a leaf. Then cut around the leaf, leaving a ¼ inch edge of contact paper all around to prevent the contact paper from peeling off the leaf. Make several contact-covered leaves. Tape a string on each leaf.

Tie each leaf to a small piece of wood, so it will dangle like a mobile. Hang the mobile from the ceiling.

Weed Painting

Weeds; tempera paint; manila paper.

The children dip a weed in the tempera and gently brush it across the paper. Have them experiment painting with different types of weeds. Talk about the different patterns the different weeds make.

Leaf Roller Painting

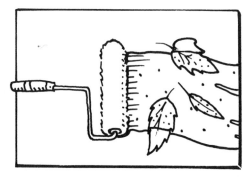

Small paint rollers (ask parents to loan some); tempera paint in fall colors; large sheets of paper (24 × 24 inch or 18 × 24 inch); styrofoam meat trays or paper plates.

Cover a work area. Let children lay dried leaves or weeds on their paper. Put a small amount of paint in a tray or on a plate. Let children dip a roller in the paint and slowly roll it back and forth over the leaves. Provide a second color of paint and let children roll the paint again. Carefully lift off the leaves to reveal the final painting.

FALL CHANGES

Leaf Badge

Real leaves; precut 3 inch circles of posterboard; safety pins; shellac; tape.

Dry the leaves by pressing them between waxed paper in heavy books for a few days. Let the children color the posterboard circles in fall colors. Then let them glue a pressed leaf on the circle. Tape a safety pin to the back of the circle so the badge may be worn.

Shellac over the leaf on the front of the circle, if desired.

Leaf Shape Painting

Tempera paint in fall colors; newsprint paper cut in large leaf shapes.

The children paint a leaf in fall colors. A brush or sponge may be used for painting.

Display in the hall or front entry windows, if possible.

Leaf Designs

Simple leaf shape stencils; manila paper; crayons or markers.

Let the children use the different leaf shapes at the end of this section to trace around on pieces of paper. Encourage them to use several different leaf shapes and to overlap the shapes for more interesting effects. Finally, let them use crayons or markers to color in designs on the stenciled shapes.

Spongy Leaves

Several varieties of leaf stencils (see patterns at end of this section); fall colors of tempera paint in meat trays; small squares or circles of sponge with a clip clothespin attached; manila paper.

The children may lay the construction paper stencil on their manila paper. Using the clothespin as a handle, they carefully dip the sponge in the tempera and paint the inside leaf shape of the template. Encourage them to "hop" the sponge when painting, so to leave a sponge effect. For an interesting outcome, suggest they use several different stencils and several fall colors of paint.

Weed and Leaf Bookmarks

Real leaves and weeds collected by the children; clear contact paper; 3 × 6 inch strips of construction paper.

Dry collected leaves and weeds by pressing them in sheets of waxed paper between the pages of a heavy book for a few days. Cut a 3 × 6 inch strip of construction paper for each child.

Let the children arrange and glue the dried leaves and weeds on the strip of paper. Then cover the strip with clear contact paper or iron it between two pieces of waxed paper, to increase the usefulness of the bookmark.

**Leaf-Framed
Finger Paint**

Liquid starch; dry tempera paint of fall colors; large pieces of paper for finger painting and for picture frame.

Cover the work area. Let the children finger paint. (Sprinkle dry fall-colored tempera over a dollop of liquid starch on a 12 × 18 inch piece of paper for each child.) Encourage them to mix two colors to see what new color they make.

Lay the paintings aside to dry thoroughly. Then have an adult cut large leaf shapes out of the center part of another 12 × 18 inch paper. Staple or tape a paper with the leaf shape cut out of it on top of the finger painting to make a leaf frame for the painting.

BLOCKS

Making Shapes

The teacher may call for two children to bring long blocks, another two to bring short blocks. As a group, use the blocks to make a rectangle.

Ask for three long blocks and assemble a triangle. Ask for four short blocks to make a square.

Outside Play

Add a bucket of small wooden or plastic people from commercial play sets to the block area this week. Talk about people cleaning up and playing in the leaves outside.

BULLETIN BOARD

Paper towels; fall colors of tempera paint or food coloring; eye dropper.

Tack a large bare tree on the bulletin board. Cut leaf shapes from paper towels. Let children use an eye dropper to drop fall colors of food coloring or tempera paint on the towel leaves. The colors will run and create a "different" leaf for the tree. When dry, glue to the tree or staple on the board. Let each child make several so there will be plenty for the display. Add squirrels, nuts, birds, bird feeders, a sun with a cloud partially covering it, etc.

COOKING

**Warm Spiced
Apple Juice**

*4 sticks of cinnamon
4 whole cloves
½ gallon apple juice*

Slightly heat the juice with the spices left whole in it. Let it simmer for ten minutes while the yummy smell fills the air. Talk about the special smells in the fall.

FALL CHANGES

Caramel Apple Fondue

1 small can evaporated milk
1 cup brown sugar
2 tablespoons margarine
Apples cut into slices
Toothpicks

Bring first three ingredients to a boil in a fondue pot or electric skillet. Turn off the heat and beat the mixture for one minute. Let it cool slightly.

Using a toothpick, each child pokes an apple slice, then dips the end of it into the caramel. The caramel mixture may be poured into several small dishes to make it easier and faster for several children to dip their apple slices. (Also tastes great when marshmallows are dipped in the caramel!)

Caramel Apples on Sticks

1 package of caramel candies
½ stick of margarine
1 apple for each child
Popsicle sticks

Melt the caramel candies and the margarine together in a fondue pot or electric skillet. Wash hands. Each child pushes a stick into one apple, then carefully dips the end of the apple into the caramel. (It isn't necessary to cover more than ⅓ - ½ of the apple with caramel.)

Place the caramel apples on pieces of waxed paper to cool. Enjoy!

LANGUAGE ARTS

Books

Anno, Mitsumasa. *Anno's Counting Book*. Crowell, 1977.
Barrett, Judi. *An Apple a Day*. Il. by Tim Lewis. Atheneum, 1973.
Blough, Glenor Orlando. *Wait for the Sunshine: The Story of Seasons and Growing Things*. Whittlesay House, 1954.
Burningham, John. *Seasons*. Bobbs-Merrill, 1970.
Buscaglia, Leo F. *The Fall of Freddie the Leaf: A Story of Life for All Ages*. Holt, Rinehart and Winston, 1982.
Casey, Patricia. *Autumn Days*. Putman Publishing Group, 1984.
Fisher, Aileen. *I Like Weather*. Thomas Y. Crowell, 1963.
Greydanus, Rose. *Changing Seasons*. Troll Associates, 1982.
Hogrogian, Nonny. *Apples*. Il. by author. Macmillan, 1972.
Lambert, David. *The Seasons*. Watts, 1983.
Lapp, Eleanor. *The Mice Came Early This Year*. A. Whitman, 1976.
Lenski, Lois. *Now It's Fall*. Henry Z. Walck, 1948.
Lobel, Arnold. *Frog and Toad All Year*. Harper and Row, 1976.
McNaughton, Colin. *Autumn*. Dial Books Young, 1983.
McNaughton, Colin. *Seasons*. Dial Books Young, 1984.
Podendorf, Illa. *Seasons*. Children's Press, 1981.

Santrey, Louis. *Fall*. Troll Associates, 1982.
Udry, Janice. *A Tree Is Nice*. Harper and Row, 1956.
Venino, Suzanne. *What Happens in the Autumn?* National Geographic, 1982.
Wensel, U. and J.M. Parramon. *Autumn*. Children's Press, 1981.

Fingerplays

Fall Tree

I am a large fall tree.	(Raise arms overhead.)
Winds blow and blow at me.	(Sway back and forth.)
My leaves come tumbling down.	(Swirl hands in downward movement.)
And make a blanket on the ground.	(Lay down on the floor.)

The Riddle of the Star

Read or tell the story "The Riddle of the Star" (found at end of this section) to the class. As you finish the story, cut an apple in half across the round middle part—to show the children the star pattern formed by the seeds inside.

"Autumn Boy" and/or "Autumn Girl"

Large paper doll cut from tagboard (can draw a capital "A" on the chest and laminate doll(s) for repeated use); glue felt or sandpaper strips on the shoulders and waist; fall clothes cut from fabric scraps or felt.

The children can dress and undress the doll. You may devise a game or riddle statements to vary the method of taking turns dressing the figure. For example: "Dress Autumn Girl for walking in the rain," or "Autumn Boy will need to wear this since it is cool outside."

Nutty Classification

Provide a bowl with several different kinds of nuts in their shells. Ask the children to sort the nuts, grouping them by size, color, or by kind of nut.

Our Fall Story

Write an experience story, as a group, based on collecting the items needed for Nature Collages (see ART). The teacher may have to ask leading questions to elicit statements from the children. Encourage sentences rather than one- or two-word answers. Write the sentences on the chalkboard or chart paper.

When finished, children may each glue a leaf from the Nature Walk around the border of the paper.

Clothing Game

Catalogue; glue or tape; sandpaper; various clothes items.

Cut several examples of fall clothing out of a catalogue. Glue or tape a small square of sandpaper to the back of each, so the picture will stick to the flannel board.

Lay three to five clothes items out in a row in front of the flannel board. Call for a certain clothes item: ''I am looking for a jacket.'' Let one child find it and put it up on the flannel board. Continue until all the items have been selected. Next, change the types of clothes and play the game again.

Feel Box

(To make a feel box, see two-year-olds, LANGUAGE ARTS, in the Spring and Growing Things section of the April Curriculum guide.)

Without the children seeing, put fall objects—nuts, leaves, pine cones, apples, and other things you've discussed—one at a time into the feel box. Let children take turns reaching inside the box to feel an object and guess what it is.

Water Leaf Prints
(Outside Activity)

Provide paintbrushes and small buckets of water. Children paint fall leaves with water, then press them on the cement. Observe the pattern the print makes. Point out and discuss the vein in the leaf.

Make two prints of different kinds of leaves. Let the children look at the prints and find the leaf that matches each.

Leaf Game

Using the leaf patterns on page 83, cut out pairs of leaves in several fall colors.
1. *Colors*
   Mix up the color pairs and let children match them together again. Talk about the color names.
2. *Position Directions*
   Provide a small, real tree branch. Ask children to take turns following a direction—''Put the yellow leaf on top of the branch... Put the brown leaf beside the branch... Put the red leaf under the branch.''

Leaf Press

Fall leaves; play dough.

Roll or pat out four circles of play dough. Press a different kind of leaf in each circle of dough to make a print. Take the real leaves off the doughprint, then let the children match the leaf to the print.

Provide play dough and collected leaves. Let the children make prints for each other to match.

Clothesline

Clothesline; catalogues; pinch-type clothespins.

String a clothesline across a corner or in a nontraffic area. Children cut out pictures of fall clothes from catalogues, then hang on the line with pinch-type clothespins.

Weather Doll

Provide a large (human baby sized) doll and baby clothes, including play shorts, shoes, a sweater, pants, a light blanket, and a dress. The children take turns dressing the doll in an appropriate outfit for the day after you have talked about the weather.

MATH

NUMBER CONCEPTS

Counting

1. *Nuts, Leaves, Apples*
   Use real groups of nuts, leaves, or apples. Let the children count each group. Change the number of things and count again.
2. *"Fall Leaves"*

One fall leaf, two fall leaves,	(Hold up finger for each.)
Three fall leaves, Hooray!	
Four fall leaves, five fall leaves,	
The wind blows them away!	(Blow on fingers and then let the fingers wiggle and swirl away.)

Squirrels and Nuts

Cut out several squirrels using the pattern shown. Staple a small dixie cup to the front of each squirrel so it will stand up by itself. Then print a numeral on each cup.

Provide a bowl of small nuts, such as acorns collected outside. Let the children count out the correct number of nuts to put in each cup.

SIZE RELATIONSHIPS

Apple, Apple

Purchase two-to-four apples of each variety and size from the supermarket. Put them all into a large bowl. The children sort and categorize in as many ways as possible—by color, kind, size. Then count the apples in each group. (This is a good opportunity to talk about sets and combining two smaller sets, etc.)

Blindfold Game

Take turns blindfolding each child. Hand them two objects, one large and one small. They are to pick the size that you indicate just by feeling the objects. As the children become more efficient at this task, make the game more challenging by choosing objects closer in size to each other.

Large Leaf/Small Leaf

Provide two boxes with lids, with a slit cut in each lid. Label the boxes with the words *large* on one box, *small* on the other. Also, be sure to use picture clues for each. Have a basket with either real leaves or construction paper leaves. The children take turns drawing a leaf from the basket, deciding if the leaf is large or small, then depositing it in the appropriate box via the slit in the lid.

MOVEMENT

Falling Leaves

Lay out a long rope in a spiral pattern. Let children walk barefooted on the rope to make a movement like a leaf might make as it falls.

Raking Leaves (Outside Activity)

Provide a few real leaf rakes and one or two yard baskets. Let children take turns raking leaves, putting the leaves in the baskets, then dumping the baskets.

Raking Leaves (Pretend)

We like to rake the dry fall leaves	(Pretend to rake leaves.)
Into a giant hump.	(Make round shape with arms.)
Then back up a little way,	(Walk backwards.)
And bend our knees, and jump!	(Everyone jump as high as possible.)

Little Squirrel

Little squirrel, little squirrel
Swish your bushy tail.   (Children wiggle bottoms as if swishing
                                                            tails.)

Little squirrel, little squirrel
Swish your bushy tail.   (Wiggle bottoms.)
Hold a nut way up tall,   (Pretend to hold up a nut between two
                                                            hands.)

Wrinkle up your nose so small,   (Wrinkle and wiggle noses.)
Little squirrel, little squirrel
Swish your bushy tail.

MUSIC

Seed Shakers

Make rhythm instruments by stapling large seeds or small collected nuts between two small paper plates. Shake the instruments and dance as a record is played.

Falling Leaves

Play slow, graceful music on a record. Let the children move to the music and gently swirl and fall to the ground. Try to watch real leaves fall. Talk about what you see. Play the music and let the children move to the music again as they try to remember how the real leaves fell.

When the Leaves Turn Red and Yellow

(Tune: "She'll Be Coming Round the Mountain")

When the leaves turn red and yellow in the fall
When the leaves turn red and yellow in the fall
When the leaves turn red and yellow, then the apples taste so mellow,
When the leaves turn red and yellow in the fall.

Sing a Song of Fall

(Tune:"Happy Birthday")

Let's sing a song of fall,
Let's sing a song of fall.
With cooler days and falling leaves,
Let's sing a song of fall.

ROLE PLAY

Collecting Nuts and Picking Apples

Provide small baskets that can be carried. Let the children pretend to harvest and pick apples from trees and nuts from the ground.

Raking Leaves

Provide a plastic, toy leaf rake. Let the children pretend to rake leaves and pile them in baskets.

SCIENCE

Signs of Fall (Table Display)

Let children bring in objects to put on the table which show that fall is here. Include an insect house and a magnifying glass.

82

Nature Walk

Take the children on a walk around the area or walk around at a park. Give each child a paper sack to collect leaves, nuts, pine cones, weeds, etc., as signs of fall. Observe and point out changes in nature and in the color of natural things.

Carefully observe trees. Have children find and touch roots, bark, and leaves. "Are *all* the trees losing their leaves?" Point out and talk about evergreens.

**Green Leaf—
Colored Leaf—
Dried Leaf**

Pick some green leaves and some colored leaves from trees. Put the leaves beside each other on a table, then observe and discuss how they change each day. On a chart or paper, note the day and draw/color a leaf picture beside the day's name—to show how the leaf looked on Monday, Tuesday, etc.

Put two-to-four of the picked leaves in a heavy book between sheets of waxed paper for a few days. Then take out the dried/pressed leaves to compare with the leaves left laying out on the table.

Dried Corn on the Cob

Let children pick out one dried kernel of corn and use a magnifying glass to observe the kernel and the place it was on the cob.

Leaf Shapes for Tracing

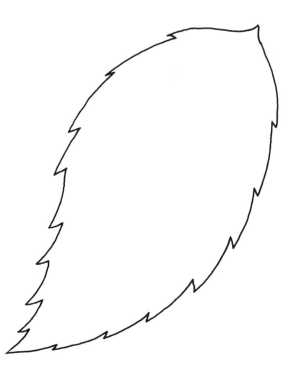

The Riddle of the Star

Retold by Bertie W. Kingore

Once upon a time a little girl was bored and had nothing to do. When she asked her mother to help her think of something fun, her mother said, ''Be a detective. See if you can find the answer to this riddle:

''I'm a little, round house,
Colored yellow, green or red.
I have no doors or windows,
But a chimney is on my head.''

''You'll know when you find the right house,'' said her mother, ''because when you open it up there's a star inside.''

So the little girl skipped off to figure out the riddle. She had only skipped a short distance when she saw a police car and her police friend, Miss Owens.

''Miss Owens,'' called the little girl. ''Can you help me solve this riddle:

''I'm a little round house,
Colored yellow, green or red.
I have no doors or windows,
But a chimney is on my head.''

''I'll know when I find the right house,'' said the little girl, ''because there's a star inside.''

''I'm sorry,'' said Miss Owens. ''I've been assigned to patrol this area for eight months now. But I don't remember a house like the one you've described. You might ask Mr. Matthews, the mailman. He surely knows every house in this area.''

So again the little girl skipped off. She had only skipped a short distance when she found Mr. Matthews delivering mail to a neighbor's mailbox.

''Mr. Matthews! Mr. Matthews!'' yelled the little girl as she ran up to the mailbox. ''Can you help me solve this riddle:

''I'm a little round house,
Colored yellow, green or red.
I have no doors or windows,
But a chimney is on my head.''

''I'll know when I find the house,'' said the little girl, ''because there's a star inside.''

''Dear me,'' said Mr. Matthews. ''I've been delivering mail to this area for nine years now. But I don't remember a house like the one you've described. Say, you might ask Granny Smith. She's lived here longer than anyone else. She surely knows every house in this area.''

So once again the little girl skipped a short distance when she found Granny Smith working in the orchard beside her house.

''Granny Smith,'' called the little girl as she ran up to her. ''Can you help me solve this riddle:

''I'm a little round house,
Colored yellow, green or red.
I have no doors or windows,
But a chimney is on my head.''

''I'll know when I find the house,'' said the little girl, ''because there's a star inside.''

Granny Smith just laughed and laughed. She picked an apple off of one of her trees and then sat down on the ground to talk with the little girl.

''When I was just a little girl like you,'' Granny said, ''I planted some apple seeds in this rich ground. I watered the seeds and cared for them and they grew into these lovely trees. Now I have an apple orchard:

''My apples are little and round,
They are yellow, green or red.
They have no doors or windows,
But a chimney is on each head.''

Then Granny pointed to the stem on the top of the apple. ''Oh,'' said the little girl. ''The stem *is* like a chimney and your apples *are* like little round houses. But I've eaten lots of apples and I've never seen a star inside.''

Granny smiled and said, ''Take this apple home and ask your mother to help you open it to find the star inside.''

''Thank you, Granny Smith!'' called the little girl as she skipped back to her house. She quickly ran inside and showed her mother the apple.

''Look Mom,'' said the little girl:

''An apple is a little, round house.
It is yellow, green or red.
It has no doors or windows,
But a chimney is on its head.''

''You are a clever detective,'' laughed her mother.

''But you have to show me if there's a star inside!'' pleaded the girl.

Her mother took the apple and got a knife. She cut the apple in half. But she did not cut it in half from the stem down to the bottom. She cut it in half by cutting in the middle of the round part of the apple. And, when the little girl lifted the pieces apart, there *was* a star. The beautiful seeds made a star; a star was inside the apple.

FALL CHANGES

Fun and Safety at Halloween

CONCEPTS

- Halloween is celebrated on October 31 every year.
- Some symbols we use as we celebrate Halloween are: scarecrows, pumpkins, black cats, witches, and ghosts.
- Orange and black are Halloween colors.
- It is important to practice safety at Halloween and throughout the year.

ART

Ghostipops

Individually wrapped suckers; white paper napkins or kleenex; black construction paper scraps; black or orange yarn; glue.

Let children place a napkin over the wrapped candy, as shown. Help them tie the napkin in place with a 6 inch piece of yarn. Then let them cut or tear eyes and a mouth out of black construction paper to glue on the ghostipop.

Orange and Black Play Dough

Prepare a batch of play dough and color one half of it orange, one half black. Dramatic changes in colors often spark new interest in play dough.

Using the special colors of play dough, let the children model jack-o-lanterns, black cats, spiders, and other Halloween characters. The creations may be saved for math time. Then count the variety of characters to see how many there are in each group.

Ghost Prints

White tempera paint; black construction paper, 12 × 18 inches; water; towels.

Do this activity on a tile floor or old shower curtain with plenty of water and towels handy.

Hint: Before starting this activity, let the children practice bending over and putting their hands flat on the floor in front of their feet.

Pour tempera in a shallow pan. Let the children, barefoot, step into the paint. Next, they step onto a piece of newsprint, then onto the back edge of the black construction paper. While standing there, let them dip their hands into the white paint, bend over at the waist, and make their hand prints on the black paper in front of their feet.

Help them stand upright, step off the paper and into a bucket/pan with a little water in the bottom. You help them wipe or sponge off their feet and hands.

**Pumpkin—
Jack-o-Lantern Game**

Pumpkin cutouts or stencils; scraps of construction paper; glue.

Provide small orange construction paper cutouts of pumpkins or stencils of pumpkins for the children to trace to make their own pumpkin out of orange construction paper.

The pumpkin on the front of the October Curriculum guide may be used as a pattern, if desired.

The children then glue a green stem to both the front side and the back side of the cutout. Also, provide construction paper cutouts or scraps so they can glue a jack-o-lantern face to one side.

Game: Hide the pumpkin—jack-o-lantern behind your backs. Then hold out the pumpkin side and say: ''Pumpkin, pumpkin, round and fat.'' Quickly put the shape back behind your backs, turn it around to the jack-o-lantern side, hold that side out and say: ''Turn into a jack-o-lantern just like that!''

Repeat the game as many times as the children choose. Encourage them to say the simple verse each time with you.

Halloween Party Art

1. *Jack-o-Lantern Placemats*
   Orange construction paper, 12 × 18 inches; large pumpkin stencil; scrap construction paper; glue.

   Each child makes a jack-o-lantern from a 12 × 18 inch sheet of orange construction paper. Let the children trace a stencil and cut it out according to their capabilities. Glue on black eyes, nose, and mouth. Add names and save for the party.

2. *Sipping Pumpkins*
Manila paper; pumpkin stencils; crayons or markers; hole punch; straws.

Provide small manila cutouts of pumpkins or stencils of pumpkins for the children to trace to make their own pumpkin out of manila paper. The pumpkin shape on the front of the October Curriculum guide may be used as a pattern. A ghost or other Halloween symbol could also be used.

Let the children color the pumpkin using crayons or markers. (Some children will want to draw a face to make their pumpkin a jack-o-lantern.) Then use a hole punch to punch a hole in the center of the pumpkin. Push a straw through the hole, and the cutout becomes a straw decoration and a "sipping pumpkin" to use for extra fun during a party.

3. *Centerpiece*
Orange construction paper; markers; scrap construction paper or paint; stapler.

You or the children cut out three, six, or nine pumpkins of the same size. Let a group of two or three children decide how to decorate one of the pumpkins and make a jack-o-lantern. Staple three of the jack-o-lanterns together at the sides to form a triangular centerpiece.

The children may each want to make one to take home for their table.

Fingerprint Jack-o-Lanterns

Small pumpkin cutouts; stamp pad or black tempera paint.

Provide small orange construction paper cutouts of pumpkins and ink pads or meat trays with a very small amount of black tempera paint on them. Let the children touch the ink pad or paint with a fingertip, then press the fingertip on the pumpkin cutouts to make eyes, nose, and mouth.

Spooky Designs

Black construction paper; white chalk.

Children use the chalk to draw designs on the black paper. Perhaps play a Halloween record as they work. Lightly spray the finished designs with hair spray, so the chalk is less easily rubbed off.

Rubberband Spiders

Black construction paper spider cutouts; rubber bands; ¼ inch elastic.

Provide simple black construction paper or posterboard cutouts of a spider's body. The children use white crayons to add eyes and designs to the cutout. Then let the children cut rubber bands in half and glue or tape on eight rubberband pieces as wobbly legs for each spider. Suspend the spiders from the ceiling with a length of elastic purchased from a fabric store.

Ghost Prints

White tempera paint in meat trays or paper plates; sponge pieces; clothespins; (pinch a clothespin on each piece of sponge to use as a handle and limit messy fingers); 9 × 12 inch black construction paper; black yarn; glue.

The children sponge paint on the paper. Encourage them to gently dab on the paint rather than rubbing it around. Ask them to make the shape of a ghost. When dry, let each child glue on 3 inch pieces of black yarn for eyes.

Black Batik

9 × 12 inch manila paper; crayons; very thin mixture of black tempera paint.

Let the children draw pictures and designs of their choice on the manila paper. When the picture is finished, let them brush the thin black paint over the picture for a nighttime effect. (The paint, which does not stick to the crayon, creates an interesting finish to the picture.)

Pumpkin Puppets

4½ inch squares of orange construction paper; black construction paper cutouts of small triangles and circles; green rectangle cutouts for stems; glue; stapler.

The children glue on the triangles and circles to make a face on one of the orange squares. Glue a rectangle on the top for the stem. Then help them staple a second square to the first square on three sides to make a simple hand puppet, as shown.

The Great Halloween

Plaster of paris or ceramic dough (see Art Recipes); styrofoam meat trays; popsicle sticks; tempera paint; shellac.

Help the children plan a Halloween character or design on paper, which they will later mold with the plaster. Allow the class to help mix the plaster or clay. Provide each child with a meat tray to hold the molding medium. Give each child some of the plaster in the tray and a popsicle stick. The children then mold their planned Halloween shape. Encourage them to etch details into their creation with the popsicle stick. Dry thoroughly. Paint and shellac, if desired.

3-D Ghosts

Black construction paper; white tissue paper; glue; chalk.

The children draw a simple ghost shape on black construction paper. (Using chalk to draw the shape will make the drawing easier to see.) Provide 2 inch white tissue paper squares for the children to twist and glue on to cover and fill in the shape. If preferred, cotton balls could be glued on instead.

Halloween Child Flip-Over Drawing

Child pattern; crayons or markers.

Duplicate both sides of the simple pattern of a child on one paper. Let the children use crayons or markers on the front of the paper to draw facial features and clothing on the child, as he or she would normally look.

Then let them fold down the top of the paper so the head on the back of the paper covers up the head on the front. Now let the children draw a mask, wig, and/or hat on the folded-over face. Then the children have a flip-over picture of both a child as usually dressed, and as disguised for Halloween!

A good art activity for the day after Halloween. The children can draw how they looked.

Hanger Halloween Creatures

Wire coat hangers bent out of shape as shown and covered with a nylon hose tied on the top; glue; yarn; constructon paper scraps.

Give each child a hose-covered hanger. Let them glue on construction paper and yarn to make the facial features and hair or whiskers of any Halloween creature.

Decorate the room by hanging the creatures from the ceiling as mobiles.

BLOCKS

Large—Small

While in circle time or waiting for lunch, ask one child to bring you a large block and another child to bring a small block. Compare the two blocks side by side.

During free time or block time encourage the children to use the large blocks to make something large. Then nearby make a structure with small blocks and discuss the differences.

Pumpkin Patch

Construct a path from the block area to a pumpkin patch. Let the children use a bus with little people inside to travel along the road to visit the pumpkins.

BULLETIN BOARD

It's Halloween Time

For a bulletin board with great "feel appeal," cut several large pumpkin shapes from a variety of textures: orange fake fur, sandpaper, an acetate sheet cutout with orange construction paper pumpkin behind it, adhesive-backed paper displayed with the sticky side out, a piece of upholstery, etc. Think of additional ideas for pumpkins and make great jack-o-lanterns for the children to feel on the bulletin board. Tape or staple wrapped candies and gum all around the board.

Halloween Child Flip-Over Drawing

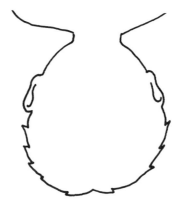

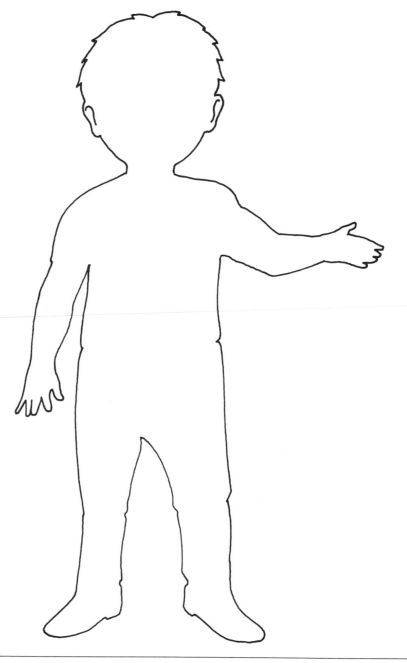

FUN AND SAFETY AT HALLOWEEN

If possible, also fasten several small flashlights to the board to stress carrying lights for safety. On Halloween or on the last day of the week, distribute the candy as you dismantle the board.

Variation: Make a large clock face on the bulletin board using jack-o-lanterns where the numbers belong. Use the candy and the flashlight idea as above.

COOKING

Sand-Witches

Wash hands. Let children use a witch-shaped cookie cutter to cut bread witches out of a slice of bread. Let them spread peanut butter and honey mixed together to top their witch shapes.

Eat the bread scraps or feed them to birds.

Witch's Brew

Each child mixes in a cup:

> *1/3 cup orange juice*
> *1/3 cup 7-Up*

Stir. Add an ice cube if desired and enjoy.

Variation: Using a black kettle, if possible, combine a quart of orange juice and one quart of 7-Up. Drop in a small piece of dry ice to give a real witch's brew effect.

Pumpkin Cookie

Wash hands. Provide or bake sugar cookies cut in pumpkin or circle shapes. (Graham crackers may be used if preferred.) As a group, mix up the frosting recipe. Then let each child put a spoonful of frosting in a small paper cup and stir in one small drop of red and one drop of yellow food coloring to make their own pumpkin-colored frosting. Let the children use table knives or plastic knives to frost a cookie.

Frosting Recipe

Mix together using a small electric mixer:

> *2 cups powdered sugar*
> *2 tablespoons shortening*
> *½ cup marshmallow creme*
> *Milk added to spreading consistency*

Older children may enjoy setting up a "Frosting Center" where each child prepares an individual portion.

3-4 tablespoons powdered sugar
1 teaspoon shortening
2 teaspoons marshmallow creme
Milk to mix
1 small drop red food coloring
1 small drop yellow food coloring

After the frosting is spread, give the children raisins or chocolate chips to make a face on their cookie.

Toasted Pumpkin Seeds

2 cups rinsed seeds
2 tablespoons melted margarine
1½ teaspoons garlic salt
Electric fry pan

Rinse off the fiber from the pumpkin seeds. Mix the ingredients together. Cook in an electric fry pan at 250° for 30-60 minutes (until lightly brown and crisp). Stir the mixture every 15 minutes. Spread on paper towels to cool.

LANGUAGE ARTS

Books

Halloween

Balian, Lorna. *Humbug Witch*. Abingdon Press, 1965.
Brewton, John, Lorraine Blackburn and George Blackburn. *In the Witch's Kitchen: Poems for Halloween*. Crowell, 1980.
Bridwell, Norman. *Clifford's Halloween*. Four Winds Press, 1967.
Carlson, Nancy. *Harriet's Halloween Candy*. Penguin, 1984.
Charles, Donald. *Shaggy Dog's Halloween*. Children's Press, 1984.
Cole, Babette. *The Trouble with Mom*. Coward-McCann, 1983.
Gibbons, Gail. *Halloween*. Holiday, 1984.
Green, Carol. *The Thirteen Days of Halloween*. Children's Press, 1983.
Karlin, Nurit. *The Tooth Witch*. Harper and Row, 1985.
Katz, Ruth. *Pumpkin Personalities*. Walker and Co., 1979.
Kessler, Leonard. *Riddles that Rhyme for Halloween Time*. Garrard, 1978.
Myra, Harold. *Halloween, Is It for Real?* Nelson, 1983.
Reese, Colleen L. *My First Halloween Book*. Children's Press, 1984.

Safety

Berry, Joy. *Danger*. Peter Pan, 1984.
Boyer. *Let's Walk Safely*. Oddo, 1981.
Chlad, Dorothy. *Strangers*. Children's Press, 1982.
Cray, Elizabeth. *I'm Lost*. Parenting Press, 1985.
Gordon, Sol and Judith Gordon. *A Better Safe Than Sorry Book*. Ed-U-Press, 1984.

FUN AND SAFETY AT HALLOWEEN

Hubbard, Kate and Evelyn Berlin. *Help Yourself to Safety: A Guide to Avoiding Dangerous Situations With Strangers and Friends.* Charles Franklin Press, 1985.

Teacher Resource Books

Halloween

Gibbons, Gail. *Things to Make and Do for Halloween.* Watts, 1976.
Ludwig, Nancy. *Halloween Plays and Art Projects.* Carson-Dellos, 1983.

Safety

Write for free sample copies:
Let's Be Safe Coloring Book. Texas Traffic Safety, S.D.H.P.T., Austin, TX 78701.
Traffic Safety Teacher's Guide for Grades K-3. American Automobile Association, 3000 Southwest Frwy., Houston, TX 77098.

Fingerplays

Jack-o-Lantern

There's a scary jack-o-lantern	(Circle shape with two arms.)
It's staring straight your way!	(Open eyes wide and extend head forward.)
Don't be scared! Don't be afraid!	(Hide eyes with hand.)
It probably just wants to play!	

Halloween Witch

If I was a Halloween witch,	(Make high peaked hat with fingers touching high over head.)
I'd ride with my cat on a broom	(One fist rides on top of one arm, moving through the air.)
I'd fly around scaring everyone,	(Wave arms.)
Watch out! Here I come! Zoom!	(Hold flattened palms together close to body; quickly zoom hands out toward group.)

Crossing Safely

Stop at the corner. Watch for the light.
Look carefully to the left, look carefully to the right.
When you're sure it's safe, then you may go.
Walk across so safely because we love you so!

Buy a Pumpkin—Carve a Pumpkin

As a class go to a vegetable stand or grocery store to buy a class pumpkin. Talk about the different sizes and shapes. Preplan how much money to spend so the children can also discuss which ones are too expensive, which are within their price range.

Back in the classroom, plan a face for the pumpkin on paper or on the chalkboard. Let the children suggest shapes to try. You sketch several different faces, and the class votes on which one to use.

Cut an opening at the top of the pumpkin. Discuss how the pumpkin and seeds look and feel inside. Take turns pulling out the seeds and fiber. Save the seeds.

Use a marker to draw the planned face on the pumpkin. The teacher *ONLY* cuts the face using a small, sharp knife.

Police Visit or Field Trip

Let a police officer talk to the children about safety at Halloween and all year through. Discuss safety in walking, crossing streets, playing by a street, riding a pedaled vehicle, riding in a car, carrying a light while trick-or-treating, and not eating any treats until an adult at home has checked them.

Traffic Light, Traffic Light

Precut traffic light shapes or duplicate traffic light pattern on manila paper; red, yellow, green construction paper circles; glue.

Cut out traffic signals and circles. Discuss the order in which to glue the circles. The children lay them in the correct sequence, then glue the circles in place.

Discuss the importance of traffic signals for motor vehicles as well as for pedestrians and bicycles.

Game—Tape the Nose on the Jack-o-Lantern

Provide a large cutout of a jack-o-lantern with the nose missing. Pin or tape it to the wall at the children's eye level. Have a cutout of a nose with a loop of tape on the back. Let children take turns being blindfolded and trying to tape the nose on the jack-o-lantern.

Safety Rules

As a group, let the children talk about safety rules. Talk about what they will wear and where they will go on Halloween evening. Encourage waiting in turn to speak, listening to others, and speaking in complete sentences.

Quiet Time

Just before going home each day, sit the class together for smiles and to discuss what was done at school that day. Try to create a happy frame of mind for the children and help them to look forward to coming back to school for a good day tomorrow. Remind the children to think about safety as they go home.

Progressive Story

The teacher begins a Halloween story about a friendly ghost family, a class of children adopting a scarecrow, or maybe a jack-o-lantern who wants to run away. Let each child add to the story where the teacher leaves off.

Not all the children will want to do this, but all will benefit from the exposure and, perhaps, will participate at a later date. If possible, write the final story on a large chart for all to enjoy. It's also fun to tape record the children's voices as they tell the story, so the tape may be enjoyed again and again later.

FUN AND SAFETY AT HALLOWEEN

Signs of Safety

Show and discuss signs along the street which help people drive and walk safely. Talk about traffic lights and what each color means. Repeat the finger-play "Crossing Safely" several times.

Illustrated Chart Stories

Make a large sketch of a Halloween symbol. Write sentence starters for a story to be written inside the shape as shown on the next page.

Read the starters to the class. Talk about what words to use to best complete the story. Carefully print the children's words to finish the story. Read the completed story together every day for a few days.

Dolls in Traffic

Talk about and experiment with traffic safety by using a doll in a toy car, truck, or wagon. Run the toy vehicle down an incline with the doll standing, then sitting, and then belted in as if wearing a seatbelt. Talk about what happens each time. While words might be easily forgotten, this experiment can make a lasting impression on the children!

MATH   COUNTING AND NUMERAL RECOGNITION

Lima Bean Ghosts

Use a permanent black marker to add eyes on lima beans so they look like ghosts. Use the ghosts for counting. Store them in a small plastic jack-o-lantern (like the ones used for trick-or-treating).

If desired, write numerals inside the egg cups of an egg carton. Let the children place the correct number of "ghosts" in each cup. Randomly number the cups from 0-3 or 0-5, using each numeral more than once; or number them in order from 0-11 or 1-12, if appropriate for the ability level of some of the children.

Pumpkin Flannel Board Cutouts

Use the pumpkin on the front of the October Curriculum guide as a pattern and make several felt cutouts. As a class, pick a number. Then direct the children, "Quietly tell me to stop when I have put up _____ pumpkins." *SLOWLY* add one pumpkin at a time to the board. Repeat the activity using a different number. Let the children also take turns putting up the figures. Children love to use the flannel board.

Halloween Story

I am a _____ .

I wear a _____ .

My face is _____ .

I like to _____

_____

_____

I am a _____

I am colored _____

and _____

I am good for _____

_____

Trick-or-Treat Math

Have a sack and pull out real objects as you name each one. Use wrapped candies, gum, seeds, pennies, buttons, popcorn, etc. Let the children count each set again to check that you have the right number.

''Know what I found on Halloween night?
I opened my bag and had quite a sight!

One _____(name object)_____

Two _____

Three _____

Four _____ .''

Continue counting objects as appropriate for the ability level of the group.

Scarecrow Match

Let the children use brads or glue to put together the scarecrow on the pattern at the end of this section by matching the numerals. They may make a face on the scarecrow and color him if they wish.

MATH VOCABULARY

Large—Small

Provide the children with two small and two large construction paper pumpkins or ghosts. Let the children decorate the figures with crayons or markers. Assist the children in stapling the figures together, leaving a small opening in each size for putting two or three pieces of large and small candy inside the appropriate sized figure.

**Large—Small/
Big—Little**

Teacher Preparation: Tie shower-curtain hooks on a heavy 2-3 foot length of string at 4-6 inch intervals.

Using large and small Halloween symbols, with a hole punched in the top, let the children take turns hanging up their symbol on the same hook with others of the same size.

For an individual activity, let the children classify the above objects according to other attributes. Supply pictures in other categories, hole punched and laminated, for the children to use.

MOVEMENT

Pumpkin Jump

Tie a small real or cardboard pumpkin to a rope and string it over a tree limb outside, or inside through an eye hook on the ceiling. Pull the rope to make the pumpkin jump.

Let the children try to jump the same height as the pumpkin—close to ground, higher, higher. Also, let the children stand under the pumpkin and then jump to try to catch it.

Bean Bags

Make bean bags in ghost or pumpkin shapes. Use masking tape to tape a shape on the floor. Let the children practice tossing underhanded to get the bags inside the shape. Each time, talk about whether the bag lands *inside* or *outside* the shape.

Ghost Hunt

Make several tissue paper ghosts by using a rubber band to secure a white kleenex over the top of a small lollypop. (See ART, Ghostipops) Have at least one ghost for each child in the group.

While the children turn their backs, hide the ghosts around the room. Group the children together at a starting place. Choose a movement for the children to do, such as hop, crawl, or tiptoe. Begin playing a record. When the music starts, the children perform the directed movement around the room while trying to find the ghosts. If they find a ghost, they pick it up and continue moving around, hunting for more ghosts.

Stop the music several times. Each time the music stops the children hurry back to the starting place.

Collect the ghosts and hide them again, if desired. When the hunt is finished, let everyone share the ghosts and all sit down to lick a lollypop together. (A great time to read a Halloween book aloud to the group as they rest and relax.)

Black Cat

Black cat, black cat turn around.
Black cat, black cat jump up and down.

Black cat, black cat close one eye.
Black cat, black cat stretch to the sky.

Black cat, black cat wiggle your nose.
Black cat, black cat touch your toes.

Black cat, black cat shake your head.
Black cat, black cat lay down in bed.

Chant the verse as the children do the actions with exaggerated movements. Let the children invent new verses and actions. Repeat the verses, varying the speed from fast to faster. End the activity by doing the verse very slowly to calm the group back down.

MUSIC

Musical Pumpkin Walk

Lay pumpkin cutouts in a pattern or shape on the floor. Play a record and let children step on the pumpkins as they march in rhythm. Vary the tempo of the music. Talk about marching, walking, and sliding to the music.

FUN AND SAFETY AT HALLOWEEN

Flapping Scarecrow

(Tune: "Did You Ever See a Lassie?")

Did you ever see a scarecrow, a scarecrow, a scarecrow,
Did you ever see a scarecrow flap this way and that?
With his loose arms and wobbly head and straw hands and long legs,
Did you ever see a scarecrow flap this way and that?

The children move their bodies like scarecrows, waving and wobbling each body part as it is mentioned in the song. For a second verse, let everyone hum the tune while parading and moving like scarecrows around in a circle.

Halloween Musical Sounds

Let the children explore using their voices, their bodies, and lots of objects in the room to create Halloween musical sounds. Some suggestions are:
1. Try singing "oh" or "boo" as your voices move four or five notes up the musical scale.
2. Try stamping your feet in place in *very* slow rhythm, as if a giant were marching.
3. Try using rhythm sticks to tap on various objects in the room. Talk about what Halloween sound each might be.
4. Swish hands slowly back and forth together as if a ghost were flying by.
Play a record and let the children use their Halloween musical sounds to accompany the record.

Pumpkin Patch

(Tune: "Farmer in the Dell")

1. The pumpkin in the patch,
   The pumpkin in the patch,
   Scary-O Halloween,
   The pumpkin in the patch.
2. The pumpkin takes a scarecrow . . .
3. The scarecrow takes a cat . . .

4. The cat takes a bat . . .
5. The bat takes a ghost . . .
6. The ghost takes a spider . . .
7. They go to trick or treat . . .

ROLE PLAY

Costumes

Provide old Halloween costumes and a mirror. Let the children try on the costumes and look at themselves in the mirror. Encourage them to talk about who they are dressed up to be.

Halloween Parade

The children act out different characters (witch, bat, scarecrow, etc.) as they walk around the room in parade fashion. Choose different characters and continue the parade. Perhaps play a record as the parade goes on.

Safety

Make a "street" with two lengths of masking tape on the floor and role play crossing the street safely. Let one child hold up red or green circles to tell the other children to stop or go.

Safety at School

Role play the safe way for everyone to do things at school. Dramatize putting away toys so children will not trip, carrying chairs, keeping feet out of walkways, carrying and using scissors, and walking rather than running to the door.

SCIENCE

Spiders

Halloween is a good time to learn about real spiders. Try to locate a complete web. Observe it undisturbed. Let children look at it with a magnifying glass. Try to watch a spider as a web is being made.

If a partial web or broken web is found, let the children touch the strands. Discuss how they feel. Why does the web stick to us? Why would a spider need a sticky web? *National Geographic* is an excellent source of pictures and information about spiders.

Pumpkins

Observe a real pumpkin as it is being cut into a jack-o-lantern. Talk about how the seeds grow inside the pumpkin. What is all that fiber inside the pumpkin?

Plant several pumpkin seeds. Soak a few seeds overnight. Plant them in a large pan and care for them. Make a chart detailing when the seeds were planted, when they first sprouted, and measuring the growth of the plants.

FUN AND SAFETY AT HALLOWEEN

Scarecrow Match

November Curriculum

1. Shapes and Sizes

2. Shopping

3. Thanksgiving and Life in Early America

Shapes and Sizes

CONCEPTS

- Introduction of basic shapes: circle, square, triangle, rectangle.
- A shape may come in different sizes, yet still be the same shape.
- Awareness of shapes in their everyday world. Many things we see and use each day contain basic shapes.

ART

Shapes Greeting

Door-size white butcher paper; different shapes in different sizes and papers; glue.

Cut shapes from construction paper, wallpaper samples, sandpaper, aluminum foil, gift wrap, plus any other paper that you or the children can brainstorm. Lay the butcher paper on the floor or tabletop and, as a group, glue the shapes onto the paper. Let dry, write the caption, "Learning Our Shapes," then hang the paper on the door for all to enjoy.

Box Creatures

Cardboard boxes in several different sizes and shapes; tape; tempera paint; construction paper scraps.

As a group, stack the boxes in different ways to see how many different people or creatures you can create. Decide on your favorite and tape it together. Let the children paint the creature and add detail and facial features with construction paper. Consider using empty spools to make funny eyes and a bottle cap for a nose.

Coin Rubbings

Variety of coins; manila paper; crayons with the paper removed.

Show the children how to lay a paper on top of a coin and then rub over the coin area with the side of a crayon to make the coin impression appear. Use different coins, rubbing one at a time, to fill up the paper with rubbings. Using different colors and different coins makes the art more interesting.

Collages

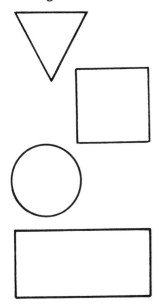

1. *Construction paper shapes; glue; manila paper.*

   Provide precut circles, squares, rectangles, and triangles to glue on construction or manila paper. If desired, separate the precut shapes and let children glue a circle collage, a square collage, a rectangle collage, and a triangle collage. Staple the pages together to make a shapes book.

2. *Tissue paper shapes; white construction paper; liquid starch.*

   The children brush liquid starch on white construction paper, then place precut tissue paper shapes on the starch. Let it dry.

3. *Inexpensive paper plates; shapes precut from fabric scraps; glue.*

   Let the children experiment placing the shapes in different designs on their paper plates. When they design an object or collage that they like, let them glue the shapes to the plate.

Crayon Peel

Old crayons with the paper removed; manila paper.

Peel off the paper around several crayons. (This is a good way to use those broken crayon pieces!) Use a knife or scissor blade to put notches or grooves along the sides of the crayons. Have the children color, using the crayon sides, on a piece of manila paper.

Wallpaper Shapes

Precut wallpaper circles, triangles, squares, rectangles (choose only one shape per week); glue; newspapers.

Working on a table or the floor, use one-half page from the newspaper per child for this project. Encourage the children to glue each shape so the patterned side shows: "Put the glue on the plain, white side." Glue shapes all over the newspaper sheet. The contrasting patterns of wallpaper on newspaper make an interesting wall display.

Shape Mobile

Precut, 3 inch construction paper shapes; yarn; glue; glitter.

Let the children choose three or four shapes. Let them make a glue design by dripping glue on each shape then sprinkle glitter on the glue before it dries. Shake off the excess. Help the children tape their shapes to a long piece of yarn to make individual mobiles. Hang the mobiles from the ceiling with a paper clip hook or a push pin.

Print-a-Shape

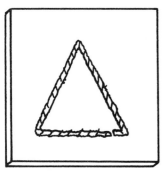

2 inch square cardboard pieces; 8 inch lengths of yarn; glue.

Draw a shape, as chosen by each child, on the cardboard. Each child then dips a length of yarn in the glue, strips off the excess glue, and lays the yarn along the shape outline. Let dry. Turn the cardboard over and glue a thread spool to the back, to serve as a handle. When dry, the children may carefully dip the yarn-shape into tempera paint, then print on construction paper or newsprint. Trade stamps with friends to print a variety of shapes.

Play Dough Shapes

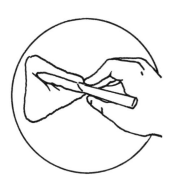

Play dough (see Art Recipes); cardboard or posterboard patterns of circles, triangles, squares, and rectangles; popsicle sticks or plastic knives; 1 inch dowel rods cut into 6 to 8 inch lengths (optional).

Give each child a ball of play dough to pat out like a pancake (or let the children use the dowel rods to roll out the dough). Then let them choose shape patterns to put over the play dough, then cut out with a stick or knife.

Shape Delights

Multiple colors of construction paper cut into three different sizes of circles, triangles, rectangles, and squares; glue; yarn; tree branch set in a can of cement or plaster.

The children choose three different colors and different sizes of one shape. They glue their three choices together, one atop another, to make a colorful shape delight. Glue or tape on a loop of yarn. Let the children hang their shapes on the tree branch.

Finger Rounds

12 to 18 inch circles cut from white shelf paper; liquid starch; dry tempera paint powder.

Cover tabletops with newspapers. Let the children finger paint on the circles. Put a 1 inch dollop of starch on each circle. Sprinkle tempera powder on the starch, then ask the children to stir the mix with their fingers to make the finger paint. Talk about using circular movements with their fingers or hand. Sprinkle on different colors of tempera to make multiple-colored finger rounds.

Shape-Up Mobiles

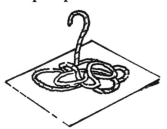

Yarn; liquid starch; glue; waxed paper.

Children dip pieces of yarn into a dish of starch, then arrange the yarn in an interesting shape or design on a piece of waxed paper. A second and even third color of yarn may be dipped and laid on top of the first piece. Let the shape dry for twenty-four to thirty-six hours. Then peel off the waxed paper. Tie a piece of yarn to the shape-up and hang it from the ceiling, like a mobile.

Shape-a-Person

Shapes cut from construction paper: 3 inch circles (heads), 1 inch circles (hands), 1 × 4 inch rectangles (arms), 1½ × 5 inch rectangles (legs), ⅓ × 2 inch rectangles (feet), 3 inch square (body trunk); glue; 9 × 12 inch pieces of paper.

Talk about the parts of our body. Give each child a set of shapes. Work together arranging the shapes to make people. Once arranged let the children glue their shape-a-person onto a 9 × 12 inch piece of paper. Then ask them to add facial details with construction paper or markers.

Shape Box

Cardboard grocery box; glue; scissors; magazines; large cutout letters spelling "Shapes."

Glue the word "Shapes" across the top of the box. Then on one of each of the four sides print: Squares, Circles, Rectangles, and Triangles.

Tear out magazine pages picturing objects that contain one of the four shapes: doors, road signs, tables, stamps, buttons, clocks, mirrors, etc. Let the children cut around each object and glue it on the appropriate side of the shape box. Work to cover each side of the box with the appropriate shapes.

Pea and Toothpick Sculptures

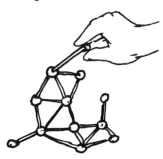

Dried peas; round toothpicks; small cups or bowls.

Soak the dried peas overnight in water. Give each child a cup of softened peas and a pile of toothpicks. Let the children build sculptures by sticking toothpicks into the peas. Let them create designs as complex as they wish. Then set aside the sculptures to dry. As the peas dry out they shrink, and . . .fantastic! . . . the sculpture becomes strong and tightly bound together.

BLOCKS

1. Talk about and name the different shapes of the blocks. Encourage the children to say the shape name when using any block.
2. Let the children experiment to discover which blocks can be put together to create a new shape. For example, two triangles make a square, two squares make a rectangle.
3. Consider tracing around each shape on the shelf where blocks are stored. Then when it's cleanup time, the children match each real block to its drawn outline to help organize storage, simplify cleanup, and increase their shape awareness.
4. Explore making exciting block structures. Then have the children count how many of each shape they used in their structure.

BULLETIN BOARD

Shapes Around Us

Prepare the bulletin board caption "SHAPES AROUND US," as shown. Use brightly colored construction-paper cutouts of shapes in different sizes to create several objects exhibiting the basic shapes of triangle, circle, rectangle, and square.

SHAPES AND SIZES

Cracker Shape-Ups

Snack crackers
Cheese spread
Peanut butter

Buy snack crackers made in the basic shapes. Let the children spread cheese or peanut butter with a plastic knife or table knife. For two-year-olds, use the cracker shape of the week.

Shape-Up Cereal

½ cup margarine
2 teaspoons seasoned salt
5 teaspoons Worcestershire sauce
6 cups varied cereals (Chex, Cheerios, etc.)
1 cup peanuts
1 cup miniature marshmallows (optional)

Use an electric fry pan, set at 250°. Melt butter. Stir in the seasonings, cereals, and peanuts. Mix to coat well. Heat 1 hour, stirring every 15 minutes. Spread on paper towels to cool before eating.

Discuss how the Shape-Up Cereal is like this class: "We are all a little different in our shape. But when we get together we can be friends and do good things together."

Shape Sandwiches

Have children use cookie cutters in various shapes to make mini-sandwiches out of bread and cheese.

A Square Meal

Have "a square meal" by serving only square-shaped snacks. Some possibilities include: Chex cereal, cheese slices, bread slices, lunch meats, and crackers. Talk about the square shapes.

Variations: *Circle Snacks*—pizzas made from English muffins; crackers; lunch meats; grapes; banana slices.

Triangle Snacks—cheese triangles; bread cut diagonally; crackers.

Rectangle Snacks—crackers; cheese slices cut in half; bread cut in half; pretzel sticks.

Banana Wheels

½ banana per child
1 package of jello
Plastic knives
Waxed paper
Plastic sandwich bags
Round toothpicks

Wash hands. Working on squares of waxed paper, let each child peel and slice a banana half into round "wheels." The child then puts the slices into a plastic sandwich bag with one tablespoon of the jello powder and shakes them together. Pour the banana wheels back out on the waxed paper. For added fun, let the children eat the banana wheels by picking them up with a toothpick.

LANGUAGE ARTS

Books

Allington, Richard. *Shapes*. Raintree, 1979.
Bendick, Jeanne. *Shapes*. Franklin Watts, 1968.
Bruna, Dick. *I Know About Shapes*. Price-Stern, 1984.
Curry, Peter. *Shapes*. Price-Stern, 1983.
Hargraves, Roger. *Little Miss Sunshine's Shapes*. Price-Stern, 1982.
Hoban, Tana. *Circles, Triangles and Squares*. MacMillan, 1974.
Hoban, Tana. *Look Again!* MacMillan, 1971.
Hoban, Tana. *Round and Round and Round*. Greenwillow, 1983.
Hoban, Tana. *Shapes and Things*. MacMillan, 1970.
Holmes, Kenneth. *Basic Shapes...Plus*. Enrich, 1980.
Hoff, Syd. *Syd Hoff Shows You How to Draw Cartoons*. Scholastic, 1979.
Hooker, Yvonne. *Round in a Circle*. Putman Publishing Group, 1983.
Hutchins, Pat. *Changes, Changes*. MacMillan, 1971.
Mahnay, Patricia. *Shapes and Things*. Standard Publishing, 1984.
Rarrett, Peter and Susan Barrett. *The Circle Sarah Drew*. Scroll Press, 1973.
Rarrett, Peter and Susan Barrett. *The Line Sophie Drew*. Scroll Press, 1973.
Rarrett, Peter and Susan Barrett. *The Square Ben Drew*. Scroll Press, 1973.
Silverstein, Shel. *The Missing Piece*. Harper and Row, 1976.
Silverstein, Shel. *The Missing Piece Meets the Big O*. Harper and Row, 1981.
Turk, Hanne. *Max Versus the Cube*. Neugebauer Press, 1982.
Wildsmith, Brian. *Puzzles*. Franklin Watts, 1970.

Teacher Resource Books

Froman, Robert. *Rubber Bands, Baseballs and Doughnuts*. Thomas Y. Crowell Co., 1972.

Fingerplays

Circle

I can make a big round ball.   (Form circle with arms.)
It's a circle, don't you see?
I'll throw to you my big round ball,   (Throwing motion.)
And you'll roll it back to me.   (Repeatedly roll one hand over other.)

Creative Thinking

Ask the children to respond to: ''If I were a circle, I'd be a...'', ''If I were a square, I'd be a...'', etc. Record their responses on paper or with a tape recorder. Older children might draw or paint a shape picture, to which you could write the caption. For two-year-olds, ask the question using the shape of the week.

Floor Shapes with Tape

Using masking tape, make large shapes on the floor (at the door where children line up is one good location). Then, perhaps while waiting a minute between activities, ask children to do any of the following (be sure to name the shape each time):

1. Walk around the outside.
2. Walk with one foot outside and one foot inside.
3. Hop into.
4. Sit inside.
5. Stand beside.
6. Stand between the _____ and the _____ shapes.
7. Jump over.
8. See how many children will fit together standing on the lines of the shape.

Shape Walk

Go on a walk, inside or outside, to hunt for objects made with circles, triangles, squares, and rectangles. Talk about how many different shapes you find.

Circles: Wheels, doorknobs, bowls, jars, records, clocks, coins, buttons, glasses, tires.

Triangles: Rooftops, sailboat sails, "Yield" traffic signs, side windows on cars, swingsets.

Rectangles: Tabletops, bulletin boards, picture frames, doors, cereal boxes, books.

Squares: Windows, pockets, crackers, cheese slices, signs, floor tiles.

Changeable Shapes

After reading *Changes, Changes* by Pat Hutchins, use the flannel board to build an object using different felt shapes. The children take turns changing the object into something else by moving the shapes around. They might need to brainstorm ideas at first. (This activity is also very effective using table blocks.)

I See a Shape

Say: "I see a circle, you can too." Then give clues until the children figure out what round thing you saw in the room. As children become adept at the game, let them lead. Vary the shapes.

Flying Shapes

Package of small, round paper plates; shapes cut out of construction paper; glue.

Glue one of the basic shapes on each paper plate. Go outside and let the children take turns choosing a plate, naming the shape on it, and then sailing the plate into the air. When all the shapes have been tossed, call for flying shapes pickup by searching for one shape at a time: "Find all the flying shapes with triangles on them."

Shape Verses

Draw a shape person on the chalkboard or use felt or construction paper shapes on the flannel board or tabletop. (With felt or paper shapes, the children can make the shape people again and again as the verse is recited.)

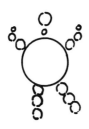 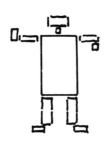  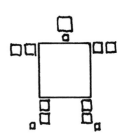

Cynthia Circle is nice and round.
No corners on her are ever found.

Ricky Rectangle is a funny sort.
Two sides are long and two sides are short.

Tilly Triangle is here to see you.
She has three sides and three points too.

Samuel Square, that is my name.
I have four sides that are just the same.

Flannel Board Fun

Make the following circles and triangles out of felt. Explore with the children how many different ways the shapes may be arranged to create bunnies and birds. Later, leave the pieces by the flannel board, stored in an envelope or folder with a pocket, and let the children take turns creating bunnies and birds.

A. 2 two inch circles
B. 1 four inch circle
C. 4 one inch circles
D. 3 one-half inch circles
E. 1 three inch circle, cut in half
F. 5 triangles with one-half inch sides

Shape Combs

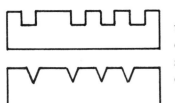

Provide several shape combs by cutting 2 × 5 inch pieces of cardboard and then cutting triangle, square, or rectangle notches along one side. Let the children use the shape combs in a plastic tub of cornmeal or sand. The children enjoy seeing the designs made as they draw each comb along the top of the cornmeal or sand.

SHAPES AND SIZES

Flannel Board Fun

Puppet Time

Use one or more puppets to explain the characteristics on each of the basic shapes. Have the puppet go for a walk and find the shapes one at a time. With each shape, the puppet examines the shape for clues to figure out what it is. Let the children help by speaking with the puppet to decide if each shape is the same or different than the one before.

Fishing

Tie a piece of string to a dowel or rod stick. Tie a magnet on the other end of the string. Let the children "fish" in a bucket of paper shapes (with a paper clip on each so it can be picked up by the magnet).

Sandpaper Shapes

Cut the basic shapes from sandpaper. Let the children put a mask over their eyes, or close their eyes, then try to identify the shapes by feeling each.

Shape Sacks

Using glue and construction paper—or else markers—decorate lunch sacks with the shape of the day (or week). Send the sacks home with a note to the parents to assist the children in finding objects or pictures of the sack shapes. Show and tell the items each child brings back with his/her sack.

Memory Game

Have a tray with three or four round things on it. Talk about how they are the same. Cover the tray with a cloth and secretly remove one item. Let the children figure out which round thing is missing. Repeat the game several times. Play the game using items for each of the other basic shapes.

Variation: Put one of each of the basic shapes on the tray. Cover the tray, remove one of the shapes, and let the children identify which shape is missing.

Shape Riddles

Make up simple riddles for each of the basic shapes. Have the shapes beside you as you say the riddles for the children to guess. One or two of your most able students may want to make up their own riddles to ask the group.

1. I have three sides and three points. What am I?
2. I am round like a pancake. What am I?
3. A door has my shape. What am I?
4. I have four sides that are all the same size. What am I?

Cut and Paste Shapes

Make a copy of the shapes page for each child. Talk about the shapes. Name each shape on the top, then find the shape on the bottom that is the same size. Talk about how shapes can be turned around in different directions but still be the same shape. Let the children cut out the bottom shapes to paste on the appropriate top shape. Talk about the remaining shapes.

Shape-O Bingo

Make a copy of the bingo page for each child. Let the children color each shape red, blue, or yellow. Let them randomly use the colors so each bingo board is individual. Provide buttons, lima beans, or construction paper squares for markers.

Have a set of red, blue, and yellow circles, triangles, squares, and rectangles in a box or sack. Draw one and show it to the group. The children who have that same color shape get to put a marker on that space. Continue until several children "bingo."

MATH   NUMBER CONCEPTS

Shapes

1. Fold a paper napkin to show the relationships of one shape to another. Fold a square napkin into rectangles and then another napkin into triangles.
2. Have the children go on a shape scavenger hunt in the classroom, finding one or more objects of each shape.
3. Discuss the concepts of "smaller" and "larger" and have the children put cutout shapes in order from smallest to largest.

Mystery Shape

Cover a shoe box with plain newsprint. Randomly glue construction paper shapes on the outside of the box. Cut a small hole in the lid big enough to allow a child's hand to fit in. Glue the top of an old, washed sock around the opening so it creates a "tunnel." Children can reach inside but not see into the box.

Put into the box small objects of the shapes appropriate for your class. The children take turns reaching in and feeling for a predetermined shape, or they can feel an object and tell the class what shape it is before taking it from the box.

Sequencing

Provide the children with shapes of various sizes and colors, depending on the abilities of your class. Two-year-olds should work with only one variable. Using the flannel board, display a pattern of three to six shapes. The children then try to duplicate this pattern with their shapes at the table.

Variation: As the older children master this concept, start a repeating sequence and let them tell or show what comes next.

From *We Care,* Copyright © 1988 Scott, Foresman and Company.

Cut and Paste Shapes

Shape-O Bingo

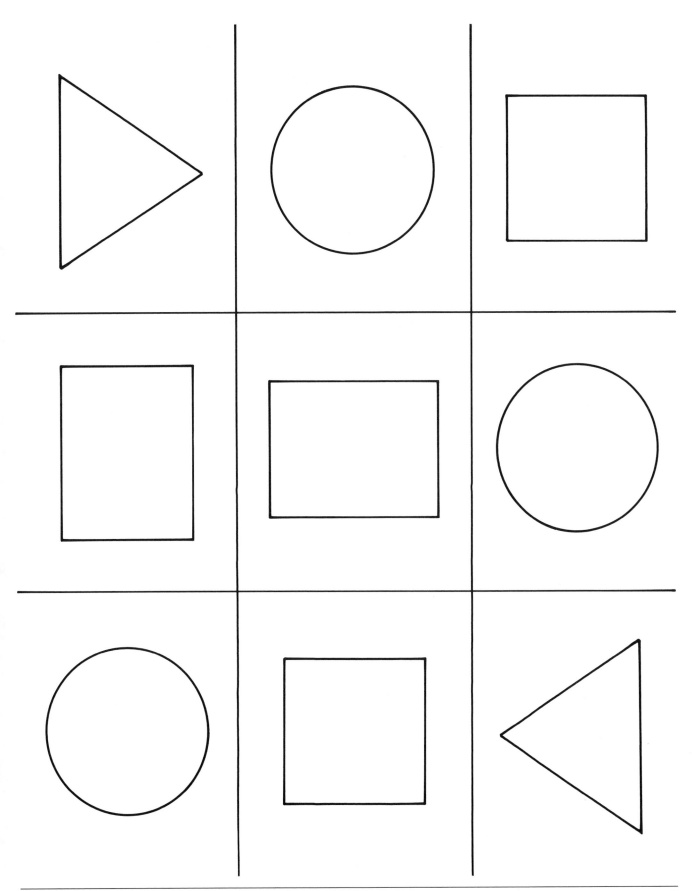

Pound-a-Shape

   Either you draw or the children may trace a stencil of a shape on a styrofoam meat tray. Then let the children stick golf tees along the perimeter, thus outlining the shape.
   Variation 1: Hold the meat tray to the light and look at the shape pattern made by the holes.
   Variation 2: With a crewel needle or bobby pin and yarn, sew along the outline with the yarn.

MATH VOCABULARY: Circle, Triangle, Square, Rectangle

Shape Flash

1. You flash a shape to the class. The children whisper the name of the shape.
2. Pass out a variety of shapes to the children. As you flash a shape, the children with that shape hold it up high over their heads.
3. Either you or the children call out the name of a shape. The children then draw the shape in the air with their arm or finger.

Human Shapes

   The children lay together on the floor, end to end, to form each of the basic shapes.

MOVEMENT

Shape-a-Sizes Exercises

1. With legs apart, extend arms and rotate them in circles.
2. Move extended arms in a square, triangle, and rectangle shape.
3. Bend over at the waist, then move the trunk at the waist in the shape of a square or circle.
4. Lay on the floor, raise one or both legs, and move in the shape of a square and a circle. This is harder than it sounds!
5. Let the children stand and draw a circle in the air with their fingers. Next, let them draw a circle with their noses. Vary the task by having them draw a tiny circle and then a large circle.

Tape Movements

   Fix masking tape or a large rope on the floor in the basic shapes. Let the children walk the pattern forward, backward, side-step, hopping, etc.

Bean Bag Toss

Cut a large triangle, square, circle, and a rectangle in the bottom of a large over-turned cardboard box. Make sure the holes are large enough to let bean bags fall through easily.

Put the box in a corner or against the wall, out of the traffic area in the room. Let the children toss the bean bags underhand, trying to get them into the shape holes.

Relay Race

Each child stands by a pile of shapes. At the signal, pick up one shape from the pile and run to the opposite side of the room to put it down. Then return and run with another shape until all of the shapes are at the other side of the room. The relay works well with three or four children racing at a time, so everyone gets a turn quickly.

MUSIC

Rhythm

Let the children choose a rhythm instrument to correspond with each shape.

△ = triangle

☐ = blocks

◯ = drum

▯ = rhythm sticks (dowel rods)

As a group, clap the rhythm on the rhythm chart. (An adult touches each shape in turn on the chart to guide the children from left to right.) After the group is doing well clapping the rhythm, let them use the instruments to "play" the rhythm on the chart.

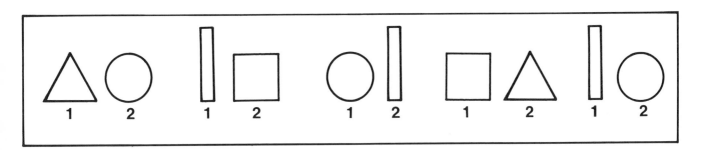

Shape Song

(Tune: "Farmer in the Dell")

1. A circle is a round ball,
   A circle is a round ball.
   A line that just goes round and round,
   A circle is a round ball.

2. A square has four sides,
   A square has four sides.
   Straight over, down, across, and up,
   A square has four sides.

3. Triangles have three points,
   And triangles have three sides.
   Draw up, down, then back again,
   Triangles have three sides.

4. Rectangles look like doors,
   Rectangles look like doors.
   Two sides short and two sides long,
   Rectangles look like doors.

SCIENCE

Orange Seeds

Talk about the shape of fruits. Save the seeds from oranges or grapefruits. Soak them overnight in water. Plant several in a large styrofoam cup of potting soil with a hole punched in the bottom for drainage.

Water well. Keep in a shady place until the seedlings have several leaves. These seeds grow well in a greenhouse bag (see April Curriculum guide, Spring and Growing Things, SCIENCE section).

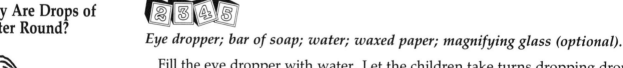

Why Are Drops of Water Round?

Eye dropper; bar of soap; water; waxed paper; magnifying glass (optional).

Fill the eye dropper with water. Let the children take turns dropping drops of water on the waxed paper. Look at the drops with a magnifying glass. Talk about their shape.

The outside of a drop of water is like a skin holding the drop together in its round shape. If the "skin" is broken, the water will lose its round shape.

Take a bar of soap. Wet the end and gently touch it to a drop of water. Ask the children to watch closely! The skin breaks and the drop spreads out.

Let the children repeat the experiment several times, if interested. Talk about why the drop is round and what makes it change its shape.

SHAPES AND SIZES

Shopping

CONCEPTS

- Many different kinds of stores sell things we need and want.
- Some of the most common types of stores are grocery, clothing, shoe, discount, drug, toy, and book stores.
- Stores sell things to make money, which is called ''making a profit.''
- Advertisements tell us about stores and what they sell.
- People work in stores to earn money. The money they are paid is called wages.

ART

Paper Plate Pouch

1 whole paper plate, luncheon size; 1 half of a paper plate, luncheon size; yarn for shoulder strap; stapler; hole punch; markers or crayons.

Decorate each plate with markers or crayons. Staple the half plate to the whole plate to form a pouch. With a hole punch, punch two holes at the top for attaching the yarn shoulder strap. The pouches may be used to carry play money to buy items in the class stores.

Sack Puppets

Lunch-size paper sacks; glue; markers or crayons; sack puppet pattern (or draw own faces).

Glue or draw a face on the bottom of the sack so the fold in the sack is used for the mouth opening, as shown. Let the children add details on the puppet to show what kind of store the puppet works in. Glue a picture on the front of the puppet, in the puppet's hands, to show what he/she sells.

Encourage the children to let their puppets talk with each other about what they do in their store. Let the puppets help children role play about shopping in different types of stores.

Logo Collage

9 × 12 inch construction paper; newspapers; old telephone books; glue.

The children cut around the ads and logos for the stores they recognize. Then let them make a collage by gluing the logos onto construction paper.

Art Store

Using paints, crayons, or markers, the children create their own pictures. Print each child's name in the bottom right-hand corner of the picture. Discuss how artists always sign their artworks.

Display all the pictures under the title "Art Store." Add a small price tag to each artwork, if desired. Discuss how people can go to art stores to buy art to display in their homes.

Potato Carving and Printing

Waxed paper; plastic table knives or spoons; potatoes cut in half; tempera paint on paper plates or meat trays; 12 × 18 inch paper.

Give each child a potato half and a knife or spoon. (For extra safety, space all the children sitting at a table apart from one another.) Let the children cut designs into the potato with the knife or spoon. When their design is finished, let them lightly touch the potato into the paint, then print the design by pressing the potato several times onto the paper. Repeat using different colors.

Paper Bead Necklace

Using the triangle pattern below, cut triangles out of bright wrapping paper or the comic section of the Sunday newspaper.

Starting at the wide end of the paper, let the children roll each triangle around a pencil, as shown. Spread a thin layer of glue on the last half of the triangle, so it glues together when rolled. Slip out the pencil, set the bead aside to dry, and make more beads.

When all the beads are dry, the children string them on a piece of colored yarn or string. Help the children tie the bead necklaces around their necks. (If desired, the store shrink art may be hung in the center of the necklace as a pendant.)

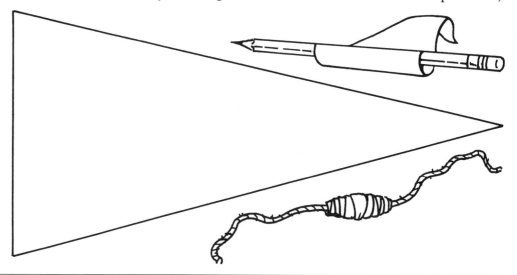

Shrink Art

Warm a gallon plastic milk carton to make it easier to cut. Using the pattern on the front of the November Curriculum guide, cut a store shape for each child out of the milk carton.

Let the children use permanent markers to color and decorate their store. If desired, punch a hole in the top of each shape so it can be strung later.

Lay the finished stores on a cookie tray and bake in a 200° oven for 4-6 minutes. Watch them carefully, as they shrink very fast all of a sudden. (If overcooked, they shrivel up rather than lay flat.)

Nail Designs

Small hammers; large head (roofing) nails; soft wood scraps (pine wood scraps are usually available for the asking at construction site scrap piles) or styrofoam pieces.

Let the children draw an outline of a store on a small piece of soft wood or styrofoam. Let them carefully hammer in the nails using the store outline as a guide. Talk about safety. Be sure the children are seated and spaced well apart as they work.

When finished, the children will have a very special store design. Color may be added with paints or markers, if desired.

Safety comment: As long as *soft* wood is used, this activity goes very well since the children do not have to pound very hard to get the nails in. Children love this project!

BLOCKS

Add trucks to the block area. Encourage the children to build stores and have the trucks drive back and forth to deliver supplies and equipment.

BULLETIN BOARD

Let's Go Shopping

Use 12 × 18 inch papers to make several store fronts with large display windows. Add a name for each store and a few details with markers or construction paper. Display as if side-by-side along a street, or clustered together in a shopping mall.

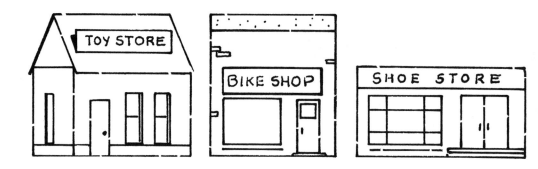

Let the children use magazines and catalogues to cut out items to glue or pin (with push pins) in each window to show what that store sells. For extra learning, use the names of local stores which the children know.

Variation: Quarter the bulletin board lengthwise with yarn dividers. Make each quarter a "display window" for a different type of store by putting a store name on a sign in the "window." You could also add picture clues on the signs. Provide the children with pictures of typical items found in each store. The children may classify the pictures by pinning the articles in the appropriate "store" with push pins. Effective suggestions include shoe store, grocery store, toy store, and restaurant.

COOKING

Jello Wiggle Creatures

Packages of jello (sugarless works well, also)
½ of the water called for on the package

Wash hands. Let the children mix the jello following package directions, but using only half the water called for. This makes a jello that is easily cut and handled.

Spray cookie sheets (with 1 inch sides) with Pam or rub with a light coating of shortening. Pour the jello mixture into the cookie sheets and refrigerate until set.

Wash hands. Give each child a piece of waxed paper to work on. Cut each child a large square of the jello. Let the children use cookie cutters or table knives to cut their jello squares into wiggle creatures. Eat the creatures.

Smacking-Good Snack

2 tablespoons whipped topping
1 teaspoon cocoa mix
1 teaspoon chopped nuts or chocolate chips

Wash hands. Let each child measure the ingredients and mix the snack in a small cup. Easy and delicious. Banana slices may also be added, if desired.

Banana Creme Pudding

Instant banana creme pudding
Vanilla wafers
Bananas
Milk

Wash hands. Let the children help measure and mix the pudding following package directions. Pour into small cups. Let the children add a couple of wafers and banana slices to each cup.

Peach Delight

Waxed paper
Rolling pin

Individual recipe:

1 canned peach half
1 rounded tablespoon whipped topping
2 vanilla wafers

Wash hands. Let each child make a snack by placing a peach half in a bowl and putting whipped topping on top of the peach. Then use a rolling pin to crumble two vanilla wafers between layers of waxed paper, and put the crumbs on top of the whipped topping. Eat and enjoy!

During cooking or snack time, talk about where people shop for food. Discuss grocery stores, open-air or farmers markets, and convenience stores.

LANGUAGE ARTS

Books

Adams, Pam, illus. *Shopping Day*. Playspaces, 1974.
Bograd, Larry. *Lost in the Store*. Macmillan, 1981.
Campbell, Rod. *Pet Shop*. Scholastic, Inc., 1984.
Koelling, Caryl. *Molly Mouse Goes Shopping*. Price-Stern, 1982.
Mayer, Mercer. *Possum Child Goes Shopping*. Scholastic, Inc., 1983.
Spier, Peter. *The Food Market*. Doubleday, 1981.
Spier, Peter. *The Pet Store*. Doubleday, 1981.
Spier, Peter. *The Toy Store*. Doubleday, 1981.

Fingerplays and Nursery Rhymes

Recite with the children "To Market, to Market" and "Hot Cross Buns."

Things to Buy

Three things to buy in the baker's shop.
Creamy and rich with a cherry on top.
Along came a girl with money to pay.
She paid a quarter and took one thing away.

Two things to buy in the baker's shop...

One thing to buy in the baker's shop...

No things to buy in the baker's shop.
No creamy things. No cherries on top.
No one comes with money to pay.
So the baker closes shop and goes home today.

Visit to a Grocery Store

Plan a class trip to a grocery store. If possible, arrange a tour. Take a small amount of money and let the children locate and buy the few simple items needed for one of the cooking projects. Once back to the classroom, let them prepare the snack with the purchased items.

Visit to a Pet Store

Plan a class trip to tour a pet store. If possible, take a small amount of money and buy a small item needed for a classroom pet, such as fish food.

Logo Book

Make a class logo book by pasting on separate pages the logos for stores that the children know. "Read" the book together several times.

Hide and Say

Hide something small behind your back, in your hand, or in some container. Ask the children to guess what it is. Describe the object by giving one clue at a time until the children guess correctly. Then encourage different children to be the leader and take turns hiding something.

Vary the game by telling the class what kind of store the item is from: "I'm hiding something I bought at a pet store."

Logo Match and Concentration

Cut out two of each kind of logo for three to six stores the children know. Glue each logo on an index card or on a piece of construction paper.
1. Mix up the cards and let the children take turns putting the matched pairs together.
2. Turn all of the cards face down in rows. Let the children play Concentration, taking turns turning over two cards at a time trying to make a match. If they match, they keep the cards. If not, they must turn the cards back over.

Going to the Store Maze

Give each child a copy of the maze on page 131. Talk about going to the store. Use fingers to follow the path for the child to get to the store without crossing any lines.

Let the children use crayons to color in a face and hair for the child on the handout. Then let them draw in the correct path to the store.

Directions Game

Cut out of newspapers and telephone books several logos of stores the children know. Glue each on a piece of construction paper and laminate them, if possible. Use masking tape to tape the logos to the floor.

Give one or two oral directions, using the logos, for the children to follow: "Put two feet on the hamburger store and two hands on the toy store." (Use commercial names for the stores if the children recognize such stores by name.)

Signs

Cut out several 4 × 8 inch cards. Print on each card a simple word repeatedly found on stores: Open, Closed, Push, Pull, Exit, etc. Talk about what each word says. Make pairs of the cards for the children to match.

Drink Stand

Discuss simple economics. Talk about how stores sell items to make money, which is called "making a profit." Discuss how people who work in stores are paid money, which is called "wages." Talk about the expenses involved in running a store: inventory, electricity, rent, etc.

Set up a simple drink stand. Mix a drink. Provide small cups. Let the children take turns buying and selling the drinks using play money. (Developmental Learning Materials (DLM) has some very realistic-looking paper coins. DLM is a publisher of early childhood equipment, located in Allen, Texas.)

Use the play money to show the children what happens to the money a store takes in. Put some of the money on a paper marked "Expenses," some on a paper marked "Wages," and some on a paper marked "Profit."

SHOPPING

127

Grocery Sack

1. Secretly put several large grocery store items in a grocery sack. Ask the children to look at the bag and guess how many things were bought at the store. Then let the children take the items out one at a time as the group counts them.

 Repeat the procedure several times. Children love to guess first, and it increases their interest in counting.

2. Begin with an empty sack. "I need to buy four things at the store." Let the children help put four items in the sack. Repeat the activity using any appropriate number.

Real Money

Have two to ten real pennies available. Let the group count them together. Then let individual children count the pennies.

One More—One Less

Have several items from stores on a table. Put one item in a sack, saying, "I bought one thing at the _____ store. Then I bought one more. How many things did I buy?" Continue adding one more item as appropriate for the ability of the group.

 Later, reverse the process. "I bought three things from the store. Then I gave one to _____ (a child's name). How many things do I have now?"

MATH VOCABULARY

Big—Little/Large—Small

 The children draw a large window of a store on manila paper. Some suggestions are a toy store, grocery store, or shoe store. Inside the window the children may draw one large and one small object appropriate for that store window. If desired, pictures of objects may be glued on the paper instead. The toy store could have a large and a small ball; the grocery store could have a large apple and a small banana, or a large and a small box of cereal, etc.

SIZE RELATIONSHIPS

1. Arrange items from the grocery store or shoes from the shoe store from little to big, and from big to bigger to biggest.
2. Have three sizes of shoes and three sizes of shoe boxes: baby shoes, children's shoes, and adult shoes. Let the children match the correct shoes to each box.

MOVEMENT

Grocery Cart Path

Have a plastic play grocery store cart, if possible. Make a winding path with a long rope. Let children carefully steer the cart along the path.

Variations: 1. Walk on tiptoes.
2. Walk toe to heel.
3. Walk backwards.
4. Walk in giant steps.

Color Up

Have the children squat on the floor. You or a child names a color. Anyone wearing that color stands. The leader then names another color, and the children go up or down depending on whether or not they are wearing the color.

Store Categories

Name a type of store, such as shoe store or bookstore. Then name different items. The children squat down and quickly stand up every time they hear an item that doesn't fit the category. Name incorrect items often enough to keep the children moving.

Imagining

You and the class imagine and act out the following ideas. Use exaggerated movements.

1. Walking on gravel with bare feet.
2. Walking on hot asphalt or cement in a shopping center.
3. Climbing long staircase at the store. Hurry down the other side.
4. Stepping on different tiles to get across the floor.
5. Stubbing a toe on the table leg. It hurts!

MUSIC

High and Low

Talk about high musical sounds and low musical sounds. Have instruments, records, and tapes to demonstrate high and low. Have the children sing high and low notes after you demonstrate.

Shopping Lassie

(Tune: ''Did You Ever See a Lassie?'')

Did you ever see a lassie, a lassie, a lassie?
Did you ever see a lassie go shopping like that?
Buy this thing, and that thing, and this thing, and that thing,
   (Pretend to be grabbing things off of shelves as quickly as possible.)
Did you ever see a lassie go shopping like that?

Talk about how silly it would be just to buy everything we see. Talk about how we need to be careful shoppers and think about what we buy: "We need to shop with our brains, not just with our eyes." Then sing the second version of the song.

Did you ever see a smart child, a smart child, a smart child?
Did you ever see a smart child go shopping like this?
Look at this thing, and that thing, but only buy needed things,
   (Pretend to look at items and check them carefully.)
Did you ever see a smart child go shopping like this?

The Worker in the Store

(Tune: "The Farmer in the Dell")

Decide on a type of store, then name items appropriate for that store. Continue until three to six verses have named different items.

The worker in the store, the worker in the store,
Heigh-ho the derry-o, the worker in the store.
The worker sells some _____ .
The worker sells some _____ .
Heigh-ho the derry-o, the worker sells some _____ .

ROLE PLAY

Stores

Set up a special kind of a store. A shoe store or a grocery store works very well. Let the children help bring in items to sell at the store. (Mark each of the children's things with their names to prevent problems later.) If using a grocery store, bring in several real but empty boxes and cans. For a shoe store, bring in several pairs of different kinds and sizes of shoes and shoe boxes.

Provide as many props as possible: sacks, toy cash register, play money, purses, shelves, and a check-out table. Shelves are easily built by the children from short boards and blocks. A toy doll buggy or plastic grocery cart really adds to the role play.

It is very important to let the children set up their own store by placing all the items on the shelves and by deciding how to arrange all the other props.

Let the children take turns being the worker and the shoppers.

Sack Puppets

Use the sack puppets made in ART to shop and work in the store. Let the children use the puppets to talk about what they need to buy, etc.

Containers

1. Provide a plastic tub of dry beans or rice. Let children use the beans or rice to fill up different kinds of containers. Ask which contains the most, the least.
2. Provide a short, wide plastic glass and a tall, thin plastic glass. Put the same amount of liquid in each. Show the children. Ask which has the most liquid. Demonstrate by pouring the liquid into measuring cups. Most children will not be ready to understand that the containers have the same volume of liquid. The shape of the container tricks them.
3. Talk about the different kinds of containers stores use for the things they sell. Display numerous containers on the science table. Let the children classify them in several different ways. Explain how the containers are the same and how they are different.

Musical Glasses

Fill four to six glasses with different amounts of water. Tap each glass lightly with a spoon. Listen for the different tones. Help children arrange the sounds from low to high. Then arrange them from high to low.

Thanksgiving and Life in Early America

CONCEPTS

- Thanksgiving is a time to give thanks and to share with others.
- Pilgrims and Indians celebrated the first Thanksgiving.
- The Indians and Pilgrims taught each other many useful and helpful things.
- We serve turkey, cranberries, vegetables, popcorn, and pumpkin pie for Thanksgiving dinner to remember and celebrate the foods that the Pilgrims and Indians grew and ate together on the first Thanksgiving feast.
- Indians today dress and act differently than the way Indians did in early America. Similarly, we dress differently than the Pilgrims did.

Note: Be alert to children's statements which may reflect misinformation or stereotypes about Indians. Similarly, you should avoid terms such as "how," "chief," "squaw," "papoose," and "savage"—often used to stereotype the Indian people. Avoid using the phrase "sit like an Indian" when sitting cross-legged at circle time, since that leads children to believe Indians sit without chairs today. Accent the cooperation between Pilgrims and Indians—exemplified in the first Thanksgiving feast—which we continue to celebrate. Children need to develop an understanding of a realistic view of Indian life in early America and today.

ART · THANKSGIVING FEAST PILGRIM AND INDIAN COSTUMES

Pilgrim Collar

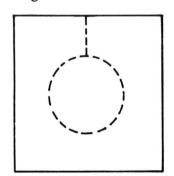

12 inch white paper squares; scissors.

Use a square of construction paper or butcher paper. Cut from the back to the neck and cut out a circle as shown. This provides an opening for the child to put the collar around the neck to wear like a Pilgrim collar.

Pilgrim Hats

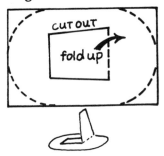

Aluminum foil; black 12 × 15 inch construction paper rectangles.

Cut out a Pilgrim hat shape by rounding off the corners of the black construction paper. Cut the opening large enough for the child's head to fit through. Fold up the cutout area so it will stand up to make the top shape of the hat. Use aluminum foil to make the buckle for the front of the hat. Staple a wide band across the front of the hat.

Indian Vests

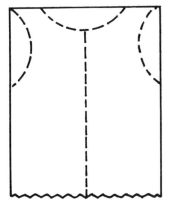

Paper grocery sacks; markers, crayons, or tempera paint; Q-Tips; scissors.

Make paper-sack Indian vests by cutting large grocery sacks, as shown. The children use markers or crayons (or tempera with Q-Tips for brushes) to decorate the vests with Indian signs (see Indian Signs page at the end of this section).

Show the children how to make short cuts to "fringe" the paper. Let them carefully fringe around the bottom edges of the vest.

Indian Necklaces

Rigatoni or macaroni; tempera paint; newspapers; yarn or string.

Color rigatoni or macaroni by shaking or stirring it in a jar of tempera paint or food coloring and water. Spoon out the pasta and spread it on newspapers to dry.

Once dry, the children string the pasta on 24 inch pieces of yarn or heavy string to tie and wear as necklaces. Discuss colors and repeating patterns.

Indian Drums

Cans with plastic lids or oatmeal boxes; tempera paint or markers.

Make drums out of cans or oatmeal boxes by letting the children paint the drums and decorate them with Indian signs or Thanksgiving symbols.

Thanksgiving Easel Painting

Newsprint paper; tempera paint; brushes.

1. Cut tepee shapes from large pieces of newsprint for painting at the easel. Discuss the concept of the triangle shape as children paint.
2. Provide large Pilgrim hat shapes to paint on at the easel.
3. Provide large turkey cutouts and several colors of paint.

Sand Drawing

Box lids or rectangle cake pans with 2 inch sides; sand, salt, or cornmeal; sticks.

Provide one or more box lids or large rectangle cake pans. Put a ½ inch layer of fine sand, salt, or cornmeal in the bottom of each pan. Provide sticks of different sizes. Let the children explore smoothing the sand layer, then using a stick or finger to draw figures and designs in the sand. They can "erase" the picture by smoothing the sand again, creating new designs. (Children thoroughly enjoy this process even though they cannot take their "art product" home to show.)

Mosaic Turkey

Turkey outlines; glue; various collage materials, as listed.

1. Provide copies of a small turkey outline for each child. The children use glue and beans, rice, macaroni, seeds, and/or kernels of corn to fill in the turkey outline.
2. Copy the turkey outline onto brown construction paper. Break off pieces from a pine cone. Let the children glue the pine cone pieces inside the outline to make turkey "feathers."

Feather Painting

Large and small feathers; tempera paint; paper.

Let the children paint using feathers dipped into tempera paint. Encourage gentle strokes so they see the soft lines the feather will make as they lightly brush it across the paper.

Experiment using different sizes of feathers and different colors for a more interesting effect.

Sand/Salt/ Cornmeal Painting

Use sand, salt, or cornmeal (whichever is readily available); dry tempera powder; shakers; glue; paper.

Color the sand/salt/cornmeal by mixing it with dry tempera powder. Mix several colors. Put the mixtures in shakers. (Empty garlic salt containers work well. Also, you can make shakers by taping waxed paper over the opening of a paper cup with the mixture already in it, then carefully poking small holes in the waxed paper.)

Let the children freely squirt out designs with the glue, then shake the colored mixture over the glue. Carefully shake off the excess on a sheet of waxed paper so it can be recycled.

Talk about the sand pictures Indians made. If possible, show examples from reference books. If you use cornmeal, discuss the importance of corn to the Indians; discuss how they made cornmeal.

THANKSGIVING AND LIFE IN EARLY AMERICA

Handy Turkey Puppets

Manila paper; construction paper scraps; glue; crayons or markers; hole punch (optional).

Let the children trace around their hands without tracing their thumbs. (Some children may need help.) You then cut holes for two fingers, to serve as the legs of the turkey puppet. (A hole punch works well if you can make three or four overlapping punches in a circle, to create a hole large enough for small fingers to use.)

Provide, or let children cut out, construction paper circles for the puppet head and eyes, a yellow triangle beak, and a red wattle. The children glue these on their hand turkey, as shown.

Finally, the children color the turkey using bright colors for each feather.

Indian Sign Finger Painting

Finger paint; white shelf paper or finger painting paper.

Provide a finger painting mixture and large pieces of paper. The children use their fingers to finger paint several Indian signs on their paper. Display a large chart of signs for them to look at, or provide several copies of the Indian Signs page at the end of this section for them to use as they paint.

Indian Beads and Necklaces

Ceramic dough (see Art Recipes); drinking straw; tempera paint; yarn.

Provide each child with a ball of dough. Let the children pinch dough off the large ball and roll 12-18 marble-sized balls for beads.

Using a drinking straw, poke a hole through each bead. Let the beads harden a day or two. When hard, paint them with bright colors of tempera paint. Allow to dry again. String 6-9 beads on a length of yarn to make an Indian-style necklace. Let each child make two necklaces, then trade one with another child—as the Indians traded with the Pilgrims!

Indian Head Puppets

Brown or tan construction paper; ½ inch strips of construction paper for headbands; crayons or markers; popsicle sticks; glue.

The children draw on construction paper around their hand, with their fingers closed together, as shown. They then glue on a headband and a popsicle stick, for a handle. Finally, each child adds designs and details to complete an Indian Puppet.

Tepees

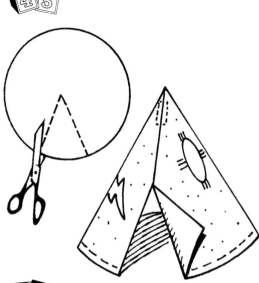

9 inch circles cut from brown butcher paper or brown grocery sacks (cut out a triangle, as shown); markers; crayons or tempera paint; tape; oil.

The children draw and paint (or color) Indian signs on the tepee paper. When dry, tape the tepee together on the inside at the top. Then fold the door flap open.

Set the tepee on newspaper. Use a paint or basting brush to lightly brush the entire outside of the tepee with pure vegetable oil. The oil makes the brown paper look like leather!

Pilgrim Cabin

Popsicle sticks; glue; paper.

The children draw a simple outline of a large house on a piece of paper. Then they glue popsicle sticks atop each other, over the outline, to make a log cabin similar to a Pilgrim's cabin.

BLOCKS

Build houses to play in and tables on which to serve the Thanksgiving feast. Provide toy logs, if possible, and encourage the children to build log cabins. Set up an Indian village with plastic figures. Build block corrals for the horses.

BULLETIN BOARD

We Are Thankful

We are Thankful

Print the caption on the board, as shown. Pin up a large cornucopia. Provide patterns or cutouts of different kinds of fruits and vegetables. Give each child a cutout, or let each child make one fruit or vegetable out of construction paper scraps. Have each child name something for which to be thankful. Print each idea on the child's fruit or vegetable. You may also print the child's name or initials on the food item. Then pin or staple each finished fruit/vegetable on the board, as if pouring out of the cornucopia.

THANKSGIVING AND LIFE IN EARLY AMERICA

Pumpkin Drop Cookies

½ cup butter/margarine
1½ cups sugar
1 egg
1 cup cooked or canned pumpkin
2½ cups all-purpose flour
1 teaspoon baking powder

1 teaspoon baking soda
½ teaspoon salt
1 teaspoon nutmeg
1 teaspoon cinnamon
½ cup diced roasted almonds
1 cup chocolate pieces

Cream butter and sugar until light and fluffy. Beat in egg, pumpkin, and vanilla. Mix and sift flour, baking powder, baking soda, salt, nutmeg, and cinnamon. Add to creamed mixture; mix well. Add almonds and chocolate pieces; mix thoroughly. Drop dough by teaspoons onto well-greased cookie sheets. Bake at 350° for 15 minutes or until lightly browned. Remove from cookie sheets while still warm; cool on racks. Makes about 6 dozen.

Hot Dog Canoes

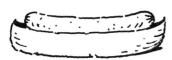

Wash hands. Cut hot dogs in half. Use two refrigerator biscuits. Let the children pat and stretch each biscuit so it makes a rectangle longer than the hot dog. Wrap the biscuits around the hot dog and pinch up the ends as shown. Bake about 10 minutes at 375°.

Indian Popcorn

8 cups of popped corn
⅓ cup maple-flavored syrup
Large bowl or plastic tub
Paper cups

Wash hands. Let the children help mix the syrup and the popped corn together until the corn is well coated. Serve in paper cups. Sticky, but good!

Talk about how the Indians made maple syrup from maple trees. Most sources suggest that the Indians popped corn in clay pots, which they set in a campfire. Some sources, however, suggest that the Indians tossed corn kernels on the hot rocks of their fire and then caught the popped kernels as they flew out in all directions.

No Bake Pumpkin Pie

Individual recipe:

Small custard-sized pie crusts
2 tablespoons canned pumpkin
1 tablespoon marshmallow creme
1 tablespoon prepared whipped topping
Sprinkle of cinnamon

Mix all ingredients together and pour into the crust. The recipe is then ready to eat; if you wish, it may be refrigerated or frozen.

Pumpkin Pudding Cones

⅓ can of pumpkin with spices
8 oz. prepared whipped topping
2 packages of vanilla pudding
3½ cups milk
Ice cream cones
Large bowl

Let the children help mix the pudding with the milk. Then add the pumpkin mix and stir well. The children then spoon the mixture into ice cream cones. ''Frost'' the tops with whipped topping.

Thanksgiving Feast

Feast possibilities include: cornbread, vegetable stew, pumpkin pie or pudding, popcorn, milk, baked apples.... Any or all of these may be prepared in the classroom starting a day or so in advance or by inviting other classes to share in the feast, with each class making one part of the dinner.

To prepare the vegetable stew, let each child in the class contribute a vegetable. The children may peel and cut up all but the carrots with a peeler and a plastic knife. (The carrots are too hard to cut easily with a plastic knife.)

Children may wear the Thanksgiving costumes they made. A parade down the hall would be fun. Also, parents would enjoy attending this activity.

LANGUAGE ARTS

Books

Batherman, Muriel. *Before Columbus*. Houghton-Mifflin, 1981.
Barrlett, Robert Merrill. *Thanksgiving Day*. Crowell, 1965.
Brown, Marc Tolon. *Arthur's Thanksgiving*. Little, Brown, 1983.
Cohen, Barbara. *Molly's Pilgrim*. Lothrop, Lee and Shepard, 1983.
Friskey, Margaret. *Indian Two Feet and His Eagle Feather*. Children's Press, 1967.
Gibbons, Gail. *Thanksgiving Day*. Holiday House, 1983.
Goble, Paul. *The Girl Who Loved Wild Horses*. Bradbury, 1978.
Kroll, Steven. *One Tough Turkey*. Holiday House, 1982.
Moncure, Jane Belk. *My First Thanksgiving Book*. Children's Press, 1984.
Schulz, Charles. *A Charlie Brown Thanksgiving*. Scholastic, 1974.
Ward, Elains. *The Thanksgiving Feast*. Argus Communications, 1981.
Whitehead, Patricia. *Best Thanksgiving Book*. Troll Associates, 1985.

Teacher Resource Books

Anderson, Joan. *The First Thanksgiving Feast*. Clarion Books, 1984.
Corwin, Judith Hoffman. *Thanksgiving Fun*. Messner, 1984.
Hopkins, Lee Bennett. *Merrily Comes Our Harvest In: Poems for Thanksgiving*. Harcourt Brace Jovanovich, 1978.
Kessel, Joyce. *Squanto and the First Thanksgiving*. Carolrhoda Books, 1983.
Sandak, Cass R. *Thanksgiving*. Watts, 1980.

Fingerplays

This Is My Turkey

(Right hand makes a fist with thumb extended; left hand, with fingers close
   together, is placed with palm against right hand fist.)
This is my turkey
You know what he can do?
He can spread his tail   (Spread out fingers.)
And wave it at you!   (Wave fingers.)

Ten Little Indians

Ten little Indians dancing around,   (Extend ten fingers and
                                               wiggle them.)

Ten little Indians planting corn in the ground. (Close one hand; push index
                                               finger of other hand into
                                               the hole in the first hand.)

Ten little Indians crawl in a tepee;   (Bring finger tips together to
                                               make a point over head.)

Ten little Indians as quiet as can be!   (Fold hands and lay head
                                               on hands.)

Shhhh!

Ten Little Pilgrims

Ten little Pilgrim children are we.   (Hold both hands up with fingers
                                          extended.)

1-2-3-4-5 Pilgrim boys.   (Wiggle each finger in turn.)
1-2-3-4-5 Pilgrim girls.   (Wiggle each finger in turn.)
Working together so carefully,   (Use appropriate actions.)
Playing together so fancy-free,
Happy to live in a land that's free!   (Hold hands together as if praying.)

Colored Feather Match

Color feathers by using permanent
markers to color all along the tips of
the feathers. Prepare two feathers for
each color you wish to use. Put all the
feathers together in a box or sack and
let the children find the matching colored pairs.

Variation: Staple one half of a
heavy-duty paper plate to a whole
paper plate to form a storage pocket.
Cut an even number of notches along
the top edge of the paper plate, as shown. Store the colored feather pairs in the
pocket. Let the children dump the feathers out, then stick the matching colored
pairs beside one another in the notches along the top of the plate.

Indian Names

Indian names are usually based on things in nature. Many girls were named after plants, such as Cactus Flower, Spring Blossom, and Morning Rose. Many boys were named after animals, such as Little Beaver, Raging Bull, or Swift Deer. Discuss Indian names with the children. Let each child choose an Indian name. Make Indian name tags with yarn attached, so children may wear their names around their necks if they choose. The Indian names may also be printed on the backs of the vests (see ART).

Being Thankful

Discuss the meaning of "being thankful." Talk with the children about things for which they are thankful. Read to the children the poems "All in a Word—Thanks" by Aileen Fisher and "The Little Girl and the Turkey" by Dorothy Aldis in Lee Bennett Hopkins's book.

Sticker Match

Use Thanksgiving stickers of various kinds to create matching games, a concentration game, and/or a bingo game. Limit the number of stickers for matching to a number appropriate to the ability of the children. Begin with four to six matches.

Indian Headdress

Talk about how Indians earned feathers to wear in their headband by the difficult feats and achievements they accomplished. "What could each of us do that would be an important achievement and earn us a feather?" Encourage interested children to set realistic goals to work toward. Reward each child with a feather when they achieve their goal.

Storytelling

Telling stories was an important part of Indian culture. The stories taught Indian children the ways and beliefs of their people. The Pilgrims also told stories to children and adults, because so few books were available.

Prepare a story to tell the children. Choose one which includes interesting and accurate information about life in early America. Use a lot of facial expressions and voice changes as you tell the story. Children are fascinated by storytelling, and will probably ask you to tell it again and again.

Our Thanks Tree

Tree branch; can of rocks or plaster of paris; construction paper; crayons or markers; hole punch; yarn.

Secure a real tree branch in a can of rocks or plaster of paris. Using 3 × 5 inch pieces of construction paper, have the children draw or cut out a picture of something for which they are thankful. Let each child carefully use a hole punch to make a hole in the upper left-hand corner of each card. Tie on a 6 inch piece of yarn. Then let the children hang their "thanks" pictures on the branches.

Early America

Display and talk about real items representing life in early America. Some examples are: a pestle for grinding seeds, models of log cabins and/or tepees, Indian blankets and/or jewelry, pottery, and clothing. Parents and other community members may have items they would be willing to share.

Guest Speaker

Invite a Boy Scout leader or Y.M.C.A. Indian Guide leader to talk to your class about early Indians. Perhaps they might teach the children some Indian sign language or some early-American craft.

Indian Sign Language

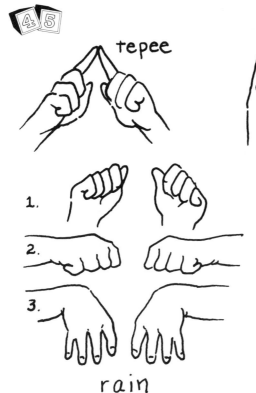

Indians used sign language to communicate with other tribes that spoke different languages. Talk about how we use our hands to tell people "come here," "good-bye," etc. Teach the children a few simple Indian signs, such as those shown.

Classification: Today vs. the Past

Prepare a folder game by providing pictures of homes, clothing, vehicles, and other items either typical of the past or used today. At the bottom of the folder tape or glue an envelope in which to store the set of pictures. The children dump out all the pictures, then classify them appropriately.

For more able children, you might provide some items that are used similarly today as in the past, such as a picture of a canoe or a horse. Talk about how while many things change, some things remain the same.

Thanksgiving Feast Game

The children sit in a circle. The first child says, "At my Thanksgiving Feast, I ate turkey." The second person repeats the sentence and adds another food. Continue around the circle, adding a food each time, until someone gets mixed up. Then let all the children say "Gobble-gobble-gobble!" and start the game over with the child who is next in the circle.

MATH   NUMBER CONCEPTS

Lace-a-Canoe

Provide two cutouts of a canoe. Punch four holes along the bottom and number them 1-4 from left to right, as shown. Tape a piece of yarn or string to the left edge of one canoe. Let the children lace the two canoe cutouts together by lacing the numerals in order. Provide a plastic figure to fit inside the canoe after it's laced, if desired.

To make a good lacing string, wrap the end of the string in tape or dip it in glue and let it dry. The number of holes to lace may range from three to six or more, according to the children's ability.

Corn Count

Provide a 4 cup section cut from an egg carton and a small bowl of corn kernels. Write a numeral in each cup and let the children count out the appropriate number of kernels to place in each cup.

Pilgrims

Make three Pilgrim heads out of paper, as shown. Put small squares of sandpaper on the back so they will stick to a flannel board, or glue a ½ × 2 inch strip of paper in a loop on the back of each to make finger puppets. Move the Pilgrims while saying the following verse. Repeat the verse and let the children act it out with the Pilgrim figures.

"Three Little Pilgrims"

The first little Pilgrim wanted corn to eat.
The second little Pilgrim thought pumpkin pie would be neat!
The third little Pilgrim asked for turkey and dressing.
Then they all bowed their heads for a Thanksgiving blessing.

THANKSGIVING AND LIFE IN EARLY AMERICA

Pretzel Shapes

Provide ten pretzel sticks for each child.
1. The children count out three sticks, then lay them together to make a triangle.
2. The children count out four sticks, then lay them together to make a square.
3. The children carefully break one pretzel stick in half. They then lay together the remaining two whole sticks and two half sticks to make a rectangle.
4. Each child mixes together his/her sticks and starts over again—making a triangle, square, and rectangle.

Shape-a-Turkey

For each turkey:
1 three inch circle (body)
1 one inch circle (head)
2 1 × ½ inch rectangles (legs)
1 ½ inch triangle (beak)
2 ½ inch squares (eyes)
5 two inch triangles (feathers)

Make the pieces out of felt for the flannel board or out of paper to use on a tabletop. Show the children how the shapes can go together to make a turkey. Let the children take turns mixing up the shapes, then putting them together again to make the turkey.

Talk about the shapes, naming each one as you work together.

MOVEMENT

Dancing Indians

(Say with a strong four-beat rhythm.)

The Indians are dancing	(Move bodies rhythmically.)
Drum...drum...drum..drum...	(Pat hands on legs.)
The Indians are dancing	(Repeat first instruction.)
Drum...drum...drum...drum...	(Repeat second instruction.)
Toe-heel, toe-heel along the ground	(Continue to act out movements.)
Toe-heel, toe-heel without a sound.	
The Indians are dancing	
Drum...drum...drum...drum.	

Thanksgiving Movements

Walk toe-heel, toe-heel single file in rhythm to Indian music.
Strut like turkeys with arms tucked as wings.

1) Strut from a starting line to a finish line.
2) Lay a long rope down on the floor in a pattern. Let the children, in single file, strut along following the rope pattern.

THANKSGIVING AND LIFE IN EARLY AMERICA

The Little Pilgrim Hunter
(An Action Story)

(Act out each underlined movement as the story progresses.)

Bent over—Legs straight, touch hands to floor.
Fell down—Drop to floor.
Walked—Pat legs and walk in place.
See/looked/saw—Hands over eyes to shade them; look both directions.
Jumped—Jump in place, raising hands over head.
Hopped—Hop in place like a rabbit.
Crawled—Move in place on all fours.
Yelled—Oh!
Ran—Pat legs quickly and run in place.

Once upon a time a little Pilgrim hunter went hunting for a turkey. He bent over to pick up his trusty gun but oops, lost his balance and fell down. He jumped back, brushed off his clothes, bent over again, and picked up his gun. Then he went walking toward the woods to find a turkey.

He walked a little way until he saw a squirrel in a tree. He looked up at the squirrel. But he didn't want a squirrel so he walked on.

He walked a little further and he came to a big hole. He looked in the hole. No turkey. So he backed up, ran fast...faster...faster and jummmmmped over the hole. Then he walked on.

He walked a little further and he saw a rabbit hopping through the grass. He looked at the rabbit. He laughed and tried to hop like the rabbit. Hop...hop... hop. But he didn't want a rabbit so he walked on.

The little Pilgrim hunter walked a little further until he came to a cave. He looked into the cave. But it was too dark to see. So he got down on his knees and crawled into the cave. He crawled on until he bumped something! It was soft and warm. Was it a turkey? No, it was a big bear!

He yelled and quickly crawled back out of the cave. (Spoken and acted out quickly.) He ran back toward home. He hopped by the rabbit. He ran toward the hole and jummmmmped across. He ran by the squirrel, out of the woods and back to his log cabin. He was out of breath and so worn out that he never went hunting for a turkey again until he was grown up!

The End

Indian Toss Game

Foam rubber cubes or scraps; 2-4 baskets.

The Crow Indians played a game in which they tossed stones into the air to catch them in a basket. Let two to four children at a time hold a basket and try to catch pieces of foam rubber in the basket as the pieces are gently tossed toward them.

Variation: Try tossing a foam piece into the air with one hand, then catching it in a basket held by the other hand.

MUSIC

Paddle Your Canoe

Children sit in pairs facing one another with their feet together and holding hands. They alternately rock back and forth as they sing, "Paddle, paddle, paddle your canoe..." Vary the speed. Sing and move at a regular tempo—very fast, then *very* slowly. (Tune "Row, Row, Row Your Boat")

We Love Turkey

(Tune: "Are You Sleeping?")

We love turkey, we love turkey
So good to eat, so good to eat.
We serve it on Thanksgiving, we serve it on Thanksgiving
What a yummy treat! What a yummy treat!

Thanksgiving Ways

(Tune: "Mulberry Bush")

This is the way to paddle canoes,
Paddle canoes, paddle canoes.
This is the way to paddle canoes,
On Thanksgiving morning.
This is the way the Pilgrims work...
This is the way the turkey struts...
This is the way the popcorn pops...
This is the way they ate the feast...

Drum Rhythms

Practice typical 4/4 drum beat rhythms, varying where you place the accent.

1—2—3—4
1—2—3—4
1—2—3—4
1—2—3—4

Begin clapping a rhythm and let the children join in, following your model. Use knees or tabletops as drums and beat the same rhythm together several times before switching the rhythm accent. Provide drums and let the children take turns playing the rhythm while the other children walk, dance, hop, or jump to the rhythm.

ROLE PLAY

Dramatize the First Thanksgiving

1. Divide the children into three groups to act as men, women, and children. Let each group role play the way they think the Pilgrims prepared for the feast. Encourage movements and conversation among the children as they improvise props and decide on the location of the forest, houses, tables, etc.

2. Regroup the children into two groups to act as Pilgrims and Indians. If they wish, they may use some of the costumes made in ART. Let the children decide how the tables should be arranged, where everyone should sit, etc. Encourage the children to talk about the things for which they think the Pilgrims and Indians were thankful. Stress the friendship between the Pilgrims and the Indians.

SCIENCE

Seeds

Provide seeds like those the Indians gave to the Pilgrims, such as pumpkin, corn, etc. Let the children examine the seeds. Try to provide pictures of the seeds as grown plants, ready to be harvested. Help the children match the seeds to the pictures of the grown plants.

Corn Shelling

Set out an ear of dried corn. Let the children shell the corn. Encourage them to use a magnifying glass to examine the place where a kernel came off the cob and to examine a single kernel. Cut a kernel in half and let the children examine it again.

Grinding Corn

Provide a grinding stone and kernels of dried corn. Show the children how to grind the corn. (Grinding corn down to corn meal is very hard work. You may want to start the process at home, using a blender to grind up some kernels into small pieces. Then let the children try to further grind the pieces using the grinding stone.)

Feathers

Let the children examine and compare turkey feathers with chicken feathers. Talk about size, feel, shape, etc.

Apple Faces

Apple dolls were made by the Iroquois Indians. Show the children how to make a head for such a doll. Peel a firm apple. Carve large features, as shown. (The apple will shrink to one-quarter its size, so don't cut too much away.) Stick in cloves for eyes.

Leave the carved apple face on a plate, away from drafts, so it does not mildew. It takes about four weeks for the apple to shrink and harden. Since the apple will become more and more distorted, the children will not know what it will look like for a whole month! Take photographs of the fresh apple, of the newly carved apple, then one photograph each week. Display the pictures and discuss what happened. Then mix up the pictures and ask the children to arrange them in the correct sequence.

Indian Signs

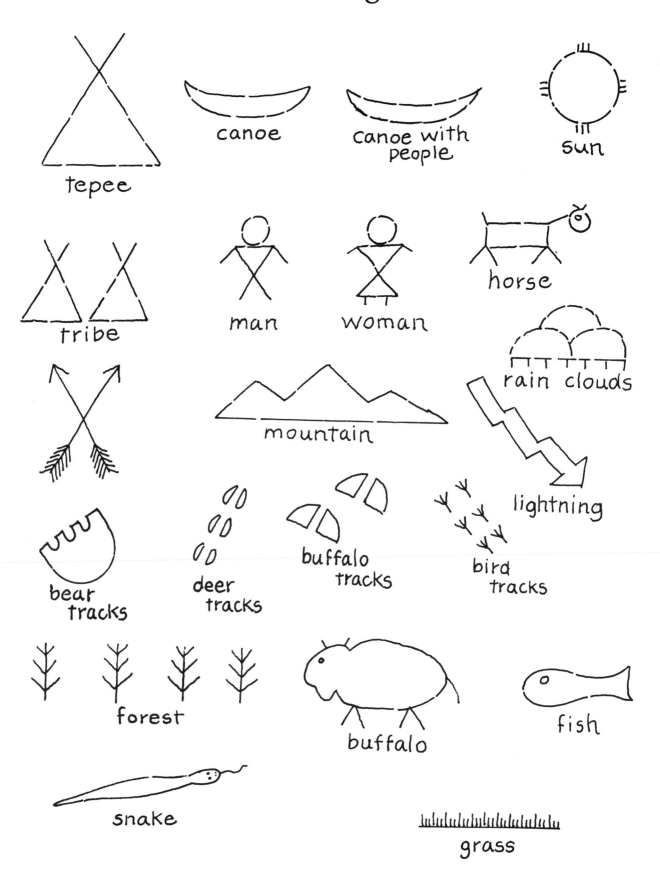

tepee

canoe

canoe with people

sun

tribe

man

woman

horse

mountain

rain clouds

lightning

bear tracks

deer tracks

buffalo tracks

bird tracks

forest

buffalo

fish

snake

grass

December Curriculum

1. Celebrations Around the World

2. Christmas

3. Toys

Celebrations Around the World

CONCEPTS

- Children live in many different countries and do different things.
- Children in other countries may celebrate Christmas in different ways.
- Some children do not celebrate Christmas because they have different beliefs.
- Children around the world may still be friends.

ART

Cereal Friendly Face

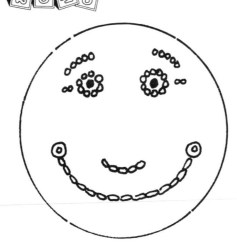

Construction paper; Cheerios cereal; glue; crayons or markers (optional).

Give each child a large circle cut from a 9 × 12 inch piece of construction paper. Use several different colors as appropriate for skin colors around the world. The children glue the cereal on their circle to create eyes, a nose, and a mouth. The children may add construction paper strips for hair, if desired. They may create other details with crayons or markers.

Starch Collage of Children

Cutouts of children from magazines; construction paper; liquid starch in small containers (less messy than glue); paintbrushes.

Provide or let the children cut out pictures of children who are different sizes and who are doing different things. Give each child a piece of paper. Have the children "paint" some starch on an area of their paper, lay a cutout picture on top of the starch, and then brush more starch over the picture. Let them use several pictures to make their collage. The starch will dry clear.

Encourage the children to overlap the edges of the pictures as they create a collage. Let it dry thoroughly.

**Fish Piñata
(Whole Class Project)**

Large brown paper bag (not a heavyweight one); crepe paper; tissue paper, crepe paper, or thin wrapping paper; glue or tape; construction paper scraps; wrapped candy; a piece of string or yarn.

Put the wrapped candy in the bag and tie the end shut with the string. Fan the opening out for the tail of the fish.

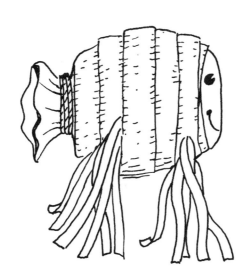

Cut several 2 inch strips of the paper. Starting at the tied end, the children glue or tape a strip of paper around the sack. Next, they tape or glue on another strip so it slightly overlaps the first one. Continue putting on strips until the bag is covered. Cut eyes out of scraps and glue them on. Add a few strips of paper, hanging down like streamers, for fins.

Hang up the piñata in a safe area. The children take turns being blindfolded and trying to hit the piñata with a stick. When the piñata breaks open, all the children scatter and collect the candy. Encourage equal sharing so all can enjoy the fun.

**Class Christmas Chain:
How Many Days
Until Christmas?**

2 × 9 inch strips of red and green construction paper; glue.

Count together on a calendar the number of days until Christmas Day. Let all the children help glue together alternate strips of red and green to make a paper chain with that number of strips. (They may also make extra chains to decorate the room and the tree.)

Print a numeral on each strip of the chain if desired. Hang the chain under the sign: "How many days until Christmas?" Each day, tear off one strip of the chain and count together the remaining strips to keep track of how many days remain before Christmas arrives.

Candy Canes

Ceramic play dough in red and white (see Art Recipes).

Simple Version: The children roll balls of each color of play dough into long snake shapes. Then they form the long rolls into candy cane shapes. The candy canes must dry for thirty-six hours at room temperature on a rack or screen.

1. *Small Candy Canes*
   Tape a safety pin to the back of each cane so the children can wear candy cane pins.
2. *Large Candy Canes*
   Hang large canes on Christmas trees—these decorations last for years. (They are also great for counting activities in math!)

Two-Color Candy Canes: The children roll white and red dough into long snake shapes. Then they twist together one white and one red roll to form a candy cane shape. Pinch the ends together so the two colors of dough do not separate when dry. The candy canes must dry for thirty-six hours at room temperature on a rack or screen.

Rudolph Reindeer

9 inch brown construction paper triangles for face; white circles for eyes; smaller black circles for pupils in eyes; red circle for nose; yellow or light brown antler cutouts; glue; red glitter (optional).

Give each child the cutout pieces to make one reindeer. Show the children how to put together the pieces by letting them glue together their own pieces. Glue red glitter on the nose to increase the "red-nosed" effect if desired.

Variation: To make special antlers, help the children trace around each of their hands on construction paper. Cut them out and glue them to the top of the reindeer head.

Hanger-Head Friends

One clothes hanger for each child; one leg from panty hose per child; glue; yarn for hair; construction paper scraps.

Pull the hanger into a circle shape. Bend the open hook of the hanger to form a complete circle and eliminate the sharp point. Stretch the panty hose over the hanger and tie as shown. Talk with the children about all the features they could add to this hanger head to make it look like a face. Let them use the yarn and construction paper scraps to complete their hanger-head friend.

CELEBRATIONS AROUND THE WORLD

Pop-Out Friendly Cards

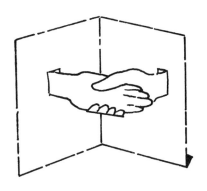

9 × 12 inch manila paper; markers or crayons; construction paper scraps; glue.

Have the children help each other trace around both hands and cut them out. Glue the hands together as if shaking hands. Fold a 9 × 12 inch paper in half. Show the children how to glue just the edges of the wrists on each side of the paper so the hands will "pop out" when the card is opened.

Print "Be My Friend" on the outside of each card for each child. Let each child dictate to you any other words he/she wants you to print on the card.

The children use markers, crayons, and construction paper to finish decorating their cards. Encourage them to give the card to a child whom they would like to have for a friend.

BLOCKS

Heavy—Light

Help the children classify the blocks into two groups, the heavy blocks and the light blocks. If possible, provide a simple scale and have the children weigh each block as they decide if it is heavy or light.

Friends

Suggest that the children build square outlines for two or more houses. Have them build roads or sidewalks between each of the houses so friends could walk or drive back and forth to visit one another.

BULLETIN BOARD

Let's All Sing Together

Cut simple child-shaped patterns on the fold of construction paper as shown on the next page. Make the cutouts from different colors of construction paper to represent children from different countries. Let the children use crayons, markers, or construction paper scraps to add details to each of the characters. Make the cutouts look like they are singing with open mouths. Cut out a music book for each character. Slit the characters' hands and insert the paper books. Display the characters on the bulletin board with the caption: "Let's All Sing Together." Place a few cutouts of musical notes randomly among the characters. If desired, use a world map as the backing on the bulletin board.

COOKING

Sugar Cookies
(A United States Favorite)

Packaged refrigerated sugar cookie dough or your favorite recipe
Rolling pins
Christmas cookie cutters
Frosting or sprinkle decorations (optional)

Wash hands. Let each child roll out some dough, choose a cookie cutter, and cut out a cookie. Use a toothpick to make the child's initials on the cookie. Bake and enjoy.

Make an extra batch of cookies to share with another class. Talk about Christmas being a time to share with friends.

Tortillas
(A Mexican Favorite)

Wash hands. Make tortilla dough according to the recipe on a cornmeal package. Wash hands. Give each child a small ball of the stiff dough. Have the children pat the dough on a piece of waxed paper to make a round, thin tortilla.

Cook the tortillas on a grill (like pancakes). Turn them over once to cook on both sides. Let the children use table knives to spread butter on the warm tortillas. Delicious to eat.

CELEBRATIONS AROUND THE WORLD

Gingerbread People
(A European Favorite)

No cookie cutter is needed!

5 cups flour
1½ teaspoons soda
½ teaspoon salt
2 teaspoons ginger
1 teaspoon cinnamon
1 teaspoon cloves
1 cup shortening
1 cup sugar
1 egg
1 cup molasses
2 tablespoons vinegar
Raisins

Sift the dry ingredients together. Cream together the shortening and sugar. Stir in egg, molasses, and vinegar. Beat well. Stir in the sifted dry ingredients and mix well. Chill.

Wash hands. Let the children help roll the dough in pecan-sized balls. Use three balls for each cookie. Place one ball on a greased baking sheet and flatten it with thumb to make the head. Roll one ball into a fat rope for the arms. Roll one into a rope and curve it for legs. Add raisins for eyes and buttons. Bake at 350° for 10-12 minutes.

Open-Face Sandwich
(A Swedish Favorite)

One thin, dense piece of bread (light or dark) per child
Several brightly colored toppings: lettuce, sliced ham, sliced hard-boiled
*   eggs, cheese slices, cucumbers, shrimp, watercress*
Cream cheese

Wash hands. The children use table knives to spread the cream cheese on the bread. Next they pick two or more of the toppings and use them to create their open-face sandwich.

Crispa
(A Mexican Favorite)

Deep frying pan and grease
One triangle of refrigerator crescent rolls per child
Cinnamon sugar (½ cup sugar + ½ teaspoon cinnamon)
Rolling pins

Wash hands. Allow the children to take turns rolling the dough thin with a rolling pin. Cut into two or three pieces with a plastic knife. Deep fry. Sprinkle with cinnamon sugar. Cool and eat.

Potato Latkes
(A Chanukah
Tradition)

2 cups grated potatoes
1 egg
¼ cup flour
1 teaspoon salt
½ teaspoon baking soda
½ cup finely chopped onion (optional)
Vegetable oil for frying
Applesauce

Wash hands. Let the children help grate the potatoes. Mix the potatoes with the soda and let set for a few minutes. Then squeeze the liquid out of the potatoes and mix all ingredients together. Carefully drop the mixture by spoonfuls into the hot oil. Turn when golden brown. Drain on paper towels and serve warm with applesauce.

LANGUAGE ARTS

Books

Bragg, Juliana. *The Nativity*. Golden Press, 1982.
Carle, Eric. *Do You Want to Be My Friend?* Crowell, 1971.
De Regniers, Beatrice Schenk. *May I Bring a Friend?* Atheneum, 1965.
Ets, Marie Hall. *Nine Days to Christmas*. Viking Press, 1959.
Hildebrandt, Greg. *A Christmas Treasury*. Unicorn, 1984.
Ichikawa, Satomi. *Merry Christmas: Children at Christmastime Around the World*. Philomel Books, 1983.
Riley, Sue. *Sharing*. Child's World, 1978.
Spier, Peter. *People*. Doubleday, 1980.
Whitehead, Pat. *Christmas Alphabet Book: ABC Adventures*. Troll, 1985.

**Teacher Resource
Books**

Bradshaw, Angela. *World Costumes*. Macmillan, 1963.
Fowler, Virginia. *Folk Toys Around the World: And How to Make Them*. Prentice-Hall, 1984.
Gardner, Horace J. *Let's Celebrate Christmas*. Ronald Press, 1950.
International Council on Health, Physical Education, and Recreation. *Book of Worldwide Games and Dances*. 1967.
Renberg, Dalia Hardof. *The Complete Family Guide to Jewish Holidays*. Adama Books, 1985.
Wernecke, Herbert H. *Celebrating Christmas Around the World*. Westminster Press, 1962.

CELEBRATIONS AROUND THE WORLD

Fingerplays

Chanukah Lights

One light, two lights, three lights, four,
  (Hold up four fingers, one at a time.)
Five lights, six lights, then light three more;
  (Hold up five more fingers.)
For Chanukah watch the nine pretty lights
On the Menorah burning bright.
  (Wiggle fingers as if flickering flames.)

Sharing

Encourage the children to bring dolls or other items from other countries to share with the class. Enlist the help of any parents who are from other countries or have lived or visited abroad.

What's in the Package?

Gift wrap a piece of cardboard, complete with a bow. Attach felt or velcro to the back so it may be used on a flannel board. From a catalogue, cut out pictures of gifts for children. Glue a small piece of velcro or felt to the back of each picture.

Place one picture on the flannel board. Hide it under the wrapped cardboard. Have the class guess what gift might be in the "package." Give clues as necessary. Each child may take turns being the teacher and hiding a picture under the package. Encourage the use of complete sentences.

Children in the World

Provide books, magazine pictures, or posters of children in native dress. Discuss each. Does the type of clothing give clues to the type of climate in that country? How? Encourage the use of complete sentences. Write sentences on a chart to show the children how their words look written down.

Trees of Many Colors

Copy the handout, found at the end of this section, for each child. Let the children use a paper hole punch to punch out small circles of construction paper. Have them glue red hole-punched circles on one tree, and blue, yellow, and all colors on the other trees (you may change the color words on the handout to any colors you desire). Talk about the size of the circles on the trees and the size of the hole-punched circles. Which are larger? smaller? Talk about the colors. Let them color the rest of the tree with crayons if they wish.

To help younger children know which color to glue on which tree, hang up a finished example, with the correct colors, where they can easily see it. Older children may underline or circle each color word with a crayon of that color to help them remember the proper color for each tree.

Chanukah

Ask someone in your community to visit the class and talk about the Chanukah season. The children will be interested in some of the customs and symbols, such as the Star of David, the Menorah, and the dreidel.

Make a dreidel using the dreidel pattern at the end of this section or a wooden block with a small dowel rod glued in place. Have someone teach the children how to spin the dreidel and perhaps teach them a song about using a dreidel during Chanukah.

Friends Are Special

Have the children draw a picture of themselves and a pretend friend doing a special activity. Discuss the possibility of each child having a friend from a far-away country come to visit. What one special activity would they choose to do? Let each child tell about an activity. Then they may draw a picture.

Christmas Around the World

Show the class a globe or world map. Show them where the United States is. Talk about how other people live around the world and how some celebrate Christmas differently than we do. Point out the country on the map or globe as you talk about it.

Great Britain

British people call Santa Claus "St. Nicholas." The day after Christmas is Boxing Day, named for the custom of churches opening their poor box after Christmas to distribute the money. Today Boxing Day is the day that mail-carriers, newspaper-carriers, and other public servants go from house to house to receive their Christmas gifts.

France

French people exchange presents on New Year's Day instead of at Christmas.

Denmark

Gingerbread is very popular in Denmark. Many vendors sell it during Christmastime. Many people hang it on their Christmas trees for decoration.

Switzerland

The Swiss people also call Santa Claus "St. Nicholas." St. Nicholas does not come to Switzerland on Christmas Eve. He visits Swiss homes on December 6 (the anniversary of the first St. Nicholas, fourth century, who gave secret presents to the poor and was known for his kindness to children).

Mexico

One of the ways that Mexicans celebrate is by breaking a piñata full of candy, peanuts, and fruits.

Pen Pals

Try to arrange time to write letters to a class of children in another country. Let the children dictate their ideas about Christmas and friends for you to write and mail. Imagine the excitement when the children receive their first letter from children in another part of the world!

The Night Before Christmas

Read ''The Night Before Christmas'' out loud to the children. Remind the children that Great Britain, Switzerland, and other European countries call Santa Claus ''St. Nicholas.''

Santa Paste-Together

Dotted Santa—copy on white paper (pattern at end of this section).
Santa Clothes—copy on red paper or have the children color the clothes before they cut them out (pattern at end of this section).

Give a copy of each of the two patterns to every child. Let them color, cut out, and paste Santa together. Lots of fun—and good for developing visual discrimination and motor coordination.

MATH

NUMBER CONCEPTS

Counting

1. Count the play dough candy canes the children made in ART. Talk about adding one more and/or taking away one to make one less.
2. You can cut out felt star shapes using the pattern on the front of the December Curriculum guide. Provide a flannel board and let the children take turns putting up the number of felt stars called for by the teacher.

Count Down to Christmas

Four ideas for interesting ways to help the children know how many days remain before Christmas!

1. Use a wreath made from construction paper and tag board. Cut twenty-five windows in it. Number each window. Put a picture behind each window. Take turns opening a window each day until Christmas.
2. Start with a blank calendar. The children take turns adding a sticker to the calendar each day. Have a large special sticker already on the calendar marking Christmas Day.
3. Make a large Santa head. On his beard, draw twenty-five quarter-sized circles. Write a numeral (1-25) in each circle. Each day, let a child glue a cotton ball to cover up one of the numerals. (Be sure to start with numeral ''24'' and work backward so the numerals remaining show how many days until Christmas.) The children can ''see'' Christmas getting closer as the beard gets fluffier and fluffier!
4. Also see Class Christmas Chain in ART.

Numeral Trees

Use the Trees of Many Colors handout, found at the end of this section. Cover up or white-out the color words. Print a numeral (1-4) by each tree. Provide circles with 1-4 on each. Let children match the number 1 circles to the number 1 tree, match the circles with ''2'' on them to the number 2 tree, etc.

One Half

1. Make Gingerbread people (see COOKING). Cut one in half and ask the children to count the pieces.
2. Cut two stars out of construction paper. Cut one in half. Count the pieces. Compare one half to one whole star.

MATH VOCABULARY

Heavy—Light/ Big—Little

Provide two balls of play dough for each child. Ask the children which ball is big and which is little. Ask which feels heavy and which feels light. Give each child more play dough. ''Does more dough make your ball heavy or light?'' ''Does more dough make it look big or little?''

Bring in a simple balance scale. Let the children take turns making two play dough balls or other shapes. Ask them to predict which of the two shapes is heavy and which is light. Weigh the shapes on the balance scale to confirm if they are correct in what they predicted.

MOVEMENT

Games from Other Countries

Australia—Coconut Shell Relay

Use bean bags instead of coconut shell halves. Divide the class into two groups. Each group stands in a circle. Give the first person in each group seven bean bags. On ''GO,'' pass each bean bag from person to person as fast as possible. The goal is to have one group pass all seven bags around the circle before the other group finishes.

Talk about how Australian children use coconut halves when they play this game. ''Has anyone seen a coconut shell?'' (You might want to bring a coconut to class to share.)

Great Britain—Hop Scotch

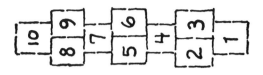

Each player has a small stone or bean bag. A child tosses the bag or stone into square one. The child then hops into the square, picks up the bag, and hops out. The child then tosses the bag to square two, etc. Follow the same procedure until the child gets all the way to ten. (Younger children may play using only squares one to four or one to six.)

You may draw the hop scotch board with chalk outside or make it with masking tape on the floor or rug.

Sweden—Are You Awake, Mr. Bear?

One child pretends to be the bear lying asleep (hibernating) in his den. The rest of the children slowly crawl on their hands and knees toward the bear and repeatedly ask in a whisper: "Are you awake, Mr. Bear?" The bear snores loudly until he/she decides to jump up and try to tag the children as they try to run home. Tagged children become bear cubs and next time help the bear chase the other children. Continue until all the children are bear cubs.

Around the World in Eighty Days

Use a recording of "Around the World in Eighty Days." Provide scarves or crepe paper streamers for individual creative movements or dancing as the music plays.

It's a Small, Small World

Use "It's a Small, Small World" recording in the same way. Discuss whether or not the music tells us to move in different ways with each song. Encourage the children to sing along with the record.

Ring Around the World

(Tune: "Ring Around the Rosie")

Ring around the world,
We like to play together,
Friends, friends,
Let's all fall down.

MUSIC

Jolly Old St. Nicholas

Sing the song together, reminding the children that St. Nicholas is another name for Santa Claus in other countries.

Piñata

(Tune: ''Oh Christmas Tree, Oh Christmas Tree'')

A piñata is fun to make!
A piñata is fun to break!
  (Repeat)
Take a stick and turn 'round and 'round;
Make the candy fall to the ground.
A piñata is fun to make!
A piñata is fun to break!

Hopping with Friends

(Tune: ''Mulberry Bush'')

We go hopping 'round the room,
'Round the room, 'round the room.
We go hopping 'round the room,
It's fun to be with friends.

ROLE PLAY

People Around the World

Pin up pictures of the way people dress in other countries. Provide clothing items that suggest the costumes worn by the people in the pictures. Have the children dress up and talk about what country they represent. If possible, take photographs of the children to display along with the original pictures.

Presents

Provide empty boxes wrapped as presents. The children arrange the presents under a real or pretend tree. The children role play handing out the presents among family members for Chanukah or Christmas.

CELEBRATIONS AROUND THE WORLD

SCIENCE

Ice

Place ice cubes in a zip-lock plastic bag. Have the children feel the bag. List the words they use to describe how it feels, such as cold and hard.

Put the bag on a table. Ask the children: "What will happen next? Why?" As you do other activities, have the children check the bag from time to time to observe what is happening. When the cubes are completely melted, talk about what has taken place and use the terms "melted" and "liquid." Have the children feel the bag again. List the words they use to describe how it feels.

Finally, put the bag of water in a freezer. Ask the children: "What will happen? Why?" Examine the bag the next day and talk about the changes that occurred.

Trees of Many Colors

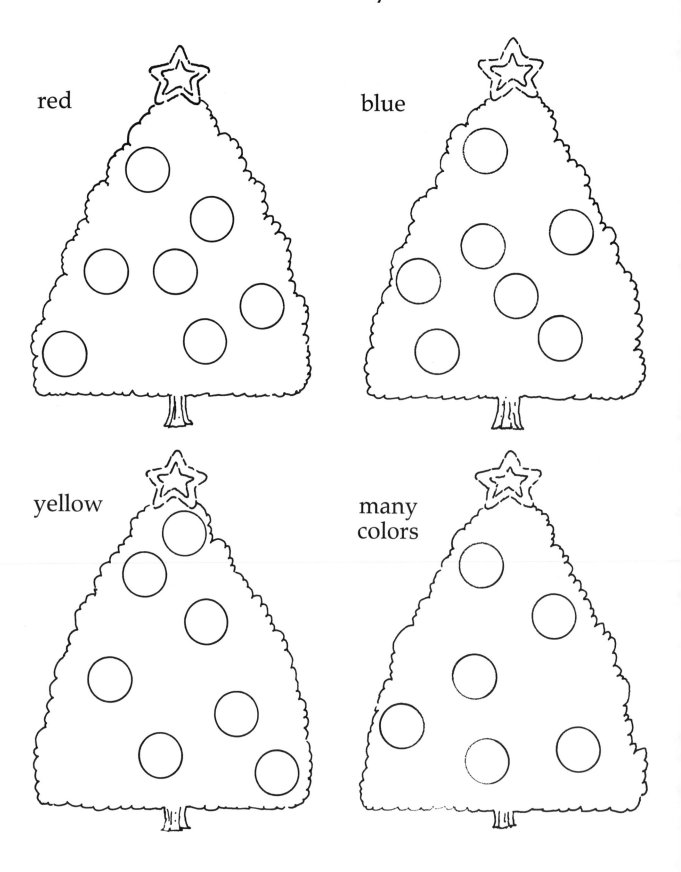

red

blue

yellow

many
colors

Dreidel Pattern

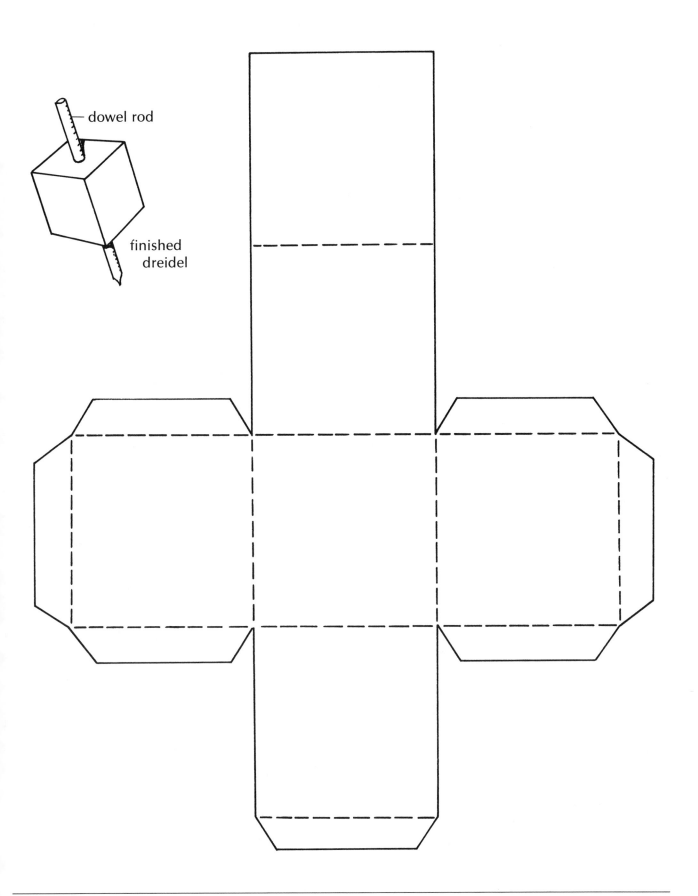

dowel rod

finished
dreidel

Dotted Santa

Santa Clothes

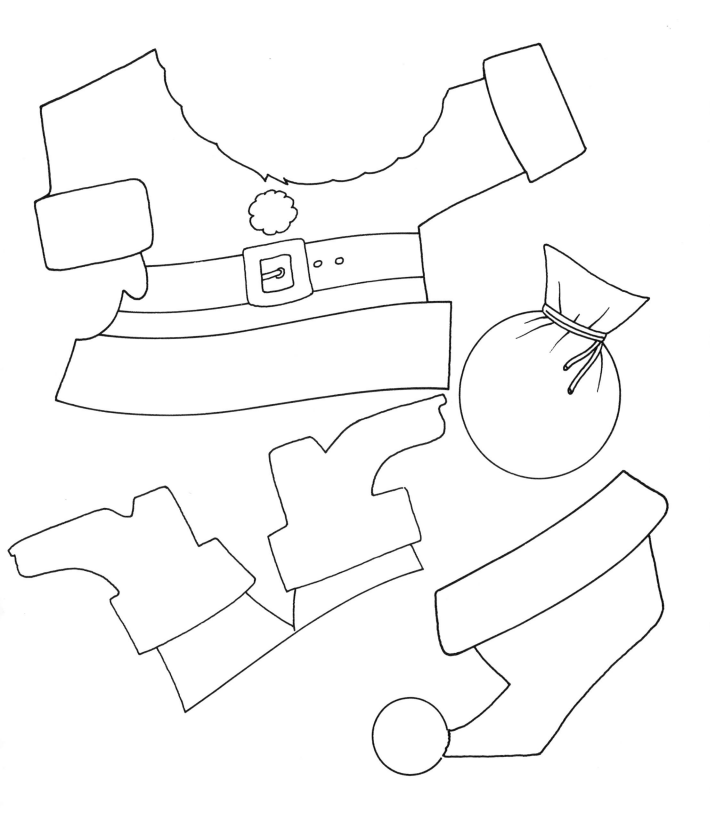

Christmas

CONCEPTS

- Christmas is a national holiday celebrated on December 25 each year.
- Christians celebrate Christmas as the birth of Jesus, the Son of God.
- Some symbols we use as we celebrate Christmas are: angels, stars, wreaths, evergreen trees, tree decorations, bells, candles, Santa Claus, reindeer, and Christmas stockings.
- Red and green are Christmas colors.
- Christmas is a time for sharing. Many people like to give and receive gifts.

ART

Remember Me

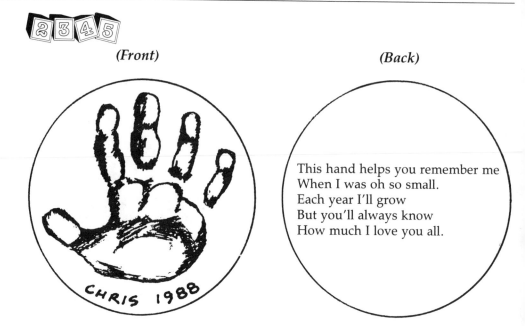

(Front)   *(Back)*

This hand helps you remember me
When I was oh so small.
Each year I'll grow
But you'll always know
How much I love you all.

5 inch wooden circles painted white; ¼ inch ribbon or rickrack; glue; tempera paint; meat tray.

Pour a small amount of paint on the meat tray. Help each child press a hand in the paint and then on one of the circles. When dry, print the year and the child's name below the handprint. Then print the verse on the back and glue the ribbon around the outside, leaving a loop at the top for hanging on the tree.

Snow Friends

White paper cut into 3 × 4 inch pieces; snow friend pattern on posterboard; construction paper scraps; markers or crayons; glue.

Give each child a piece of paper. Let the children trace the pattern and cut out a snow friend, or provide cutouts of the snow friend pattern, if you prefer. Have the children draw or glue on details to individualize their snow friend. Pin or tape the snow friends together to make a continuous chain. Display along the wall, around the door, or across the chalkboard.

Creative Christmas Experiences

Wrapping Paper—The children can create their own Christmas wrapping paper. It's simple and fun. (See ART, Mothers and Mother's Day.)

Play Dough—Provide red play dough. As children work with the play dough, talk about all the red things seen at Christmastime.

Tempera Painting—Provide large cutouts of Christmas trees and several colors of tempera paint. Let children "decorate" the trees by painting ornaments, candy canes, and garlands on them.

Christmas Tree Decorations

Garlands. Using a large plastic needle (or a bobby pin as a needle), the children string styrofoam packing pieces, Fruit Loops cereal, and/or small marshmallows onto long pieces of string or yarn. (Stringing popcorn is too frustrating for young children, because many of the kernels break apart as children try to string them.)

Silver Bells. Cut out individual egg cup sections from egg cartons. Let the children wrap each egg cup in a piece of foil to make a silver bell. Loop a piece of yarn through a hole punched in the top so the bells can hang on the tree. You may tie a small jingle bell to the inside of the silver bell, if desired.

Tinsel or Icicles. Cut aluminum foil in strips ½ inch wide and 4-6 inches long. Have the children wrap the strips around pencils in candy cane fashion. Then slide the pencil out and use a hole punch to punch a hole in one end. Add a piece of yarn and hang the icicles on the tree.

Candy Canes. Cut white cane shapes out of construction paper and let the children glue red pompom balls on them.

Cookie Cutter Ornaments. Make Ceramic Dough (See Art Recipes.) or Art Bread Dough (See Art Recipes). Provide rolling pins or 1 inch dowel rods to roll out the dough. Have the children choose cookie cutters and cut out ornament shapes. Push a hole through the top of each ornament with a pencil. When the ornaments are dry, let the children decorate them with markers or paint. Add a loop of yarn for hanging.

Pine Cone Decorations. Collect small pine cones. The children brush the tips of each cone with glue. Then, sprinkle the cones with glitter and sequins.

Variations: The children may paint the pine cones first, using red, silver, or gold tempera paint. Hang the decorations with a loop of yarn or with a pipe cleaner twisted around the top of the cone.

Christmas Friendship Tree

Cut a wall size Christmas tree from butcher paper. Lay it on a table or on the floor. Using different colors of tempera paint, the children dip their hand in the paint and make a handprint on the tree. Each child may make one of several colors, if desired. (For those who do not wish to put their hand in paint, the teacher may trace the child's hand on construction paper and cut it out. The child may then glue the handprint on the tree.) Write each child's name under his/her print.

This activity is wonderful when done as a school project with a very large tree cutout. Lay the tree on the floor; each class takes turns making the handprints. Display the finished tree on a wall near the main office or front entrance. Add the caption: ''Christmas Friendship Tree.''

Play Dough Wreaths

Red and green play dough.

Show the children how to roll ''snakes'' out of the green play dough. Help them form the snakes into a wreath shape and pinch the ends together. Then have the children use the red dough to make *small* red balls to add as berries on the wreath.

Window Stencils

Glass wax; Christmas stencils; small sponges.

The children can decorate windows and mirrors. Dip the sponges in the glass wax and then dab it on the inside of a stencil taped to the window. When the whole decoration is filled in with wax, carefully remove the stencil and do another. (The wax easily washes or rubs off.) Do the activity on tabletops just for the fun of doing it, if desired.

Christmas Symbols

Red and green tempera paint; paper; other art materials as needed for the activity chosen.

The children freely create designs on paper using red and green paint. Let them experiment with different art methods such as finger painting, sponge painting, string painting, splatter painting, or straw blowing. When the paintings are dry, you can use them to cut out *large* Christmas symbols —such as stars, trees, bells, wreaths, and candles—to display around the room. Or, cut large Christmas symbols out of the center of construction paper, keeping both the cutout symbol and the cutout frame. Glue the frame from the cutout over a painting so the Christmas symbol shape appears to have been painted. Glue the other part of the construction paper cutout to the back of the painting. Hang like mobiles so both parts of the cutouts show as the painting turns in the air.

Evergreen Painting

Small cuttings from evergreen trees; tempera paints; paper.

Let the children explore using evergreen branches as paintbrushes. Encourage gentle movements to make delicate lines.

Glitterball Mobiles

Round toothpicks; glitter; glue; newspapers.

For each child: one 1-2 inch styrofoam ball; one 6 inch pipe cleaner.
You should carefully push the pipe cleaner completely through the center of the ball. Make a small hook at one end and pull it back up into the ball to secure the pipe cleaner. Curve the top of the pipe cleaner into a hook shape for hanging on the mobile.
Let the children dip one end of each toothpick into the glue. Then, push the glued end into the styrofoam ball so one-half to three-quarters of the toothpick sticks out. (The glue helps prevent the toothpicks from falling out later.) Have them continue until the toothpicks stick out all over the ball. Then set aside to dry overnight.

When the glue is dry, cover an area with newspapers and let the children dip their balls into a small bowl of glue. Hold them for a minute, so the excess glue drips back into the bowl. Then, the children use a spoon or a saltshaker container to sprinkle the glitter all over the toothpicks and ball. (Have the children use the glitter over a piece of paper so it may be folded and the excess glitter poured back for reuse.)

Tie the glitterballs to strings or yarn and hang them from the ceiling like mobiles. Children love to watch their movements and their sparkle as they catch the light.

Christmas Hanging Soap Balls

Hanging Soap Ball mixture (see Art Recipes); one 24 inch piece of wide yarn for each child; waxed paper.

Each child molds the mixture around the knotted yarn as directed. Instead of just making a ball, the children may mold other simple shapes, such as a bell. Children love to wear these while bathing.

Bearded Santas

7-8 inch circle stencil; 7 inch triangle stencil; construction paper; glue; cotton; styrofoam packing material or elbow macaroni; meat trays.

Make the stencils from posterboard or cardboard. Each child draws around the circle stencil to make one circle for the face and one white circle for the beard. Cut out the circles and have the children glue the face about halfway down over the white circle so it looks like a beard.

Let the children draw around the triangle stencil, cut the triangle out, and glue it on the top of Santa for a hat. Glue on cotton for the trim on the hat. Have the children use construction paper scraps or markers to add eyes, a nose, and a mouth to their Santa.

Pour small amounts of glue into meat trays. The children dip styrofoam pieces into the glue and stick them on the Santas to make eyebrows and a moustache, and to cover the beard area.

Paper Plate Wreath

Small paper plates with centers cut out; green tissue paper cut into 2 inch squares; one package of fresh cranberries; glue; meat trays; red yarn or ribbon.

Pour small amounts of glue on the trays. Show the children how to pinch a square of tissue around their finger, touch the end of it in the glue, and press it onto the rim of the plate. Have the children continue gluing on squares until the rim is covered. Then let them glue on five or more cranberries to make the berries on their wreaths.

Use a paper punch or scissors point to punch a hole at the top of each wreath. Tie a ribbon through the hole so the wreath can hang. The results are very attractive.

BLOCKS

Building Tall Structures

Working with the children, experiment with several ways to stack the blocks safely for building tall structures. Have them look at a brick wall to see how the bricks are stacked. Talk about which stacking method is the strongest and safest.

Fireplace

The children use the blocks to build a fireplace with a chimney.
Variation: Build just the chimney for Santa to come down.

BULLETIN BOARD

A Sock Full of Wishes

Provide a large sock pattern. The children decorate their socks as they desire. Print each child's name at the top or bottom of the sock. Then, the children draw or cut out toys and other things they wish to get or give for Christmas.

A Sock Full of Wishes

COOKING

Christmas Punch

2 quarts chilled cranberry juice
1 quart chilled ginger ale
1 box frozen red raspberries, thawed (optional)

Carefully pour the cranberry juice into a large bowl. Add the ginger ale and raspberries. Stir well and serve over ice cubes. Makes 3 quarts.

Sugar Plums

Powdered sugar
2 egg whites, beaten
Dried prunes

Wash hands. Have the children dip each prune into egg white. Wait for drips to stop. Then dip the prune in sugar. Place on paper towel to dry.

No-Cook Fudge

Individual recipe:

> *1 cup powdered sugar*
> *2 tablespoons cocoa*
> *1/8 cup peanut butter*
> *1 tablespoon milk*

Wash hands. Mix all the ingredients. Let the children roll the mixture into balls. Keep refrigerated.

Christmas Sugar Cookies

Provide refrigerator cookie dough or use your favorite sugar cookie recipe. Provide Christmas cookie cutters. Have the children help roll out the dough and cut out the cookies.

After the cookies are baked, provide white frosting and food coloring so the children can create many different colors of frosting. Let them use table knives to spread the frosting on the cookies. They may also use small candies and chocolate chips to decorate the cookies.

LANGUAGE ARTS

Books

Aoki, Hisako and Ivan Gantschev. *Santa's Favorite Story.* Neugebauer, 1982.
Berenstein, Stan and Jan Berenstein. *The Bear's Christmas.* Random House, 1970.
Bragg, Juliana. *The Nativity.* Golden Press, 1982.
Bright, Robert. *Georgie's Christmas Carol.* Doubleday and Co., 1975.
Brooke, Roger. *Santa's Christmas Journey.* Raintree Publishers, 1985.
Davidson, Amanda. *Teddy's First Christmas.* Holt, Rinehart and Winston, 1982.
Hildebrandt, Greg. *A Christmas Treasury.* Unicorn, 1984.
Jeffers, Susan. *Silent Night.* Dutton, 1984.
Keller, Irene. *A Thingumajig Christmas.* Children's Press, 1982.
Keats, Ezra Jack. *The Little Drummer Boy.* Collier Books, 1968.
Mayer, Mercer. *Merry Christmas Mom and Dad.* Western, 1982.
Moore, Clement. *The Night Before Christmas.* Knopf, 1984.
Nedobeck, Don. *Twelve Days of Christmas.* Children's Press, 1982.
Oakley, Graham. *The Church Mice at Christmas.* Atheneum, 1980.
Olson, Arielle North. *Hurry Home, Grandma!* Dutton, 1984.
Pearson, Tracey Campbell. *We Wish You a Merry Christmas.* Dutton, 1983.
Reece, Colleen L. *My First Christmas Book.* Children's Press, 1984.
Scarry, Richard. *Richard Scarry's Best Christmas Book Ever!* Random House, 1981.
Schweninger, Ann. *Christmas Secrets.* Penguin Books, 1984.
Seuss, Dr. *How the Grinch Stole Christmas.* Random House, 1957.
Spier, Peter. *Peter Spier's Christmas.* Doubleday and Co., 1983.
Tornborg, Pat. *A Sesame Street Christmas.* Western Publishing, 1982.
Weiler, Beverly. *Santa's Christmas Tree: A Story with Songs to Sing and Play.* Great Western Publications, 1980.
Whitehead, Pat. *Christmas Alphabet Book: ABC Adventures.* Troll, 1985.

Teacher Resource Books

Creative Educational Society. *How to Have Fun Making Christmas Decorations.* Creative Craft Book, 1974.

Livingston, Myra Cohn. *Christmas Poems.* Holiday House, 1984.

Lohan, Robert. *Christmas Tales for Reading Aloud.* Daye Press, 1966.

Fingerplays

Santa's Helper Elves

Santa's little helper elves are standing in a row.
  (Hold up five fingers.)
Santa comes in and they bow just so.
  (Wave; bend fingers in a bow.)
They stack toys to the left,
  (Move hand to the left.)
They stack toys to the right.
  (Move hand to the right.)
Then Santa's little helper elves sleep all night.
  (Curl fingers; hide hand behind back.)

Five Little Reindeer

(Hold up five fingers. Wiggle or point to each in turn.)

Five little reindeer waiting in a row.
The first reindeer said, "Santa, drive me slow."
The second reindeer said, "Santa, drive me fast."
The third reindeer said, "Santa, drive me last."
The fourth reindeer said, "Let's go bye, bye."
The fifth reindeer said, "It's Christmas Eve. Let's fly!"

Christmas Stickers Games

Purchase sets of Christmas stickers to use in preparing learning games and activities.

1. *Match-Ups*
   Cut 2×2 inch pieces of tagboard or posterboard. Put one sticker on each piece, using two copies of each sticker. Prepare six to twelve matched pairs. Then let the children work independently to match the pairs by spreading the cards out in a row and placing the matching pair on top.
2. *Concentration*
   Use the matched pairs of stickers prepared for the Match-Ups game. Two children use four to twelve matching pairs to play Concentration. The number of pairs used depends on the ability of the children.

Felt Christmas Tree

Provide a large felt cutout of a Christmas tree. Also have a box of felt ornaments, sequins, tinsel cut in one-quarter to one-half lengths, and wide yarn for garlands. The children may decorate the felt tree again and again.

**Ho-Ho-Ho:
Listening Game**

One child ("it") stands with back to the rest of the group. Choose another child to pretend to be Santa Claus and say: "Ho-ho-ho! Merry Christmas." The child who is "it" tries to guess who is playing Santa.

**Santa and Elves
(Observation Game)**

The child who is "it" pretends to be Santa and hides his/her eyes. All of the other children are elves. Choose one of the "elves" to hide. The child who is it tries to figure out which elf is missing.

**Field Trip
Opportunities**

1. Plan a field trip to a shopping area to see Santa and all the Christmas decorations. Walk around a short while to count the number of bells, reindeer, or other Christmas symbols the class can see.
2. Plan a field trip to a nursery where they sell Christmas trees. Point out the many different kinds and shapes of trees. (Consider purchasing a small tree for the classroom.) Ask the owner of the nursery if you may collect some of the evergreen branches that have fallen off the trees to use on a science table in the classroom.

Little Jack Horner

Recite with the children the familiar nursery rhyme "Little Jack Horner." Let the children act out the rhyme.

**Ring Those
Christmas Bells
(Listening Game)**

Provide two or three bells that have very different sounds. Ring the bells several times to let the children hear each sound. Have the children close or hide their eyes. Play one bell and have the group guess which bell was rung. Some children may realize that the size of the bell is related to its sound.

The Night Before Christmas

Read or recite to the children Clement Moore's classic poem "The Night Before Christmas." The children may eat Sugar Plums (see COOKING) as they listen to the poem.

Recipes for Christmas Dinner

As you write, let each child dictate a recipe for making some favorite dish for Christmas dinner. The children will have some rather fantastic versions to share! Have the children illustrate their recipes. Put all the recipes together in a class book. (Consider making a copy of the recipes for parents. The children's recipe book makes a lovely and comical Christmas present for families to enjoy.)

Letter to Santa

The children dictate a letter to Santa. The following form may be duplicated to speed up the writing proccss.

Dear Santa,

My name is _____ and I am _____ years old. My teacher is helping me write this letter at ____ (school's name) ____.

I have been very good (or at least I have tried to be)! Please bring me _____

_____ for Christmas. Also, please bring

_____ for _____. Thank you for all the good you do.

Love,

_____

Christmas Cards

Help the children fold manila paper into fourths, like a card. Have them create Christmas cards to give to whomever they choose. Some children may want you to print a Christmas message on their card.

MATH

Santa's Bag

Bring in a large bag or pillowcase. Fill it with stuffed animals and toys from the classroom. Have the children count each item as it is pulled from the bag. Call out items for the children to find and put in the bag: "Find two red things that can fit in Santa's bag." "Find four round things that can fit in Santa's bag."

Christmas Stars

Provide construction paper Christmas trees for each child. Give each child several gummed stars or paper reinforcements. You should then hold up a card with a numeral on it. The children glue the appropriate number of stars or reinforcements on their tree.

Snowpeople

Provide precut white circles of various sizes (from 2 inches to 4 inches in diameter). Make a set of cards with numerals on them from 1-5 or more. Let the children spread out the numeral cards and use the circles to create a snowperson with the number of circles specified by the numeral on the card. Also provide construction paper cutouts of hats, scarves, and small black circles for facial features. Do not provide glue. Have the children put the snowperson together and then replace the pieces for rebuilding by another child.

MATH VOCABULARY

Heavy—Light

Review the idea of heavy and light by having one bucket or sack full of bricks or rocks and another full of feathers, crushed newspaper, or styrofoam packing pieces. The children take turns carrying the bags. Discuss which is heavy and which is light for them.

Game: Use two plastic eggs of the same color; those in which women's hose are sold work well. Put something heavy in one egg and something light in the other, such as a ball of play dough and a cotton ball. The children take turns holding one egg in each hand to decide which is heavy and which is light.

Variation: As the children master this concept, use three eggs of the same color and discuss heavy, heavier, and heaviest—or light, lighter, and lightest.

Heavy-Light Packages

Wrap several boxes of different sizes with Christmas wrap. Put something in the boxes to provide weight. Make at least one small box heavy and one big box light. Have the children predict which boxes might be heavy or light. After they guess, let the children lift each box and discover which are heavy and which are light.

Shape Trees

Provide precut, small shapes for the children to place on Christmas trees. Have one construction paper tree for round ornaments, one for square ornaments, one for rectangular ornaments, and one for triangular ornaments.

Baskets of Shapes

1. Bring in one round, one square, and one rectangular basket. Using actual items or pictures of Christmas items, instruct the children to put an ornament in the round basket, a small toy in the square basket, or a large star in the rectangular basket. As a culminating activity, count the items in each basket together.
2. From the previous shapes activity, use the biggest basket, the littlest basket, and the Christmas items or pictures. This time, have the children classify each item or picture as big or little and put it in or beside the appropriate basket.

Triangle Stars

Provide triangles of equal sizes or provide a triangle pattern for tracing. Show the children how two triangles can be put together to make a star.

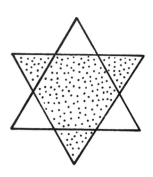

COOKING

Pudding Pops

2 three ounce boxes of instant pudding
4 cups cold milk

Wash hands. Let the children help measure and prepare the pudding according to directions. Quickly pour the pudding into small paper cups and insert a popsicle stick. Put cups into a freezer and enjoy the next day.

Nachos

Round corn chips
Cheddar cheese
Waxed paper

Wash hands. Lay chips on a cookie sheet in a single layer. Let the children help grate the cheese on pieces of waxed paper and put the cheese on each chip. You should put the nachos under the broiler until the cheese melts, or put them in the oven at 400° until the cheese melts. Eat carefully and enjoy! Talk about crunchy sounds as the children munch the chips.

Doughnuts

Refrigerator biscuits
Cinnamon sugar (1 cup sugar + 1 teaspoon cinnamon)
Grease for frying
Lid from pop bottle
Electric frying pan

Wash hands. Let the children use the lid to cut out "holes" from the center of each refrigerator biscuit. Talk about the circle shapes. You should fry the doughnuts and the holes in 2 inches of grease in an electric frying pan. Drain the doughnuts and holes, then have children take turns shaking the doughnuts in the sugar mixture.

LANGUAGE ARTS

Books

Bianco, Margery Williams. *The Velveteen Rabbit*. Avon Books, 1975.
Billam, Rosemary. *Fuzzy Rabbit*. Random House, 1984.
Davidson, Amanda. *Teddy's First Christmas*. Holt, Rinehart and Winston, 1982.
DiFiori, Lawrence. *My Toys*. Macmillan, 1983.
Freeman, Don. *Corduroy*. Puffin Books, 1977.
Jaques, Faith. *Tilly's Rescue*. Atheneum, 1981.
Johnson, Crockett. *Ellen's Lion*. Godine, 1984.
Matthiesen, Thomas, photos by. *A Child's Book of Everyday Things*. Putnam Publishing Group, 1981.
McPhail, David. *Those Terrible Toy-Breakers*. Parents Magazine Press, 1980.
Milne, A.A. *The World of Pooh*. Dutton, 1957.
Muntean, Michaela. *Alligator's Garden*. Dial Books Young, 1984.

Pin the Star on the Tree

Pin up a paper Christmas tree. Have the children take turns being blindfolded and trying to pin a star on the top of the tree.

Santa Toss

Tape a large Santa figure to a wastepaper basket. Provide bean bags or aluminum foil crushed into ball shapes. The children try to toss underhanded into the basket. Vary the distance at which the children stand from the basket for the tossing activity.

Red, Red, Green

Tie a string around a small ball (a nerf ball works well) and suspend the ball from the ceiling. Paint a dowel rod red on one end and green on the other end.

A child stands directly in front of the ball and places both hands on the stick, about one-third of the way from each end. The teacher calls out a color and the child bats the ball with the same-colored part of the stick. As children become proficient at the task, you may say a simple pattern for the child to bat, such as red, red, green.

Obstacle Course for Santa

Set up an obstacle course throughout the room for Santa to travel to deliver his presents.

Christmas Pop-Up

Repeat the action verse several times. Children love to pop up again and again.

Santa puts some toys down deep in a sock.
(Crouch down as close to the floor as possible.)
Christmas morning comes and out they POP!
(Jump up, arms stretching into the air.)

MUSIC

Santa's On His Way

(Tune: "London Bridge")

Santa Claus is on his way, on his way, on his way;
Santa Claus is on his way to celebrate Christmas.
Santa Claus is in his sleigh, in his sleigh, in his sleigh;
Santa Claus is in his sleigh with lots of toys.
It will be so fun to share, fun to share, fun to share;
It will be so fun to share celebrating Christmas.

Santa

(Tune: "Bingo")

There is a fat and bearded man
And Santa is his name-o.
S-A-N-T-A, S-A-N-T-A, S-A-N-T-A,
And Santa is his name-o.

Favorite Christmas Songs

Sing together the children's favorite songs, such as "Twinkle, Twinkle, Little Star," "Jingle Bells," and "Rudolph the Red-Nosed Reindeer." Sing "Happy Birthday" to Jesus. Provide rhythm instruments, so the children can accompany their singing.

Hot Potato-Bell Game

Sit together in a circle. While singing "Jingle Bells," the children pass around a bell like a hot potato. Note who gets it last, without much fanfare, and continue the game.

Silent Night

Explain that the song was originally performed in a church on Christmas Eve with only the composer singing as he played his guitar. If possible, play "Silent Night" on a guitar while the children softly sing.

Nutcracker Suite

Play a recording of the "Nutcracker Suite." Let the children move freely in rhythm to the music. You may provide scarves or crepe paper streamers for the children to wave as they move.

Santa Props

Provide a cardboard beard covered with cotton balls, a red stocking cap, a bag or pillowcase, stuffed animals, small toys, and stockings to fill. Let the children pretend to be Santa and deliver presents from the bag.

Decorate the Tree

Provide a small artificial Christmas tree and a box of unbreakable ornaments. Have the children pretend to be a family decorating their tree.

One Horse Open Sleigh

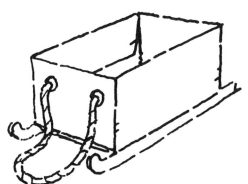

Provide cardboard boxes, large enough for a child to stand in. One box should be slightly larger than the other. Tuck the flaps down on the inside of the smaller box to provide reinforcement. Cut a large rectangle from the bottom of the box, leaving 3-4 inches as a frame. From the other box, cut out two sleigh runners. Attach the runners to the sleigh box along the bottom of each side.

Allow the children to take turns painting the sleigh with tempera paint. When the paint is dry, punch two holes in the sleigh's front and add a tow rope. A child may step inside the box and hold it up around the waist. Another child may pretend to be the horse that pulls the sleigh. The children hold the sleigh and walk, pretending to ride in the sleigh.

Santa's Sleigh

Use the one horse open sleigh as Santa's sleigh. Provide a construction paper headband with reindeer antlers stapled to each side.

Down the Chimney

Use a large, tall box—big enough for one child to get into. Use tempera paints or a black marker to draw bricks on the sides of the box to make it look like a chimney. The children use the Santa Props and pretend to be Santa going down the chimney and coming back out.

Evergreen

Provide different kinds of evergreen branches. Have the children smell and feel each. Compare the needles from the branches. Classify the needles by their length.

Pull off one needle from a branch. Use a magnifying glass to examine the newly exposed end of the needle. On the branch, examine the point that held the needle. Talk about the sap. Let the children feel its stickiness.

Reindeer

Bring in an encyclopedia and photographs of real reindeer. Tell the children about the life of reindeer. Show them how reindeer look, where they live, and what they eat.

Toys

CONCEPTS

- Toys are devices people use for playing and for learning.
- Creative toys enable children to invent, to discover, and to solve problems.
- Toys allow imaginative participation among children.
- Toys may be commercially made or handmade.

ART

Box Playhouse

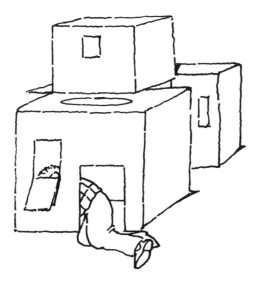

Empty furniture or refrigerator boxes; heavy tape or nonpincher type clothespins; knife; paints or markers.

The children help arrange several boxes so they touch together to create "rooms" in a box playhouse. Then, you cut openings in the boxes and tape them together securely around the open edges, so children can crawl through them into the different rooms of the house.

Tape a smaller box on top of one or two of the large boxes. Cut openings, so the children can stand up and peek out the top of the stacked boxes. Cut openings for windows. Then let the whole class help paint designs on the house or decorate it using markers.

Allow two or three children to play together in the house at one time. The structure will easily last for a week or two if used for quiet play activity.

Styrofoam Prints

Styrofoam meat trays; paintbrushes or pencils with the point broken off; manila or construction paper; tempera paint.

The children use the end of the brush handle or a pencil to draw (scratch) a design or picture on the underside of a meat tray. Then brush the picture with tempera paint and press it on a paper to make a print.

Roly Poly Spin-Around Spool

One large empty thread spool per child; heavy duty rubber bands; short stub of a pencil or a popsicle stick; small flat washer; large-headed nails; hammer; paints.

Let each child paint one spool. When it's dry, help the children hammer a nail part way into the top of the spool. Then help them thread a rubber band through the spool and hook one end over the nail. Finally, slip the washer over the other end of the rubber band and push the stick through the rubber band loop.

To play, use the stick to wind the rubber band. While still holding the stick, set the spool on the floor and let go. The spool will spin across the floor. Mark off a distance with strips of masking tape. Have the children try to aim their spool so it spins the whole distance.

What makes the spool travel and spin around? What happens if it is wound with just a few turns? A lot of turns? Which is the most fun to watch?

Treasure Toy Box

Each child should bring a small box with lid from home. The kind checks come in are the perfect size. Paint both parts separately. Allow them to dry, then decorate them by gluing on dried beans, popcorn, buttons, small shells, sequins, discarded beads, etc. Take home and store a special little toy inside.

Toy Art Graffiti

2 × 4 foot pieces of butcher paper; crayons, markers, or tempera paints.

Cut out one or more large, simple toy shapes. Put them on the floor or tabletop and let the children work together freely to make designs on the shapes. When the shapes are covered with art graffiti, display them along the wall for all to enjoy.

Toy Booklet

Catalogues; 9 × 12 inch construction paper; yarn; hole punch.

Cut pictures of different kinds of toys out of catalogues or advertisements. Cut construction paper in half. Each child should have three to five pages for the booklet. The children glue pictures of toys of their choosing on each page. Add a cover. Print "Toys by (child's name)" on each cover. Then punch three to five holes along the left side and have each child lace with yarn to hold the book together.

Christmas Card Puppets

Used Christmas cards; popsicle sticks; scissors; glue.

The children choose a card they like and cut out or cut around the main figure. Then, they glue the figure to a stick. When dry, the figure becomes a stick puppet. Use the puppets to talk with one another. Or, the children may move the puppets as they recite together a favorite rhyme, poem, or song.

Sandpaper Prints

Crayons; sandpaper squares; manila paper; iron.

Have the children use crayons to draw designs and pictures on the sandpaper. Encourage them to use bright colors. Then, you should lay a piece of manila paper over the crayon design and press it with a warm iron. Now the child has a print of the design on the manila paper. Add more crayon colors and print again, if desired.

Sculpt-a-Toy

Send a note home asking for nonreturnable items to use in an art project. Suggestions include: plastic eggs from women's hose, paper rolls, styrofoam packing, pipecleaners, old watches, clocks, keys, buttons, small plastic bottles or jars, nuts and bolts, metal washers, and yarn pieces. Display the donated items on a common table for all to share. You may wish to add several items, too. Children then create a toy from scraps by gluing pieces together. Robots are especially well made in this manner, by using a styrofoam drinking cup for the body and adding some of the listed items for arms and other details.

Ring Toss Game

One toilet paper tube per child; crayons or permanent markers; string or yarn; two rubber jar rings per child.

Each child decorates a toilet paper tube with the crayons or markers. Help the children tie a 12 inch length of string to the roll. Thread one ring on the string to another ring as shown.

To play, show the children how to hold the roll in one hand with the rings hanging down. Then, show them how to swing or flip the rings and try to catch one or both of them on the roll.

Toy Stick Horses

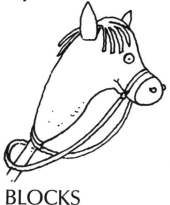

36 inch dowel rod or yardstick for each child; socks; fabric or construction paper; yarn; buttons; old newspapers.

The children decorate the socks to make a horse head. Glue on eyes, nose, yarn, or construction paper for a mane, etc. Stuff the sock-heads with crumpled newspapers. Use a rubber band to attach the heads tightly to the stick. Add yarn pieces for the reins.

Gallop around to music. Use the horses to ride back and forth to the playground.

BLOCKS

1. Use blocks to build cages for stuffed animals to live in.
2. Children may enjoy putting blocks together to build small beds for dolls.
3. If they wish, children may construct roads of a size appropriate for any of the toy cars or trucks in the room.

BULLETIN BOARD

Toys on Parade

Use simple cutouts of toys to show number sets in order. Print numerals on cards. Let children use push pins to place the correct numeral under each set of toys.

Oxenbury, Helen. *Playing*. Wanderer Books, 1981.
Razzi, Jim. *The Strawberry Shortcake Toy Book*. Random, 1980.
Spier, Peter. *The Toy Store*. Doubleday, 1981.
Stephenson, Dorothy. *The Night It Rained Toys*. Follett, 1963.

Teacher Resource Books

Buist, Charlotte A. *Toys and Games for Educationally Handicapped Children*. Thomas, 1969.
Caney, Steven. *The Toy Book*. Workman, 1972.
Fowler, Virginia. *Folk Toys Around the World: And How to Make Them*. Prentice-Hall, 1984.
Lopshire, Robert. *How to Make Snop Snappers and Other Fine Things*. Greenwillow Books, 1977.

Fingerplays

Toys on Parade

One teddy bear, I love him so.
   (Hold up one finger; hug arms around self.)
Two roller skates, they help me go!
   (Hold up two fingers; rub hands back and forth together as if skating.)
A ball, bat, and glove are here to play,
   (Hold up three fingers; act out hitting ball with bat.)
Toys on parade for me today.
   (March as soldiers.)

Toy Matching Game

Manila folder; colored pictures of several kinds of toys cut from catalogues or coloring books; yarn; sandpaper.

Cut several pictures of toys from the catalogue. Then cut each toy in half. Glue one half of the toy on the left side of the folder and the other half of the toy on the right side of the folder. Be sure the matching halves are in mixed order on the two sides, so the children will have to look and think carefully to make a match. Cut a length of yarn for each toy. Glue, tape, or staple one end of the yarn under each toy on the left side of the folder. Glue a small piece of sandpaper under each toy on the right side. Show the children how they can match the halves by sticking the loose end of the yarn to the sandpaper under the matching half. Then, have the children work the game several times by themselves.

Favorite Toys

Let each child have a turn telling about a favorite toy. Stress that it can be a toy they have or just one they would like to have.

Toy Classification

Children love to handle small things. Collect a set of inexpensive miniature toys and objects, by shopping at either a carnival supply shop or at a discount store in its birthday favors area. Let the children handle the miniatures and describe them. Talk about several different ways the objects might be classified—such as by color, wheels or no wheels, and makes noise or no sound.

Provide two to six 24 inch pieces of yarn. The children make a ring from each piece on a tabletop or on the floor. Children then use the rings to separate the miniatures into different categories. Ask the children to explain and talk about the categories they create: "Why did you put those objects in the blue ring?"

Note: You may do the same activity using toy cutouts from catalogues. However, miniatures will motivate the children more than pictures.

Teddy Bear Day

Encourage everyone to bring a teddy bear or other stuffed animal. (Label each toy animal, using a piece of masking tape with the child's name on it.) Plan the day's activities around the teddy bears.

1. Let each child show and tell about his/her animal.
2. Have a teddy bear picnic at snack time.
3. Have a parade in the room or around the school.
4. Reading choices might include the *Corduroy* books by Freeman or *Berenstein Bears Picnic*.
5. Make construction paper cutouts of teddy bear bodies, heads, and paws. Let the children glue or attach with brads the head and/or paws. Decorate the bears with markers, more construction paper, or buttons.
6. See the MOVEMENT section of this unit for teddy bear movement activities.

Christmas Card Jigsaw Puzzles

Used Christmas cards; scissors; envelopes.

Choose several interesting cards. Let the children help to cut the front of each card into three to five pieces. Code each set of pieces with a dot of color on the back of each piece so matching pieces won't get mixed up with other puzzles. Store the pieces of each puzzle in an envelope coded with the same dot of color.

Surprise Sack or Feely Box

Secretly place a toy in a sack or feely box. The children look away as they feel inside and try to guess what the toy is.

"I'm Thinking of..." Game

Think of a toy with which the children are all familiar. Give clues about the toy without naming it. Children take turns guessing. The child who guesses correctly can then think of a toy and give simple clues.

Toy Riddle Match

I am often red, and have four wheels and a tongue to pull.
  What am I? (wagon)
I go on your feet. I have four wheels and like to go on a sidewalk.
  What am I? (skates)
I am large. I have two wheels, handlebars, and a seat.
  What am I? (bike)

Let the children help you create toy riddles like the ones above. Talk together about what each riddle means. Then, print each riddle on an index card. Have the children look through catalogues until the class has found and cut out at least one picture to match each riddle. Glue each picture on an index card. You may print the name of each toy under its picture, if desired.

Display the picture cards along the chalk rail, or on the table or floor. Mix up the riddle cards. Let the children take turns drawing a riddle card, looking at it while you read it to the class, and putting the riddle card by its matching picture.

Visit to a Doughnut Shop

After making doughnuts as discussed in COOKING, make arrangements for the class to visit a doughnut shop. As you visit, emphasize the sequence involved in making doughnuts. Talk about what must be done first, second, etc. Stress four to six simplified steps in the doughnut-making process. Also, talk about the different smells. Name the different kinds of doughnuts the class sees.

When you return to the classroom, talk again about the sequence of doughnut making. On a large piece of paper, print each step as the children mention it. If a child mentions something out of sequence, say: "I'm glad you remembered that. We'll write it down in just a minute. But something else happened before that." Later, come back to that child and ask him/her to say the idea again, so you can write it where it belongs. Encourage the children to make a picture showing one of the steps. Display the pictures around the chart dictated earlier by the children.

Follow Me!

Manila folder; markers; laminating paper or clear contact paper.

Open the manila folder and draw three or more wide "roads" that curve or zigzag across both sides. Color a green dot by the left side of each and a red dot by the right side. Laminate the folder. Talk with the children about always working from left to right. Tell them that green means go and red means stop. To play this game, therefore, the children must start at the green dot and stop when they get to the red dot.

1. Provide a small ball and let children carefully roll the ball along each road from the left side (green) to the right (red).
2. Provide a small car and have children carefully "drive" the car so it stays on the road.
3. Provide markers or crayons, so the children can draw a continuous line from the left to the right side on each road.

TOYS

Toy Counting Book

Half sheets of manila or construction paper; pages torn from toy catalogues; scissors; glue; brads.

Give each child half sheets of paper with a numeral (1-5 or more) written on each page. Let the children cut around pictures of toys from the catalogues and glue the correct number of toy pictures on each page. Have each child decorate a front cover, then staple or use a brad to put the pages together to complete a toy counting book.

Penny Search

Hide five or more pennies in a plastic tub with two inches of sand, rice, or dried beans in the bottom. Let the children take turns digging gently to find the five coins.

Buy a Toy

Provide small toys or cards with pictures of toys glued on them. Have a simple price tag on each toy. The children match the appropriate number of pennies to each toy's price.

This activity could follow the Penny Search. After the children have dug for the pennies, they match them to the toys with price tags.

Measure the Distance

Provide a tape measure. Make the Roly Poly Spin-Around Spools in ART. As the children spin the spools, have them measure the distance their spools travel each time.

Count-a-Toy

1. Provide real toys.
2. Count the toys that have circle parts, square parts, triangle parts, or rectangle parts.
3. Count the toys by their colors or color combinations. ''How many black and white bears do we have?''

MATH VOCABULARY

Heavy—Light

Using toys brought from home or provided in the classroom, let each child pick a toy and discuss if it is heavy or light. (You may need to be sure there are some heavy toys, such as a metal truck, skates, or a riding toy.) The older children might be ready to have help classify three toys as heavy, heavier, and heaviest—or light, lighter, and lightest.

Variation: Divide a tabletop in half with masking tape. Label each side as ''heavy'' or ''light.'' The children put heavy toys on one side and light toys on the other. When finished telling about the toys, count the heavy toys and the light toys.

Toy Wind-Ups

You "windup" children to be toys. Children move arms, legs, head, etc., like a doll or robot or any other toys they may wish to be.

Teddy Bear Stretch

Repeat the lines in a sing-song manner. Have the children act out the suggested movements.

1. Teddy bear, teddy bear, stretch up tall.
2. Teddy bear, teddy bear, make a big ball.
3. Teddy bear, teddy bear, lean to the right.
4. Teddy bear, teddy bear, jump up with all your might!
5. Teddy bear, teddy bear, walk around.
6. Teddy bear, teddy bear, curl up on the ground.
7. Teddy bear, teddy bear, pat your head.
8. Teddy bear, teddy bear, go quietly to bed.

Teddy Bear Actions

Walk on all fours like a bear.
Pretend to climb a tree.
Curl up in a ball to hibernate.
Stretch and wake up.

The Toy Store

Look in the window of the toy store.
  (Fingers make glasses for eyes to look through.)
See the jack-in-the-box and a whole lot more!
  (Crouch down, leap up with arms over head.)
Here's a telephone that really can ring,
  (Hold receiver to ear and move arm in wide arcs in an exaggerated dialing motion.)
And a little bird that can chirp and sing.
  (Tuck hands under arms like wings. Point head up and tweet.)
Over there's a top to spin around,
  (Spin in a circle.)
And here's a ball to bounce on the ground.
  (Move arms as if bouncing and catching a ball.)
They have a robot you can program to walk,
  (Walk with stiff legs and arms.)
And a baby doll that can wave and talk.
  (Wave and say "Ma-Ma.")
Oh, it's fun to look at all the toys,
Such wonderful things for girls and boys!

Balloon Walk

Blow up several balloons and tie each end in a knot. Show the children how they may gently bat the balloons with their hands to keep them in the air.

Mark off a starting and ending line. Let the children try to walk that distance while batting their balloon to keep it in the air.

MUSIC

Here's a Toy

(Tune: "London Bridge")

Here's a toy, let's all play,
Let's all play and have fun today.
Here's a toy, let's all play,
Let's all play together.

Let the children take turns naming a toy before a verse is sung. Then, one child leads the rest of the group in acting out that toy while all are singing.

Blow My Balloon

Everyone stretches out arms, close together in front of them. Pretend to blow up a balloon. As the balloon enlarges, gradually spread arms apart. Then, quickly clap hands back together and fall down when the balloon breaks.

The children may say the words, or they may sing them by moving one note up the scale for each word sung. Children love to repeat this musical game again and again.

Blow my balloon. Whoosh!   (Pretend to blow air into balloon.)
Blow my balloon. Whoosh!
Blow, blow, blow, blow, blow. Clap!
Where did it go?

Playing Together

(Tune: "Did You Ever See a Lassie?")

The more we play together, together, together,
The more we get together, the happier we'll be.
For your friends are my friends,
And my friends are your friends.
The more we play together, the happier we'll be.

The more we share together, together, together,
The more we share together, the happier we'll be.
So I'll share and you'll share,
For when we share, we show we care.
The more we share together, the happier we'll be.

ROLE PLAY

Toy Store

Set up a toy store in the room. Provide, or have the children bring, several toys of different kinds. To display toys, create shelves with boards and blocks, or use book shelves. Let the children determine how to categorize the toys for placement on the display shelves.

Suggested props: cash register, price tags, play money or real pennies, small pads of paper for writing down sales orders, and paper sacks.

Box Play House

Provide small props to add to the fun of playing in the Box Play House made in ART. Small tea sets for tea parties and books and pillows for reading time are two possibilities.

Construction Time

Provide some type of toy construction sets, such as Legos, Lincoln Logs, or Constructs. Have a small group of children work together to create a construction site. Talk about the jobs of the different workers on real construction sites. Let the children role play the different workers as they complete the construction.

SCIENCE

Bell Sounds

Provide different sizes of bells. Demonstrate how each bell sounds. Have the children turn their backs. Play the bells one at a time. The children raise their hands high over their head when a bell sound is higher than the one before it and crouch down to the floor when the sound is lower.

Water Glass Sounds

Provide three or four glasses and one stick. Pour different amounts of water into each glass to show the children how you can make different musical notes by gently tapping each glass with the stick. Mark each glass with a piece of colored tape to show how much water to put in it.

Give the children a small pitcher of water. Allow them to refill the glasses to each marked line and test the musical sound by gently tapping each glass. Have them carefully pour the water from the glasses back into the pitcher, so others can do the experiment.

Jar Noise

Provide an empty glass jar. Hold the jar near each child's ear. Talk about the noise they hear in the jar. What makes the noise? There are little sounds in the air all around us. The sounds make the air in the jar move or vibrate. Then we hear them.

Fill the same jar with water. Have children put an ear down close to the jar and listen. Now what do they hear? They hear nothing, because the water pushed the air out of the jar.

January
Curriculum

1. Life in Winter

2. Dinosaurs

3. Five Senses

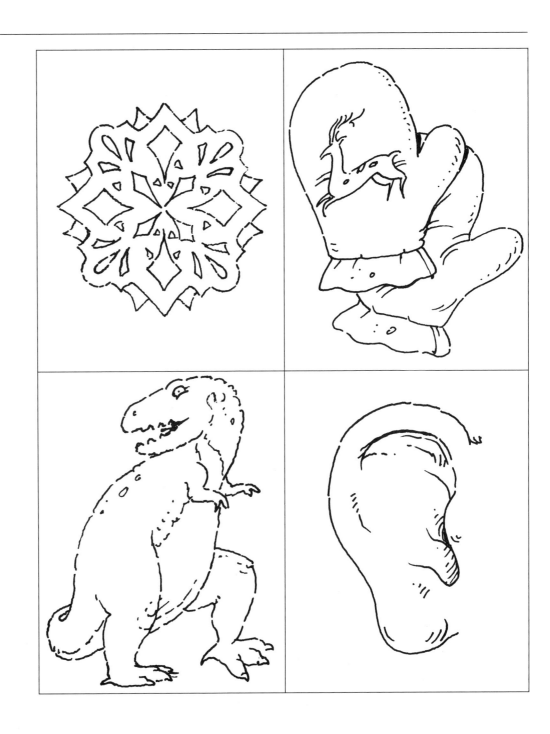

Life In Winter

CONCEPTS

- Winter is the season that comes after fall and before spring.
- The weather is often very cold in winter, but in some areas it stays warm.
- Sometimes the temperature drops below freezing (32°F, O°C). Then, water freezes and ice and icicles may form.
- It snows in some places in winter. Other areas get little or no snow in winter.
- Most outdoor plants do not grow in winter, but evergreens stay green all year.
- Some animals, such as bears and turtles, hibernate (sleep for several weeks) in the winter, when it is too cold to find food.
- Some birds migrate (fly to warmer areas) to find food and live during the winter.

ART

**Sponge Painting
Snow Pictures**

Sponge scraps; pincher-type clothespins; white tempera paint; light blue construction paper; crayons or markers.

On a piece of blue paper, each child draws a picture of any outdoor scene or object. Clip a clothespin to make a handle on each sponge piece. The children dip a sponge in the white paint and lightly hop the sponge around on the paper to create a snow scene.

**Sponge Painting
Snowpeople**

Provide sponges cut in circles of different sizes. Let the children choose three descending sizes to dip in white paint to make snowpeople prints.

Shaving Cream Art

Give each child a squirt of shaving cream to work with on a tabletop. Talk about little snowflakes and have the children dab the cream with fingertips. Talk about big snowstorms or blizzards and let children move their whole hands through the cream.

To clean up, just wipe the excess cream off with a sponge and enjoy the fresh smell and clean tabletops!

Play Dough Snowpeople

Provide white play dough. Let the children roll balls in different sizes to make snowpeople shapes. Add arms, if desired. Use different colors of play dough and let the children add details, such as hats, hair, eyes, brooms, etc., to complete their snowpeople.

Winter Easel

Provide white tempera paint and colored butcher paper at the easel for children to enjoy painting.

No-Snow Snowperson

Three white plastic garbage or lawn bags; styrofoam packing pieces or wads of newspaper; construction paper scraps; assorted hats, scarves, and clothing items.

Talk with the children about why some areas do not have snow. Let children help stuff each of the three bags with styrofoam pieces or wadded pieces of newspaper. Tie each bag tightly at the top. Then, stack the three bags or "no-snow balls" on top of one another. Stack the bags in a corner area of the room to help them stay together more securely.

Use construction paper scraps and clothing items to make facial features and other details. If desired, let the children choose different clothing items to change the snowperson's look each day. Add to the fun by naming the snowperson each day.

Safety note: Do not allow young children to stuff the plastic bags without your supervision. Talk with the children about the dangers of playing with plastic bags.

Thumbprint Winter Pictures

White tempera paint in meat trays or paper plates; twigs; glue; blue construction paper; paintbrushes.

Let the children paint a strip of white across the bottom of the construction paper to make the snowy ground. Next, they glue on one or more small twigs to make bare winter trees. Finally, they dip their thumbs in the paint and print "falling snowflake" thumbprints all over the paper.

Snowflake Snowpeople

Paper doilies in three sizes; blue construction paper; buttons or small construction paper circles for details; paper cutouts of small black top hats (optional).

On a piece of paper, the children glue three doilies in descending sizes to make a snowperson. Next, they glue on the buttons or circles for facial details and buttons. Glue on a hat, if desired.

Popcorn Snow Scenes

Popped corn; glue; blue construction paper.

The children glue popped corn all over their papers as if it were falling snow.

White Collage

Cotton balls; Q-Tips; white construction paper scraps; white buttons; popped corn; styrofoam packing pieces; any other available white things; glue; 9 × 12 inch construction or manila paper.

Talk about white being the color of winter because of the snow. Have the children glue a collage from a large variety of white items. Print ''White'' at the bottom of each child's picture.

Dainty Splatters

Paper doilies; white tempera paint on meat trays or paper plates; old toothbrushes; shallow cardboard box; screen for splatter painting that is larger than the box's opening; construction paper of dark colors.

The children put a piece of paper in the bottom of the box and lay one or more doilies in interesting arrangements on the paper. Then, lay the screen over the opening of the box, dip a brush in white paint, and have the children gently rub the brush over the screen to splatter paint on the doily and paper.

Star Prints

One or more apples and green peppers; tempera paint in meat trays or paper plates; 9 × 12 inch manila paper.

Talk about the shape of stars. Cut through the center of an apple. (Do not cut end to end; cut through the roundest part of the apple.) Separate the halves and show children the star pattern made by the seeds inside. Cut through a green pepper (not end to end) and look at the different star shape made by those seeds.

Pat the halves dry with a paper towel so paint will easily stick to them. Have the children dip the halves in the paint and print the star shapes several times on their papers. Encourage the children to use different colors and to overlap the star prints for more interesting effects.

Chalk Drawings

White chalk; 9 × 12 inch dark colored construction paper.

Let the children freely draw designs on the paper with the chalk. If desired, provide a cup of water and allow the children to dip the chalk into it before drawing to produce a different effect. Spray each finished paper with inexpensive hair spray to prevent the chalk from rubbing off.

String-Pulled Blizzards

9 × 12 inch or 12 × 18 inch dark colored construction paper; white paint in meat trays or paper plates; yarn or string, cut into 18 inch lengths.

Fold the paper in half. Have the children lay the string in the paint, keeping the ends of the string dry for holding. Lay the string inside the folded paper. Let one child *gently* hold down the paper, while the other child pulls the string around to swirl paint designs on the inside of the paper.

Open the paper to see the design. Dip the string in the paint and repeat the process on the same paper to increase the design. Talk about the swirling snows of a blizzard.

Winter Mural

24 × 35 inch or larger piece of butcher paper; blue and white tempera paints; brushes; twigs; manila paper; crayons or markers; fiberfill or paper doilies.

Let the children take turns painting the top part of the butcher paper blue for the sky and the bottom part white for snow-covered hills and ground. Have children draw people, houses, etc., on the manila paper, cut them out, and glue them on the mural. Let the children glue on twigs for bare trees and glue on snow-people made of fiberfill or doilies. Add details as desired to complete the winter mural.

Rice Snow Pictures

Liquid starch; blue dry tempera powder; slick white shelf paper or finger painting paper; raw white rice; sponge in a small pail or bowl of water.

Cover the work area with newspapers. On each piece of shelf paper, pour a dollop of the starch and sprinkle the tempera paint over the starch. The children use their fingertips to stir the color into the starch, then freely finger paint all over the paper. Squeeze a few drops of water on the painting if it becomes too dry. You may also add more starch and tempera paint to extend the color.

When the children are done finger painting, have them wash their hands and quickly sprinkle rice all over their painting before it dries. The rice will stick to the starch if the painting is dried flat. Children enjoy carefully feeling the differences in texture after the painting is dry.

Sparkly Snowflakes

6 inch circle pattern to trace around; scissors; brushes; Sparkle Paint (see Art Recipes); white paper (not construction paper, as it is too thick to cut well).

The children trace around the circle pattern and cut out their own circles. To make snowflakes that children can cut by themselves:

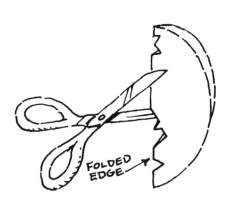

FOLDED EDGE

1. Fold the circle in half.
2. Children cut out shapes along the fold.
3. Open the circle and fold it in half another way, to make a new fold line.
4. Children cut out shapes along that fold.
5. Continue opening and refolding as long as children wish or until the snowflake design is complete.

Lay the snowflakes on newspapers on a tabletop. Have the children brush the sparkle paint on one side of the flake. When it's dry, paint the second side and let dry. (The salt in the mixture makes the finished snowflakes glisten.)

For a beautiful effect, display the finished snowflakes on a dark wall or on a bulletin board covered with black or blue paper.

Snowflake Mobiles

Tie strings from the finished flakes and hang them from the ceiling, so they dance and sparkle in the light.

Whipped Snowpeople
(Two-day Art Activity)

Using the Whipped Snowperson Pattern at the end of this section, cut out one snowperson from posterboard for each child; Whipped Snow (see Art Recipes); construction paper scraps; glue; tempera paints; Q-Tips and fabric scraps (optional).

The children spoon the Whipped Snow from the bowl and use fingers or the back of the spoon to spread it onto a snowperson pattern. Let the snowperson dry overnight.

When it's dry, the children may add details to personalize their snowperson. They may use construction paper scraps or paint applied with Q-Tips to add facial details. Fabric scraps make good scarves, hair, hats, or clothes of any kind. Encourage the children to think beyond adding just the usual eyes, nose, mouth, and buttons.

BLOCKS

Show the children some standard ice cubes. Help them decide which blocks are shaped like the ice cubes. Tell them the name of that shape (probably rectangle, square, or cube). Encourage the children to build ice castles using the blocks shaped like ice cubes. Add other blocks, if needed.

BULLETIN BOARD

New Year's Resolutions

Discuss what "resolutions" mean. Cover the bulletin board with brightly colored butcher paper or fabric. Pin up the caption: "Our New Year's Resolutions." Cut out a 9 inch circle, balloon, party hat, or party horn for each child. On each shape, print a resolution stated by the child. Print the child's name under the resolution. Sample resolutions might include: To make my bed every morning; to be nicer to my brother; to help my dad work in the garage.

COOKING

Popcorn Snow Storm

Pop popcorn without putting the lid on the popper. Place the popper on a clean, spread-out sheet so the popcorn stays clean. (Some popcorn poppers get very hot on the bottom. For added safety, set the popper on a cookie sheet before placing it on the sheet for popping.) Talk about how the popping corn looks like falling snow.

Snow Cones

Crushed ice
Concentrated grape or apple juice
Paper cups

Pour some crushed ice into a cup for each child. Cover the ice with the concentrated juice.

Cold Day Cocoa

For each child:

> **1 tablespoon instant cocoa mix**
> **2 tablespoons dry powdered milk**
> **1 teaspoon powdered sugar**
> **3/4 cup hot water**

Let the children measure their own mix into a cup. Add the water and have the children stir the mixture with a spoon until it's thoroughly mixed and cooled.

LANGUAGE ARTS

Books

Allington, Richard and Kathleen Krull. *Beginning to Learn About Winter.* Raintree, 1981.

Anno, Mitsumasa. *Anno's Counting Book.* Crowell, 1977.

Blough, Glenn. *Soon After September: The Story of Living Things in Winter.* Whittlesey House, 1959.

Briggs, Raymond. *The Snowman.* Random House, 1978.

Brooks, Sandra. *What Happens in Winter.* Standard Publishing, 1982.

Brown, Margaret. *The Dead Bird.* Addison-Wesley, 1958.

Brown, Margaret. *The Winter Noisy Book.* Harper & Row, 1947.

Casey, Patricia. *Winter Days.* Putnam, 1984.

Cosgrove, Margaret. *Wintertime for Animals.* Dodd, Mead, 1975.

Duvoisin, Roger. *White Snow, Bright Snow.* Lothrop, 1947.

Freedman, Russell. *When Winter Comes.* Dutton, 1981.

Hader, Berta and Elmer Hader. *The Big Snow.* Macmillan, 1948.

Keats, Ezra Jack. *The Snowy Day.* Viking, 1962.

Lenski, Lois. *I Like Winter.* Henry Z. Walck, 1950.

Levine, Caroline A. *Snow Fun.* Watts, 1981.

Lobe, Mira. *The Snowman Who Went for a Walk.* Morrow, 1984.

McCauley, Jane R. *Ways Animals Sleep.* National Geographic, 1982.

Miskovits, Christine. *Where Do Insects Go in Winter?* Denison, 1973.

Parish, Peggy. *Ootah's Lucky Day.* Harper & Row, 1970.

Parker, Bertha and Eloise Wilkin. *My Big Book of Seasons.* Western Publishing, 1983.

Podendorf, Zila. *Animal Homes.* Children's Press, 1982.

Prelutsky, Jack. *It's Snowing! It's Snowing!* Greenwillow Books, 1984.

Sendak, Maurice. *Chicken Soup with Rice.* Harper & Row, 1962.

Shaw, Charles. *It Looked Like Spilt Milk.* Harper & Row, 1947.

Silverstein, Shel. "Snowman." *Where the Sidewalk Ends.* Harper & Row, 1974.

Sole-Vendtell, Carme. *Winter.* Children's Press, 1981.

Watson, Jane Werner. *Frosty the Snowman.* Golden Press, 1951.

Teacher Reference Books

Barker, Will. *Winter-Sleeping Wildlife.* Harper & Brothers, 1958.

Hylander, Clarence John. *Out of Doors in Winter.* Macmillan, 1943.

Youngpeter, John M. *Winter Science Activities.* Holiday House, 1966.

Fingerplays

Three Little Kittens

   Recite the familiar nursery rhyme. Talk about why we need to wear mittens in the winter.

Snowflakes

Snowflakes, snowflakes spinning all around.
   (Flutter fingers high above head, in the air, slowly falling to ground.)
Snowflakes, snowflakes falling to the ground.
Snowflakes, snowflakes so cold and white.
Snowflakes, snowflakes, will you stay all night?

White Day

   Talk about why white is a winter color. Ask each child to wear something white on White Day. Cut out pictures of white things and make a group collage called "Winter White." Serve white things for a snack, such as marshmallows, popcorn, milk, white bread, cream cheese spread, or whipped topping.

Unique: Snowflakes and Children

   Talk about how both snowflakes and children are unique—every one is a little bit different and every one is special. All snowflakes have six sides but have different designs. All children have bodies and faces, yet each child is different and special. Nobody is exactly like you!.
   If possible, catch snowflakes on hands and paper and examine them closely. Try to count the six sides.

Memory Game

   Put some winter-related items on a tray or tabletop. Cover and secretly remove or add one item. Uncover and let the children tell you what is different. Just before you remove the cover, you may want to recite:

   "Remember, remember what you see.
   Now something is different; what can it be?"

   Vary the number of items from two to six, depending on the expertise of the children. Two-year-olds should start with just two or three items to remember.
   Possible winter items include: paper snowflakes, paper snowperson, mitten, scarf, dead leaf, bird seed, etc. You may also use the pictures on the front of the January Curriculum guide.
   To extend the fun, try removing or adding more than one item at a time and see if the children can still successfully tell what is different. You may end the game by removing all of the items for them to recall.

Skiing

Some people travel by ski or sled in the winter. Bring in pictures or books that show people skiing or traveling on sleds. You may borrow posters from travel agencies—they are a good source for skiing pictures.

Read to the class *Ootah's Lucky Day* by Peggy Parish, which is one fun-to-read book with sleds in it.

Ask a person who owns skis to bring them to the class and show them to the children. If possible, let the children take turns slipping their feet into the ski boots and pretending to ski.

Matched Pairs

Bring in several pairs of mittens (or use the children's mittens, if available). You may also use cutouts of differently colored pairs of mittens. Mix up the pairs. Have the children find the matches. Repeat the game as long as it holds the children's interest.

Weather Dolls

Bring in some paper dolls or real dolls. Provide a variety of outfits for different temperatures. Let the children take turns dressing the dolls as if the dolls were going to play outside in the snow, to play inside, etc.

Igloo

Read *Ootah's Lucky Day* by Peggy Parish to the class. Help the children make a small igloo model. Mix up the Whipped Snow recipe (see Art Recipes), but use less water so the mixture is thicker. Tape a small shoebox and a toilet paper tube together to make the igloo shape. Let the children help spread the Whipped Snow thickly all over the structure, piling up a round dome look. Be sure to leave a hole for the tunnel opening.

January Calendar

Fill in the numerals, days, and month name on the January Calendar at the end of this section. Duplicate one calendar for each child. The children draw a winter scene to complete their personal calendar. As a group, mark any special days in January on the calendar.

Winter Riddles

You begin by making up two or three riddles for the children. When the children catch on, let them enjoy making up their own riddles to try to stump their friends. For example: "Children have fun sitting on me and riding down a snowy hill. What am I?"

Numeral Recognition: Snowballs

Provide a ball of white (uncolored) play dough (see Art Recipes) for each child. Write a numeral on the board or chart. Using their play dough, the children make as many "snowballs" as the numeral indicates. Use the numerals known by the children for fun practice.

MATH VOCABULARY

Long—Short

If possible in your area, compare lengths of icicles. Go on an icicle hunt, looking for long and short ones. See who can find the longest and the shortest. Measure in a hurry!

Where icicle hunting is out of the question, have the children model icicles with play dough. Make long ones and short ones.

Shapes: Circles

Talk about how a snowperson is usually made by rolling round shapes.

1. Make the Circle Snowperson pattern (at the end of this section) from felt. Let the children take turns building the snowperson by putting the felt circles together on a flannel board.
2. Use the Circle Snowperson pattern and the felt circles made from that pattern. Let the children take turns matching the felt circles on the same size circles of the pattern copy.
3. A few older children might use a copy of the pattern, cut it out by themselves, and glue it together to make the snowperson.

Ordinal Numbers

To practice "first," "second," and "third," put three shoe boxes on the floor, in a corner area away from traffic. Label the boxes "first," "second," and "third." Give one child a white beanbag or a white styrofoam ball (like those used to make tree ornaments). Ask the children to take turns throwing the "snowball" into whichever box you call out: "Toss the snowball into the third box."

Measurement: One Cup; One-Half Cup; Time

Crush enough ice cubes to fill one cup and one half of another cup. (Measuring cups for cooking work best.) Write down the time you put the ice in the cups. Ask the children: "Which do you think will melt faster, the cup or the half cup of ice?" Keep track of how many minutes each takes to melt at room temperature. Measure the water after the ice has melted. Is it still filling the one cup and half cup? Which takes more room—ice or water?

Measurement:
Inches; Time; Cup;
One-Half Cup

Find several icicles to bring inside. Measure the length of each one. Let the children predict which will melt first and which will have the most water.

Put each of the icicles in a separate bowl. Note how many minutes each takes to melt. Measure how much water each has left.

Make a chart. Draw the shape of each icicle. Show how long it was in inches, how long it took to melt, and how much water was measured from it. Label the chart "Measuring Icicles."

MOVEMENT

Winter Movements

Ask the children to:

- Lie down inside the classroom and pretend to make angels in the snow.
- Pretend to melt like snowpeople. Sink as slowly as you can to the floor.
- Pretend to go ice skating or skiing. Slide smoothly and carefully in your stocking feet.
- Pretend to roll big balls for a snowperson. Lift them carefully.
- Stretch to put each ball on top of the other. Stretch very tall to put a hat way up on top.
- Pretend to make snowballs and throw them overhanded and underhanded.

Footprints in the Snow

Make footprint cutouts. Lay them on the carpet or tape them to the floor, so they won't slip when stepped on. Let the children walk in the footprints.

Vary the pattern of the prints. Make it curve or zig zag. Vary the length between steps, so the children have to stretch or tip toe.

An Action Poem

Playing in the Snow

Five little children playing in the snow,	(Wave five fingers over head.)
Jumping up and down in a row.	(Children jump up and down.)
One fell down and hurt his toe,	(Fall down.)
Oooooh!	(Hold foot and rock back and forth.)

Four little children playing in the snow...	(Repeat above action)
Three little children playing...	
Two little children playing...	
One little child playing...	

No little children playing in the snow,	(Shake heads sadly.)
In to see mother they must go.	(Walk in place.)
Mother smiles and fixes the toe.	(Clap hands.)
Five little children playing in the snow.	(Wave five fingers over head.)

LIFE IN WINTER

From *We Care*, Copyright © 1988 Scott, Foresman and Company.

MUSIC

Frosty the Snowman

Play the record, if available. Sing the song with the children several times.

Skater's Waltz

Play a record of "Skater's Waltz" or another smooth, gliding type of music. Let the children take off their shoes and pretend to skate by moving smoothly to the music.

Hibernation Song

(Tune: "Are You Sleeping?")

Are you sleeping? Are you sleeping?
Little bears, little bears.
Winter time has come now. Winter time has come now.
Hibernate. Hibernate.

The children stretch arms as the song begins and end the song by curling up on the floor as if hibernating like little bear cubs.

ROLE PLAY

Dolls

Provide doll clothes, so children can dress dolls appropriately for the weather each day. Talk about getting the dolls ready to go out shopping, to go to the doctor for a flu shot, to go next door to play with a friend, etc.

Winter Clothes

Provide lots of winter clothing items for the children to try on and use for role play. Some suggested items are: mittens, winter coats of different sizes and styles, scarves, boots, and hats.

Snow Shoveling

Provide cardboard cutouts of snow shovels. Have the children pretend to shovel the snow off the driveways so the cars and trucks can get out of the garage.

If desired, provide a box of small styrofoam packing pieces. Let the children shovel the pieces from one box into another.

SCIENCE

Hibernation

Discuss how some living creatures, such as bears and turtles, sleep for several weeks in the winter when it is too cold to find food.

If possible, invite a zookeeper to visit the class and talk about hibernating animals and migrating birds.

Migration

Discuss how some birds migrate to warmer areas where they can more easily find food and live during the winter. Try to find out which birds are in your area in the winter. Talk about why it is harder for birds to find food in the winter. Talk about what birds like to eat.

Bird Feeder

Make a bird feeder to hang outside a window or wherever the children can see birds using it and care for it.

1. *Pine Cone Feeders*—Tie a long string around a pine cone. Spread it with peanut butter mixed with bird seed. (Be sure to mix the seeds and the peanut butter together well, as peanut butter by itself may cause birds' beaks to stick together.) Hang the feeder on a tree branch.
2. *Milk Jug Feeder*—Clean out an empty milk jug. Cut a hole near the bottom large enough for a bird to fit through.

   To make a perch, cut a small hole under the opening and attach a small stick or dowel rod inside this small hole. Fill the bottom of the feeder with bird seed. Hang the feeder securely on a tree limb or rafter, away from people-traffic areas.
3. *Milk Carton Feeder*—Clean out a small milk carton. Attach a long string firmly to the top. Cut an opening large enough for a bird to fit through. Attach a small dowel rod beneath it for a bird perch.

   Fill the bottom of the feeder with bird seed and hang it securely outside.

Reminder: Be sure to keep the feeders cared for and full of seed once the birds have come to rely on them.

Window Fog

Let children breathe on classroom windows or glass doors and draw pictures with their fingers in the "window fog." Talk about how water vapor forms on the glass as their warm breath contacts the cold glass.

Signs of Winter

Discuss what things we can see, hear, and touch outside that tell us it is winter. If weather permits, go for a short walk and look for frost, dead leaves, bare trees, evergreens, snow, ice, icicles, warm clothing on people, water vapor from noses and mouths, and winter birds.

Ice Melts

Bring in a piece of ice or an icicle from outside (or from the freezer if outside temperatures are above freezing). Talk about how the ice looks and feels. Ask: ''What happens when it gets warm?'' Let some children hold a piece of ice in their hands for a few seconds. Ask them: ''How does it feel?'' Point out any water from the ice on their hands.

Providing Food for Outside Animals

Discuss how most outdoor plants do not grow in winter. Therefore, some people provide hay or other food for outside animals, such as cattle, sheep, horses, or deer. Try to find pictures of outside animals being fed and show them to the children.

Whipped Snowperson Pattern

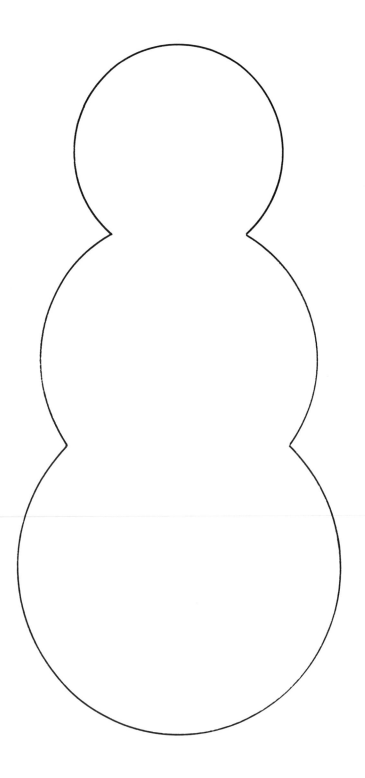

January Picture

January

Circle Snowperson

Dinosaurs

CONCEPTS

- The word "dinosaur" means "terrible lizard."
- No people were alive when dinosaurs lived on the earth, so no one has ever really seen a dinosaur.
- Some dinosaurs ate only plants; others ate meat.
- Most dinosaurs were very large but some were small.
- People have found dinosaur fossils, such as footprints, bones, and teeth.
- No one knows for sure why the dinosaurs died (i.e., became extinct).

ART

**Stuffed Dinosaurs
(Whole Class Activity)**

Butcher paper; tempera paint; newspapers; strings.

Cut two matching dinosaur shapes from two pieces of 24 × 36 inch (or larger) paper. The children use tempera paint to paint each shape. (Cover a tabletop or floor area with newspapers. Children do the painting on the newspapers to minimize messes and clean up.)

Staple the shapes together, leaving an opening at the top of the dinosaur's back for stuffing. The children wad up pages of the newspaper to push gently inside the stapled dinosaur until it is nicely stuffed.

Staple shut the opening. Attach one or more strings and hang the stuffed dinosaur from the ceiling like a mobile.

For added interest and involvement, make more than one dinosaur for the children to work on. Vary the shapes to look like different kinds of dinosaurs.

Play Dough Dinosaurs

Make two or more batches of play dough (see Art Recipes) in dinosaur colors—dark green, grey, etc. Let the children roll ball and cylinder shapes for bodies and heads. Roll long, fat snake shapes for tails. Add small balls for spots, eyes, and other details. Use a shoebox to cut out a cave for the dinosaurs.

Lime Play Dough

To increase the fun, make play dough according to the usual recipe (see Art Recipes) but add one package of lime-flavored gelatin before adding the boiling water. Looks dinosaur green and smells great too!

Kid-asaurus Tracks

Green tempera paint; butcher paper; pan of soapy water; towels.

After discussing fossils and dinosaur tracks, let the children make "Kid Tracks" by stepping in green tempera paint and walking on the large paper. Provide a chair and the pan of water so the children may sit down and wash their feet. Display with a caption: "Kid-asaurus Tracks."

Paper Mache Dinosaur

Chicken wire; newspaper; wallpaper or flour paste; tempera paint.

A large paper mache dinosaur is an exciting classroom addition that will last a long time. Make a dinosaur shape by twisting and hooking together chicken wire. The shape should resemble some type of dinosaur known by the children. The shape may be smaller, but a 3-5 foot size is most impressive and fun.

Provide cut 1½ × 12 inch strips of newspaper. Make a paste from commercial wallpaper paste or by gradually mixing flour with water until it forms a smooth paste. It is best to have the paste in a 3-5 gallon plastic dishpan to limit spills and messes.

Place the dinosaur model on a plastic drip cloth. Let children take turns putting a strip of paper into the paste, removing the excess paste by pulling the paper between two fingers, and placing the paper strip on the dinosaur. Encourage children to "pet" the dinosaur each time they add a strip to help them remember to smooth down each edge as well as they can.

After the model is completely covered with one coat of pasted strips, dry it (still sitting on the plastic cloth) for one day. Then add at least two more coats, letting it dry completely between each coat. Since this is a large project, more than one class may take turns working on it. When the third coat is dry, the dinosaur is ready for painting with tempera paint.

Dinosaur Macaroni Collage

Macaroni; construction paper dinosaurs; glue.

Provide 9 × 12 inch construction paper cutouts of dinosaurs. Cover the work area. Give each child a handful of uncooked macaroni. The children add texture to the dinosaur body by gluing the macaroni all over the shape.

Dinosaur Painting

Easel paper; tempera paint; dinosaur stencils.

Cut dinosaur shapes out of large pieces (18 × 24 inch) of the paper used for easel painting. Have each child use brushes and tempera paint to paint on one of the shapes.

The painting may be done at an easel, on a covered tabletop or floor, or by taping the paper to a wall area that has been covered with a piece of plastic.

Dinosaur Tooth Necklace

Modeling Goop (see Art Recipes); knitting needle; string or yarn.

Leave the mixture white. Let children knead, roll, and play with a small amount of the mixture. Then, demonstrate how to roll a piece and taper one end to resemble a tooth. Have each child make several teeth.

Gently push a knitting needle through the thick end of each tooth. Wiggle it around gently to form a hole large enough for string or yarn to slip through *easily*. Let dry on a rack or piece of screen for one or two days at room temperature.

Provide string or yarn. Let the children string and wear their dinosaur tooth necklace.

Dinosaur Prints

Dinosaur-shaped sponges; clip clothespins; tempera paint; manila paper.

Using the Dinosaur Figures pattern at the end of this section, cut small, simple dinosaur shapes from sponges. Use a pincher-type clothespin to hold the back of each sponge.

Cover a work area. Pour a small amount of tempera paint into meat trays or paper plates. Provide manila paper (9 × 12 or 12 × 18 inch). The children dip the sponges into the paint and repeatedly press the shape on their paper until it no longer prints. Then, they use another shape dipped into another color. Continue until the paper is covered.

Dinosaur Diorama

Use a shoebox to create a class diorama. Cut off one long side of the box.

Color scenes of trees, rocks, mountains, a cave, and other background details to glue on the inside back and sides of the diorama. Paint the outside of the box and the floor of the diorama with tempera paints, if desired.

Have the children draw their own small dinosaurs. Glue a piece of tagboard on the bottom of each dinosaur. Fold the tagboard to create a stand for the animals.

Let the children take turns making scenes in the diorama with the dinosaurs and plants.

BLOCKS

Build caves or other hiding places for dinosaurs to live in. If possible, provide plastic dinosaurs to add to the fun.

BULLETIN BOARD

Where the Dinosaurs Lived

On butcher paper, draw several trees and other large plants, large boulders, a cave opening, a lake, etc. The children may then paint the scene with tempera paint. Allow the scene to dry and staple it to the bulletin board. To make "vines," add lengths of yarn with cutout leaves glued to them. Add an example of several varieties of dinosaurs to the bulletin board. Print the caption "Where the Dinosaurs Lived" to complete the board.

Work-asaurus

Make a large dinosaur for the center of the board. Surround the dinosaur with large eggs. On each egg, print a job frequently done in the classroom, such as "lead," "erase board," and "serve snack." Make a small dinosaur for each child. Print a child's name on each baby dinosaur. Pin the child's baby dinosaur next to each job egg when it is that child's turn to do that work. Print the caption: "Work-asaurus." Change the job assignments daily to sustain interest in the board.

COOKING

Dinosaur Stew

3 carrots, cut into small pieces	*1 teaspoon Worcestershire sauce*
3 potatoes, cut into small pieces	*1 teaspoon garlic salt*
1 pound stew meat in small chunks	*1 bay leaf*
3 cups water	*2 teaspoons salt*
3 beef-flavored bouillon cubes	*½ teaspoon pepper*

Wash hands. Let the children use table knives or plastic knives. Each child works on a paper towel or a piece of waxed paper and cuts part of one vegetable into very small pieces. (The smaller the pieces, the faster the cooking.)

Put the ingredients into a crock pot. Cook on high for 4-5 hours. Serve in dishes or paper cups.

For added fun and imagination, get a *large* bone from a meat shop. Boil the bone clean. Then use the "dinosaur" bone to stir the ingredients as they are put into the pot. Use the bone to stir the stew again just before eating.

Cave Rocks
(Delicious Candied Peanuts)

Electric frying pan
1½ pounds peanuts (shelled)
2 egg whites
2 teaspoons water
1 cup sugar
2 tablespoons chili powder
1 teaspoon cumin

Whip egg whites and water together. Stir in everything but the peanuts. Add peanuts. Cook at 250° for 1 hour.

Stir every 15 minutes until coating is hard and crunchy. Do not overcook or it will burn quickly.

Spread on waxed paper to cool for 10 minutes.

Dino-Dough

1 cup peanut butter
¼ cup dry milk powder
3 tablespoons honey
Vanilla wafers
Raisins
Pretzel sticks

Mix the first three ingredients. Have each child form some of the mixture into a dinosaur shape. Add raisin eyes, vanilla wafers for plates of bone down the dinosaur's back, and pretzels for a spiked tail. Eat!

Dinosaur Eggs

¼ cup margarine
10 oz. marshmallows
5-6 cups Rice Krispies–type cereal

Melt butter and marshmallows over low heat. Add cereal and stir well. Cook for 5 minutes.

Wash hands. Let the mixture cool before giving each child a spoonful of the mixture to form into an egg shape. Let them work on a paper towel or piece of waxed paper to limit clean up mess.

LANGUAGE ARTS

Books

Aliki. *Digging Up Dinosaurs*. Thomas Y. Crowell, 1981.
Althea. *Desmond at the Carnival*. Rourke, 1981.
Althea. *Desmond the Dusty Dinosaur*. Rourke, 1981.
Brandreth, Gyles. *Amazing Facts About Prehistoric Animals*. Doubleday, 1981.
Brown, Marc and Stephen Krensky. *Dinosaurs, Beware! A Safety Guide*. Little, Brown, 1982.
Charlton, Elizabeth. *Terrible Tyrannosaurus*. Dandelion Press, 1982.
Curran, Eileen. *Home for a Dinosaur*. Troll, 1985.
Cutts, David. *More About Dinosaurs*. Troll, 1982.
Eastman, David. *I Can Read About Prehistoric Animals*. Troll Associates, 1977.
Fuchshuber, Annegert. *From Dinosaurs to Fossils*. Carolrhoda Books, 1981.
Gabriele, Joseph. *First Days of the Dinosaurs*. Penny Lane Publishers, 1984.
Harvey, Anthony. *The World of the Dinosaur*. Lerner Publications, 1980.
Hoff, Syd. *Danny and the Dinosaur*. Harper and Row, 1958.
Howard, John. *I Can Read About Dinosaurs*. Troll Associates, 1972.
Martin, Alice. *Dinosaurs*. Western Publishing Co., 1973.
Packard, Ann and Shirley Stafford. *Time of the Dinosaurs*. S. Stafford, 1981.
Parish, Peggy. *Dinosaur Time*. Harper and Row, 1974.
Petty, Kate. *Dinosaurs*. Franklin Watts, 1984.
Sattler, Helen R. *Baby Dinosaurs*. Lothrop, 1984.
Sharmat, Marjorie. *Mitchell Is Moving*. Macmillan, 1978.
Whitehead, Patricia. *Dinosaur Alphabet Book*. Troll, 1985.

Teacher Resource Book

Glovach, Linda. *The Little Witch's Dinosaur Book*. Prentice-Hall, 1984.

Poems

Kredenser, Gail. "Brontosaurus." In Jack Prelutsky's *The Random House Book of Poetry for Children*. Random House, 1983.
Prelutsky, Jack. "Long Gone." In Jack Prelutsky's *The Random House Book of Poetry for Children*. Random House, 1983.
Silverstein, Shel. "If I Had a Brontosaurus." In Shel Silverstein's *Where the Sidewalk Ends*. Harper and Row, 1974.

Fingerplays

The Dinosaurs

The dinosaurs lived so long ago	
What happened to them we do not know!	
Some were tall,	(Stretch hand upward to show height.)
And some were small.	(Crouch down low to show height.)
They lived in water,	(Make swimming motions.)
And on the land.	(Stomp feet.)
The stegosaurus had big plates of bone	(Make a pointed shape with both hands.)
On its tail and back.	
The brontosaurus had a long, long neck	
And a tail that could give you a WHACK!	(Clap hands together sharply.)
But the meanest dinosaur of all, no doubt,	(Shake finger warningly.)
Was the tyrannosaurus rex! Watch out!	(Jump at each other with hands clawlike; scowl and growl.)

Dinosaur Pronunciation Guide

Stegosaurus	(steg - uh - SO - rus)
Tyrannosaurus	(tih - ran - uh - SO - rus)
Brontosaurus	(bron - tuh - SO - rus)
Diplodocus	(dip - LAH - duh - cuss)
Ornithomimus	(or - nith - oh - MY - muss)

Flannel Board Dinosaurs

Make several dinosaurs from felt or nonwoven interfacing. The nonwoven interfacing is thin, so you can easily trace any dinosaur picture on it, color it with markers, and make flannel board figures quickly.

Let the children enjoy putting the dinosaur figures on and taking them off the board. Help children name some of the dinosaurs.

To extend the fun, make up a class flannel board story, writing it on chart paper as you go along. Let the children have fun making up the story, then ''reading'' it to the class while adding the dinosaur figures to the flannel board at the appropriate times.

Dinosaurs, Beware!

Read *Dinosaurs, Beware! A Safety Guide* by Marc Brown and Stephen Krensky. The children may freely discuss the comical pictures and talk about the safety ideas represented in each scene.

Danny and the Dinosaur

Read *Danny and the Dinosaur* by Syd Hoff. Make a stick puppet of Danny and one of the brontosaurus. Reread or retell the story using the puppets. Later, have the children use the puppets to retell the story.

Dinosaur Wishes

1. If you could go back to dinosaur times and you met a dinosaur face to face, what would you do?
2. What do you wish you could say to a dinosaur?
3. What would you tell a dinosaur to try to help him?

Dino-mite Learning

Provide a dinosaur shape with handwriting lines on it. Encourage children to say something they have learned about dinosaurs. Print each idea on a dinosaur shape for the child to take home.

Dinosaur Information

Children are really curious about dinosaurs! Read some dinosaur books to the children to increase their knowledge about kinds of dinosaurs, what they ate, and what they did.

With younger children, you may prefer to show them the best pictures in the books and simply tell the information in your own words.

Dinosaur Land Game

Make a simple gameboard or use the Candyland Game board. Play, using cutouts of dinosaurs for markers to move.

Build a Dinosaur

Trace a large, simple dinosaur shape on the nonwoven interfacing. Color it with markers. Cut it out, then cut it into 3-5 pieces. Have the children place the parts on the flannel board and put them together to make the dinosaur whole.

Mix up the parts and play again.

Dinosaur Concentration

Make two copies of several small dinosaur shapes. Cut loosely around each dinosaur shape, so each dinosaur is in a box or "cloud" cutout. Put the cutout pairs on a tabletop. Turn the pieces over and mix them up. Let children take turns turning over two shapes and trying to find the two that match. When a match is made, leave it turned face up.

Great fun and excellent for memory. Use the names of the dinosaurs, when appropriate: "You found one brontosaurus and one stegosaurus."

DINOSAURS

Brontosaurus Maze

Give each child a Brontosaurus Maze handout from the end of this section. The children use their finger to follow the path and discover the correct way out. Then, they color the correct path to the tree leaves.

Discuss with the children that the brontosaurus was very large but that it ate only plants. Emphasize working from top to bottom and from left to right as children do the maze.

Dinosaur Recipes

Ask the children how they think they could cook a dinosaur. Use a tape recorder to record individual answers. Let them play it back and listen again, if they wish.

Make a class chart story: "How to Cook a Dinosaur." List each child's name and write a sentence or two for each. Joel said: "I would make dinosaur pizza. But it would take a really big pan!"

Make a copy for each child to take home. Parents will enjoy sharing the fun.

MATH NUMBER CONCEPTS

Counting Dinosaurs

Use the Dinosaur Figures pattern at the end of this section to make sets of dinosaurs from nonwoven interfacing (for the flannel board) or from construction paper (for tabletop use). Count how many of each kind: how many tall ones, how many with long tails, etc.

Addition/Subtraction

Make a set of two or three dinosaurs. Ask the children: "How many will there be if I add one more?" "How many will there be if one goes away?" Have the children help you make up simple story problems with the dinosaurs.

Dinosaur Eggs

Tape or write a numeral on the outside of several plastic eggs (the type that come apart in halves). Provide small cutouts of dinosaurs. Have the children place the appropriate number of baby dinosaurs inside each egg.

MATH VOCABULARY

Long—Short/Shapes

Hold up pictures or models of dinosaurs and have the children find ones with long necks or short legs or long tails or short tails, etc.

Provide two silhouettes of each variety of dinosaur. Ask the children to match the shapes. You may also prepare the silhouettes for use on the flannel board.

Big—Bigger—Biggest

Cut out three dinosaurs of graduated sizes. Talk about the size of each dinosaur. Have children place them in order from big to biggest. Then, mix them up and ask children to place them in order from biggest down to big.

The Biggest Plop

One big dinosaur was standing on a rock.
He jumped into some water and made a *big* plop!
Two big dinosaurs were standing on a rock.
They jumped into some water and made a *bigger* plop!
But the three big dinosaurs standing on a rock
Jumped into some water and made the *biggest* plop!
(Let the children help with some appropriate movements. Hold up the appropriate number of fingers for each verse. Clap hands together for the "plop!")

MOVEMENT

Stilts

Provide one or two pairs of stilts. You may make stilts using large empty cans with yarn strung through the top to make a rope to hold. Let the children walk around on the stilts and pretend they are dinosaurs.

Dino and His Bone

Let one child be Dino. Have other children try to tiptoe up behind to steal the bone without Dino knowing!

Dinosaur Tracks

Cut out large dinosaur footprints. Tape them to the floor. Children follow the prints using long steps. Ask them to walk forward and then backward following the footprints.

Tape baby dinosaur footprints to the floor beside the large prints. Children use smaller steps to follow the baby prints forward and backward.

MUSIC

Dinosaur Walk

Have children move like dinosaurs as a record is played. Choose music to go with:

1. Walking slow, giant steps of the brontosaurus;
2. Running with fierceness of tyrannosaurus;
3. Walking, stretching out long dinosaur neck;
4. Walking, waving long dinosaur tail.

Rhythmastics

Clap a rhythmic pattern. The children softly clap to repeat the pattern. Then, a new leader claps a different pattern for the group to repeat. (Reinforces listening skills.)

Dinosaur Tune

(Tune: ''Where, Oh, Where Has My Little Dog Gone?'')

Where, oh, where has my dinosaur gone?
Where, oh, where can he be?
I searched on the mountain,
But not in the sea.
Where, oh, where can he be?

Let the children suggest other places to look for the dinosaur. Substitute those places in the song and sing another verse.

ROLE PLAY

Museum

Set up a dinosaur museum. The children may build shelves with blocks. Set up rocks, bones, and dinosaur ''fossils'' made by the children. Provide a hat or badge for the museum owner to wear. Have the children make tickets, so they may go into the museum. Provide magnifying glasses and other appropriate props.

Cave Dwellings

Use a blanket or large box to make a cave. Let the children pretend to be dinosaurs living in a cave for shelter.

SCIENCE

Skeleton Match

Provide a copy of the Dinosaur Skelton Match at the end of this section for each child. Have them cut out the parts of the whole dinosaur body to match to the skeleton. Talk about how bones provide our bodies' shape and strength.

Bones/Skeleton

Bring a complete skeleton from a boiled chicken. Compare the skeleton to a photograph of a chicken. Have children feel the size of their own leg bone and compare that to the size of the chicken bone.

Ask the children to look carefully at the skeleton. Then, have them close their eyes. Take one bone from the skeleton and let the children decide where it belongs.

Dinosaur Fossil Eggs

Press a layer of play dough in the bottom of a small box or shoebox lid. Press six to ten pebbles or marbles into the clay (close together). Gently remove the marbles so their indentations remain.

Mix one cup of plaster of paris with enough water to make it pour easily. Pour the plaster over the indentations in the play dough.

After it hardens, lift the plaster out of the box. The shapes will look like fossils of dinosaur eggs.

Fossils

Use Modeling Goop (see Art Recipes) or plaster of paris. Give each child some ''goop'' in a meat tray. Provide a supply of leaves, rocks, bones, and small paper cutouts of dinosaur shapes. Let the children choose some items to press into the goop and then remove.

Dry the ''fossils'' for one day.

DINOSAURS

Dinosaur Figures

Brontosaurus Maze

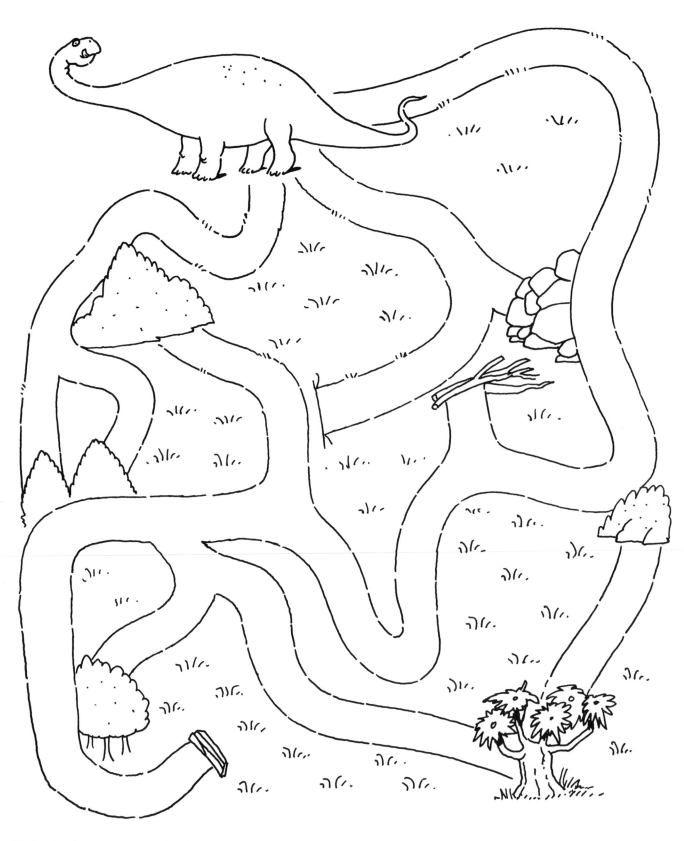

Help the brontosaurus find some leaves to eat.

Dinosaur Skeleton Match

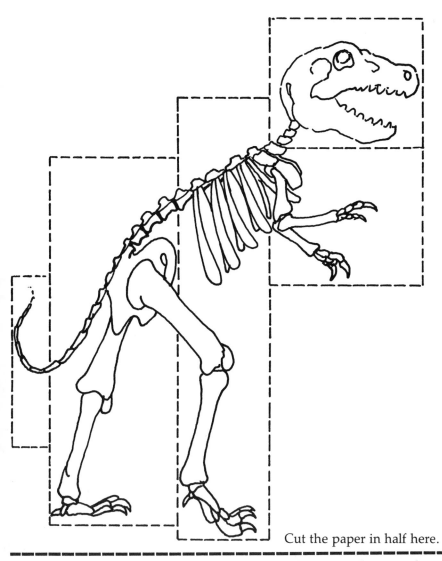

Cut the paper in half here.

Color these dinosaur parts. Cut out each one and match it to the skeleton.

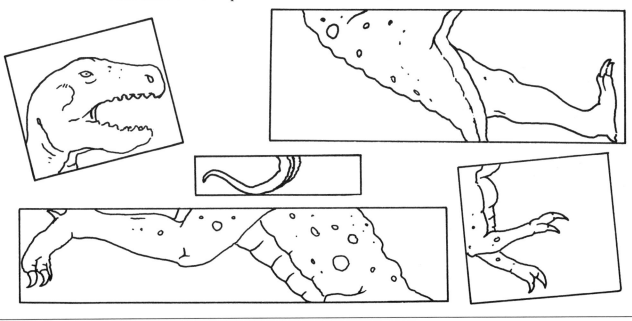

Five Senses

CONCEPTS

- People have five senses: We see with our eyes.
  - We hear with our ears.
  - We smell with our nose.
  - We taste with our tongue.
  - We feel primarily with our fingers, but all the parts of our body have feeling.
- We learn things by using our senses.
- Our senses help us to enjoy life and the things around us.
- Some people do not have use of one or more of the senses.

ART

Sniff Art

Cupcake papers or nut cups; construction paper or gummed art paper; cotton balls; powdered tempera paint; plastic sandwich bags; odds and ends of perfume; an eye dropper.

The children glue a cupcake paper or small nut cup on a piece of construction paper to represent the blossom of a flower. Add a construction paper or gummed art paper stem and leaves. The children color a cotton ball with a color they desire by putting it into a sandwich bag with a teaspoon of powdered tempera paint and shaking the bag gently. Glue the cotton ball in the center of the cupcake paper. After it is dry, gently pull it apart slightly. The children add a few drops of perfume with the aid of an eye dropper.

Variation I. *Real twigs or small tree limb; tissue paper or real leaves; construction paper; cotton balls; lemon and orange extract.*

Glue a twig, or a small limb with several smaller limbs branching off, to a piece of construction paper. Add either tissue paper leaves or real leaves to the tree. Color cotton balls yellow (for a lemon tree) or orange (for an orange tree). Glue several half pieces of cotton balls on each ''tree.'' Add a drop of lemon or orange extract to each cotton ball with an eye dropper.

Variation II. Do either of the above two art activities as a group project by putting a large piece of butcher paper on the wall. Paint a sky, a sun, the ground, a pond, and houses. Then ''plant'' a grove of lemon trees, orange trees, and a flower garden for the class and parents to sniff and enjoy.

Texture Banner

Large piece of muslin or burlap; fabric of various textures; dowel rod; glue (Sobo fabric glue works best).

Provide fabric of different colors and textures in different sizes and shapes. Using a piece of unbleached muslin or burlap, have the children glue the pieces of fabric to the muslin or burlap. Fold down 1½ inches at the top and stitch, glue, or staple the fabric in place. Insert a dowel rod, broom handle, or yardstick. Tie a string or yarn to each end of the dowel. Use as a hanger for the texture banner. Suggested fabrics include satin, net, corduroy, velour, velvet, suede, upholstery fabric, vinyl, and rubber or plastic doormat. You may also assemble banners as an individual project.

Finger Paint Textures

Finger paint; sand, rice, or cornmeal.

Finger paint with any color and any design. Sprinkle sand, rice, or cornmeal on the painting while it's still wet. Let it dry. Gently rub fingers over the painting. Is it rough or smooth? Can you find parts of the painting that are smooth and parts that are rough?

Play Dough

Three batches of play dough (see Art Recipes); food coloring; peppermint, lemon, and orange extract.

Add red coloring and peppermint extract to one batch of dough, yellow coloring and lemon extract to the second, and orange coloring and orange extract to the third.

Encourage the children to really squeeze and feel the play dough. Talk about how it feels squishing through their fingers. Have them close their eyes and guess which batch you are holding under their nose.

Food Collage

Various kinds of dry cereal, pretzel sticks, popcorn, dried beans, and miniature marshmallows; tagboard or shirt cardboard glue; markers or crayons.

Make a collage by gluing the various food items to a piece of construction paper. If desired, have children use a marker or crayon and make a creature or vehicle using the cereal as facial features or wheels.

Finger Painting with Sniff Appeal

Prepared pudding; menthol shaving cream.

Let the children finger paint using something with a distinct aroma. Pudding and menthol shaving cream are only two of several alternatives.   To make cleanup easier, the children may finger paint inside cookie sheets or pizza pans.

Easel Painting

Tempera paint in shallow containers; bucket of water near the easel.

Show the children how to paint at the easel using only one finger (no brushes allowed). Wash your finger and repeat with another color. Encourage them to wash the paint off completely before dipping into a new color. Talk about painting a design to cover the entire area. Encourage them to create new colors on their painting by mixing colors on their paper.

Chalk Talk

Colored chalk; black construction paper; inexpensive hair spray.

Let the children explore drawing a design or a picture with colored chalk. Encourage them to use a variety of colors. Spray lightly with hair spray to prevent the chalk from smearing. Talk about which color(s) of chalk they like best. Which looks darkest? Which looks lightest?

Texture Puzzle

Fabrics in several different textures; tagboard or posterboard; glue; exacto knife or single-edge razor blade.

Cut the fabrics into approximately 2 × 2 inch or 2 × 3 inch pieces. Provide an 8 × 8 inch piece of posterboard for each child. Dilute the glue slightly and put into a bowl. The children use a pastry brush or paintbrush to apply glue to the back of the fabric. With this method, the corners have a better chance of being glued down. Allow to dry overnight. When it's dry, cut into several pieces, using the exacto knife, to create a puzzle. Put the child's initials on the back of each piece and provide an envelope for storage. You may make the envelope from folded construction paper, if desired.

Encourage the children to assemble their puzzle and feel the different textures. Trade puzzles with a friend.

Shiny, Shiny Mobile

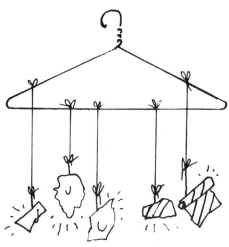

Coat hangers; yarn; paper clips; aluminum foil; shiny metallic wrapping papers; mirrored window film.

Tie varying lengths of yarn to the sides of the hanger. Tie a paper clip hook at the end of each piece. Let the children choose shiny materials for the mobile. Have the children cut out irregular shapes and use a hole punch to make a hole in each shape. Hang each shape on a paper clip to complete the mobile. Each child may make a small mobile, or the whole class may create a large one.

Fluffy Painting

2 cups of soap flakes; powdered tempera paint; liquid starch; portable electric mixer; large bowl.

In a large bowl, combine the soap, powdered tempera paint, and ½ cup of starch. Mix with the mixer (low speed). Add more starch if necessary to achieve a finger painting consistency. The children finger paint on paper with this mixture. Encourage them to talk about how this paint feels in their fingers. Also talk about how it looks and smells in comparison with regular paint.

Silly Mr. Senses

Oatmeal boxes or round snack cans with plastic lids; wallpaper; construction paper; sewing notions; junk items; styrofoam pieces; glue.

Each child brings an oatmeal box or round snack can from home. Glue a piece of construction paper or plain wallpaper sample around each can. Make the top third of the covered can look like a face by gluing on facial features as shown. Add texture all over the can by having the children glue on construction paper, buttons, brads, sewing notions, and other junk items. Show the children how to make accordion folded arms. Glue on a paper hat, if desired. Make funny shoes by having the children trace around a baby's shoes and glue them on the bottom of the can, so they stick out from under the can.

Senses Book

Magazine pictures; 9 × 12 inch construction paper; liquid starch; brushes; glue.

Provide lots of magazine pictures for the children to use. Cut the construction paper in half and provide five pages for each child to make a book. Print the name of one sense on each page. Encourage the children to glue pictures depicting the sense being used to the appropriate page. The children need to use only one or two drops of glue to hold the pictures in place. When the glue is dry, the children brush a thin layer of liquid starch over the entire page. Allow the starch to dry thoroughly before assembling the pages into a book. The starch will seal down the edges of the pictures and create a shiny appearance.

Color Mosaics

Water colors or thinned tempera paints; brushes; manila paper; plastic wrap (as used for food storage).

The children drop blobs of paint all over their paper. Use several different colors. Then, carefully lay a sheet of clear plastic wrap on top of the colors. The children crumple the plastic wrap gently to mix and move the color blobs. *Leave the plastic wrap in place on top of the colors until they're completely dry.* Then, lift off the plastic wrap. The children will be amazed to see the mosaic patterns created by the way the plastic wrap touched the paper!

BLOCKS

1. Take two to four children at a time with you to the block area. Give each child a selection of blocks on the floor in front of them. Blindfold each child in the group and tell them what to build, such as "build a tower" or "build a wall as long and as high as you can." The children may request that you supply them with more blocks. See if the children can pick out the different shapes of blocks, such as cylinder, square, or triangle. Ask them which of their senses they are not using and which they are using to help build the items.
2. Add a firetruck, train, or airplane to the block area. Talk about the sounds each makes.

BULLETIN BOARD

What Sense Is This?

On a paper plate, print either "taste," "see," "smell," "feel," or "hear" and glue on a picture clue for that sense. Make one plate for each of the five senses. Place these randomly on the bulletin board. Provide laminated pictures of children or animals doing different daily activities. The children may use push pins to place each picture under the sense they think is being used. Some pictures may fit under several categories! Talk about their choices.

COOKING

Mystery Snacks

You may prepare a mystery snack each day! *Before* they taste it, the children try to guess what the snack is from the smell, touch, or sound. Use items that have a distinct smell. Pickles, toasted garlic bread, cinnamon toast, most fruits, some types of cookies or brownies, peanut butter, and popped corn are possible choices. Have all of the children hide their eyes while they trying to guess the Mystery Snack of the day.

Knox Blox

Prepare Knox Blox from gelatin. This type of gelatin is different from the flavored kind. The children may handle and feel it in their hands.

> *4 envelopes Knox Gelatin*
> *3 pkg. flavored gelatin (3 oz.), any flavor*
> *4 cups boiling water*

In a large bowl, combine the gelatins. Add the water and stir until dissolved. Pour into a shallow pan and chill until firm. You may cut the Knox Blox into squares and eat them with hands. Encourage the children to wiggle the squares. Watch the movements and talk about how the Knox Blox look and feel. If preferred, you may cut the Knox Blox with cookie cutters to create many different shapes.

Jello Taste Quiz

As a class, prepare three distinctly different flavors of gelatin. When it is set, give everyone a taste of all three. Talk about how it tastes and the name of the flavor. Blindfold the children and have them hold their noses shut. Now let them taste and try to guess the flavor. Most of the children will not know which flavor is which! Later, discuss how our taste also depends on our sight and our smell.

Nutritious-Delicious

Cut apples in half and remove the seeds. Give each child half of an apple and a plastic knife. Pass around a jar of peanut butter and let each child fill the seed hole with peanut butter. Eat and lick your lips!

LANGUAGE ARTS

Books

Aliki. *My Five Senses.* Harper & Row, 1962.
Allington, Richard L. and Kathleen Krull. *Hearing.* Raintree, 1980.
Allington, Richard L. and Kathleen Krull. *Looking.* Raintree, 1980.
Allington, Richard L. and Kathleen Krull. *Smelling.* Raintree, 1980.
Allington, Richard L. and Kathleen Krull. *Tasting.* Raintree, 1980.
Allington, Richard L. and Kathleen Krull. *Touching.* Raintree, 1980.
Brenner, Barbara. *Faces.* Dutton, 1970.
Brown, Marcia. *Walk with Your Eyes.* Watts, 1979.
Curry, Peter. *I Can Hear.* Price-Stern, 1984.
Curry, Peter. *I Can See.* Price-Stern, 1984.
Hoover, Rosalie and Barbara Murphy. *Learning About Our Five Senses.* Good Apple, 1981.
Leigh, Tom. *Sesame Street What's Inside.* Western Publishing, 1980.
Moncure, Jane B. *The Look Book.* Children's Press, 1982.
Moncure, Jane B. *Sounds All Around.* Children's Press, 1982.
Moncure, Jane B. *A Tasting Party.* Children's Press, 1982.

Moncure, Jane B. *The Touch Book.* Children's Press, 1982.
Moncure, Jane B. *What Your Nose Knows!* Children's Press, 1982.
Sullivan, Tom. *Common Senses.* Children's Press, 1982.
Thomas, Anthony. *Things We Hear.* Watts, 1976.
Watson, Jean. *Sounds, Sounds, All Around.* Winston Press, 1983.

Fingerplays

My Hands

My hands can do a lot of things.
I'd like to name a few.
  They can turn a knob,
  Pat a pet,
  Do hard jobs,
  And have fun. Yet,
The favorite thing these hands can do
Is make the signs that mean "I love you!"

My Friend and I

We both have eyes to help us see,
My friend and I.
  (Make glasses by circling fingers over eyes.)
We both have a nose to help us smell,
My friend and I.
  (Sniff.)
We both have a mouth to help us taste,
My friend and I.
  (Lick lips with tongue.)
We both have ears to help us hear,
My friend and I.
  (Cup ear with hand.)
We both have hands to help us touch,
My friend and I.
  (Hug self, or touch or hug someone else.)
Our senses help us to be friends.
Let's play, my friend and I!

Loss of Senses

Have a qualified person talk with the children about the handicap of losing one or more senses. Talk about how people compensate for the loss of a sense.

Listen and Choose: Sound Cans

1. Gather small containers with lids (35mm film containers are good). Add some of the following to make two containers of each: rice, pebbles, pennies, sand, cotton balls, pencil erasers, or water. Have the children listen to the sound each makes as the container is filled. After finishing the pairs of sound cans, try to determine which is which. Do this as a class activity several times. Then, have the children work independently and try to match each pair according to the sound.
2. Arrange the containers in order to show loud, louder, and loudest.

Feel Cans

Empty the containers used as sound cans or get additional cans. Fill the containers with liquids: hot, cold, room temperature, frozen. Have the children feel the containers and arrange them in cold, colder, coldest or hot, hotter, and hottest order.

Smell Cans

Using the small containers with lids, put a cotton ball inside each. Pour a small amount of a familiar-smelling liquid on each cotton ball and put the lid back on. Open the top, pass the container around the table, and have the children guess what the smell is. Suggested liquids include vanilla extract, dill pickle juice, lemon juice, pine cleaner, after shave, onion juice, liquid smoke, and others you desire.

Mystery Bag or Box

An old leg from a pair of jeans sewed across one end with a draw string placed at the other end makes a quick and easy mystery bag. Put something smooth, rough, prickly, soft, bumpy, spongy, and hard in the bag. Without peeking, children take turns finding things of different textures within the bag. You may suggest to each child what to pull out of the bag.

What's That!

Gather several familiar objects that make a sound. Some examples could be keys, a pan and spoon, jingle bells, two blocks to bang together, and chalk on a chalkboard. Have the children hide their eyes while you make a noise. They try to guess what made the noise.

Tasting

Blindfold the children as they each take a turn tasting items and guessing what each item is. Items used must be fairly familiar to small children. Avoid using any food substance that will be spicy hot to them.

Talk about the four taste sensations our taste buds can sense. These are sweet, salty, sour, and bitter. Mix a sample of each for the children to taste. Use bottles of water and add a little sugar in one, a little salt in one, a little lemon juice in one, and a little vinegar or alum in the last. Using an eye dropper, put a drop from each bottle, one at a time, on the children's finger and let them taste. Discuss their reactions. Which did they like best? least? Can they think of any foods that taste similar?

Blindfold children again. This time, hold something with a pungent odor under their nose as you have them taste something else. For instance, put a dill pickle under the nose while the child is tasting an orange slice. ''Does the smell make it harder to know what you've tasted?'' Talk about how smell affects our sense of taste.

Senses Flash

Using pictures cut out from magazines, have the children decide what sense would be involved to experience the picture. Cards of each of the five senses should be available. (Paper plates like those used on the bulletin board may be used effectively.) Hold up the card that the children name for each picture. Some children may begin to read those words. Some children may discover that pictures may use two or more senses. Ask the children to explain the reason for their answers.

Riddles

Make up riddles with one of the senses as the answer. The children will enjoy making them up after they catch on to what you are doing.
Examples: ''My sense will help you tell if something is hot or prickly. What sense am I?'' ''Using my sense, a person can tell if something is music or noise. What sense am I?''

Hard or Soft

Prepare two shallow boxes. Print the word ''soft'' in the bottom of one box and the word ''hard'' in the bottom of the other. Glue a picture of a stuffed animal with the word ''soft'' and a picture of a rock or block with the word ''hard.'' Collect several objects for each category. Let the children take turns choosing an object and deciding the correct box in which to put it. After playing several times, this can become an activity for independent use. The children will enjoy a ''seek and find'' time to locate new objects in the room to use in the game.

FIVE SENSES

From *We Care*, Copyright © 1988 Scott, Foresman and Company.

Tactile Names

Provide each child with a card that has his or her name printed on it in large letters. Laminate each card. Give each child a portion of play dough (see Art Recipes). Let them roll small balls of dough into long snake shapes. They then form the dough over the letters on the card. You may use the name cards repeatedly to make play dough names.

MATH NUMBER CONCEPTS

Rings on Fingers

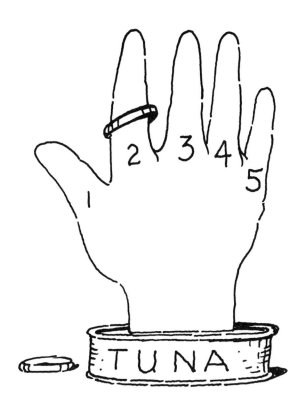

Cut an adult size hand from poster board. Leave a section of the arm to insert into plaster of paris in a small box or tuna can. Let the plaster of paris dry with the hand cutout in it, so the hand will be free-standing.

Print a numeral on each finger, starting at the left and going across in numerical order. Let the child or children take turns putting the correct number of rings on each finger. You can purchase rings in the party favor section of a discount store.

Variation: Put two cutouts side by side. Number across, left to right, from one to ten.

Number Necklace

Use push pins to pin number cards from one to five along the bottom of a bulletin board. Provide a bowl of *large* macaroni and five lengths of yarn. (For easier stringing, dip the ends of the yarn in glue and dry overnight, or tape around one end of each yarn.) Working independently, the child strings onto each length of yarn the number of macaroni pieces indicated by the card. You assist by tying the yarn into a knot. Then, hang the necklace on the appropriate push pin with the appropriate number card.

Math Movement

The children take turns doing a movement, such as hopping or jumping jacks or marching, while the remainder of the children count as the child does the movement. When the child stops, the children tell how many times he/she did the movement. Then, the other children repeat the movement the same number of times, while you and the child count. Change leaders and repeat the game.

Tactile Numeral Cards

Prepare cards with sandpaper numerals and/or glue numerals from one to five or more as appropriate for your group. After the glue drys, the children can close their eyes and trace each numeral with their fingers.

Note: You can obtain a thicker line of glue by squeezing glue from a liquid dishwashing soap bottle. Also, you may use nubby upholstery fabric for making the numerals.

MATH VOCABULARY

Long—Short

1. Using objects within the classroom, you and later the children make up riddles about long or short items. You may give clues until someone guesses the object.
2. The children may also play the game "Mother, May I?" and take either long or short steps.

MOVEMENT

Wiggle Time

Wiggle your shoulders,
Wiggle your nose,
Wiggle your fingers,
Wiggle your toes.
Now wiggle, wiggle all of you,
From the top of your head to the tip of your shoe!

Stretching

Stretch up, up we go.
Stretch way up above your nose.
Bend over, down we go.
Stretch way down and touch your toes.

FIVE SENSES

**All the Colors
Sit Down**

Pat your tummy if you have on red.
If you're wearing yellow, shake your head.
Find something black and make a big frown.
All the colors sit down!
Wave both arms if you have on blue,
Spy something green and tap your shoe.
Bend way over if orange is what you see.
All colors down and count to three!

Parachute Fun

Use a flat bedsheet if you don't have access to a parachute. For all parachute activities, the children hold the parachute with a thumbs-up grip. That means the fists are under the parachute or sheet and the thumbs are on the top. You may do the parachute activities indoors or out.

1. The children sit or stand while holding the parachute with a thumbs-up grip. They take turns calling out a number between one and five (or more). Then, they all *gently* flick the chute that number of times while counting. This should be a slow moving activity.
2. Billow up the parachute. Call out one child's name. That child tries to run to the center and back before the chute falls. To enhance the fun, put an object on the floor in the center. The child tries to grab the object and get out before the chute falls.
3. Use a lightweight ball or beach ball to roll around on top of the parachute. See how long the children can keep it rolling while keeping it on the chute.
4. Hold the chute while doing exercises. Open and close feet and legs; bend at waist and touch chute to toes; hop on one foot; swing legs in and out. Let the children suggest other exercises.

MUSIC

Rhythm Instruments

1. Use the rhythm instruments to let the children accompany a record.
2. Use the instruments for the children to copy a simple rhythm pattern played by you.
3. Use the instruments to make a high and a low sound.

Make Some Music

(Tune: "She'll Be Coming Around the Mountain")

Let's make music with our fingers; go rap, rap, rap.
   (Drum fingers on some surface.)
Let's make music with our fingers; go rap, rap, rap.
Let's make music with our finger; let's make music with our fingers,
Let's make music with our fingers; go rap, rap, rap.
2. Let's make music with our feet; go tap, tap, tap.
3. Let's make music with our hands; go clap, clap, clap.
4. Let's just put them all together; go rap, tap, clap.

FIVE SENSES

Put Your Finger

(Tune: "If You're Happy and You Know It")

Put your finger by your eye, by your eye.
Put your finger by your eye, by your eye.
Put your finger by your eye, and don't you tell a lie!
Put your finger by your eye, by your eye.

Put your finger on your cheek, on your cheek.
Put your finger on your cheek, on your cheek.
Put your finger on your cheek, but don't fall in the creek!
Put your finger on your cheek, on your cheek.

Put your finger on your ear, on your ear.
Put your finger on your ear, on your ear.
Put your finger on your ear and leave it there for a year!
Put your finger on your ear, on your ear.

Put your finger on your knee, on your knee.
Put your finger on your knee, on your knee.
Put your finger on your knee and pretend that you're a bee.
  (Wiggle bottoms and make a buzzing sound.)
Put your finger on your knee, on your knee.

ROLE PLAY

Appealing to Your Senses

Provide sunglasses, old glass frames with different colors of cellophane in them, play telephones or tin can and string telephones, and gloves of several different fabrics.

Eye Examination

Let the children role play checking each other's eyesight. Use a poster board and duplicate the Snellen sight chart that uses the letter "E" in different positions. A white jacket, a yardstick for a pointer, and an eye patch are a few props that might add to the fun.

Senses Museum

Set up one or more tables with multiple items to see, hear, touch and smell. (Avoid tasting at this time.) Provide a magnifying glass and stethoscope. One child may be the guide and show the other children (museum visitors) around the museum.

FIVE SENSES

SCIENCE

What Sound Is This?

Make a tape of sounds with which the children are familiar. Be sure to include animal sounds, if available. (Pet stores are a good place for recording some animal sounds.) Include high and low sounds, as well as loud and soft sounds. Play the tape, stopping after each sound to let the children identify it.

Sugar and Salt Mystery

Bring examples of both sugar and salt in unmarked containers. Set up the activity like a scientific experiment, by referring to the substances as "Sample A" and "Sample B." Spread a few grains of each on black construction paper. Ask leading questions of the children to spur curiosity. Is one larger than the other? Is the shape of A different from B? Do the grains have sides that we can see? Bring out a magnifying glass. Let each child look at both samples. Next, carefully smell each sample. Caution the children not to take a big sniff, for fear of inhaling the grains into the nostrils. Can the samples be identified by smell? Ask: "Is there any other sense we can use to find out what these are?" Someone should mention tasting. The mystery should then be solved!

February
Curriculum

1. Health and Nutrition

2. Valentines

3. Famous People and Birthdays

4. Care of Pets

Health and Nutrition

CONCEPTS

- Healthy people eat nutritious foods that provide energy and help them grow.
- A balanced diet includes foods from each of the four food groups: meat, dairy products, fruits and vegetables, and bread and cereals.
- Too much junk food—such as cookies, candy, and other sweets—is not good for our bodies.
- Doctors and dentists help to keep us healthy.
- Exercise, adequate rest, and a good night's sleep are important to keep bodies fit.
- Children can learn to keep themselves clean and healthy.
- February is National Dental Health month.

ART

Toothbrush Painting

Newsprint or manila paper; tempera paint; old toothbrushes.

The children use toothbrushes instead of paintbrushes to paint designs on paper.

Water Tempera

Paintbrushes; water; powdered tempera paint; paper.

Have the children dip a brush into water. Then, touch the damp brush in powdered tempera paint and paint. The water plus powdered tempera paint produces color with texture as the children paint. Have them wash their brush and repeat the process using another color.

Paper Mache Fruits and Vegetables

Newspaper; masking tape; 1 × 6 inch strips of paper for paper mache; wallpaper paste; paint.

Make the form for bananas, cucumbers, zucchini, carrots, apples, etc., by using crushed newspaper and taping it in shape. Paper mache around the form in several layers. Allow it to dry, then paint it with the appropriate colors.

Note: Two-year-olds may need help making the initial form resemble a fruit or vegetable shape, but they can definitely take it on their own after that.

Fruit Folks Puppets

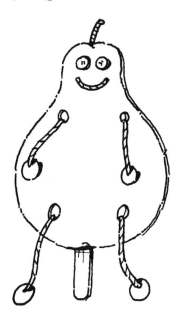

Fruit shapes—either precut or a pattern for children to trace and cut out; small buttons; markers; yarn; glue; popsicle sticks.

Provide the fruit shapes and have the children add eyes, nose, and mouth with small buttons or markers.

Punch two holes on each side of the fruit shape in the lower quarter and two holes on each side in the upper quarter. Thread a 6–8 inch piece of yarn through each set of holes for arms and legs. Glue small circles at the ends of the yarn for hands and feet. Glue a popsicle stick to the back to complete a Fruit Folks Puppet.

Floor Puzzle

Cut a large, simple shape, appropriate for health or nutrition, from a piece of cardboard. A tooth or fruit shape would work well. Let the group help paint the shape. Then, cut it into as many pieces as appropriate for challenging the children. Try to make interesting and distinct pieces, so children recognize how to match them together. Store in a zip-lock bag or small box.

Happy Teeth Toothbrush

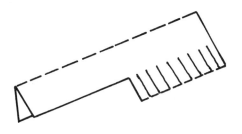

12 × 18 inch construction paper; 1½ × 8 inch white paper strips; glue; scissors; gummed stars.

The children fold the construction paper in half the long way. They then glue the white paper strip between the pieces of construction paper. The children fringe the white paper strip so it resembles a brush. They complete the toothbrush by gluing the edges of the brush handle together. The children get to put on a gummed star every time they remember to brush their teeth. Talk about the importance of brushing their teeth.

Play Dough Foods

Cookie cutters; play dough (see Art Recipes).

The children pat out the play dough and shape their favorite foods. Discuss what they make. Talk about why those are their favorite foods.

Carbon Paper Drawing

Carbon paper; manila paper or newsprint; crayons.

Place carbon paper between two pieces of paper. The children use crayons to create designs on their paper. Have them then lift off the top paper to see what designs they have created on the carbon drawing. You may place the carbon so that the design is copied on the back of the original drawing, if desired. Then, the children create a front and back drawing simultaneously.

3-D Circles

Multicolored construction paper strips of various lengths; glue or tape; manila or construction paper.

Let the children choose a variety of colors and lengths of strips. Demonstrate how to make a circle by gluing or taping the overlapped ends together. Allow the children to make all of their strips into separate circles. Glue or tape the circles to manila paper with some standing on their sides and some lying on edge. Circles arranged both ways on the paper will make an attractive three-dimensional display.

Pizza Pan Print

One or more pizza pans; mixture of ½ water, ½ honey, and a squirt of detergent; tempera paint; manila paper or newsprint; paintbrush.

Work on the *underside* bottom of the pan. Have the children brush the honey mixture all over the surface (to help the tempera paint adhere to the metal). Let them paint a picture or design with the tempera paint. Then, press the pan on a large paper to make a neat, round print of the picture.

Rubber Cement Magic Designs

Rubber cement; manila paper; tempera or watercolor paints.

The children use the rubber cement brush to paint rubber cement designs on the manila paper. Some children may wish to draw a healthy person or a fruit shape with the rubber cement. Let the rubber cement dry for one half hour. Then, have the children paint with tempera or watercolor paints. Encourage them to cover all of the paper with bright colors. When the paint is thoroughly dry, the magic starts! The children rub fingers over the rubber cement so it comes off, leaving a white design all through their painted creation.

Egg Carton Sculpting

Round toothpicks; cups cut from egg cartons; tops of egg cartons; scissors.

Provide the cut egg cups or let the children cut their own, if possible. Give each child an egg carton top to use as the base for the sculpture. The children use toothpicks to stick cups together and to stick them into the base, so the sculpture will stand up.

BLOCKS

Add-a-Block

All of the children put their chairs in a large semicircle around the block area. You start a structure with two or three blocks in the center of the block area. Then, call the children, one at a time, to add two or three blocks to the structure and sit back down and watch as other people take a turn. "What can the new structure be?" "What kind of blocks will Don add when it is his turn?" Your questions will help keep the children's interest while they await their turn.

BULLETIN BOARD

Take Care of Your Teeth

Print the caption "Take Care of Your Teeth" across the top of the board. Divide the bulletin board in half with a length of yarn. On one half, put the words "Happy Tooth" and display actual objects that promote healthy teeth, such as new toothbrush, floss, X-rays from a dentist, pictures of nutritious foods, toothpaste, and fluoride rinse. On the other half, put the words "Sad Tooth" and display gum, candy bars, worn out toothbrush, soda can, and cake and cookie wrappers.

Provide a tooth pattern and have the children use markers to make a happy tooth and a sad tooth. Display their creations around the outside of the bulletin board.

My Wonderful Body

Print the caption "My Wonderful Body" across the top of the board. Put up a large cutout of a child. Have pieces of yarn connecting body parts to callouts for each part.

Provide a separate cutout of the heart, lungs, and stomach. Let the children take turns using push pins to put the organs in the appropriate place on the child.

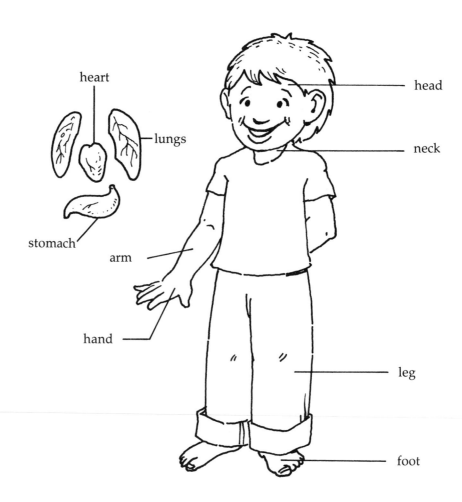

COOKING

Fantastic Fruit Fun

Each child contributes a piece of favorite fruit from home. (You might provide a fresh pineapple, strawberries, or blueberries.) Miniature marshmallows add fun to the salad. Wash hands. Have the children peel and cut up fruit in a large bowl. The children may cut soft fruit, such as bananas, orange sections, and strawberries, with a plastic knife. They will enjoy participating rather than just watching you do all the cutting. Mix the fruits together and enjoy.

Applesauce

½ apple for each child
1 cup cinnamon red hot candies
Water
Plastic or table knife
Waxed paper
Electric frying pan

Wash hands. Give each child a piece of waxed paper, a plastic knife, and half an apple with the seeds cut out. Let the children cut their apple into small pieces. (This is a safe cutting activity. It is fun and good eye-hand coordination practice for the children.)

Place all the apple pieces in the pan. Pour in the candies. Pour in just enough water to cover the apples. Cook at medium-high setting until apples are very soft—approximately 45 minutes.

Wonderful smells will fill the air. The taste is delicious!

Fruity Fondue

Ice cream topping (caramel is a good choice if some children have chocolate allergies)
Small individual bowls or paper cups for the topping
Toothpicks for each child

Cut a variety of fruits in bite-sized pieces and serve on plates in the center of the table, where all can reach them. Suggested fruits include: bananas, pineapple, strawberries, apples, or pears. Angel food cake also is a good choice.

The children use toothpicks for picking up fruit pieces. Children dip the fruit pieces in their own bowl of fondue sauce. Fruit flavored yogurt also makes an excellent fruit dip.

Ideas for Fun, Nutritious Snacks

1. Crackers with peanut butter topped with raisins or nuts.
2. Peanut butter stuffed celery with raisins on top. (Ants on a Log)
3. Peanut butter spread on a leaf of cabbage (rolled up).
4. Peanut butter, honey, and wheat germ mixed to make a spread for bread or crackers.

LANGUAGE ARTS

Books

Aemmer, Gail. *Good Health Fun Book.* Carson-Dellos, 1984.
Baldwin, Dorothy. *Your Body Fuel.* Bookwright Press, 1983.
Burshad, Carol. *Bodyworks.* Random House, 1981.
Carle, Eric. *What's for Lunch?* Philomel Books, 1982.
Keller, Irene. *The Thingumajig Book of Health and Safety.* Children's Press, 1982.
Moncure, Jane. *Healthkins Help.* Children's Press, 1982.

Moncure, Jane. *Magic Monsters Learn About Health.* Children's Press, 1980.
Peavy, Linda. *Food, Nutrition and You.* Scribner, 1982.
Rhodes, Janis. *Nutrition Mission.* Good Apple, 1982.
Sharmat, Mitchell. *Gregory, the Terrible Eater.* Four Winds Press, 1980.
Simon, Seymour. *Body Sense/Body Nonsense.* Lippincott, 1981.
Steig, William. *Doctor De Soto.* Farrar, Straus, and Giroux, 1982.
Williams, Barbara. *Albert's Toothache.* Dutton, 1974.

Teacher Resource Books

Write to the following addresses or contact a local dentist for free dental health materials.

1. American Dental Association
   Bureau of Dental Health, Education and Audio-Visual Services
   211 Chicago Avenue
   Chicago, IL 60611

2. Colgate-Palmolive Company
   300 Park Avenue
   New York, NY 10010

3. Lever Brothers Company
   390 Park Avenue
   New York, NY 10022

Frompovich, Catherine J. *Child's ABC's for Nutrition Coloring Book.* C.J. Frompovich, 1981.
Marbach, Ellen. *Nutrition in a Changing World.* Brigham Young Univ. Press, 1979.
Taylor, Clara. *An Annotated International Bibliography of Nutrition Education.* Teachers College Press, 1971.

Fingerplays

Where Is Your Mouth?

(Add motions as appropriate)

Where is your mouth? There is your mouth.
Let it open wide.
Where is your mouth? Look in my mouth.
How many teeth are inside?
   (Count teeth.)

Teeth

I use my teeth to chew my food.
   (Make a loose fist, then a chewing motion with fingers on top of thumb.)
I keep them very healthy.
I always brush them every day.
   (Pretend to brush, using finger.)
Now isn't that smart of me!
   (Smile proudly; point to self.)

HEALTH AND NUTRITION

Guest Speakers

Ask a dentist to speak to your class. Call to make arrangements well in advance. They will generally bring several props and handouts for the children.

Ask the school cook or a dietitian to talk to the children regarding the importance of a nutritious, balanced diet. Ask that speaker to emphasize the four food groups.

Healthy Teeth Mobile

Provide a large cutout of a healthy tooth and suspend it from the middle of a hanger. Hang actual dental objects from either side of the coat hanger to finish the mobile. Some ideas are toothbrush, toothpaste, floss, picture of nutritious food, and a dental mirror.

Visit to a Doctor's Office

Visit a doctor's office and look at all the equipment. Have the doctor tell how she/he uses each piece. The doctor may also show the children how she/he gives a health checkup.

Doctor's Bag

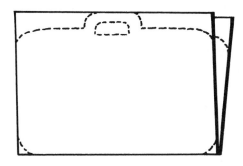

12 × 18 inch black construction paper; Band-Aids; cotton balls; tongue depressors; Q-Tips; syringes (needle removed).

Fold the paper in half to make a 12 × 9 inch rectangle. Round off the corners and cut out a handle. The children open the ''bag'' and glue the health items listed above on the inside of it. They then have a doctor's bag ready for role play. Print each child's name on the outside of the bag: ''Dr. Chris.'' Talk about how and why the doctor uses each item.

Oral Language Development

One of the goals of this unit is to introduce the children to the special nutrition vocabulary. A few suggestions include: food groups, nutrition, balanced diet, exercise, vitamins, dentist, toothbrush, mouthwash, floss, and dental mirror. Talk about junk food—what it is and why it is called ''junk food.''

Talk about the four food groups. Discuss the importance of eating something from each group every day. Talk about who likes what from each food group.

Nutrition Classification

Hang a large piece of butcher paper on the wall. Provide a wide selection of women's magazines for cutting out pictures of food. Use a marker to divide the paper into four sections: milk group, bread and cereal group, meat group, and fruit and vegetable group. Children cut out pictures and decide, as a class, where each food belongs. The children may take turns gluing the pictures in the appropriate classification.

Nutrition Completion

Laminate numerous individual food pictures from each of the food groups. On the flannel board, place several pictures of food that might be included in a balanced meal. Leave out items from one food group. Children decide which food to add to complete the meal. You can make this an individual activity or a class activity.

Logos

Use logos of foods and eating places. Have children identify familiar logos and make their own logo book.

Table Settings

Teach children to set the table correctly. Draw outlines of utensils on large construction paper. Children place corresponding items on the outlines.

Homemade Toothpaste

2 parts soda; 1 part salt; drop of oil of peppermint.

The children make their own toothpaste by combining the ingredients. Give small toothbrushes to the children and let them experiment with the proper way of brushing teeth.

Teeth Model

Pink posterboard; white egg cartons.

Cut out the egg cups. Cut a 12 inch long oval from the posterboard. Crease it in half width-wise to form the roof and bottom of a mouth. Staple the egg cups for teeth along each small end of the oval. Add a posterboard strip along the top to form the "gum."

With the model, show the children the most effective way to brush teeth. Use a nonpermanent marker to make "food particles" on the teeth. Let the children use a toothbrush covered with a piece of fabric to "brush the teeth clean."

Feel Box

Put personal care items, one at a time, inside the feel box for children to feel and identify. Use a toothbrush, comb, hairbrush, bar of soap, fingernail clippers, toothpaste tube, and barette.

Hand Cleanliness

Simple yet thorough handwashing is one of the best ways to keep disease from spreading throughout the class! Model careful hand cleanliness by always washing: 1) before eating or preparing food, 2) after toileting, and 3) after helping children in the bathroom.

Food Group Riddles

1. I'm in the bread and cereal group. I am in a loaf shape.
   You use me to make sandwiches. What am I? (Bread)
2. I'm in the dairy group. I'm white. People drink me out of a glass. What am I? (Milk)
3. I'm in the fruit and vegetables group. I am yellow and long. You peel me to eat me. What am I? (Banana)

Make up other riddles for the food the children like best.

MATH
NUMBER CONCEPTS

Fruits and Vegetables

1. Have real, plastic, or paper mache fruits and vegetables available. Ask the children to count them. Group them according to color and/or size. Count each group.
2. Have the children arrange them according to size, from smallest to largest.

Walking Math

As you're walking down the hall, count how many steps it is from your classroom to your destination. Also count the number of doors, doorknobs, and windows.

Worms in the Apple

1. Make several copies of the apple that's at the beginning of the February Curriculum unit. Make "worm" holes in each apple with a hole punch. The children hold up each apple and count the number of holes. Match each apple to a card with the appropriate numeral on it.
2. Have extra apple patterns available. Let the children take turns using the hole punch to make the number of worm holes dictated.

Bean Bag Toss

Provide two or three boxes or cartons with numerals printed on the sides. The child names a numeral and tries to throw the bean bag into the appropriate box.

HEALTH AND NUTRITION

Nutrition Graph

Tape to the wall a large piece of butcher paper or chart paper with a grid drawn on it. Print the number of children on one side and names of foods or food groups on the other. Tally the number of children that eat their meat, peas, corn, milk, etc., during lunch each day. Record the number on the graph by filling in the columns with different colors.

	1	2	3	4	5	6	7	8	9	10	11	12
meat												
milk												
bread												
potatoes												
corn												
peas												
jello												

Number of children

MATH VOCABULARY

Near—Far/Heavy—Light

1. Give each child real, plastic, or paper mache foods—such as cucumbers, corn, potatoes, apples, and oranges—to manipulate at the table. Give instructions: "Put the ear of corn far away from the edge of your table." "Put the potato near the green bean." "Move the cucumber far away from the apple."
2. Ask: "Which food is heavy, a banana or a bean?" "Which is light, a piece of bread or an apple?"
3. Hold a cotton ball contest. Children stand behind a mark and take turns tossing a cotton ball as far as they can. Measure or discuss which went the farthest.

MOVEMENT

Roll Ups

Roll fruits or vegetables across the room using different body parts:
"Use your elbow to roll this orange from the edge of the rug to the door."
"Use your nose to roll this cucumber...."

Ring Toss Game

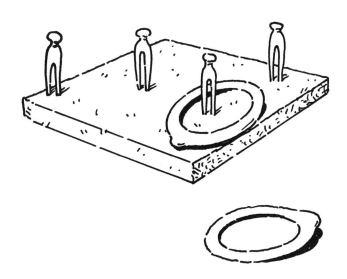

Styrofoam piece; non-pincher type clothespins; rubber canning-jar rings.

Push clothespins into the styrofoam so the rounded ends are standing up. The children stand near the game and try to toss rings underhanded onto the pins.

Variation: Place the game on the floor. The children stand over the game and try to drop the rings onto the pins.

Exercise Chant

Begin by asking children if they can jump and run. Explain that you can only do these if you are healthy. Ask them if they know what "healthy" means. Discuss. Run in place while you repeat the exercise chant.

Let's all run, run, run.
Because it's fun, fun, fun.
It's good for our legs.
It's good for our heart.
Let's exercise with a running start!

Food Acting

Pretend to be each of the suggested foods and do the appropriate movements or sound for each.

Bacon sizzling
Toast in the toaster—pop up
Popcorn popping
Jello—wiggle
Chocolate shake—shake
Fish—swim on the floor
Crab—crawl

HEALTH AND NUTRITION

257

MUSIC

Food Is Good

(Tune: "Twinkle, Twinkle Little Star")

Food is good for us you know,
It gives us energy and helps us grow.
So choose your food so carefully.
Make it as healthy as can be.
Food is good for us you know.
Nutritious food will help you grow.

Healthy Way

(Tune: "Mulberry Bush")

1. This is the healthy way we live.
2. This is the way we wash ourselves.
3. This is the way we comb our hair.
4. This is the way we brush our teeth.
5. This is the way we eat good foods.
6. This is the way we exercise.

Feather Game

Play soft, flowing music. Provide feathers. When the music plays, the children blow the feathers to keep them floating in the air. When the music stops, watch the feathers float down. Start the music again and repeat the process. Later, let the children act as if they were feathers. Move slowly to the music, then lie down. Stretch out and rest for a minute or so. Talk quietly about how bodies need rest to be healthy.

ROLE PLAY

Ready for School

Have available comb, brush, toothbrush, toothpaste, soap, washcloth, towel, mirror, tissue, and nail file. Discuss what each one is. Let the children role play getting up in the morning and doing what they should to get ready for school.

**Doctor's Office:
Time for a Physical!**

Let the children listen to their heartbeat, have their temperature taken, have their reflexes checked, be weighed and measured, and have their throat and teeth examined.

Give a balloon to each patient as they leave.

Restaurant

Provide a table and chairs, dishes, menus, napkins, and silverware. Help the children read the menu and order balanced meals.

Eye Doctor

Set out an eye chart, doctor's coat, flashlight, mirror, and empty frames of glasses. Talk about what an eye doctor does and discuss nearsightedness. Let the children role play getting an eye examination or buying glasses.

SCIENCE

Hearts

Bring in a live small animal, such as a guinea pig. Provide a stethoscope. Let the children listen to each other's heartbeat and to the heartbeat of the animal. Is one faster?

Weather Calendar

Help the children become more aware of the weather by making a weather calendar. Each day, have the children give the "weather report" by checking on the weather outside. Then, paste an appropriate symbol or two on each day: sun, rain, wind, clouds, etc.

Talk about the variety of the weather. Count the number of days you've had sun, wind, etc.

Steam

Demonstrate how steam can cook foods by steaming a few vegetables in the classroom. Be sure to taste the vegetables before and after steaming. Show the children the water in the bottom of the pan, with the steamer basket sitting in the water and the vegetables in the basket. Tell the children that the holes let the steam from the water through to cook the vegetable. Carefully take the lid off the pan to see the steam coming up. (Caution the children that steam can burn them.) Tell them more vitamins are left in the food with this cooking method.

Coughing Germs

Fill two deflated balloons with a little confetti. Inflate one balloon, being careful to remove your mouth each time you inhale. When it's inflated, quickly release the air from the balloon. Watch the confetti escape with the air. Tell the children that it is like germs, which spread when you cough.

Carefully inflate the second balloon. When you release the air from that one, place a tissue and your hand over the mouth of the balloon. This time, most of the confetti stays inside. Explain that covering your mouth when you sneeze or cough helps to keep most germs from spreading.

HEALTH AND NUTRITION

Valentines

CONCEPTS

- The tradition of sharing valentines is fun for young children.
- Friendship, sharing, and love should be the focus of the holiday.
- Traditional valentine colors are red, pink, and white.
- We have a heart inside our body, but the human heart does not look like a valentine.
- A balanced diet, exercise, and rest are important in caring for the heart.

ART

**Valentine Bags
(Easiest to slightly
more difficult)**

1. *Heart Collage Bag*
   White paper bags; small, precut, pink and red heart shapes of various sizes; glue.

   The children paste the precut pink and red hearts all over the bag. Print each child's name in large letters on the bag.

2. *Valentine Train Bags*
   White paper bags; 2 inch construction paper circles.

   The children paste two circles at the bottom of each bag for train car wheels. Then, they decorate the bags as desired. Print each child's name in large letters on the bag.

   You should make two paper bags yourself, one decorated as an engine and one as a caboose. Display all the class's bags in a line to make a train.

3. *Laced Plates Bag*
   White paper plates; hole punch; red yarn; crayons or construction paper hearts.

   Use one whole paper plate and half of a second paper plate. Punch holes around the edges of the plates. Children lace the plates together with red yarn to form a "pocket." Print each child's name in large letters on the bag. Decorate as desired with construction paper hearts or with crayons.

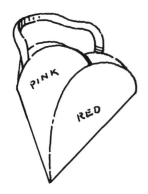

4. *Folded-Hearts Bag*
   9 × 9 inch red, white, and pink construction paper; glue; glitter.

   Each child uses one white or pink 9 × 9 inch construction paper and one red 9 × 9 inch construction paper. Cut as large of a heart as possible from each paper. Fold each heart in half. Overlap the halves and glue together to form a bag. Staple or glue on a handle. Print each child's name in large letters on the bag. Decorate with glue and glitter.

Valentine Piñata

Two <u>large</u> hearts cut from butcher paper; red tempera paint; pink and red tissue paper; glue; newspapers; yarn.

Have the children paint the two hearts. When they're dry, put the hearts together and staple around the edge, leaving an opening for stuffing. The children help wad up newspapers and stuff them inside the hearts. Add wrapped candy, gum, trinkets, etc. Staple the piñata shut and hang it from the ceiling to enjoy for a few days. (Reinforce the piñata with masking tape, in the area you punch the holes for hanging.)

Plan a Valentine's Day piñata party. Let the children take turns trying to break it by using a plastic bat or a stick. For safety, have all the other children *sitting* a safe distance away.

Two-for-One Hearts

One 6 inch and one 3 inch construction paper heart for each child; glue; glitter; candy conversation hearts; yarn.

The children apply glue in a free design on each heart. Sprinkle glitter on the glue, dry, and shake off the excess glitter. Next, the children glue the smaller heart to the middle of the large heart and glue a candy conversation heart to the center of the smaller heart. (Have enough candy so that the children may eat one piece and glue on one piece.) Punch a hole at the top of each finished heart and hang the hearts from the ceiling like mobiles.

Doily Prints

Paper doilies; white tempera paint; red construction paper.

The children gently paint lacy paper doilies with white paint. They then press the doily on red construction paper to leave a lacy print.

Heart Traces

Posterboard heart shapes of 4, 6, and 8 inches; crayons or markers; manila paper.

Show the children how to hold down the heart shape with one hand while drawing around it. Encourage them to use different colors of crayons or markers to draw around each heart. Encourage them to overlap the different heart sizes in a collage effect.

Stencil Painting

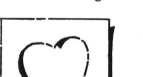

negative stencil

positive stencil

Posterboard for making heart-shaped stencils; red and pink construction paper; thin glue (mix 1/2 glue and 1/2 warm water in baby food jar); corn powder paint (mix one part of tempera paint powder and two parts of cornmeal; store in an old salt shaker or a spice jar).

When you cut a stencil, you actually get two: one positive and one negative stencil.
1. The children trace around the positive stencil on red paper, cut out the heart, and decorate it for valentines.
2. Place the negative stencil on pink construction paper. The children brush the stencil's heart-shaped opening with the thin glue. Then, they gently shake corn powder paint on top of the glue.

Let it dry. Then, lift off the negative stencil. Spray with hair spray to prevent flaking.

Heart Creatures

White, pink, and red construction paper; glue; crayons or markers.

Show children how to fold and cut hearts, or provide precut hearts in several sizes and in white, pink, and red colors.

As a class, experiment by arranging the hearts on a piece of paper so they form Heart Creatures: snowpeople, butterflies, people, animals, monsters, etc. Encourage children to try several different arrangements.

When children finish experimenting, have them glue their Heart Creature to a colored paper and add details (faces, hair, clothes, etc.) with crayons or markers.

VALENTINES

Heart Puppets

4 inch red construction paper hearts; popsicle sticks; crayons or markers; construction paper scraps; stapler.

The children decorate the hearts by coloring faces on them. Encourage the children to show different emotions on the faces—happy, sad, tired, scared. Use construction paper to add hair and other details. Then, staple each heart face to a popsicle stick to make a puppet.

Provide time for the children to play with their puppets, talking to other puppets about what made them feel the way they do.

Heart Fold-Overs

9 inch white construction paper hearts; red and pink tempera paint.

Show the children how to fold the hearts in half. Then, open the hearts and have the children use spoons or brushes to put dots of white, red, or pink paint on one side of the heart. Fold over and rub across the heart lightly to spread the paint. Open and lay aside to dry.

BLOCKS

Suggest that the children build a house or a store in the block area. Then, build a parking garage near the store and a parking lot far from the store. As they play, ask who is building with a heavy block and who is using a lighter block.

BULLETIN BOARD

A Valentine Means Love

Use heavy-duty aluminum foil to cut out two large heart shapes. Use construction paper or butcher paper to cut out two large pink heart shapes and two large red heart shapes. (If desired, use white butcher paper and have the children paint the hearts before assembling.) Staple each matching pair of hearts together, leaving an opening for stuffing. Let the children help lightly stuff each heart with newspapers or nylon hose. Staple the opening.

Staple or pin the three stuffed hearts on the bulletin board. Add the caption ''A Valentine Means Love'' at the top. Provide small hearts cut from white, pink, and red construction paper. Let the children cut out pictures of things they love and glue one on each small heart. Randomly arrange the small hearts all over the board. Outline the board with red and pink crepe paper or yarn, if desired.

Variation: Use photographs of the children. Place the photos on the small hearts.

COOKING

Rice Krispies Hearts

½ cup margarine
10 oz. pkg. marshmallows
Red food coloring
5 cups Rice Krispies cereal
Waxed paper

Melt margarine and marshmallows together. Cook over low heat for 3 minutes, stirring constantly.

Stir in red food coloring and cereal.

Cool slightly. Wash hands. Give a small amount to each child. Have each shape a heart on a waxed piece of paper. Eat!

If there is enough mixture, let each child mold an extra heart and wrap it in plastic wrap to *share* with someone else—perhaps in another class.

Cinnamon Hearts

2 pieces of bread per child
Heart-shaped cookie cutters
Butter
1 teaspoon cinnamon
½ cup sugar
Toaster oven

Wash hands. The children use the cookie cutters to cut hearts out of two pieces of bread. Then, they spread butter on the hearts.

Mix the cinnamon and sugar together and put it in an empty salt shaker. The children sprinkle the buttered hearts with the cinnamon sugar.

Toast in a toaster oven. Eat!

Valentine Cookies

Sugar cookie recipe or packaged cookie dough
Heart-shaped cookie cutters
Canned frosting
Red hot cinnamon candy or candy conversation hearts
Plastic knives

Wash hands. After following your own sugar cookie recipe or package dough directions, have the children use the cookie cutters to cut hearts out of the dough. Then bake the amount of cookies desired. Let the children spread frosting on the baked cookies and then decorate them with the candy.

LANGUAGE ARTS

Books

Cohen, Miriam. *Bee My Valentine!* William Morrow and Co., 1978.
Eastman, David. *I Can Read About My Own Body.* Troll Associates, 1973.
Gibbons, Gail. *The Post Office Book.* Harper and Row, 1982.
Glovach, Linda. *The Little Witch's Valentine Book.* Prentice Hall, 1984.
Hopkins, Lee Bennett. *Good Morning to You, Valentine.* Harcourt Brace Jovanovich, 1976.
Kelley, True. *A Valentine for Fuzzboom.* Houghton-Mifflin, 1981.
Kessel, Joyce K. *Valentine's Day.* Carolrhoda Books, Inc., 1981.
Krahn, Fernando. *Little Love Story.* Lippincott, 1976.
Moncure, Jane Belk. *Our Valentine Book.* Children's Press, 1976.
Sandak, Cass R. *Valentine's Day.* Franklin Watts, 1980.
Schultz, Gwen. *The Blue Valentine.* William Morrow and Co., 1979.
Schulz, Charles M. *Be My Valentine, Charlie Brown.* Random House, 1976.
Whitehead, Patricia. *Best Valentine Book.* Troll Associates, 1985.
Williams, Barbara. *A Valentine for Cousin Archie.* Dutton, 1981.

Teacher Resource Books

Burnett, Bernice. *Holidays.* Watts, 1983.
Chapman, Jean. *Pancakes and Painted Eggs: A Book for Easter and All the Days of the Year.* Childrens Press, 1983.
Corwin, Judith. *Valentine Fun.* J. Messner, 1982.
DePaola, Tomie. *Things to Make and Do for Valentine's Day.* Scholastic, 1985.
McGovern, Ann. *The Human Body.* Random House, 1965.
McGuire, Leslie. *Human Body Book.* Platt and Munk, 1977.
Quackenbush, Robert. *The Holiday Song Book.* Lothrop, Lee and Shepard, 1977.
Sarnoff, Jane. *Light the Candles! Beat the Drums! A Book of Holidays.* Scribner, 1979.

Fingerplays

Valentine Hearts

Three little hearts, happy all day;   (Hold up three fingers.)
One got a job and moved away.
Two little hearts, looking so neat!   (Two fingers.)
One got hungry and went home to eat.
One little heart, lonely and blue.   (One finger.)
I made him happy; I gave him to you!   (Point to child.)

(For extra fun, make finger puppet hearts to use while saying this fingerplay. Sew together the top and sides of two small hearts made from red felt.)

Heart Resources

Contact your local American Heart Association to learn what films and materials are available for your class's use.

Love Mobile

Use a dowel rod or clothes hanger to make the base. Use thread to hang 9 inch letters that spell "love." In the center, hang 6 inch hearts of white, pink, and red.

On the center hearts, you may write messages similar to those on the valentine candy hearts: "I love you," "hug me," "my friend," etc.

Discuss: Why does a heart shape mean love?

Field Trip

Visit a post office. Have children bring stamps from home and mail a valentine they have made to someone special.

Visit from a Mail Carrier

Invite a mail carrier to your class to show the children his/her uniform, bag, etc. Ask him/her to discuss the sequence of the mailing process: "How does a letter get from the mail box or post office to our house?"

Mail Call Game

Have the children *stand* in a circle. One child ("it") stands in the middle holding a valentine. Provide a spinner in the middle. The child spins the spinner. When it stops, the child "delivers" the valentine to the person nearest the spinner arrow by saying: "I have a valentine for _____ ." The child who was "it" sits down where the other child was standing. The second child now goes to the center to be "it." Repeat the game until everyone is *sitting* and has therefore had a chance to play.

This game is great fun and lets the children practice using each other's names.

Mail Carrier

Provide enough sacks so that each child has his/her name on one. Have a set of envelopes with a child's name on each. Let the children take turns being the mail carrier and matching some or all of the envelopes to the "mail sacks."

Variation: Have each child draw a picture of a house. Print the child's name on it in large letters. Use real envelopes. Write one child's name on each one. Children match the name on the envelope to the name on each house and take turns "delivering" the mail.

Happy Little Valentine

Let the group work together to dictate a creative chart story about the happy little valentine: where it goes, who sends it, who receives it, etc.

Loving, Caring, Sharing

Put up a 24 × 36 inch piece of paper with the label: "Loving, Caring, Sharing." Ask the children to find magazine and newspaper pictures that show people loving or caring or sharing. Glue the pictures on the paper.

To increase the interest, include on the collage some snapshots of children in the classroom helping and sharing with each other.

Hidden Message Hearts

Cut out large white hearts and smaller red hearts. Attach the two together with a brad.

Print a message on the white heart for each child. Hide the message by gently turning down the red heart.

Let the children decorate their hidden message hearts any way they please.

Mail Carrier

Shoeboxes; envelopes; marker.

Provide several shoeboxes or small boxes. Write a numeral on each. Provide a set of envelopes with a numeral written on each. The children ''deliver'' the mail (envelopes) by matching the numerals and placing the envelope in the correct box.

Valentine Jump

Each child has a valentine with a numeral on it. You hold up a numeral. The child holding that numeral jumps that number of times. Any other movement may be substituted, such as clapping, nodding head, turning around, etc.

Variation: Instead of numerals, put shapes on each valentine. The child holding that shape gets to jump, clap, etc., three times.

Felt Hearts

Make a set of red felt hearts. Add one at a time to a flannel board as students count. Older students may be able to take away one at a time and count backwards.

See ''Valentine Hearts'' Fingerplay (in LANGUAGE ARTS section) and ''Ten Pretty Valentines'' (in MUSIC section)

**Measurement—
The Weight of a Heart**

Almost everyone's heart is about the same size and weighs less than one pound. Use a scale to show the children about how big one pound is. Use a ball of play dough. Adjust the amount until the play dough ball measures one pound.

Size Relationships

Cut positive and negative stencils of hearts in four sizes.

The children match each positive stencil to the negative stencil of the same size—like a puzzle.

Arrange the stencils in smallest to largest order. Have children trace them on a paper in that order.

Arrange the stencils in largest to smallest order. Trace on paper.

Whole—Half

1. Fold hearts in half. Discuss whole; one half.
2. Cut snacks in half. Count how many pieces.

Near—Far

Lay valentines with numerals printed on them around the classroom floor. You call out a number and someone's name. The class or the child decides if that child is near or far from the valentine designated by you.

MOVEMENT

Floor Valentines

Two children lie down with their arms stretched out and curved over their heads. Have them gradually curve their legs and arms toward each other until they touch to form a valentine shape.

Bean Bag Toss

Cut out a large valentine shape and tape it on one end of a box. Put the box in a corner or low-traffic area. Let the children take turns tossing two or three bean bags into the valentine box.

Variation: Make heart-shaped bean bags by cutting out two heart-shaped pieces of red felt, sewing the edges together around three-quarters of the outside, filling the bags with rice, styrofoam, or dried beans, and sewing the remaining edges together.

Valentine Hop

Scatter several large valentine cutouts on the floor. Let the children hop from one to another. Vary the activity by using different movements: walk, slide, crawl, etc.

Hopping to Stay Healthy

(Tune: "Mulberry Bush")

Here we go hopping 'round the room,
'Round the room, 'round the room.
Here we go hopping 'round the room.
It's fun to exercise.

Variation: Substitute any other action word, such as jogging, walking, marching, etc.

MUSIC

Musical Chairs

Play a record. Have the children stop on hearts arranged in a circle on the floor.

Ten Pretty Valentines

(Tune: ''Ten Little Indians'')

One pretty, two pretty, three pretty valentines.
Four pretty, five pretty, six pretty valentines.
Seven pretty, eight pretty, nine pretty valentines.
Ten valentines today.

Ten pretty, nine pretty, eight pretty valentines.
Seven pretty, six pretty, five pretty valentines.
Four pretty, three pretty, two pretty valentines.
One valentine today.

   Have ten children stand in a row, each holding a valentine with a numeral from 1-10 on it. Let them sit down as their number is sung and stand up as the numbers are sung backwards.

Delivering a Valentine

(Tune: ''Mulberry Bush'')

   The children stand in a circle. One child walks around the circle and delivers the valentine to another child. The child who delivered the valentine sits down, and the receiver continues the game. Repeat the song until all have played.

Delivering a valentine, valentine, valentine!
Will you be my valentine
And be a friend to me.
Yes, I'll be your valentine, valentine, valentine.
It's fun to get a valentine,
As you can see.

Valentine's Day

(Tune: ''Muffin Man'')

Oh, will you be my valentine, valentine, valentine.
Will you be my valentine and play with me each day.

Oh, yes, I'll be your valentine, valentine, valentine.
Yes, I'll be your valentine and play with you each day.

   Variation: Let the children talk about things they enjoy doing with a friend. Sing the song and substitute other words for ''play,'' such as skate, eat, read, etc.

ROLE PLAY

**Mail Carrier
Delivering Mail**

   Any old large purse becomes a ''mail bag'' when the imaginations of young children are turned loose. Ask parents to provide their throwaway ''junk'' mail from home to add to the fun.

Giving and Receiving Courtesy

Children learn through positive models how to act courteously.

Role play giving and receiving a valentine or sharing pieces of candy.

What we say makes people feel good or bad: "What are good things to say?" Try to stretch children's talk beyond a simple thank you and you're welcome. "What else could we say when someone gives us something?"

Heart Checkup

Let the children role play going to the doctor for a heart checkup. Provide a stethoscope to use to listen to heartbeats.

SCIENCE

Mixing Colors: Red + White = Pink

1. Finger paint with white and red. Discuss with the children what is happening to the colors.
2. *Color Blendings*
   Wet paper towels. (Put a pad of newspaper underneath to protect table surfaces.) Put drops of red paint or food coloring on the wet towel. Watch how it spreads. Add drops of white. Discuss the color blendings.
3. *Play Dough* (four- to five-year olds)
   Make a batch of play dough (see Art Recipes) without adding any color, so it remains white. Give a quarter-sized ball to each child. Let each child push a thumb hole into the ball. Put a drop of *red food coloring* in the thumb hole. Let children squeeze and work the dough until the color is mixed in.

   Watch the dough change from white to pink. Add another drop of red coloring to make a brighter red play dough.

Does a Real Heart Look Like a Valentine?

Show a picture or drawing of a real human heart. (Check in an encyclopedia or in the materials from the American Heart Association.) Talk about how the heart looks a little like a valentine shape. Talk about the ways the heart looks different from a valentine.

Make a chart on which you list all the differences stated by the children.

Why Does a Heart Make a Sound?

Listen to each other's chests to hear the heart beating. Talk about a stethoscope and how it helps doctors to hear heartbeats more clearly.

Discuss how the beating is the sound the heart makes as it pumps our blood all through our bodies.

Famous People and Birthdays

CONCEPTS

- "Famous" means that many people know about a person and usually know what that person has done.
- President Lincoln and President Washington are famous people whose birthdays are celebrated in February.
- Birthdays of many famous people are celebrated as holidays.
- Our birthday is a special day for all of us.

ART

Happy Birthday, Mr. Washington and Mr. Lincoln

2 half-sheets of manila paper per child; markers or crayons.

Fold the manila paper in half. Let the children decorate a birthday card for each famous president. These cards may be displayed on a bulletin board surrounding a large silhouette of each.

Un-Birthday Card for Other Famous People

½ piece of manila paper per child; markers or crayons.

Have the children each think of a person who is special to them. Fold the paper in half. Decorate an un-birthday card for that famous person. You may write a caption for the card, if the child requests.

Un-Birthday Cake Festival

One cake pattern; construction paper; 2-6 halves of straws per child; yellow construction paper scraps; crayons or markers; glue.

The children each cut out and decorate an un-birthday cake. They glue the number of straws in place on the top of the cake to show how old they are. Cut or tear a flame for each candle using the yellow construction paper scraps. Tape each flame to the "candle." You may print the child's name and actual birthdate on the cake, if desired. Display in a group on the wall, or tape the cake to the back of each child's chair.

Three-Cornered Hats

Three 8½ × 5 inch blue or brown construction paper strips per child; 3-8½ × ½ inch yellow strips per child; scissors; crayons or markers; stapler; glue.

The children glue the yellow strip along the top edges of the rectangles. Staple the rectangles together to form a triangular, three-cornered hat.

Variation. Make newspaper hats using the pattern at the end of this section.

Splatter Painting

Dress box; screening; old toothbrushes; posterboard silhouettes of Lincoln and Washington (see pattern at end of section); tempera paint; manila paper.

Lay the silhouettes on the manila paper in the bottom of the box. Lay the screening on top of the box. Let the children paint by brushing paint-filled tooth-brushes over the screen.

Famous Cherry Tree

1 piece of blue construction paper per child; 1 large twig or part of a small limb (to fit on paper)) per child; 2 × 3 inch pieces of red tissue paper; crayons: glue.

Have the children color some grass or ground at the bottom of the construction paper. Glue the ''tree'' on the paper. Wad up pieces of red tissue paper and glue them on the ''tree'' or paper to look like cherries.

Finger Painting Silhouettes

Black finger paint (2 inch ''drop'' of liquid starch sprinkled with dry black tempera powder).

Put the starch and tempera powder in the center of each child's paper. They mix the tempera powder into the starch with their fingers and proceed to finger paint.

After each painting is dry, cut it into the silhouette of either Lincoln or Washington (see pattern).

Variation: Cut out a silhouette of Lincoln or Washington. The child uses the framed outline of the silhouette to glue onto the black finger painting. The frame makes the silhouette appear as if it were finger painted.

Un-Birthday Tree

A bare tree branch (painted, if desired) "planted" in an ice cream container using rocks, dirt, or plaster of paris; empty toilet paper rolls, 1 or 2 per child; scraps of yellow construction paper; tempera paint; glue; yarn.

The children paint the tree and a toilet paper roll and allow them to dry. Cut a "flame" from a scrap of yellow construction paper. You write the name and birthday of the child on one side of the flame. You may write the name of another famous person (Martin Luther King, etc.) on the other side, if the child wishes. Glue the flame on the top of the toilet paper roll to make an un-birthday candle. Attach a piece of yarn. Hang the candles on the tree.

Framing Lincoln

One Silhouette of Lincoln per child; one piece of manila paper per child; twigs; glue.

Glue the silhouette of Lincoln on the manila paper. As a class, go for a walk to find twigs to make a pretend log frame around the picture. The children glue the twigs around the edge of the manila to resemble a log frame.

Personal Stamps or Money

6 inch posterboard circle to design a coin; 8 x 3 inch posterboard rectangle to design a bill; 3 x 3 inch square posterboard to design a stamp; paper; crayons or markers; Washington and Lincoln postage stamps; camera (optional).

Show the children how pictures of famous people are printed on both stamps and money. Especially show children samples of postage stamps and paper money bearing Lincoln's and Washington's pictures.

Give each child a blank sheet of paper and let each design a stamp or money by tracing a posterboard shape. Decorate with crayons or markers.

Variation: Take snapshots of each child to form the center of each stamp or dollar bill! Special!

George Washington's Wig

One black construction paper silhouette of George Washington (see pattern) per child; glue; cotton balls; yarn.

Give each child a cutout silhouette of George Washington. You outline the hairline with a piece of yarn glued in place. The children glue cotton balls to the black silhouette. Encourage the children to glue the cotton balls on the appropriate side of the yarn, so it looks like a wig on his head.

FAMOUS PEOPLE AND BIRTHDAYS

Lincoln 'n' Logs

Half-pint milk carton for each child (empty and clean); box of popsicle sticks (found at craft stores); glue.

Staple the milk carton closed. The children then glue the sticks to the sides and top of the milk carton. Encourage the children to glue the sticks with the edges touching so they look like logs on a log cabin. Let dry overnight. The children may then paint the log cabin, if desired.

Lincoln—Washington Rubbings

Pennies; nickels; old crayons with the paper removed; newsprint.

Show the children how to place a coin under their paper and carefully rub over the coin make a rubbing. Move the coins and use another color. Rub again. Let the children continue until the paper is covered. Encourage them to overlap the coins to add to the interesting effect.

BLOCKS

Build a cabin or house with blocks or Lincoln Logs, if available. Talk about building outside with real logs to make a real cabin: "Would real logs be heavy or light?"

If possible, visit a construction site where a house is being built. Ask the children how boards used today in house-building are different from logs: "Are the boards heavy for the builders to handle?"

BULLETIN BOARD

Happy Birthday to All of Us!

Pin up silhouettes of Washington, Lincoln, and other famous faces that the children would recognize. Use red, white, and blue crepe paper streamers for a border. Add more visual interest with red, white, and blue balloons taped to the bulletin board. Put a large birthday cake in the center, using straws with a construction paper flame for candles. Tack white stars randomly all over the board, with a picture of each child taped to a star.

Washington Cherry Tarts

(This recipe makes a *delicious* dough that small hands can handle.)

8 oz. cream cheese—cut into 16 equal parts
2 sticks of margarine—cut each into tablespoon slices (8 slices per stick)
2 cups flour (equals 32 tablespoons of flour)
1 can cherry pie filling

Give each child the following amounts to make one individual muffin-tin tart:

1 piece of cream cheese
1 tablespoon slice of margarine
2 tablespoons flour

Wash hands. Put the ingredients in small bowls. Let the children mix their own ingredients until a smooth dough ball is formed. Then, press the dough into a tart shape in a muffin tin.

Fill each tart with the canned cherry pie filling. Bake at 350° for 29 minutes.

Famous Milk

(A famous drink for special people.)
Individual recipe:

1½ teaspoons honey
Pinch of cinnamon
1 glass cold milk
Food coloring, if desired

Stir and drink.

Lincoln Logs

Individual recipe:

1 clean piece of celery
1 tablespoon peanut butter
1 teaspoon honey

Wash hands. In a small bowl, mix the honey and peanut butter. Fill the celery stick with the peanut butter mixture.

Un-Birthday Cake Cones

Prepare one cake mix according to directions. Fill 20-24 flat-bottomed ice cream cones about two-thirds full. Bake 20 minutes at 350°.

Invite another class to share a glass of Famous Milk and Un-Birthday Cake Cones.

FAMOUS PEOPLE AND BIRTHDAYS

Candy Axe

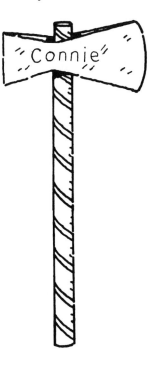

One wrapped peppermint stick per child; two axe cutouts per child.

Cut axe head patterns from a piece of construction paper. Glue the ends together, leaving the center free to put a candy stick through. Print the child's name on the axe head and insert a candy stick. Use as a place card at the unbirthday celebration. (Discuss why the axe is a symbol for George Washington.)

LANGUAGE ARTS

Books

Bains, Rae. *Abraham Lincoln.* Troll Associates, 1985.
Behrens, June. *Martin Luther King, Jr.: The Story of a Dream.* Children's Press, 1979.
Blocksma, Mary. *Grandma Dragon's Birthday.* Hampton-Brown, 1983.
Bulla, Clyde R. *Lincoln's Birthday.* Harper and Row, 1966.
Bulla, Clyde R. *Washington's Birthday.* Harper and Row, 1967.
Calmenson, Stephanie. *The Birthday Hat.* Putnam Publishing Group, 1983.
d'Aulaire, Ingri and Edgar Parin. *George Washington.* Doubleday and Co., Inc., 1936.
Glovah, Linda. *The Little Witch's Birthday Book.* Prentice-Hall, 1981.
Hutchins, Pat. *Happy Birthday, Sam.* Puffin Books, 1978.
Iwaski, Chihiro. *The Birthday Wish.* McGraw-Hill Book Co., 1972.
Jaynes, Ruth. *What Is a Birthday Child?* Bowmar Publishing Co., 1967.
Koral, Belle. *George Washington, Father of Our Country.* Random House, 1954.
Lorian, Nicole. *A Birthday Present for Mama.* Random House, 1984.
Moncure, Jane Belk. *Our Birthday Book.* The Child's World, 1977.
Moskin, Marietta. *Rosie's Birthday Present.* Atheneum, 1981.
Oxenbury, Helen. *The Birthday Party.* Walker Books, 1983.
Pomerantz, Charlotte. *The Half-Birthday Party.* Clarion, 1984.
Richards, Dorothy F. *Abe Lincoln, Make It Right!* Child's World, 1978.
Rockwell, Anne and Harlow Rockwell. *Happy Birthday to Me.* Macmillan, 1981.
Shannon, George. *The Surprise.* Greenwillow, 1983.

Teacher Resource Books

D'Amato, Janet and Alex. *Colonial Crafts for You to Make*. Julian Messner, 1975.
Hoople, Cheryl. *The Heritage Sampler, A Book of Colonial Arts and Crafts*. Dial Press, 1975.
Kay, Helen. *Lincoln: A Big Man*. Hastings House, 1958.
McGovern, Ann. *If You Grew Up With Abraham Lincoln*. Four Winds Press, 1966.
Ostendorf, Lloyd. *A Picture Story of Abraham Lincoln*. Lothrop, Lee, Shepard Co., 1962.

Picture People

Use pictures of famous people the children will recognize— perhaps Martin Luther King, the President, or some Sesame Street characters. Cut each picture into four equal quarters. As the children put the picture people back together like puzzles, discuss top, bottom, and parts of a face.

Lincoln and Washington Silhouettes

Using the silhouettes pattern, discuss what it means to be president of the United States. Talk briefly about Lincoln and Washington as people who were presidents and helped their country.

Cut each silhouette into four simple pieces for children to put together like a puzzle. If a child works the puzzle with ease, cut one or two of the large pieces in two so the puzzle has more pieces to manipulate.

Lincoln and Washington Match

Show the children detailed, full-face, and profile pictures of these famous people. Discuss their features, using as much "face" vocabulary as possible: face, nose, beard, hair, eyes, mouth, etc.

Compare the full-face pictures with the silhouettes. Play a game in which you hold up one picture and the children match it to the correct silhouette.

Mobile of Famous Faces

Discuss what it means to be famous. Ask each child to bring in a picture (from a magazine or newspaper) of a famous person. Have each child tell the class who that person is and why/how that person is famous. Hang the pictures on a class mobile of famous faces.

VIP Awards

One 3 inch posterboard circle or square per child; one 5 inch length of blue ribbon (available from a florist) for each child; tape; safety pins; crayons.

Explain that "VIP" means "very important person." "Famous people are VIPs, and so are the children in this class! You are a very important person to me!"

Print the child's name at the top of a circle or square. Have the children draw their picture on the shape.

Cut out strips of blue ribbon. (You may use paper, but fabric will be more special.) Tape a ribbon on the back of each award. Also tape on a *safety pin*.

Children love to wear these VIP Awards!

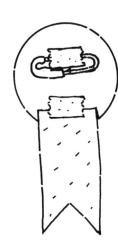

Log Cabins

Talk about logs, log cabins, etc. If possible, take a field trip to see an actual log house. Show pictures of log cabins to the class.

Quill Writing Pens

Stiff feather; bottle of ink or paint; typing paper.

Show the children how to dip the point of the feather into the ink. A very small amount of ink is all they need. Let the children write with the quill until the ink is gone. The children may practice writing their names or may write a famous person's name.

Talk about how quill pens were used for writing when Washington and Lincoln were presidents. Have the children discuss their thoughts on why we don't use quill pens today.

MATH

Counting Fun

1. Use the children's faces and bodies to talk about sets and to do counting activities.
   "What do we have on us that is in two's?"
     (eyes, ears, hands, etc.)
   "What do we have that is in five's?"
     (fingers, toes)
   "What do we have that is just one?"
     (mouth, tummy, nose, etc.)
   "What do we have that is more than one or two or five?"
     (teeth, hairs, freckles, etc.)
2. Count the number of faces in your class. Number of hands. Number of eyes. "Can we count the number of hairs on all of us?"
3. Provide a supply of pennies and put them in the center of the table. On several small pieces of paper, write one numeral that the children know or are ready to learn. Put all the papers in a small container. The children take turns drawing one piece of paper from the container. Each child counts out the required number of pennies from the center of the table. Return the pennies to the center pile after each turn.

Size Discrimination Game

Draw three simple tree shapes: small, medium, and large. Cut several red cherries: small, medium, and large. Store the tree shapes and the cherries in a small, flat box. Children place the appropriate size of cherries on the proper size of tree. When complete, have them "pick" the cherries and return them to the game box.

Cakes and Candles

Cut cake shapes from construction paper. Decorate them with markers, if desired. Write one numeral, 0 - 5 or higher, on each cake and laminate them to preserve them. Provide a bowl of real birthday candles. The children lay the appropriate number of real candles on each cake.

MATH VOCABULARY

Near—Far/Short—Long

Give each child a piece of manila paper and crayons or markers. You may use the chalkboard or chart paper to demonstrate. Instruct the children to draw a long log and a short log. Then, draw a circle *near* the long log and two cherries *far* from the short log. Continue with instructions to draw simple objects using the terms "near," "far," "long," and "short."

MOVEMENT

Obstacle Game

Set up this obstacle course right in the classroom. Great fun during an un-birthday celebration!

1. A tunnel of chairs lined up. Line up chairs with the seats alternately facing each other. Children may walk on seats, with or without your hand, but you *must* be there constantly.
2. Sheets draped over the table, under which children may crawl.
3. A balance beam, either flat on the floor or off the floor, depending on expertise of the children.
4. Stairs (if available).
5. Rope or broomstick for ducking under.
6. A ladder, flat on the floor, for stepping in and out. The ladder may be laid across two folding chairs for children to crawl across on the rails. Constant supervision is required.
7. A low wall of blocks for jumping over.
8. A fishnet tied to the legs of four chairs, to make a low crawl course.

MUSIC

Happy Birthday

Sing "Happy Birthday" to Lincoln and Washington. Have a special snack time birthday celebration for the presidents. Prepare Washington Cherry Tarts and Famous Milk (see COOKING).

Marching

Play a march record. Let the children wear their three-cornered hats or newspaper hats and march in time.

The Un-Birthday Song

Sing the song and prepare for an un-birthday party (see COOKING).

(Tune: "Yankee Doodle")

Birthdays come but once a year.
We jump and shout and give a cheer.
But un-birthdays are special too.
Hip, hip, hooray, happy day to you!

Un-birthdays are lots of fun.
Happy birthday everyone.
Un-birthdays are lots of fun.
Let's sing and play together.

ROLE PLAY

TV

Pretend to be actors on television. Who do you want to be? Let children act out a part for a few seconds. The rest of the class decides whether they were acting happy, sad, scared, etc.

Presidents

What would you do if you were president of our country? Act out some of the things a U.S. president has to do: sign papers, lead meetings, appear on TV, be interviewed by the newspaper, etc.

Birthday Party

Provide empty boxes to wrap in wrapping paper for presents. Let the children pretend to serve refreshments at a party.

SCIENCE

Shadows

A silhouette is really a shadow of a person.
Use flashlights to make shadows of things in the room. If it's sunny, explore shadows outside. ''What makes a shadow?'' ''Can shadows move?''
Make silhouettes of the children in the class.

Lincoln's Light

If possible, bring to class an old-fashioned hurricane lamp. Discuss what it would be like if this kind of lamp were our source of light. President Lincoln read many books when he was a boy, using an oil lamp for light. Darken the room and light the lamp to see how much light it provides.

Silhouettes

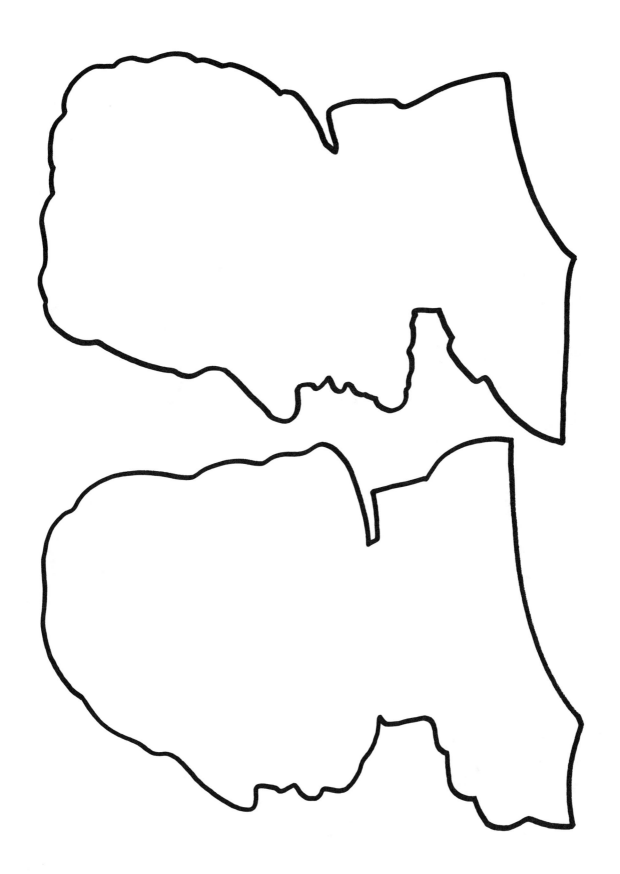

A Newspaper Hat

Directions: Use a double sheet of 30 × 23 inch newspaper.

Step 1. Fold corners to center.

Step 2. Fold up brim making a three-cornered hat.
Staple brim and folds in place.

Step 3. Decorate with markers and glitter.

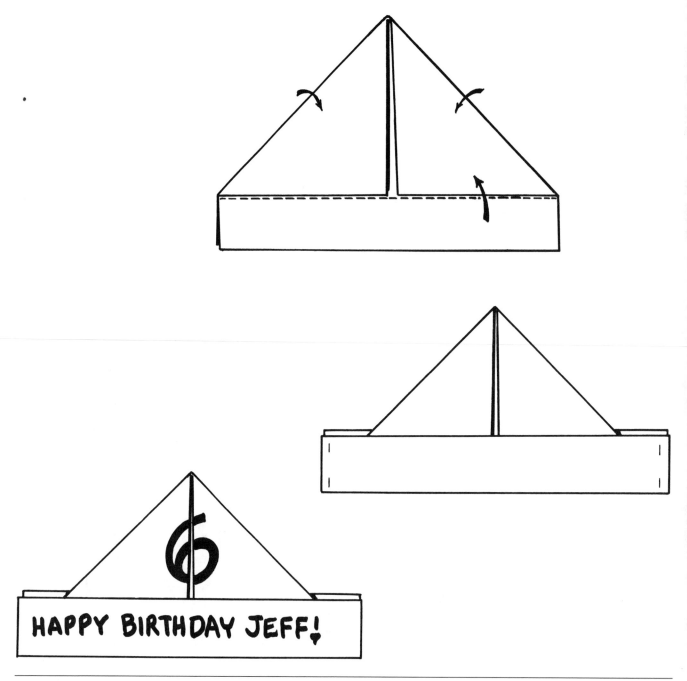

FAMOUS PEOPLE AND BIRTHDAYS

Care of Pets

CONCEPTS

- A pet is a tame animal that is taken care of and usually kept at a home because someone likes it.
- Pets need food, water, love, and sometimes special equipment, such as tanks and cages, in order to survive and be happy.
- Veterinarians are doctors who care for sick and well pets.
- The most popular pets are dogs, cats, fish, birds, hamsters, gerbils, and guinea pigs.
- Pets always need to be handled carefully and gently.

ART

Class Pet Bean Bag Pillow

Fake fur; styrofoam packing pieces; two or three ping pong balls; red felt scrap; black marker; sewing machine.

As a group, choose an animal to make as a class pet. On butcher paper, draw a *large* outline of the animal to use as a pattern. Cut two of that shape out of the fake fur. Sew around the outside edges, leaving an opening for stuffing.

Let the children help stuff the animal with styrofoam pieces. Sew the edges closed. (It's probably easiest to do this by hand, since the stuffed animal will be harder to handle at the sewing machine.) Four- and five-year-olds may take turns helping to sew the final closure using a large needle, if supervised.

Use the marker to color one ball black for the nose, if appropriate for pet choice. Color large pupils on each of the other balls to make google eyes. Glue the eyes and nose on the pet. Add other details as desired.

Make a collar for your pet and give it a name. Place it in a corner, where children may lie on it to enjoy a book or quiet moment.

Fur Finger Puppets

Fake fur scraps; for eyes, use buttons with a sequin glued in the center, construction paper circles, or purchased google eyes; felt scraps for nose, mouth, and ears; access to sewing machine.

Use a 2 by 3 inch piece of fake fur for each puppet. Use a sewing machine to stitch around three sides of the puppet, as illustrated. The children may then glue the facial features on the puppet.

Ask the children to tell what kind of pet they have made. Also, ask them to name their pet. Encourage complete sentences.

Pet Graffiti
(Group Project)

24 × 36 inch butcher paper; crayons or markers.

Cut out 24 × 36 inch simple shapes of pets, such as a dog, a cat, and a fish. Tape these to the wall with the caption: "PETS." Children use crayons or markers to color designs all over the inside of the animals. Leave the shapes up for several days and let them get more and more covered with free designs.

If working on a wall area is a problem, have the children do the group graffiti art by laying the pet cutouts on a table. After the designs are finished, pin or tape up the completed pets for several days' viewing.

Colored Glue Collage

Three to six small bottles of glue; food coloring; manila paper; scraps of yarn, fabric, and construction paper; glitter (optional).

Add a few drops of food coloring to a small bottle of glue. Replace the lid securely. Let the children help you "shake" the bottle back and forth in your hand to mix the color all through the glue. Watch and talk about how the coloring gradually spreads.

Use three to six bottles of glue and make each a different color. (Save the mixed glue for many other fun art projects.)

Have the children gently squeeze the glue on manila paper to make designs or the outline of a pet. Encourage them to try several colors. They may add bits of yarn, glitter, fabric, etc., on top of the glue, if desired. However, many children love just to "paint" a picture with the colored glue and then let it dry.

A fun way to help small muscles learn to control glue bottles!

CARE OF PETS

Group Dog House

Box; magazines; pictures of dogs; glue.

Use a *small* cardboard box or large shoebox. Cut out an opening for a door. Let the children cut around pictures of dogs they find in magazines, or provide cutouts of dogs if the children cannot cut well yet. (The children need to cut only loosely around the animal, as pictured. Do not expect them to be able to make fine, controlled cuts.)

The children glue the dog pictures all over the box, until it is covered. Put a stuffed dog in the door of the dog house for added fun.

If it is difficult to find enough dog pictures, make the project by gluing many different kinds of pets all over the box. Each day, have a different stuffed animal live in the house.

Styrofoam Pets

An assortment of styrofoam shapes and packing pieces; glue; bits of construction paper; fabric, yarn, buttons, round toothpicks, etc.

Have children glue and stick together with toothpicks a variety of styrofoam pieces and other materials to construct an imaginary styrofoam pet. Dry it thoroughly.

Encourage children to name their pets and tell what their imaginary pets can do.

These pets will float! Provide a plastic tub with a few inches of water in it. Let the children take turns teaching their pet to "swim."

Stand-Up Cat

Duplicate the cat pattern at the end of this section on construction paper for each child. The children use crayons or markers to color their cat as they desire. Glue on pipe cleaners or thin strips of construction paper for whiskers. Glue on eyes.

Show the children how to fold and glue the pieces to finish their stand-up cat. By simply changing the shape of the head, ears, and tail, you can make several other animals in the same way.

Group Pet Book

Magazines; glue; construction paper.

Let the children cut out pictures of the pets they like. Each child glues the pictures on a piece of construction paper. Print a sentence on each paper as the child dictates ideas about the pet on that page. Print the child's name under the sentence.

Staple the pages together to make a group book. Add an attractive cover. As a class, choose a name for the book and print that title on the front cover. Keep the book in the book center or where children may look at it for a long time.

Comic Pets

Transfer art mixture; spoons; paintbrushes; newspaper comic pages with pets (Pluto, Garfield, Snoopy, etc.).

Follow the procedure for the Transfer Art Mixture (see Art Recipes). Let children enjoy transferring their favorite comic pet onto plain pieces of paper to make comic collages or scenes.

Variation: Use a large piece of butcher paper and make a comic pet collage as a group project.

Origami Dog

9 inch square of construction paper; construction paper scraps; glue; markers or crayons.

The children fold a head of a dog by following the steps below.

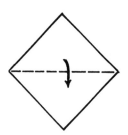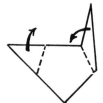

Add other details, such as a tongue, freckles, and whiskers, if desired. Lift the ears and color a pink oval on the underside, so it looks more like the inside of an ear.

Toy for a Pet

Make a small toy for a pet to play with. Use the toy with a stuffed animal and role play how to play gently with a real pet.
1. Cut several 3-4 inch pieces of yarn. Tie together tightly in the middle to make a yarn ball. Then, tie on about a 3 foot piece of yarn or string, so the yarn ball may be pulled around on the floor or ground.
2. Paint empty thread spools with non-lead paint. Thread about a 4 foot piece of yarn through the spool and tie the ends of the yarn together. Pull the yarn and let the spool roll across the floor or ground.

Pet Treat Box

Box or coffee can covered with paper; paint, markers, or crayons.

Have the children decorate a small box or coffee can to hold treats, such as dog biscuits, for their favorite pet.

Pet Shapes

Precut geometric shapes of many kinds, colors, and sizes; glue; manila or construction paper.

For several minutes, let children move the shapes around to discover what animals they can make by putting the shapes together. Encourage them to try different sizes for the body and different shapes for the head and legs: ''How would it look if we put a triangle there?'' ''How would a larger rectangle look there?''

Later, give the children the glue and have them glue their chosen shapes together to make an animal.

Print the name of the pet and the child's name on each paper—''Benny's Pet Brontosaurus.''

Pet Litterbag

Lunch sacks; construction paper scraps; glue; crayons or markers.

Duplicate the pet litterbag pattern for each child. Let the children use crayons or markers to color the pet as they wish. Glue on construction paper eyes, nose, whiskers, or freckles. After the animal is cut out, add a long red tongue, if desired.

Show the children how to fold and glue the pieces to a brown lunch-size sack. Vary the size of the ears according to the kind of animal used: long ears for a dog; shorter, pointed ears for a cat; etc. Staple on a piece of yarn so children may hang the litterbag in the car or in a room to keep it neat.

A Present for a Pet

Make a present for a pet using the book of ideas: *Make Your Pet a Present* by Eve Barwell. The book gives directions for simple presents for dogs, cats, birds, rabbits, guinea pigs, mice, and gerbils.

BLOCKS

1. Build a pet shop, using blocks and the animals from a farm set, to play pet shop for the day. If plastic animals are not available, cut small pictures from a magazine, glue to tagboard, make a ½ inch cut at the middle of the bottom, and bend one half forward and the other half back. The animals should then stand upright.
2. Encourage the children to build shelters for pets who live at someone's house.

BULLETIN BOARD

Are You My Mother?

Pin pictures of several varieties of adult pets randomly on the bulletin board. Pin pictures of the babies of the same pets randomly on the board, too. Pin a length of yarn under each adult pet and a small piece of sandpaper under each baby pet. If necessary, supply a stool for the children to stand on as they match the baby to the adult pet by connecting the piece of yarn from parent to baby.

Pet Photographs

Encourage the children to bring a photo of a family pet they have or have had. Bring a photo of your pet(s), too. Put the photos on a bulletin board or wall area within easy view. Add "Our Pets" as a caption above the photographs. Put a card by each photo with the name of the child, name of the pet, and kind of pet printed on it. You may also print something the child said about the pet by the photo.

COOKING

Peanut Butter S-Mores

Graham cracker squares
Peanut butter
Large marshmallows

Each child spreads peanut butter on one graham cracker and puts a marshmallow on top.

Broil until the marshmallow starts to melt. Remove from broiler and place another graham cracker on top.

Purple Pet Shakes

1 6-oz. can frozen grape juice concentrate
1 cup milk
2 cups vanilla ice milk or ice cream
Blender

Put all the ingredients in the blender. Blend on high speed for 30 seconds. Serve right away. Makes ½ cup for 8-10 children.

Sandwich Checkerboard

4 slices of wheat bread
4 slices of white bread
Peanut butter
Jelly

Wash hands. Trim the crusts off the bread. Make four peanut butter and jelly sandwiches, two from the wheat bread and two from the white bread. Cut each sandwich into halves, then into fourths to make four squares. On a plate or tray, arrange the sandwich squares to look like a checkerboard.

LANGUAGE ARTS

Books

Barker, A.J. and H.A. Barker. *Dogs.* Bison Books, 1983.
Barton, Byron. *Where's Al?* Seabury Press, 1972.
Barwell, Eve. *Make Your Pet a Present.* Lothrop, Lee & Shepard, 1977.
Belpre', Pura. *Santiago.* Warne & Co., 1969.
Blocksma, Mary. *The Pop Went Up.* Children's Press, 1983.
Borack, Barbara. *Someone Small.* Harper and Row, 1969.
Carle, Eric. *The Mixed-Up Chameleon.* Crowell, 1984.
De Paola, Tomie. *The Kids' Cat Book.* Holiday House, 1979.
Gag, Wanda. *Millions of Cats.* Coward, McCann & Geoghegan, 1938.
Greenley, Valerie. *Pets.* Bedrick/Blackie, 1984.
Hoban, Tana. *Where Is It?* Macmillan, 1974.
Keats, Ezra J. *Hi, Cat!* Macmillan, 1974.
Keats, Ezra J. *Pet Show.* Macmillan, 1972.
Keats, Ezra J. *Whistle for Willie.* Viking Press, 1969.
Leen, Nina. *Cats.* Holt, Rinehart & Winston, 1980.
Mayer, Mercer. *A Boy, A Dog and a Frog.* Dial, 1967.
Moncure, Jane Belk. *Pets Are Smart.* Children's Press, 1976.
Overbeck, Cynthia. *Cats.* Lerner Publications, 1983.
Parish, Peggy. *Too Many Rabbits.* Macmillan, 1974.

Pollard, Anna. *Dogs.* Cathay Books, 1981.
Roberts, Mervin F. *The T.F.H. Book of Hamsters.* TFH Publications, 1981.
Silverstein, Shel. ''Dog's Day.'' *A Light in the Attic.* Harper and Row, 1981.
Silverstein, Shel. ''The Lost Cat.'' *A Light in the Attic.* Harper and Row, 1981.
Spier, Peter. *The Pet Store.* Doubleday, 1981.
Steeh, Judith. *Cats.* Bison Books, 1983.
Thaler, Mike. *My Puppy.* Harper and Row, 1980.
Zimelman, Nathan. *Positively No Pets Allowed.* Dutton, 1980.
Zion, Gene. *Harry the Dirty Dog.* Harper and Row, 1956.

Fingerplays

Little Kitten

I have a little kitten,
With soft and shiny fur.
And when I pet my kitten,
She goes purr, purr, purr.
 (Make a fist with one hand to be the kitten. Pet the kitten with the other hand.)

There Was a Little Turtle

A favorite fingerplay, which children love to repeat, is ''There Was a Little Turtle'' by Vachel Lindsay. You can find a copy of the fingerplay in several fingerplay books. Check at your public library.

Films

Check your public library for its inventory of films about pets. Two popular films are:

''Little Dog Lost'' 48 minutes; color and sound. Disney film. Contains scenes of ranch life and outdoors. Story is about a dog that searches for an understanding master.

''Dogs, Dogs, Dogs'' 15 minutes; color and sound. Shows many kinds of dogs. Designed to motivate children to discuss their feelings about and interest in dogs.

Live Classroom Pet

If at all feasible, get a real pet of some kind to keep in the classroom. Children need the responsibility of caring for something live that depends on them. They also need practice to learn to handle a pet gently. Having a classroom pet is especially important today, because so many children no longer have pets in their homes.

Pet Un-Birthday Party

Have a classroom celebration for all pets. Pretend that the day is officially Pet Un-Birthday. Sing ''Happy Birthday.'' Serve animal crackers and Purple Pet Shakes (see COOKING) at snack time.

Stuffed Animal Day

Instead of having children bring all their real pets, invite children to bring a favorite stuffed animal to class one day. Have a few extra stuffed animals to share, if possible.

Talk about sizes, colors, shapes, and feel of the stuffed animals. Classify them into these different categories. Count how many are in each category. ''How many red? blue?'' ''How many short? tall?''

Let the children show and tell about their stuffed animals. ''What is its name?'' ''How does it move?'' ''What does it like to do?'' ''What sounds does it make?''

Use the stuffed animals to demonstrate safe care and handling of pets.

Animal Sound Recordings

Play a tape or record of the sounds of different animals. Let the children guess which animal is making that sound. Have Mattel's ''See and Say'' toy of animal sounds available for children to enjoy.

Who Am I?

Describe a common pet. Have the children guess who it is. ''I am small and furry. I purr when you pet me. Who am I?''

Nursery Rhymes

Recite with the children all of the nursery rhymes that have a pet in them, such as ''Mother Hubbard,'' ''Little Bo Peep,'' and ''Mary Had a Little Lamb.''

Pet Store

Visit a pet store to enjoy watching all the different kinds of pets. View and talk about the special supplies and equipment needed for some pets.

Have the store personnel talk with the class about the care and safe handling of the different pets.

Veterinarian Visit

Invite a veterinarian to come to your class or visit a veterinarian's office. Talk about what a veterinarian does.

The veterinarian may be able to bring a small animal to class to demonstrate safe care and handling.

As an alternative, invite someone from the Humane Society to class.

Pet Supplies

Make a display of some common pet supplies, such as a dog leash, food for different pets, cage, cedar chips, water bottle, pet dish, etc. Let children discuss what kind of pet could use each one.

Pet Rhymes

Repeat "Little Bo Peep" nursery rhyme. Ask the children to name all the different kinds of pets they can think of. Print each pet on the chalkboard or a chart so they can see the word in print.

Use the "Little Bo Peep" verse to make up a rhyme for each of the pets on the list.

Little Bo Perbil has lost her _____ (gerbil)

Little Bo Pat has lost her _____ (cat)

Little Bo Pish has lost her _____ (fish)

Little Bo Pamster has lost her _____ (hamster)

MATH

NUMBER CONCEPTS

Silent Show

Show the children a card with a numeral on it. Have the children hold up the correct number of fingers for that numeral. Do the activity in silence.

Numeral Holes

Styrofoam meat trays; wide-line black markers; round toothpicks.

On each meat tray, write a numeral with the the black marker. Have children follow the line and "write" the numeral by poking holes along the line with a toothpick. Let them hold up the finished product and see the light shining through the numeral holes.

Pet Flannel Board Cutouts

Using the pet on the front of the February Curriculum guide as a pattern, make several felt cutouts. As a class, pick a number. Then, instruct the children: "Quietly tell me to stop when I have put _____ pets on the flannel board." *Slowly* add one pet cutout at a time to the board.

Repeat the activity, using a different number. Let the children also take turns putting up the figures. Children love to use the flannel board.

MEASUREMENT

Feed the Pets

¼ cup; ½ cup; 1 cup; pictures of a small, medium, and large pet; 3 bowls; styrofoam packing pieces.

Tape a picture of one of the pets on each bowl. For the small pet, also tape a drawing of a ¼ measuring cup on the bowl. Tape ½ cup on the medium pet bowl and 1 cup on the large pet bowl.

Let the children take turns pretending to feed the animals by carefully measuring the appropriate amount of "pretend pet food" (styrofoam pieces) into each bowl.

CARE OF PETS

Matthew and His Pets

(Use a cardboard box and stuffed animals. Add animals to the box as you tell the poem.)

Matthew had a little box.
''I know what this can be.
I'll make this box a pet house
And get some pets for me.''

He put in one,
But said: ''I'm just not done.''
''I know what to do;
  Add another and make _____ .
But really it would be
  Much nicer to have _____ .
There still is room for more,
  I'll add another and make _____ .
Another pet arrives,
  So all together I have _____ .
This is a good mix,
  I'll add one more and I'll have _____ .
How many pets now do you see?
Can you count them all with me?
One, two, three, four, five, six!

Near—Far

Give half the class members a laminated numeral. Let them position themselves randomly around the classroom. The remaining children follow directions given by you or by another leader. For example: ''Chris, stand near the person holding the numeral three.'' ''Traci, stand far from the person holding the numeral five.'' The class members may switch groups, when all have had a turn. As the children understand the activity, they will enjoy being the leader who gives the instructions.

MOVEMENT

Pet Movements

Ask the children to do these movements.

Dog—Crawl on all fours; first move very slowly and then crawl faster.

Cat— On all fours, stretch the body, keeping arms and legs straight. Move the back and bottom down, then stretch back up as a cat does when it's afraid or mad.

Fish—Lie on tummies on the floor; pull forward using both arms as fins to ''swim'' across the floor; wiggle the legs together slowly like a fish tail.

Bird—Stand, arms stretched back, body bent slightly forward as a bird gliding in flight. Stretch. Run and gently flap wings as if flying.

CARE OF PETS

Walk Your Dog

    The children work in pairs, with one being a child holding an imaginary leash and the other being a pet dog (down on all fours). Ask the pairs to do the following movements. Then, have them trade places and repeat the movements.
1. Walk forward.
2. Turn around two times.
3. Ask the dog to roll over.
4. Pretend to throw a ball, which the dog pretends to catch and bring back.
5. Lie down for a pretend nap.

Dog House Toss

    Use masking tape to make a dog house shape on the floor. Have the children use beanbags and practice tossing underhanded to get the bags inside the shape. Vary the distance by putting tape on the floor to mark three different places to stand while throwing.
    You may substitute any other pet house shape, such as a bird cage.

MUSIC

Pet Music

    Choose a pet and let the children move like that animal as a record is played. Horse, cat, bird, fish, dog, and hamster movements work well.
    Stop the music. Repeat the activity using another pet. End with a slow-paced song, such as a lullaby, and have the children lie down like an animal to sleep or rest.

Songs

    Sing familiar songs about animals as pets, such as "O Where, O Where Has My Little Dog Gone?" and "Mary Had a Little Lamb."

My Pet Horsey

(Tune: "Battle Hymn of the Republic")

My pet horsey had a fly upon his back,
My pet horsey had a fly upon his back,
My pet horsey had a fly upon his back,
And he swished it to make it go away.
Swish it, swish it, little horsey,
Swish it, swish it, little horsey,
Swish it, swish it, little horsey,
Swish it till it flies away.

CARE OF PETS

Actions: horsey—Gallop in place holding imaginary reins.
fly—Wiggle index finger.
back—Stretch hand around to back.
swish it—Wiggle bottoms.

Variation: Repeat song, each time omitting the last action word and doing only the motion. Eventually the song will be only motions.

ROLE PLAY

Veterinarian's Office

Set up a veterinarian's office for children to role play having pets examined and cared for. Props may include: waiting area chairs, examination table, stethoscope, doctor's kit, and several large and small stuffed animals.

Animal Follow the Leader

Play follow the leader, imitating ways pets move and take care of themselves—washing selves, lapping up water, climbing, hopping, creeping, etc.

The children may take turns being the leader. To encourage older children to think and remember, say that an action may not be repeated by a second leader.

Pet Ball

Use soft foam balls and let children play ball without using their hands or feet. They can push the ball with their noses as pets do. (To avoid spreading germs, discourage them from picking up the ball with their teeth.)

SCIENCE

Observation of Live Pets

Have children observe the behavior of a pet over several days. Talk about what they have seen: "How does the pet eat? drink?" "What does the pet do to sleep?" "Does the pet wash?" "What does it do if a person holds it or touches it?"

If children have some misconceptions about the pet, ask them to watch some more to see if that is true. Discuss the point again after children have had a chance to watch the pet for some time.

Animal Face Shapes

Put a small amount of cereal on a napkin, meat tray, or plate for each child. Set it on a table. Ask them to try to eat it without using their hands. "Why is it hard?" "What gets in the way?"

Discuss how a dog's long nose and mouth and a bird's beak help them get food without needing hands.

CARE OF PETS

Stand-up Cat

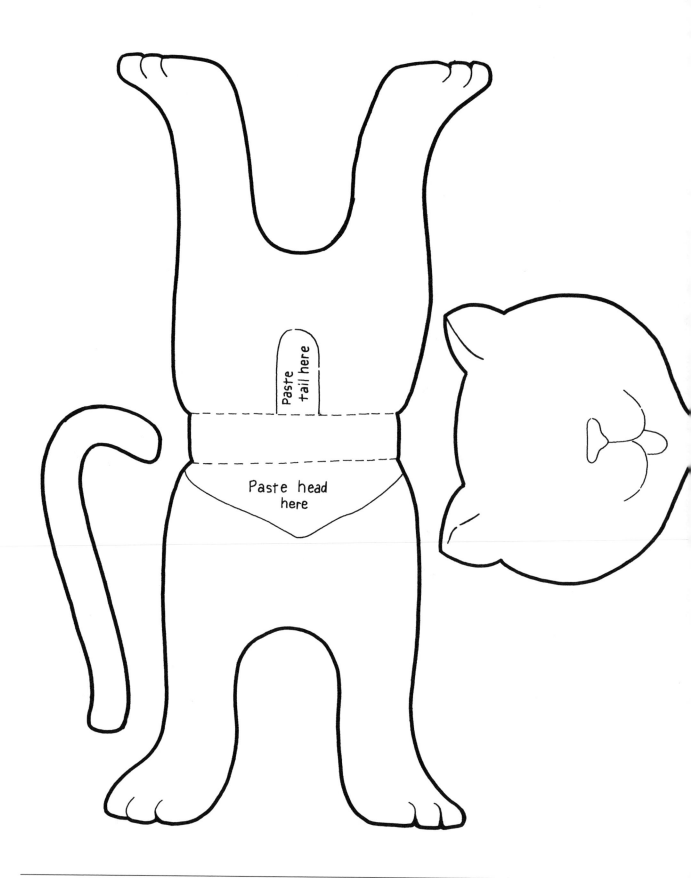

Paste tail here

Paste head here

March Curriculum

1. Ways We Travel
2. Communication
3. Feet

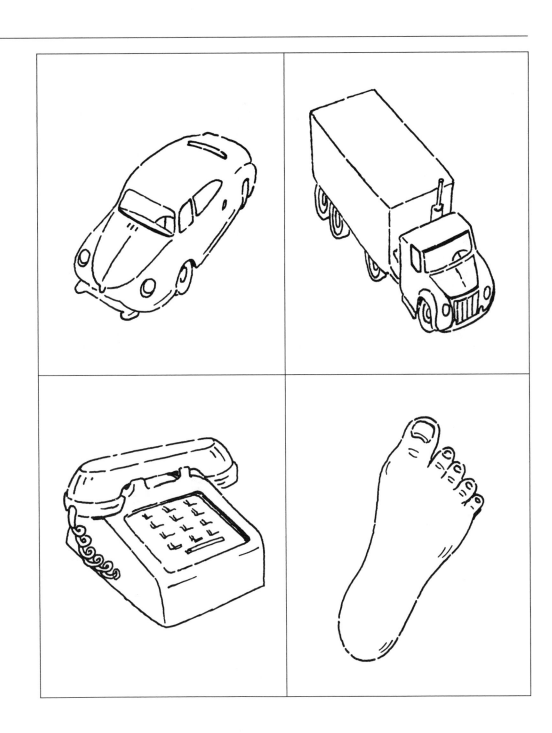

Ways We Travel

CONCEPTS

- People can move from one place to another by using their legs, an animal, or a machine.
- The machines most often used to help people travel are cars, trucks, buses, trains, planes, and boats.
- Some people travel in space. They are called astronauts and must wear special clothing when in space.

ART

**Papier Mache
Hot Air Balloon
(Whole Class Project)**

Flour and water paste; newspaper cut into 1 inch strips; dishpan; very large, heavyweight, round balloon.

Blow up the balloon and tie it tightly. The children cover the balloon with the newspaper strips dipped into the paste. Each day, add one layer and let it dry overnight. Your need to do three or four layers. Dry it completely.

The children paint the balloon with several bright colors. Tape on four yarn strings and attach a small box to make the basket under the balloon. Hang the hot air balloon like a mobile from the ceiling.

**Button-Up Cars
and Trucks**

Car- and truck-shaped stencils; glue; foil; buttons (check area fabric stores for their bargain bins of inexpensive buttons).

The children trace around a car or truck shape. Then, they glue on foil squares for windows and add buttons for wheels. Small pieces of a drinking straw make good tailpipes and smokestacks on diesel trucks.

Encourage the children to use crayons or markers to draw roads, trees, houses, etc., to complete their pictures.

Space Station

Collect several different shapes of styrofoam packing pieces. Have the children stick the pieces together with round toothpicks to create space stations that float in space.

Styrofoam Miniature Boats

Styrofoam packing pieces; round toothpicks.

Have children stick a toothpick into a styrofoam piece to make a miniature boat with a mast. Glue styrofoam pieces together for a larger and more complex creation. Glue small white triangles to the toothpick mast, if you desire a sail.

Sail the boats in the classroom in a large cake pan with 2 inch sides or in a large plastic tub. You need only 1 inch of water to sail the boats successfully. (Thus, the potential for water spill messes is greatly limited.) Encourage the children to put their boats in the water and blow gently.

Dry Tempera Stencils

A supply of simple stencils of vehicles we use for travel; dry tempera paint; manila or construction paper.

Cover the work area with newspapers. Put a small spoonful of one to three different colors of powdered tempera paint around each child's work area. The children choose a stencil and lay it on a sheet of manila or construction paper on the newspaper. They then dip a finger into the dry tempera paint and rub the finger across the edge of the stencil and onto the paper. Encourage the children to blend the colors.

Spray the finished picture with a fixative, such as hair spray.

Transportation Collage

Have children bring in envelopes containing pictures they have found in magazines and newspapers of things that they could ride in or on. After they have collected many pictures, each child pastes a collage using the pictures.

On each finished collage, print ''I like to ride in a _____'' or ''I like to ride on a _____,'' and let each child tell you what word to write to finish the sentence.

Play Dough

Make a batch of play dough (see Art Recipes). Give each child a fist-sized amount of play dough. Show the children how they can roll balls; show them how to make long rolls. Talk about sizes and shapes as they work.

Make car shapes by adding four flattened balls for wheels around a larger round shape.

Colored Chalk Drawings

Colored chalk; construction paper; small cups of sugar water—1 teaspoon sugar and 1 cup water (optional).

The children draw with the chalk on the construction paper. Dipping the chalk in sugar water helps it to slide over the paper more easily. Show the children how they may blend colors by rubbing gently with an index finger.

Spray with a fixative, such as hair spray.

Finger Paint Prints

Refer to the Art Recipes for instructions about finger painting. Discuss how waves are made by a boat; show the children how to move their whole hand to make "waves" on the paper. Discuss how an airplane takes off; show them how to move their hands diagonally to make a takeoff pattern. Discuss wheels going around on cars and trucks; show them how to move their fingers to make continuous round wheel movements, which can get larger or smaller.

Let the children continue exploring in the paint on their own paper. As each child finishes, place a piece of construction paper on top of each painting and press it to make a print of the design.

Straw Blown Pictures

Plastic straws; manila paper; tempera paint in at least three colors.

Cover the work area. Each child puts a small spoonful of one color of paint on the paper. Then, each child uses a straw to blow gently toward the paint, to make it move in interesting designs. Repeat at least two more times, using a different color each time.

Walnut Shell Boats

Have the children color and decorate walnut halves with permanent markers. They then press a small piece of clay in the bottom to hold a toothpick with a sail on it. Float the boats in a small wading pool or tub.

Toothpick Collage

White and colored flat toothpicks; glue; manila paper.

Let each child make a collage by gluing the toothpicks to make a picture or shape. Show them that they can break the toothpicks in halves or smaller pieces to make different sizes and shapes. The children may add details to the picture with crayons, if desired.

Travel Machine

Construction paper; glue; precut triangles, circles, rectangles, and squares of many sizes and colors.

Show the children how they can glue the shapes together on a paper to make a car, wagon, train, truck, airplane, etc. Without glue, let the children experiment with different arrangements on their papers. When they create their favorite, have them glue the pieces in place.

Wooden Boats

Collected wood bits and pieces (construction sites will give you their end cuts and scraps); glue; hammer; short nails with large heads (roofing nails); latex paint.

Each child glues or nails together wood scraps to make a boat. Paint with latex paint. If weather permits, inflate a wading pool outside and launch the boat creations.

3-D Transportation Mural
(3-5 Day Class Project)

3 × 3 foot butcher paper; tempera paints; manila paper; markers; camera.

As a class, take turns painting a sky, ground, and lake on the butcher paper as the background for the mural. Later, let individuals use markers or tempera paints to create cars, trucks, boats, trains, planes, etc., on 9 × 12 inch manila paper. Cut out each vehicle. (If desired, you may make stencils using simple pictures, such as the truck and car on the front of the March Curriculum guide. Children may trace the stencils and add details to individualize them.)

Glue ½ × 3 inch strips of paper into loops or rings. Glue two rings on the back of each vehicle, so it will stand out in a 3-D effect when the rings are glued or pinned to the mural. Add other details to the mural as the class desires: houses, people, trees, roads, etc.

Take photo snapshots of the children during the various stages of the mural. Display the photographs along with the finished mural. The photos are sure to generate a lot of interest, memories, and oral interaction, as the children enjoy the finished display.

Paper Airplanes

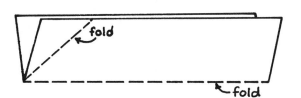

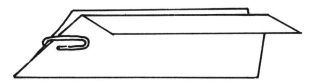

9 × 12 inch paper; markers or crayons; paper clips.

The children decorate a piece of paper with markers or crayons. They then fold the paper to make an airplane.

1. Fold the paper in half, lengthwise.
2. Fold down the triangle for the nose of the plane.
3. Fold over the top edge on each side for wings.
4. Put a paper clip on the nose for weight and to increase the flying distance.

If the weather permits, fly the planes outside by *gently* throwing them forward. (Some children will need help folding the planes. But they love trying to fly them!)

Class Shoe Box Train

Several shoe boxes of various sizes; oatmeal boxes; individual size cereal boxes; glue; tempera paint; string or yarn.

As a class, let the children cooperate in making a train. Each car is a combination of shoe boxes, box lids, and other boxes glued together. Paint each car a different color using tempera paints. Add wheels, windows, doors, and other appropriate details with paint and construction paper scraps. Empty thread spools also make good-looking wheels. Connect the cars by punching a hole and tying cars together with short string or yarn pieces.

BLOCKS

Parking Lot

Provide cards numbered 1-5 or more. Have the children build a parking lot. Put a card in each parking place to number the space, as is done in many parking lots. Provide small cars for the children to drive and park. One child may act as the parking lot attendant and assign the number of the parking space to the other children, who act as paying customers.

Highway/Runway

Use blocks to build a highway/runway. Practice driving and taking off with small cars and airplanes. Make bridges from blocks and other construction toys. Create tunnels by cutting open both ends of oatmeal containers.

Use road signs to help direct traffic flow. Children may take turns being a traffic officer or an air traffic controller in the control tower of an airport.

Make gasoline pumps. Paint wooden rectangles or leave them natural. Staple or nail on a piece of heavy string for a hose. Add other details as desired.

Maze

Build a maze with blocks around the block area. Drive the vehicles on the blocks, as a road, or on the floor, following the maze. Add stop and go fun with red and green construction paper circles glued to popsicle sticks. Let the children take turns being police officers.

BULLETIN BOARD

Ways We Travel

On the board, tack posters or other pictures or photographs that depict modes of travel. These may include pictures of the children in the classroom traveling. Let the children draw around their feet. Cut them out and tack them randomly around the pictures as a border.

Map Board

Put up a large map of the United States, with the states outlined. Let each child tell about a trip he/she has taken. If they know where they went, string a piece of yarn from where you are to the destination. Put the child's name on a flag at that point. Glue a small cutout of a car, plane, train, or bus on the yarn to show the type of vehicle in which the child traveled.

Sky-Land-Water

Use yarn to divide the board into three equal sections. Label each section, "Sky," "Land," and "Water." Make a border of transportation vehicles, if desired.

Near the board, place a small plastic container of push pins and a large coffee can full of pictures and/or small real models of bikes, motorcycles, boats, skis, planes, rockets, trucks, horses, cars, hot air balloons, blimps, fire trucks, rafts, etc.

Let individual children or pairs of children take turns pinning the pictures in the appropriate section of the bulletin board. Later, take down the pictures, so others may have a turn.

Good for vocabulary development, thinking skills, and discrimination. Children love to put things on the bulletin board and will probably want several turns to repeat this game.

COOKING

High-Energy Astronaut Shakes

2 cups milk
1/3 cup peanut butter
2 tablespoons honey
Ice
Blender

Crush eight ice cubes in the blender. Add other ingredients and blend until smooth. Makes three cups of Astronaut Shakes.

Banana Boats

1 banana per child
½ cup crushed peanuts
1 eight ounce carton frozen whipped topping (thawed)
½ cup honey

Fold together the honey and the whipped topping. Let each child peel and cut a banana in half lengthwise. Then, have each put a spoonful of the whipped mixture between the banana halves. Sprinkle with nuts, if desired.

Traveler's Snack

4 cups of any favorite cereal
1 cup peanuts
1 cup raisins
½ stick margarine, melted
1 six ounce package of milk chocolate chips
Electric frying pan

Melt the margarine in the pan. Stir in cereal, peanuts, and raisins. Mix until well coated. Stir in chips.

Put individual size servings in plastic sandwich bags.

Variation:

4 cups of any favorite cereal
2 cups pretzels
1 cup peanuts
½ stick margarine
1 tablespoon Worcestershire sauce
1 teaspoon paprika
1 teaspoon garlic salt
Electric frying pan

In the pan, melt the margarine and stir in the other ingredients until coated well. Cook at 250° stirring often, for 30 minutes. (If preferred, cook the mixture on a cookie sheet in the oven.)

Walk and Munch Necklace

String
Combination of several cereals that can be strung for a necklace: Honey-comb, Cheerios, Fruit Loops, etc. (Pretzel rings also string well.)

Cut 24 inch lengths of string. Children make a necklace by stringing as much cereal as they can, in any combination of types and colors.

Half—Whole

Occasionally serve snack or lunch items that can be cut in half. For instance, if sandwiches are on the menu, leave them whole and allow the children to cut their sandwiches in half with a plastic or table knife.

LANGUAGE ARTS

Books

Arnold, Caroline. *How Do We Travel?* Watts, 1983.

Berenstein, Stan and Jan. *Bears on Wheels*. Random House, 1969.

Crews, Donald. *Freight Train*. Greenwillow Books, 1978.

DiFiori, Lawrence. *The Truck Book*. Western Publishing, 1984.

Goodall, John S. *Paddy Goes Traveling*. Atheneum, 1982.

Gramatky, Hardie. *Little Toot*. Putnam, 1939.

Greene, Carol. *Astronauts*. Children's Press, 1984.

Hoban, Tana. *I Read Symbols*. Greenwillow Books, 1983.

Hold Everything! Why You Should Use Safety Belts. Channing L. Bete Co., 1974 ed.
   (A Scriptographic Booklet).

Hutchins, Pat. *Rosie's Walk*. Macmillan, 1968.

Jonas, Ann. *Round Trip*. Greenwillow Books, 1983.

Kessler, Ethel and Leonard. *Big Red Bus*. Doubleday and Co., Inc., 1957.

Kingore, Bertie. *Mac's Big Surprise*. Texas Instruments, 1982.

Kohn, Bernice. *The Look-It-Up Book of Transportation*. Macmillan, 1968.

Moncure, Jane Belk. *Magic Monsters Learn About Space*. Children's Press, 1980.

Piper, Watty. *The Little Engine That Could*. Platt and Munk, 1954.

Sparling, Joe. *Look Out the Car Window*. Kaplan Press, 1984.

Tester, Sylvia R. *Traffic Jam*. Child's World, 1980.

Wolcott, Patty. *Double-Decker, Double-Decker, Double-Decker Bus*. Addison-Wesley,
   1980.

Zaffo, George. All of his books on transportation.

Fingerplays

My Little Toy Train

My little toy train moves down the track.
Going, "Puff, puff, choo, choo," forward and back.
It has a bell to ring and a whistle that blows.
"Puff, choo, toot, toot," wherever it goes.
   (Move arms in train wheel motion. Pretend to pull the whistle.)

Ride in a Truck

Mr. Truck, Mr. Truck, I need a ride.
   (Make fists, thumbs up. One thumb wiggles as if talking to others.)
 All right child, just step inside.
   (Other thumb talks.)
Put on your seat belt,
   (Move first thumb as if clicking on belt.)
Turn on the gas,
   (Move thumb and finger to turn switch.)
But please drive safely and not too fast!

Films

Check your local public library for their inventory of films about the ways people travel. Two popular films are:

"Rosie's Walk," 4 minutes, color/sound. Delightful tale of a hen unwittingly leading a fox into one humorous disaster after another as the hen walks safely home.

"Little Engine That Could," 11 minutes, color/sound. Famous story of train pulling load of toys up the side of a mountain.

NASA Resources

Write to NASA to request their free pictures and informational materials.
NASA
Public Information
2101 NASA Road 1
Houston, Texas 77058

Electric Train

Set up a small electric train. Discuss train, tracks, engine, caboose, other cars, etc. Read Donald Crews' *Freight Train*.

Traveler's Walk

Make Traveler's Snack (see COOKING). Tie the individual servings in a napkin on a stick or dowel rod. Let each child carry his snack over his shoulder, like a hobo, as the class goes for a walk.

If the weather and the locale permit, take the class for a walk outside. Point out and discuss interesting things along the way. Stop at some appropriate place and eat your snack.

Peek-a-Boo Pictures

Have several pictures from magazines and/or newspapers that show ways people travel. Cut a 1 inch hole in a piece of construction paper. Put the construction paper over one of the transportation pictures so that only the 1 inch hole reveals a peek of the picture.

Discuss what it could be. Then lift the construction paper to show the class what it is. Cover a different picture and play again.

Missing Parts

Have pictures of several different kinds of transportation. Use white-out to cover up an important part in the drawing, such as a wing of an airplane. Have children look for and talk about the missing part. Encourage accurate labels, such as "wing" instead of "that thing."

Memory Game

Using transportation pictures, play Memory Game on the flannel board. Depending on the ages of the children, put three to eight pictures on the board. Cover the board and remove one or more pictures. Uncover and allow the children to determine which are missing. A good end to this game is to remove all of the pictures at once and have the children try to recall all of them. You may also play the game using real objects, such as small cars, etc., on a tray.

Mystery Bag Game

To make a mystery bag: Cut off one half of a jeans leg. Sew the bottom edge closed. Fold down the top and sew. Add a drawstring.

Put a small car, truck, horse, plane, doll's shoe, boat, etc., in the mystery bag. Show each item and talk about it. Then, go around the circle and have each child reach a hand into the bag (no peeking) and pick out a specified object to show to the group.

Variation: Child reaches in the bag without peeking, picks out one object, guesses what it is, and pulls it out to see if that is correct.

Fishing Trip in a Boat

Construction paper cut into fish shapes about 6 inches long and 4 inches wide; markers or crayons; small paper clips; 2 foot dowel rods; string; magnets.

Discuss how fish look: scales, large round eyes, fins. Have each child decorate a fish shape using crayons or markers.

Put a paper clip at the mouth area of each fish. Make "fishing poles" by tying a 3 foot length of string on one end of a dowel rod and tying a small magnet to the other end of the string. Let the children pretend to be fishing while in a boat. Putting two chairs together gives children a "boat" to sit in for fishing. A cardboard box can also make a fun fishing boat.

Put the fish on the floor. The children "catch" their fish by attracting the paper clip to the magnet. Make the activity more of a challenge by having the children try to catch a specific fish: "Catch the fish with the green scales and yellow eyes."

Delivery Trucks

If any delivery trucks come to the center, make arrangements for the children to watch the delivery from an appropriate distance. "What is inside the truck?" "Why does the driver come here?"

Perhaps the driver will talk to the children for a few moments and let them look inside the door of the truck. Also, watch the trash truck as it picks up the trash.

Classification—Moves vs. Doesn't Move

Show the class a variety of pictures. Let them decide each time if it is a picture of something that moves or does not move: house, car, person, tree, etc.

Ways We Travel Book

Ask the children to bring a photograph of themselves riding in something or on something. If no photo is available, ask them to bring a picture from a magazine or catalog of something they would like to ride.

Use a small spiral notebook. Print "Ways We Travel" on the cover or first page. On each page, paste a child's photograph or picture and print a sentence under it as the child tells you about the picture. "Jeff likes to be pulled in the wagon by his big brother." "Jennifer can ride a trike."

Display the book in the room. Children like to look through it again and again. It's a good self-concept boost!

Visit from an Officer

Invite a patrol officer to come to the center in the patrol car. Let the officer talk to the children about safety around and in cars.

Ask the officer to show the children some of the features of the car: seat belts, instrument panel, how the flashing lights work, how she/he talks to control center, etc.

Classification

1. *Wheels/No Wheels*
   Show the children pictures from magazines. Have the bulletin board divided in two sections with a piece of yarn. Place a sign "Wheels" in one section and "No Wheels" in the other section. The children pin each picture on the appropriate part of the board.
2. *Water—Sky—Land*
   Name various ways we travel and let the children tell you each time if the traveling happens in water, in sky, or on land. Some examples: by swimming, walking, plane, hot air balloon, horse, car, taxi, bus, rocket ship, etc.

Magnet Driving

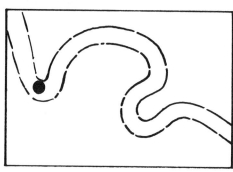

Draw a simple pathway on an 8 × 12 inch square of posterboard. Put a green dot in the upper left-hand corner, to signal the child to start at the top and work from left to right.

Use two magnets. Place the magnets on both sides of the posterboard. (They will "stick to" each other through the posterboard.)

Each child holds the board and tries to drive safely through the pathway by holding one magnet on the back of the board and moving the other magnet along the path.

Vary the pathway design for continued interest. Always arrange the path so children work from top to bottom and from left to right. If your magnet is strong, try using the magnet on the back and a small metal car on the front.

WAYS WE TRAVEL

Traffic Signs

Cut out the basic shapes of traffic signs (about one-half real size) from the appropriate colors of posterboard. Add lettering and details to complete a sign for stop, speed limit, yield, one way, railroad crossing, and others as desired.

Laminate each sign to ensure its long use.

Discuss each sign with the class: "Have you ever seen this?" "Where?" ,"What does it mean?"

Display the signs around the room. Encourage the children to use the signs as they play transportation related activities.

Visit an Airport

Observe and discuss how tickets are purchased, how baggage is checked, how passengers get on the plane, the control tower, windsock, runways, and cockpit of an airplane.

Visit from a Firefighter

Ask a firefighter to bring a real fire truck to the center. Let the children hold a hose to find out how heavy it is; try on a firefighter's coat or hat; stand on the truck; observe where the equipment is kept; look inside the cab of the truck; see which controls make the light and siren work.

Ask the firefighter to discuss with the children the difference between a fire truck and a fire engine.

Travel Riddles

Make up riddles to ask the children about the various ways to travel that you have discussed: "I have two wheels and have to be peddled to move. What am I?" "I am big and red (or yellow), have lots of wheels, and carry firefighters. What am I?"

Traffic Safety

Discuss the importance of being safe while riding in or driving a car or truck: "Why do cars have seat belts?" "What are traffic signs for?" "Why do we have speed limits?"

Show children license plates on a car and discuss why cars must have one on the front and back.

Show children a driver's license and explain how drivers must pass a driving test before they get one.

Make a "Learning to Be a Safe Driver" license for each child. Issue them after they have demonstrated safe driving and riding in role play activities.

Blastoff Countdown

Count backwards as a group—10-9-8...1, Blastoff!.

Counting

1. How many wheels does a bicycle have? tricycle? car? truck? Have models of each, so children can count.
2. Number Bingo. Divide four 9 × 12 inch cards into fourths. Draw or glue a different number of circles in each fourth. Make each card with different placements of numbers. Cut about eighty 1 inch squares of construction paper and store them in a plastic bowl with a cover.

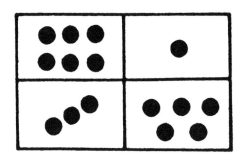

Show children how to roll a die and count the number of dots on the top. If they have that number on their card, they cover each circle in that section with a 1 inch square of paper. Continue until one child has all the circles covered.

Number Recognition Game

Twenty 2 inch squares of posterboard; package of cotton balls.

Write numerals on the squares, 0-9 or whatever numbers the group is ready to learn and practice. Write one numeral on each square. Place the squares in a small covered box, plastic bowl with lid, or drawstring bag. Place the cotton balls in a large bowl, box, or reclosable plastic bag.

Two to four children take turns picking out a square and counting out that number of cotton balls. The game is finished when all the squares or cotton balls are gone. Older children may wish to count all the cotton balls they have, before they put them away.

Number Sequence and Set Recognition

Small toy cars.

Place a square of masking tape on the top of each car. Write one numeral (0-9, or whatever numbers the children are ready to recognize and sequence) on each car.

1. *Car Parade*
   The children line up the cars in the proper sequence and pretend they are in a parade.
2. *Parking Lot*
   Divide a 10 inch square card into 2 × 5 inch sections. Draw small dots in each section to represent sets of 0-9. The children "drive" the numbered cars and park each in its appropriate place.

Half—Whole

Use the flannel board with flannel figures and shapes to demonstrate half and whole. Provide simple car or bus shapes, as well as circles and squares. Demonstrate cuttting the shapes in half. Show the children that this creates two pieces of the same size. Demonstrate that if you put the two halves back together, the shape looks whole again. Have construction paper shapes available and marked for cutting in half, if appropriate for your class. If the shapes are the same size as the flannel board pieces, the children may match their paper shapes with the flannel pieces. Use the terms "whole" and "half" as frequently as possible. Let the children use the whole and half circles and squares to build cars, wagons, and other transportation vehicles.

MOVEMENT

Imaginary Space Walk

(Played like "Going on a Bear Hunt".) Stand in the classroom and give directions to the children for a pretend walk in space. Refer to the children as astronaut Jeff, astronaut Traci, etc. Attach a string or yarn to each child for a lifeline, if desired.

As you say each direction, the "astronauts" act it out by moving in place.
1. Walk (with exaggerated slow motions) to the hatch of the ship.
2. Pull yourself up and through the hatch to go out in space.
3. Look around. Point out the stars. Find Earth.
4. Watch out for that meteor! Duck down.
5. Move to the front of the ship to repair the TV camera
    (slow motion hammering, etc.).

Continue adding events as long as the children enjoy the action. End by returning to the ship, eating astronaut food with slow-motion chewing, and lying down to sleep in space.

Great fun and great for listening skills, too.

Bicycle Fun

Have the children lie on their backs, with their legs in the air, and move their legs in bicycle fashion.

Blastoff

Pretend to be a rocket ship. Crouch down, count backwards from ten, and blastoff by standing up quickly and giving a jump up.

Row, Row, Row Your Boat

The children sit on the floor facing each other in pairs. They spread their legs in a "V," touch feet to the feet of their partner, and hold partner's hands. As the class sings the song, the children *gently* pull each other back and forth in a rocking motion.

Sandpaper Blocks

Glue or tack sandpaper to wooden 2 × 5 inch rectangles. Glue or nail a drawer pull or spool on the back of each block for a handle.

Use to make train sound and rhythms.

Record

Play a record and have the class pretend to be a train. Move around in a circle by putting one hand on the shoulder of the child in front of each child and moving the other arm in a train-wheel motion.

Control the noise level by having the train go slower and slower, quieter and quieter, until it stops when the record ends.

Take a Ride

(Tune: "Twinkle, Twinkle, Little Star")

Ride a horse or ride in a car.
Ride a train but don't go too far.
Ride a merry-go-round at the fair.
Ride a plane up in the air.
Ride a rocket to the moon.
Just be sure you are back by noon.

(The children act out each ride as it is mentioned in the song.)

Ways We Travel Song

(Tune: "Michael, Row the Boat Ashore")

Sing the verses using the names of the children in the class.

1. (child's name) drives the car to work, Hal-le-lu-jah. _____ drives the car to work, Hal-le-lu-jah.
2. _____ rides the bus to school, etc.
3. _____ rides the diesel train, etc.
4. _____ flies the plane up high, etc.
5. _____ paddles the canoe, etc.
6. _____ rides the motorcycle, etc.
7. _____ walks around in space, etc.

Blasting Off

(Tune: "Farmer in the Dell")

1. We're blasting off in space; we're blasting off in space.
   Hi ho travel-o, we're blasting off in space.
2. We're driving in a car, etc.
3. We're riding in a train, etc.
4. We're walking in a park, etc.
5. We're flying in a plane, etc.

Rest or Nap Time

Pretend you have been traveling for a long time and have stopped at a motel for the night. Get a room, unlock the door, unpack your suitcase, and lie down to rest.

Transition Times

Call children, one at a time, to join you at the door and make a human train. ''The train is now boarding for lunch time.'' Use whispered choo-choo sounds and pantomimed whistle blowings as you move together through the halls.

Snack Time

1. *Train*
   Put a sign on the door that says ''Dining Car'' and arrange the chairs like a train while you have a snack.
2. *Airplane*
   Let children take turns, two at a time, pretending to be a flight attendant. They ask another child if he/she wants a snack, then serve it to the child.

Hats

Provide an assortment of hats to encourage transportation role playing: pilot, sailor, traffic officer, bus driver, train engineer, etc. If desired, use this hat pattern to create some hats from tagboard.

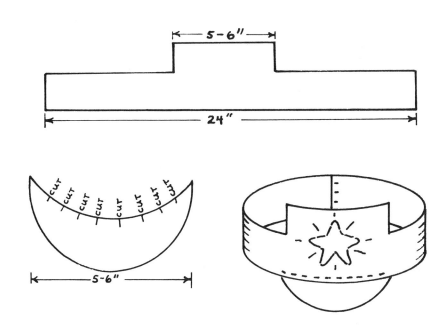

Space Helmet

Cover a 3 gallon round ice cream container with foil. Cut a window at eye level and tape plastic in it. Pretend to be an astronaut traveling in space. Attach a piece of thin plastic tubing to the helmet for a lifeline, if desired.

Travel Charades

Make a set of 3 × 5 inch cards with pictures of transportation vehicles on each one. Put all of the cards in a box. Each child pulls out one card and acts out the type of vehicle on the card. The rest of the class guess what the child is.

Box Bus

A big box and a real steering wheel provide endless hours of role play as a bus, car, or truck. Cut one door in each side. Set a small chair inside for a seat. A child gets into the box and holds the steering wheel to drive.

Make steering wheels by adding appropriate details to a sturdy paper plate or a wooden circle. Red construction paper circles for taillights and foil circles for headlights add to the fun.

Bus, Train, or Plane

Make a line of chairs, one behind another. Children pretend to buy tickets, get in, travel, etc. Play money, paper tickets, purses, and a hole punch to punch tickets will increase the role play.

Suitcases

Provide suitcases and old clothes, so children can pack and unpack for their travels.

SCIENCE

Windsock

Explain how pilots have to know which way the wind is blowing because airplanes must take off and land into the wind. Make a windsock. Attach it to a long pole. Take it outside to observe in which direction the wind is blowing.

Have the children hold out their arms as wings and take off and land into the wind.

How Does a Heavy Boat Float?

Children sometimes do not understand how heavy boats are able to float on top of the water. Tell them that the shape of the boat is one important reason. The boat must be wide to hold a lot of air. Air is lighter than water, so the boat floats.

Experiment: You need two pieces of aluminum foil, 1 foot square, and a small pan or bowl of water. Have a child tightly wad one piece of foil into a ball shape. Set it in the water and watch what happens. (It should sink.) Next, shape the second piece of foil into a boat shape by turning up and sealing the edges. Place it in the water and watch again. (It should float.) ''Why does the boat shape float?''

Ask if any child has ever floated in the water on a swimming ring or on an air mattress. ''Why was the ring or air mattress able to help you float?''

Communication

CONCEPTS

- "Communicate" means to share ideas and needs.
- People and animals need to communicate to make their needs known and to enjoy each other.
- Communication is done in many ways: through words, through pictures, through actions and gestures.

ART

Sew-Sew Designs

Blunt needles; yarn; styrofoam meat trays; pointed marker or pen.

Talk about how artists communicate their feelings and ideas through their art creations. Then, have the children sew, with blunt needle and yarn, on styrofoam meat trays. Allow the two- and three-year-olds to sew randomly and enjoy the designs that emerge. Encourage the four-year-olds to draw a simple shape, letter, etc., on the meat tray with a pointed marker or pen. Then, the children sew around the outline of their shape.

Place Cards for Snack Time

9 × 12 inch paper; crayons or markers; glue; photograph (optional).

Fold a 9 × 12 inch paper in thirds. Later you can tape it together at the bottom to make a stand-up triangle place card.

Print each child's name on one of the cards. Children then decorate the cards using crayons or markers. As a special attraction, glue on a small photograph of each child by his/her name. When finished, tape the place card so it stands up.

Young children love having a special "place" to go to at the table and will feel extra special marking that place with their own place card!

Tell Me About Your Picture

Paper; crayons; paints; markers; chalk; black marker.

Help children learn that they can communicate through art and words.

Give the children a piece of blank paper and encourage them to draw using crayons, paints, markers, or chalk. As each finishes, ask each child to "tell me about your picture." Use a black marker to print their ideas as a caption on their picture.

Developing Control of Scissors

Index cards; used greeting cards.

Two-year-olds *want* to be able to use scissors but become frustrated when they can't control scissors well. Provide them with index cards or used greeting cards

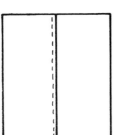 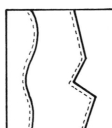

to practice cutting. The slightly stiff paper of the cards enables the two-year-olds to hold it and cut it more easily.

Later, draw line patterns on cards for the children to use as cutting lines. Begin with one straight line on each card. Then, vary the shape of the line as children increase their control of the scissors.

Finger Paint a Song

Refer to the Art Recipes for instructions about finger painting. Help the children learn that music communicates feelings and actions. Play parts of recorded songs while the children finger paint. Choose music that is slow, faster, happy sounding, etc. As they finger paint, talk with the children about letting their fingers show how the music makes them feel. Ask them which music they most like to paint to and why they enjoyed it most.

String Pictures

Heavy string; glue; paper.

Each child dips one or more pieces of string into the glue and arranges the string on the paper in any shape. After the string dries, each child uses markers or crayons to add details and color to the picture.

Encourage the children to talk with you about what their string shapes might be. Write a title or caption on the picture for the children, if they desire.

People Collage

Butcher paper or 9 × 12 inch paper; magazines; glue.

Print ''People Need People'' on a large piece of butcher paper (for a group collage) or on 9 × 12 inch pieces of paper for each child. Children cut out pictures of people from magazines to glue on the collage.

String Story

Heavy string; paper; glue; old magazines.

The children cut out or draw several pictures of figures or objects that interest them. Help them arrange some or all of their choices, so the pictures are in a sequence that tells a story. Then, the children glue the objects to the string, working from left to right, so the string story can be ''read.''

Love Mural

Muslin or old sheet; fabric crayons or markers.

Tape a large piece of inexpensive muslin (or an old sheet) to the top of a table. Print ''love'' or some other feeling in large letters in the center of the fabric. Children use fabric crayons or markers to draw pictures that communicate the chosen feeling. Print each child's name on the fabric by their picture.

Picture Postcards

9 × 12 inch paper.

Discuss how and why people send postcards to others.

Have the children fold a 9 × 12 inch paper in half. On one half, the children draw any picture they want. On the other half, print the message they want to send to someone.

BLOCKS

Provide ''block flash cards'' for children to communicate with each other. Trace around each available type and size of block on a strip of tagboard. While playing in the block area, play the silence game. The children use hand signals and flash cards to ask for the needed blocks. The children will enjoy the novelty of this game for one day.

BULLETIN BOARD

Our Message Board

Cover the board with white or light-colored butcher paper. As a border around the board, make a collage of pictures of ways of communicating, such as phone, television, billboards, tom-toms, smoke signals, computer, satellite, and pencil and paper. Let the children take turns drawing on the message board like a graffiti board. Print any word messages they want under their pictures. Children love to create this board. They will enjoy looking at it and sharing each other's messages for several days.

COOKING

Krispie Cookies
(No cook recipe)

½ cup light corn syrup
½ cup peanut butter
3 cups Rice Krispies cereal

Wash hands. Mix ingredients together. The children shape the mixture into balls. (Moisten hands slightly to eliminate sticking.)

Sharing is one way we communicate that we care. Invite another class to come in to share your Krispie Cookies. Have each child serve one guest.

As an added touch, make Place Cards for Snack Time (see ART for two-year-olds) for each guest.

Edible Letters

Refrigerated canned biscuits

Wash hands. Give each child two or more uncooked biscuits. The children roll and shape the biscuits into initials (or any other shape they choose). Bake. Provide butter or jam, if desired. Let the children eat their creations.

Create-a-Pizza

English muffins or canned biscuits flattened by each child
Pizza sauce
Grated cheese
Hamburger, browned

The children put together their own pizza. Place the pizzas on a cookie sheet to take to the kitchen to bake, or to bake in a toaster oven in the classroom. Write each name on a strip of foil and place on each pizza.

Encourage the children to communicate with each other as they are creating pizzas. Discuss which ingredient to put on first, second, etc.

LANGUAGE ARTS

Books

Foster, G. Allen. *Communication: From Primitive Tom-Toms to Telstar*. Criterion Books, 1965.
Lepthian, Emilie U. *Communication and You*. Rand McNally, 1966.
Lobel, Arnold. *Days with Frog and Toad*. Harper and Row, 1979.

Look and Learn. Field Enterprises, 1969.
Silverstein, Shel. *Where the Sidewalk Ends*. Harper and Row, 1974.

Wordless Books

DePaola, Tomie. *Pancakes for Breakfast*. Harcourt Brace Jovanovich, 1978.
Goodall, John S. *Paddy Goes Traveling*. Atheneum, 1982.
Hutchins, Pat. *Changes, Changes*. Macmillan, 1971.
Mayer, Mercer. *A Boy, a Dog and a Frog*. The Dial Press, 1967.
Mayer, Mercer. *Ah-Choo*. The Dial Press, 1976.
Mayer, Mercer and Marianna. *A Boy, a Dog, a Frog and a Friend*. The Dial Press, 1971.

Fingerplays

Wiggles

We can wiggle fingers.
We can wiggle toes.
We can wiggle shoulders.
We can wiggle a nose.
Wiggle, wiggle, wiggle all of me.
Now I can sit as still as can be.

Big Thumb

Big thumb, big thumb, where are you?
  (Make one fist; make other fist with thumb extended.)
Here I am, here I am! How do you do?
  (Extend hidden thumb and wiggle as if bowing to greet first thumb.)

Knock at My Door

Someone is knocking at my door; one, two, three, four.
  (Make a knocking motion.)
Come inside. What a nice day. I'm so glad you came to play!
  (Motion in. Two hands shake.)

Poem

Read "Deaf Donald" by Shel Silverstein (in *Where the Sidewalk Ends*) a few times to the children. Talk about deafness. Teach the class the motions to the poem.
  Invite a guest speaker to come to your class and demonstrate sign language.

School Letter

One class starts a "Have a Happy Day" message to send to the office. Each class supplies a line or two or a special picture and signs the letter. The letter then passes to the next class, etc. Deliver to the office staff and the director. Watch for smiles of delight.

**Pizza Messages
(A Sequence Craft)**

1. Cut out manila circles representing English muffins or biscuits.
2. Color the circles red (tomato sauce).
3. Glue small pieces of torn brown construction paper scraps on the circles (hamburger).
4. Glue on thin yellow strips (cheese).
5. Glue finished product on a larger sheet of construction paper.

Ask the children to think of a message to write to their parent(s). Print the dictated message.

TV Box

Cut a window for a TV screen in a *large* cardboard box. Let the children take turns standing or sitting inside to talk or sing on television.

Older children will enjoy taking turns being a newscaster and/or weather reporter. The newscaster tells what the class has been doing: birthdays, calendar, new children, etc. The weather reporter talks about what the weather was when school began, what it is like outside at the moment, and what will happen that night. Set up a table, chair, blackboard, tape recorder, etc. Play the tape back as desired.

Telephone Information

Check with your local telephone service to see if they have telephone equipment and materials to loan to your classroom.

Telephones

Use toy telephones to encourage conversations between two children. (Ask children to bring toy phones from home, if you don't have any.)

Tape record the pretend telephone conversations. Children will often speak more clearly and enthusiastically when they realize you are recording them.

Eletelephony

Read the poem "Eletelephony" by Laura E. Richards to the group.

Class Letters

Help the children understand that people write letters to communicate with each other.

As a group, write a letter to someone who's special to the class (such as another class, the school director, etc.). Let the children dictate ideas as you write them down in the letter. Begin by saying: "Let's write a letter to _____ . What do you want to say to _____ ?"

The Name Game

This game will encourage children to learn and use each other's names.

Sit in a circle. Begin by saying, "My name is Ms. Roberts. What is your name?" The child next to you says, "My name is _____," and asks the next child, "What is your name?" Continue until you have gone around the entire circle.

Classification—Talking and Not Talking

Classify pictures from magazines of people who are *talking* and *not talking*.

Recording Stars

Individually tape record each child's voice talking about self, family, etc. During group time, play the recording and have the children identify who is talking each time.

Stop and Go Signs

Make simple stop and go signs. Ask the children what they think the signs mean.

Play a game. The children tiptoe around the room when you hold up "go," but they must stop when you hold up "stop." Use each sign several times during the game.

Colored Phones Game

Using the telephone pattern on the front of the March Curriculum guide, cut out pairs of phones in several colors. Pass to the children one of each of the colors of phones. You hold up a color phone, such as yellow, and say, "Calling yellow." The child who is holding the matching color answers, "Hello. This is yellow." Continue the game until you have called all the colors.

Type a Message

Bring in an old typewriter and let children take turns experimenting with typing.

Class Books

Have each child make a picture. Print names on each picture. Put the pictures together to make a book. Make a cover for the book with construction paper or wallpaper samples. Title it: "The Best in Our Class."

Wordless Books

Share a wordless book with your class (see LANGUAGE ARTS). Discuss how a book can communicate a story when it has no words.

Tape record the class as the children help you tell the story with words. Later, let children play the tape and look at the book again by themselves.

Newspaper

Talk about the newspaper as a form of communication. Bring in the local paper and find articles that tell about local and national events. Include the weather report, comics, and advertising.

Compile a class or school newspaper on chart paper. Help the children decide what news to include. Type it up and copy it to send home with the class or the whole school. Topics might include: who is sick or on vacation, birthdays, lunch menu, a speaker coming to class, an upcoming field trip, etc.

MATH NUMBER CONCEPTS

Counting

"Five Birds"

Five pretty birds lived up in a tree.
Father, mother, babies, 1-2-3.
Father said: "Good morning."
Mother said: "Hello."
The baby birds cheeped: "It's time to eat!"
And gobbled worms like so.
One,   (Hold up finger, pretend to eat, gulp.)
Two,   (Continue action.)
Three...
          (Continue counting as far as appropriate for the ability of the children.)

Number-Up

Have cards with numerals written on each. Hold up a numeral. Each child tiptoes around the room to find that number of objects. For example, when you hold up "2," children could tiptoe to two chairs, or point to two eyes, or hold up two crayons.

Silent Show

Hold up a card with a numeral on it. Each child silently holds up that number of fingers. Fun for zero through ten. An activity for transition times.

Sixes

Provide each child with a piece of paper folded into six boxes. Write a numeral in each section with a marker. Children then put the required number of objects into each section. Small objects, such as counters, popsicle sticks, buttons, etc., are the best to use. This activity is fun for children and easy for you to check.

Telephone Math

Provide a telephone pattern for the children to cut out. Have them look through magazines or catalogs to find numerals to cut out and glue on the dial or the push buttons to complete the telephone. It is best to have a real or toy telephone for them to use as a reference. For younger children, you may put numerals 6-9 on the phone and have them glue on 0-5.

MATH VOCABULARY

Half—Whole

Review "half" and "whole" using construction paper shapes. Pass several whole shapes and several half shapes to the children in your class. Hold up a whole shape or half shape in flash card fashion. The children who have the matching shapes may hold them up, stand up, or hop on one foot.

MOVEMENT

Jogging

Jog in place to a record for one minute.

Ball Bounce

Stand in a small circle. The children bounce a large ball to one another. Call out the child's name as the ball is bounced to that child. The child catches the ball, calls out another name, and bounces the ball to that child. Continue until all the children have played several times. The activity works best for four to five children at a time, so everyone gets frequent turns. Have two or three groups playing at the same time.

Monkey See, Monkey Do

One child is the leader monkey. That child stands in front of the class and says, "Monkey see, monkey do" and does a movement that uses the arms and legs in some way. The rest of the class follows the leader by also doing the movement. Next, a different child becomes the leader monkey and repeats the activity.

Simon Says

Everyone does the suggested movement if the leader says "Simon says" before stating the movement. If the leader does not say "Simon says," the children freeze in place and do not copy the movement.

"Simon says bend over and touch your toes."
"Simon says swing one leg."
"Simon says stretch both arms up very tall."
"Simon says sit down."
"Stand up."

Continue the game using different commands that are fun and provide good exercise.

MUSIC

Farmer in the Dell

Discuss how people can sometimes make their needs known by gesturing or pointing at each other.

Play Farmer in the Dell as a circle game. Help the children choose each other to act out the parts called for in the music.

Matthew's Here Today

(Tune: "Farmer in the Dell")

Matthew's here today.
Matthew's here today.
We'll all clap our hands and say,
"Matthew's here today."

Use the names of the children in the class. Vary the action according to their suggestions: wink, nod, stomp feet, etc.

Musical Moods

Provide a scarf (or a short crepe paper streamer) for each child. Play soft recorded music and encourage the children to "float" around and around as they move the scarf with the music. Discuss how the music makes them feel.

ROLE PLAY

What Would You Say on the Telephone?

Ask the children to do the following:

"Pretend you call dad or mom at work."
"Pretend you call a friend to come and play."
"Pretend you call me, your teacher."

Communicating with Actions and Gestures

Without any words, how would you say:

I'm hungry.
Come here!
Quiet, please.
Yes.
No.

Up.
Down.
I'm cold.
That's too loud!
I don't know.

Different People Say Different Things

Try to say "hello" differently for each of the following:

a baby (How does a baby say "hello"?)
an old person
a mom
a dad
someone who feels mad
a happy child

SCIENCE

Sounds of Animals

"What sound does a _____ make?"

Animal Communication

"How do you know if a puppy or kitten likes you?"
"How do you know if a puppy or kitten is hungry?"
"How do you know if any small animal is hurt?"

Telephones

Sound is vibration. Make play telephones with two paper cups, two brads, and a long string. Punch a brad through the bottom of each cup and tie each end of the string to one brad.

Why does the "telephone" work best when the string is kept taut? (The string can vibrate better and "carry" the sound.)

Feet

CONCEPTS

- Feet are an important part of our body. They help us move.
- It's fun to do silly things with our feet.

ART

Feet Flowers

Butcher paper; construction paper.

Try a funny feet flower garden "planted" on the wall with butcher paper strip fence. Construction paper handprint cutouts become the blossoms and feet cutouts become the leaves of the flowers. Add a stem and the garden is ready to be admired.

Feet Mobiles

Construction paper; yarn; hole puncher.

Trace and cut out each child's foot on a piece of construction paper. Cut out each footprint. Print the child's name in large letters on each foot. Punch one hole on each side of the ball of the foot and one hole at the heel. Tie three pieces of yarn to the foot and hang it from the ceiling with the names showing on the bottom side, so the children can have fun looking up and seeing their names. Guaranteed a child-pleasing winner!

Hidden Feet Pictures

Manila paper; crayons or makers.

Trace around feet on manila paper. The children use crayons or markers to turn the foot into a different picture, such as a monster, an animal, a hat on a person, etc.

Feet Sponge Painting

Sponges; tempera paint; meat trays or paper plates; clothespins.

Cut flat sponges into simple foot shapes. Put small amounts of tempera paint on meat trays or paper plates.

The children dip the sponge shapes into the paint and press them on their paper. To limit the messiness, pinch a clothespin on each sponge before using it. Then, the children will have a clothespin handle to hold as they sponge paint.

Feet Tree

Paper; crayon; tempera paint; Q-Tips; real tree branch (optional).

Trace around each child's bare feet. Use a crayon to print the child's name in large letters down the middle of each foot. Have the children use Q-Tips and tempera paint to paint designs on their footprints. (The paint will not stick to the crayon name, so it will still show clearly.)

Hang the feet on a real tree branch, like leaves. Or, put a large paper tree on the wall and tape the feet on as leaves.

Paper Punch Power

Magazine pages, construction paper, or comic sections of newspapers; glue; paper plate or small box.

Using one or more paper punches, let the children take turns punching out circles from colorful magazine pages, comic sections of the newspaper, or construction paper scraps. The children decorate a foot cutout, small box, paper plate, or any shape by covering it with the circles, pasted on in mosaic fashion.

This activity is good for small muscle development and the children love it! It also helps them to learn to handle glue effectively.

Monster Feet

12 × 18 inch construction paper; Q-Tips; tempera paints.

Cut a monster foot for each child. Make it as large as possible. (Using 12 × 18 inch construction paper might work best.)

Children use Q-Tips and tempera paints to paint designs on their monster foot.

Display the feet in footprint fashion along the walls, as if a monster had walked through!

Toe Puppets

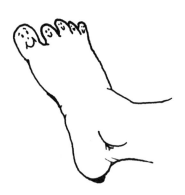

Nonpermanent markers.

Use nonpermanent markers to make puppet faces on each toe of the children's feet. Wiggle toes to make the puppets move and talk. Encourage the puppet toes to talk with others about how they feel and what they like to do.

Class Feet Collage

Butcher paper; magazines; catalogs; paste.

Cut a foot shape from a very large piece of butcher paper. Have the children cut out feet and shoes from magazines and catalogs to paste on the foot shape. Encourage the children to continue until they have covered the entire shape.

Feet Butterflies

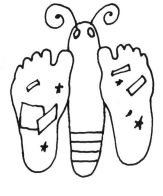

Construction paper; crayons; sponge paint; glue; torn tissue scraps.

A child puts both feet close together on a piece of construction paper. Trace around each child's pair of feet. Have the children add a body and antenna between the insides of the feet as shown. Use crayons, sponge paint, or glue and torn tissue paper squares to decorate the butterflies. Display for all to see and talk about.

Sandals

Posterboard or cardboard; hole punch; string or yarn.

Using the pattern for sandals, trace the right and left sandal onto posterboard or cardboard. Cut out each shape. Use a hole punch to punch the holes as shown. Insert string or yarn in the holes as illustrated in the small picture.

Let the children wear the sandals they've made. Discuss that these were the kind of shoes worn in Jesus' time.

Feet Painting

White shelf or butcher paper; tempera paint; meat tray or paper plate; pan of soapy water and towel.

Lay a long sheet of paper on the floor—white shelf paper or butcher paper 4-6 feet long works well.

Put a small amount of tempera paint in a meat tray or paper plate. Use a second tray with another color in it to add more interest and to make color blends.

One at a time, let children put their bare feet in the paint and immediately walk up and down on the paper to make feet prints. As children finish, have a chair, a small pan of soapy water, and a towel at the edge of the paper, so they can immediately sit down and wash the excess paint off without a mess.

The finished feet painting is very interesting and strikingly different. Children usually talk about the painting for a long time!

Tape the feet painting all along the hallways, so other classes can enjoy the effect.

Shoe Family

Magazines; catalogs; paste.

Children cut out an appropriate shoe for each member of their family from magazines and catalogs. Then, the children paste the shoes on a paper and add details to turn each shoe into a person.

As children name each member of their shoe family, print the name under each shoe. Encourage the children to make a shoe person for each member in their real family.

"Big Toe" Creatures

Manila paper; ink pad (any color but black); markers or crayons.

Make a big toe print on 4 inch squares of manila paper by pressing each child's big toe on an ink pad and then pressing it on the paper square. Let the children add eyes, nose, mouth, arms, legs, hats, etc., with markers or crayons.

BLOCKS

Cut long, narrow strips of tagboard. On each one, trace different block shapes in a repeating sequence. The children try to reproduce the sequence with the blocks on the floor. This is also a good activity to use with the smaller, tabletop blocks.

BULLETIN BOARD

Feet

Trace the children's feet on construction paper in a variety of colors. If possible, have the children cut them out. Print each child's name on his/her footprint.

Cut a large footprint from butcher paper. The children put footprints on it by stepping in tempera paint and onto the paper. Water and towels should be handy for cleanup. (See "Feet Painting" in ART.) Tack the large footprint on the bulletin board. Put the construction paper feet randomly around it.

Door Decoration

Tape several feet in a walking pattern across the door. For example, from the lower left corner across the door to the upper right, as if a child walked across the door.

COOKING

Banana Toes

½ banana for each child
1-2 marshmallows per child

Cut the banana in long slices to resemble toes. Cut a slice from a marshmallow to add to each banana toe for a toenail.
Variation: Freeze the creations to eat later and call them "Frostbitten Toes."

Feetwich Fillings

1. *Fluffernutter*
   Mix equal amounts of marshmallow creme and peanut butter. Stir until smooth.

2. *Peanutbutterandjelly*
   Mix equal amounts of peanut butter and jelly together. Stir until smooth.

3. *Honeybutter*
   Mix equal amounts of honey and peanut butter together. Stir until smooth.

   Give each child a paper cup and a popsicle stick. In each cup, put a small amount of the chosen ingredients. Have each child stir with the popsicle stick until the ingredients are well mixed. Use the same stick to spread the filling on a piece of bread or some crackers.

Toes in a Biscuit

Canned biscuits
Small smoky links

Each child flattens a biscuit as much as possible. Lay the sausage in the center, fold the sides over, and seal well by pinching them together. Lay on a cookie sheet and bake according to biscuit directions. Put the children's names on strips of aluminum foil, then lay the "toes" on top of the strips and bake them.

LANGUAGE ARTS

Books

Baker, Betty. *Walk the World's Rim*. Harper and Row, 1965.
DeRegniers, Beatrice Schenk. *What Can You Do with a Shoe?* Harper and Row, 1955.
Hutchins, Pat. *Rosie's Walk*. Macmillan, 1968.
Seuss, Dr. *The Foot Book*. Random House, 1965.
Showers, Paul. *The Listening Walk*. Crowell, 1961.
Viorst, Judith. *Try It Again, Sam: Safety When You Walk*. Lothrop, Lee and Shepard Co.
Warren, Mary Phraner. *Walk in My Moccasins*. Westminster Press, 1966.

Poems

Aldis, Dorothy. "The Sad Shoes," in *All Together* by Dorothy Aldis. Putnam, 1925.

Fallis, Edwina. "The Giant's Shoes," in *Let's Read Together Poems, Book 3*, Helen A. Brown and Harry J. Holt, eds. Harper and Row, 1954.

"Feet" Plays

These Feet Are Made For Walking

(Act out each suggested action.)

These feet are made for walking,
These feet are made to run.
These feet like to be tickled,
And play and have some fun.

Left and Right

We stamp, stamp, stamp with our left foot.
We stamp, stamp, stamp with our right.
Then we turn ourselves around and around
And *clap* with all our might.

Barefoot Day

Have a barefoot day on which no one wears shoes for a certain period of time. (More fun if you "play" too!)

Vocabulary Development: Discuss how different surfaces feel: soft, bumpy, smooth, slick, hard, etc.

Blindfold Game

Have 8 × 12 inch samples of sandpaper, carpet, satin, velvet, corduroy, tile, prickly door mat, and a scrub brush. Show the samples to the children. Feel them, discuss them, and name them. Then, take turns blindfolding children and letting them rub a bare foot over one of the samples. Remove the blindfold and ask the children to point to the sample they think they felt.

Guess the Feet Contest

Hang up or hold up a blanket, just off the floor. Children take turns, several at a time, hiding behind the blanket barefooted, with only their feet exposed. The rest of the children guess the owner of each pair of feet. Two classes together will create more fun!

Variation: Have pictures of all kinds of feet (animal, bird, human). Cover the picture with a blank sheet of construction paper so just the feet show. Let the children guess which feet belong to which animal, bird, or person.

Pick It Up!

Collect several common objects, such as a pencil, a crayon, a cotton ball, a piece of paper, etc. Let barefoot children take turns sitting in a chair and trying to pick up one of the objects placed in front of them with just their toes!

Parts of the Feet

Discuss and name the parts of the feet: heel, toe, ankle, toenail. Ask the children to point to each part on their feet as you name it.

Feet Play—This Little Piggy Went to Market

Remind the children that when they were littler, people probably played this game with them. Repeat the verse together for fun and memory.

Barefoot variation: Everyone takes off shoes. After repeating the rhyme, the children tickle their own or each other's feet and end on a laughing note!

Poem

Read "The Sad Shoes" by Dorothy Aldis (in *All Together*) to the children. If possible, bring an old pair of "sad shoes" to show the class. Discuss why these shoes are now sad shoes. Ask the children if they've ever had sad shoes. Repeat the verse several times throughout the week, so children begin to memorize some of it.

Copy the poem for the children. Let them draw a picture on the bottom and take the poem home.

Monster Feet Story

Make the Monster Feet suggested in ART. After you position the feet around the walls, discuss with the class: "What do you think these monsters look like if they have this kind of feet?" "What could we pretend that they were doing while walking around our room?"

As the children talk, write their ideas on a chart for a story.

"Feet" Begins with "F" (Class Project)

Get a large square of butcher paper and outline the paper with a repeating border of footprints (or cut the butcher paper in the shape of a large foot, then add the border). Write "'Feet' Begins with 'F'" at the top of the paper. Encourage the children to cut out pictures at home of things that begin with "F." Have them bring the pictures to school to glue on the paper. Discuss each.

Variation: Use a large posterboard or construction paper cutout of "F." Glue "F" objects all over it. Hang it from the ceiling.

Feet Play— Left and Right

You begin reading the first line of the poem "The Giant Shoes" and alternate with the children quickly learning to say the repeating line: "Left! Right! Tie them up tight!" Repeat several times throughout the week, so the children become familiar with the poem. Add actions and left to right feet stomping or marching in place as the class repeats the poem.

If Your Feet Could Talk...

Write each child's name on a chart, leaving about three lines between each name. Ask each child: "If your feet could talk, what would they want to say?" Copy their answers beside their name.

Duplicate the whole class's responses and send a copy home for the parents to enjoy!

Variation: Ask the children "If your feet could take you any place in the whole world, where would they want to go?"

MATH

NUMBER CONCEPTS

Counting Fun

1. Count the number of shoes with ties. Then, count those with buckles. Which is more? Count the number of shoes with velcro closings. Now, which is more?
2. Count the number of red shoes, blue shoes, etc. Write the numeral for each.
3. Count how many toes are on one foot. How many are on both feet together?
4. Count the number of steps it takes to walk across the room, to the door, to the table, etc. Count the same distance using giant steps, regular-size steps, and tiptoe steps.

Numeral and Number Match

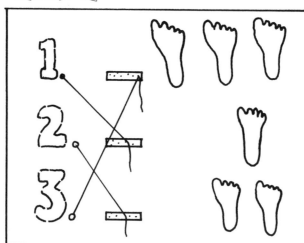

Posterboard; multiple cutouts of the foot on the front of the March Curriculum guide; markers; yarn; sandpaper or velcro.

Make a matching game with feet cutouts and numerals. Children try to attach the yarn from each numeral to the sandpaper strip by the correct set of feet.

FEET

Using a Ruler

Measure each child's foot. Write down the length of the foot by each child's name, so children can compare the numerals. Discuss: one foot; ruler; inches.

Feet Measurement

Measure a table, hall, sidewalk, or other large object with feet or steps. Use a child's foot to measure. Then, measure the same distance using your own foot. Discuss whose foot will take the most counting to measure something and why.

Size Relationships

Provide several pairs of shoes of different sizes. Have the children arrange the pairs in smallest to largest size, then arrange them in largest to smallest size.

MATH VOCABULARY

Half—Whole

If possible, bring in a saw and boards. Mark the half point of each board and let the children saw the wood in half.
CONSTANT supervision is required!

Cup—Half Cup

Empty several bags of beans or rice into a large dishpan. Provide measuring utensils of one cup and one-half cup. Let one or two children pour one cup or half cup quantities into other containers. Demonstrate filling the cups to the top.

MOVEMENT

Step Right Up

Take giant steps, baby steps, side steps, backward steps, running, skipping, hopping, skating, etc.

Feet Wiggles

Sit in a large circle on the floor with shoes and socks off. Wiggle toes, wiggle feet, stretch toes apart, stretch feet. Let the children think of feet exercises for all to do. While sitting in the circle barefoot, arrange all the class so their feet go from big to biggest. Be sure to include yourself!

Jumping Feet

Jump over a rope or a broom handle that's lying on the ground or floor. Gradually move it up as the children jump each height.

FEET

Stilts

2 empty coffee or large juice cans; 2 pieces of twine or heavy string; hammer and nail.

Using a hammer and nail, punch a hole on each side of each can near the top. Thread the twine through the holes to make a loop long enough to hold. Knot the twine securely.

Blindfoot Walk

Lay a rope in a random pattern on the floor. With shoes off and eyes closed or blindfolded, walk on the rope and follow where it leads by feeling with feet.

MUSIC

Feet Were Meant to Move to Music

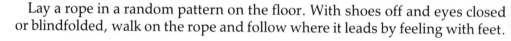

Use different speeds and styles of recorded music to show how our feet can move to music. Play records that encourage the following movements: marching, walking, hopping, sliding, skating, and tiptoeing.

Play and Sing Loopy Loo

Use the record of the song "Loopy Loo" or sing the words together as the class acts out the song.

Variation: Barefoot Loopy Loo. Everyone has shoes and socks off. Tie a piece of red yarn around each right big toe and right thumb of the children and yourself. As the class sings and dances, it is easy to distinguish left and right.

Kazoo

Make a kazoo or humboard for the children to use to make music as they march. Cover one end of a short cardboard tube (from an empty toilet paper roll) with waxed paper and fasten it tightly with a rubber band. Punch three holes in a line near the open end.

The child makes music by humming on the open end of the tube. Children love the sound.

ROLE PLAY

Work Shoes

Bring in pairs of adult-size boots, work shoes, high heels, etc. Let the children try them on and ''walk to work'' in them.

Shoe Store

Setting up a shoe store and pretending to buy and sell shoes is an excellent activity. Suggested materials: assortment of shoe boxes; large pile of shoes as varied as possible in size, style, and color; blocks or bricks and boards for building shoe display areas; paper and markers for signs and pricing; mirror; 2 or 3 chairs for customers; something with which to measure foot size; play money and a cash register are optional, as children can pretend to pay without using any props.

SCIENCE

Magnifying Prints

Use a magnifying glass to study and compare fingerprints and toeprints. Talk about size and shape.

Tracks

Examine prints of a dog, class pet, chicken, bird, cat, and child. Match each print to a picture of the animal or child. Let the children make tracks by pressing a foot or paw into a flattened circle of play dough.

Toenails

''What are toenails?'' ''Why do we have them?''
Talk about why it hurts if you cut your foot but it does not hurt when you trim a toenail.

Sandals

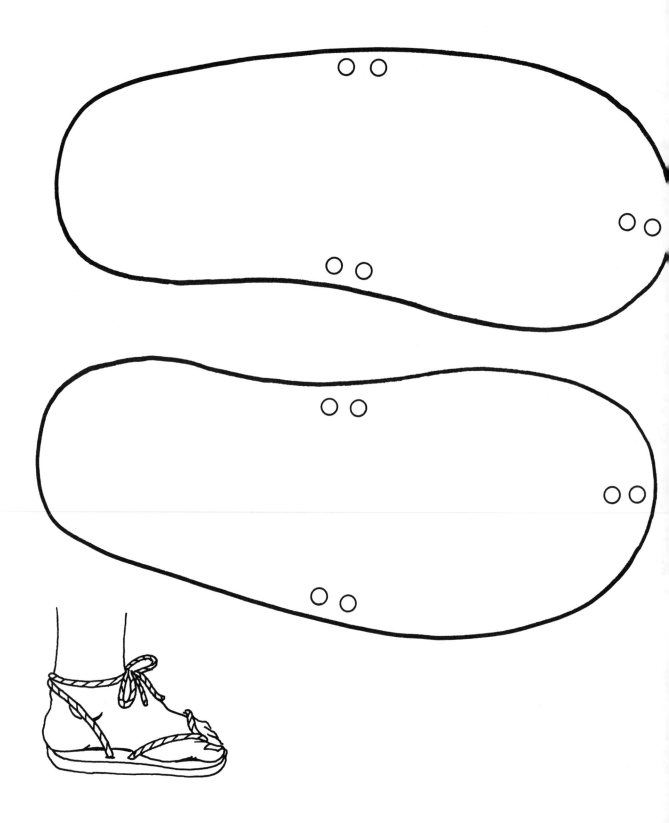

April
Curriculum

1. Easter

2. Color

3. Spring and
   Growing Things

4. Wild West

Easter

CONCEPTS

- Easter is a holiday that comes in the spring.
- Rabbits and baby chickens are popular Easter symbols.
- The egg symbolizes new life at Easter.
- It is a popular custom to decorate eggs and hide them as a fun game.
- Some people do not celebrate Easter, because they have different beliefs.

ART

Easter Baskets

1. Strawberry plastic basket. Attach two joined-together pipe cleaners as a handle. (A pipe cleaner handle is much more durable than a construction paper one! If using construction paper, make the handle from two or three thicknesses of paper, folded together for strength.)
2. Bottom of ½ gallon milk carton. Pipe cleaner handle.
3. Bottom of oatmeal box. Paint or cover with paper. Pipe cleaner handle.
4. Four-egg section of egg carton. Pipe cleaner handle.
5. Small white or brown paper lunch sack. Fold top half down to make strong ''double-walled'' sides. Pipe cleaner handle.

Let children decorate their baskets with cut paper, paint, crayons, or markers. Add Easter ''grass,'' if desired.

Dyed Eggs

Egg Dye (see Art Recipes); crayons; hard-boiled eggs.

Make one bowl of red, one of blue, and one of yellow dye. Children use a spoon to dip a hard-boiled egg into one of the colors. Encourage them to dip an egg into one color, then into a second color to see what happens to the color of the egg.

Encourage the children to draw designs and pictures gently on a hard-boiled egg with crayons before dipping the egg into the dye.

Cotton Ball Easter Bunny Head

Styrofoam wig stand head shape; glue; cotton balls; pipe cleaners; posterboard.

Let the children take turns working to cover the head completely by gluing on cotton balls. Dry overnight. Add facial features and pipe cleaner whiskers. Add posterboard ears.

From *We Care*, Copyright © 1988 Scott, Foresman and Company.

Paper Maché Easter Bunny Head

Styrofoam wig stand head shape; wire; 1 × 6 inch strips of newspaper or paper towels; thin flour and water paste or wallpaper paste; pipe cleaners.

Paper maché in layers to cover the wig stand. Have the children dip the strips into the paste, "pull" off the extra paste by sliding their fingers along the strips, and lay the strips on the head. "Pet" the strips to smooth them down. Continue until one layer covers the head. Allow the paper maché to dry overnight, then add another layer.

After two layers have dried, bend two lengths of wire to form stand-up ears. Stick the ears well into the styrofoam. The children will now need some help covering the ears with the paper maché. Add two more layers of paper maché over the ears and head.

Let the children take turns painting the rabbit head when it's totally dry. Add facial features and pipe cleaner whiskers.

Easter Tree

Bring in an actual tree branch. (The size of the branch depends on your available space.) Spray paint the branch white. "Plant" it in an ice cream container or wastebasket with dirt, rocks, or plaster of paris. (A Christmas tree stand works well, if the branch is large enough.)

Hang child-decorated eggs made from egg carton sections, paper maché, construction paper, etc. Provide sewing scraps, lace, beads, sequins, markers, Q-Tips, and paint for decorating the eggs.

Art Tissue Eggs

Colored art tissue paper cut into 1½ inch squares; diluted glue; 9 × 12 inch manila paper; brushes.

Children brush over the manila paper with diluted glue. Then, cover the glue with tissue squares like a collage.

When it's dry, glue a frame over the collage—a 9 × 12 inch piece of manila paper with a *large* egg shape cut out of it, so the tissue collage shows through in the shape of an egg.

Posterboard Eggs

Precut large egg shapes from colored posterboard or thin cardboard that children have painted with tempera paint.

Have the children glue on bits of ric-rac, lace, doilies, construction paper, etc., for decoration.

Paper Sack Bunny

White lunch-size paper sacks; construction paper; glue; yarn; newspapers.

The children stuff crushed newspapers into a paper sack. Use the yarn to tie the opening closed to make a neck.

The children glue big bunny ears, eyes, and a nose on their sack bunny.

L'eggs Eggs

One L'eggs (hose) egg or large plastic egg for each child; yarn; lace; ric-rac; construction paper; glue.

The children decorate a plastic egg by gluing on bits of the lace, ric-rac, yarn, etc. While it dries, they draw a picture on a small piece of paper to roll up inside as a surprise "gift" for someone at home.

Egg Placemat

Large cutout egg shapes; crayons; construction paper scraps; glue.

Have the children decorate the egg shapes with crayons or bits of construction paper. Print each child's name on his/her egg with large letters. Use as personalized placemats during a special Easter celebration snack.

Bunny Hop Finger Puppets

Cut a bunny shape out of stiff paper. Cut two finger-size holes on the front, as shown.

The children add details with crayons, markers, or construction paper. They may make their bunny hop and dance as you play an appropriate record.

Encourage the children to have their bunny puppets talk to each other: "What would a little bunny say to a friend?" "What would a bunny want a friend to do?"

Bunny Bracelet

Small white paper plates; construction paper; glue; wide, sturdy rubber bands.

The children use construction paper to glue large ears, eyes, nose, and (possibly) whiskers on a plate. Staple a rubber band on the middle of the back of the plate. Let children wear the bunny on their hand or arm as they act out bunny movements.

Bunny Sock Puppets

Old white socks; glue; stapler; construction paper scraps; pipe cleaners.

Have children glue or staple on old, clean white socks: construction paper ears, eyes, and nose. Glue on pipe cleaner whiskers, if desired.

Let them use their puppets to talk about how to get the eggs ready for Easter, where they are going to hide eggs, etc.

Paper Maché Eggs

Half sheets of newspaper; masking tape; 1 × 6 inch strips of newspaper or paper towels; thin flour and water paste or wallpaper paste; pastel tempera paints.

Each child crumbles one-half of a newspaper page into an egg shape. Use small tabs of masking tape to hold it in shape, if necessary.

Make a thin paste mixture by gradually stirring small amounts of warm water into 1 cup of flour in a large plastic bowl. Let two to four children at a time dip the 1 inch wide strips of newspaper or paper towel into the paste. Show them how to pull the strip gently between the index finger and thumb to take off excess paste. Then, children wrap each strip around their egg shape and gently "pet" the edges with their fingers to smooth them down. They will need four to six strips for each egg.

Let dry overnight on pieces of plastic wrap or old plastic bags. The next day, turn over the eggs to dry the underside. When dry, a second coat of paper maché may be added, if desired. Paint with pastel shades of tempera paint for an egg that will last through many Easters.

Bunny Mask

Paper plates; construction paper; pipe cleaners; glue; stapler; elastic.

Provide large white paper plates with eyes cut out. Cut around the bottom of a nose shape, so it will open and stand out from the plate.

Have the children make ears from white and pink construction paper and staple them to the plate. Make whiskers by stapling pink, white, or black pipe cleaners on the plate. Let the children use construction paper and glue to add other details as they see fit.

When finished, staple a strip of elastic on the back so the bunny head may be worn as a mask.

"Stained Glass" Eggs

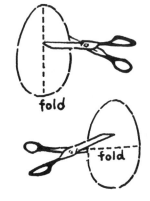

Egg shapes cut from pastel shades of 9 × 12 inch construction paper; art tissue paper in 1 inch squares; glue.

The children fold the eggs in half and cut out a few shapes along the fold, like cutting a snowflake. Open. Fold in half the other way and cut shapes on the fold. Open to see the cut design.

Provide squares of art tissue paper in several colors. The children glue a piece of tissue over each cutout on the back of the egg shape.

Turn over the egg. Display it in a window or hold up to a light.

BLOCKS

Help the children construct a block maze on the floor. Tape a cutout of an Easter bunny to a block of appropriate size. Put the Easter block bunny at one end of the maze. Place a basket of small, colored table blocks at the other end of the maze. The children take turns "hopping" the block bunny through the maze to the basket of colored blocks.

BULLETIN BOARD

The Easter Egg Hunt

Decorate and laminate Easter eggs in pairs. Display the eggs randomly on the bulletin board. Attach a length of yarn or ribbon to one of each pair. Put a piece of sandpaper under the other egg in each pair. The children match the pairs of eggs by connecting the yarn to its matching egg.

Variation: Provide a large Easter basket to display near the center of the board. As the children choose the eggs that match, they remove the eggs from the board, attach them together with a paper clip or clip clothespin, and deposit them in the basket. When all the pairs have been matched, the children mix them up and pin them back on the board, so other children may have a turn.

COOKING

Bunny or Baby Chick Sandwiches

The children use a rabbit- or chick-shaped cookie cutter to cut a shape from one slice of bread. Spread with honeybutter (½ cup of honey and ½ cup of soft butter whipped together).

Add raisins for eyes. (Save the bread scraps to feed to birds or ducks later.)

Bunny Fruit Salad

1 canned pear half for each child
Raisins
1 strawberry for each child
Cheese slices
Toothpicks

Wash hands. Place the pear half, cut side down, on a small plate. The children add raisins for eyes and use a toothpick to attach a strawberry for a nose. Add toothpick whiskers, if desired. Have children shape long ears from strips of cheese.

Admire and eat!

Bunny Cake

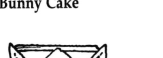

Bake a cake in a round or heart-shaped pan. Let the children use plastic or table knives to take turns spreading white frosting on the cake.

Add paper ears, large jelly bean eyes and nose, and icing or licorice for whiskers.

Easter Egg Cookies

Make a batch of rolled sugar cookie dough or use purchased refrigerator cookie dough.

Wash hands. Make an egg-shaped cookie cutter by bending and shaping the open end of a 6 ounce juice can. Or, simply give children a small amount of dough to pat with their hands into an egg shape.

Give two Lifesavers candies to each child. Let them put the candy between two pieces of waxed paper (or in a small plastic bag) and roll an unopened can over it to crush the candy slightly.

Gently push pieces of the candy into the cookie egg shapes. Bake. The candy melts slightly to decorate the Easter egg cookies!

No-Flour Passover Cookies

1 cup sugar
2 egg whites
2 cups ground nuts

Wash hands. Let the children help measure and mix all the ingredients together. Then, drop the dough by spoonfuls onto a cookie sheet lined with aluminum foil. Bake for 15-20 minutes at 325°.

LANGUAGE ARTS

Books

Baer, Jane. *The Easter Bunny Gang*. Children's Press, 1983.
Berg, Jean Horton. *The Little Red Hen*. Harper and Row, 1963.
Bracken, Carolyn. *Peter Rabbit's Pockets*. Simon and Schuster, 1982.
Brown, Margaret Wise. *The Golden Egg Book*. Western Publishing, 1943.
Brown, Margaret Wise. *Little Chicken*. Harper and Row, 1943.
Brown, Margaret Wise. *The Runaway Bunny*. Harper and Row, 1952.
Carroll, Ruth. *The Story of an Egg That Hatched*. School Book Service, 1970.
Carroll, Ruth. *Where's the Bunny?* Henry Z. Walck, 1962.

Charing, Douglas. *The Jewish World*. Silver Burdett, 1983.

Heyward, DuBose. *The Country Bunny and the Little Golden Shoes*. Houghton Mifflin, 1939.

Lenski, Lois. *Spring Is Here*. Henry Z. Walck, 1945.

Moncure, Jane Belk. *Our Easter Book*. Children's Press, 1976.

Potter, Beatrix. *The Tale of Peter Rabbit*. F. Warne, 1972.

Schenk, Esther. *Eastertime*. Lyons and Carnahan, 1953.

Schloat, G. Warren, Jr. *Wonderful Egg*. Charles Scribner's Sons, 1952.

Seuss, Dr. *Green Eggs and Ham*. Random House, 1960.

Tudor, Tasha. *A Tale for Easter*. Henry Z. Walck, 1969.

Ward, Elaine. *Sean the Bunny: An Easter Story*. Argus Communications, 1981.

Whitehead, Patricia. *What a Funny Bunny*. Troll Associates, 1985.

Zolotow, Charlotte. *Mr. Rabbit and the Lovely Present*. Harper and Row, 1962.

Teacher Resource Books

Burnett, Bernice. *Holidays*. Watts, 1983.

Chapman, Jean. *Pancakes and Painted Eggs: A Book for Easter and All the Days of the Year*. Children's Press International, 1983.

Cole, Marion and Olivia H. Cole. *Things to Make and Do for Easter*. Watts, 1979.

Hopkins, Lee Bennett. *Easter Buds Are Springing: Poems for Easter*. Harcourt Brace Jovanovich, 1979.

Livingston, Myra Cohn. *Callooh! Callay! Holiday Poems for Young Readers*. Atheneum, 1978.

Quackenbush, Robert. *The Holiday Song Book*. Lothrop, Lee and Shepard, 1977.

Renberg, Dalia Hardof. *The Complete Family Guide to Jewish Holidays*. Adama Books, 1985.

Sarnoff, Jane. *Light the Candles! Beat the Drums! A Book of Holidays*. Scribner, 1979.

Fingerplays

Wouldn't It Be Funny?

Wouldn't it be funny	
If a bunny	(Make a fist for the bunny.)
Had three ears instead of two?	(Hold up three fingers behind the bunny fist.)
Wouldn't it be funny	
If a bunny	
Could fly through the sky so blue?	(Flap fingers as if wings flying.)
Wouldn't it be funny	
If a bunny	
Had hot dogs on its menu?	(Close one hand around one finger of other hand to make a hot dog; pretend to take a bite.)
Wouldn't it be funny	
If a bunny	
Went to school like me and you?	(Point to self, then to a child.)

Wallpaper Egg Games

Using a wallpaper sample book, cut out ten to twenty different matching pairs of eggs. Play each of the following games with some or all of these matching pairs and an Easter basket.

1. *Silent Pair-Up*

   Have all the children close their eyes. Quickly give an egg to each child. Ask the children to open their eyes, silently take their egg, and walk around to find the child with the matching egg. When two children have a matched pair, they walk over and put their eggs in the Easter baskets.

   As soon as everyone has made a match, start the game over again. (If there is not an even number of children, you may hold an egg for a child to match.)

2. *Eggs in a Row*

   Use four to six pairs of eggs. You should put one of each pair in a row on the table or floor. One child takes the remaining eggs and puts them in the same sequence under your row of eggs.

3. *Lost and Found*

   Give each child one egg from each of the pairs of eggs. Holding the empty Easter basket, say:

   > "Being a bunny
   > Isn't so funny
   > When you've lost your eggs!"

   Then say "I lost a _____ egg" and describe one of the eggs being held by a child. The child with the egg says "I found it" and comes to put it in the basket. Now that child becomes the bunny and says "I lost a _____ egg." Continue until everyone has had a turn.

4. *Back-to-Back Match Up*

   Two children sit back to back. One child has three to six eggs and the other child has the matching set of eggs.

   One child describes one of the eggs. The other child tries to find the same egg in his/her set. For example: "Hold up the yellow egg with the green lines on it." When the child finds the match and holds it up, everyone claps.

   Let two other children take their places and play the game again. Continue until everyone has had a turn or until the interest wanes.

5. *Cheep-Cheep*

   You hold one set of eggs and pass out the eggs that match your set. Be sure every child has an egg to hold.

   You hold up one egg. The child who has the matching egg says "Cheep-cheep" and walks like a baby chick to put the egg in the Easter basket. Continue until all the children have played.

Easter Egg Hunt

Outside or inside, hide wrapped eggs or plastic eggs and let children search for them. Repeat the activity until they begin to tire. Encourage children to share the eggs they find: "We have enough eggs so everyone may have three. Find someone to share with if you find more than three." Be sure to compliment the children who share with another child: "Bruce, that was very polite! He gave one egg to Hector."

Easter Egg Roll

Mark off a short distance with two pieces of masking tape. Let children take turns, two at a time, rolling plastic eggs from the starting line to the finish with their noses.

For variety, let the children have another turn using a spoon to roll the eggs gently.

Visit from a Bunny (or a Baby Chick)

Invite someone who raises rabbits or chickens to come to the class and, perhaps, bring a live animal. Ask him/her to explain to the class how these animals are cared for. What do they eat? Where do they like to live? How do they drink? What sound(s) do they make?

Passover

Ask someone in your community to visit the class and talk about the Jewish holiday of Passover. Many children will be interested in the rituals and customs of this holiday.

Discuss the foods served during Passover. Let the children taste some matzoh, a flat bread made without any salt or yeast. Matzoh is available at most large grocery stores. Explain why Jewish people eat matzoh during Passover. Consider making the No-Flour Passover Cookies (see COOKING).

Classify Colored Eggs

Using plastic eggs, have the children match the ones that are of the same color.

If the plastic eggs are the type that open into two halves, children may mix up the halves and put the matching colored halves back together.

Store these plastic eggs in regular egg cartons, for convenience in handling.

Easter Match

Using the basket pattern on the front of the April Curriculm guide, cut out several eggs and baskets, all of the same color.
1. Print numerals on each basket and draw circles (or some other figure) on each egg to show that number. Have the children match the correct egg for each basket.
2. Print the name of each child in the class on each basket. Glue a picture of a child on each egg. Let children match the names and pictures.
3. Print capital alphabet letters on the eggs and lowercase letters on the baskets. Have the children complete the matches.

Bunny Nursery Rhymes

Recite several favorite nursery rhymes. For language fun, have the children say ''bunny'' any time an animal is mentioned in the rhyme.

''Old Mother Hubbard went to the cupboard to get her poor *bunny* a bone...''

''Baa, baa, black *bunny*, have you any wool...''

''Hickory dickory dock, the *bunny* ran up the clock...''

Create a Story

Copy on a large chart an Easter story dictated by the class. Start the story with an open-ended statement, such as: "Being an Easter bunny is a very hard job. First of all you have to _____ . Then _____ ." Let the children share their ideas while you print them on the paper.

Ask the children to draw pictures to go with their story. Pin up the chart story and surround it with the children's illustrations.

MATH

NUMBER CONCEPTS

Flannel Board Number Stories

Cut out several felt Easter shapes. Make up simple stories and put the figures on the flannel board as you talk.

"Two rabbits went to town. Each one wanted an umbrella. How many umbrellas did they need to buy?"

"A boy found two eggs hidden in the garden. Then, he found three more eggs by the house. How many eggs did he have all together?"

After several examples, invite children to take turns making up a number story and putting the figures on the flannel board.

Easter Match

See LANGUAGE ARTS section, four- and five-year-olds.

Eggs-Act Numbers

Use the plastic eggs that open into halves. Tape a numeral on the outside of each egg. Provide a plastic bowl full of buttons, beads, or lima beans. The children open the eggs and put the appropriate number of objects into each one. You may tape a numeral and a set of dots on the egg, instead of just the numeral.

MATH VOCABULARY

Halves

Cut out two bunnies, two eggs, and two baskets. Cut one of each shape in half lengthwise and cut the other shapes in half across their width. Write the fraction "½" on each half, if desired. Have the children match the correct halves. Talk about the fact that things can be cut in half different ways, but they are still halves.

EASTER

Inch—Foot—Yard

Use the terms "inch," "foot," and "yard" in natural conversation as opportunities arise.

Measure all of the children in the classroom. Tape a piece of butcher paper on a wall or door. Title the project "Easter Measurements." Draw and paint a tall bunny rabbit holding a yardstick. Measure the children and use an Easter egg to mark their height. Print the child's name and height on the egg.

MOVEMENT

Easter Egg Race

Mark off a start and finish line with two pieces of masking tape on the floor. Using plastic eggs, the children try the following movements from the start line to the finish line.
1. Carry an egg in a spoon.
2. Balance an egg on your head.
3. Walk with an egg between your knees.
4. Slide your feet and push the egg with your toes.

Bunny Hopping

Ask the children to do the following movements.
Pretend you are a bunny and:
1. Hop along very slowly, bending over to nibble on your vegetables.
2. Hop very quickly to get home before you're late.
3. Hop as if you were happy.
4. Hop as if you were scared.
5. Hop as if you were very sleepy.
6. Lie down very quietly, so no one can hear you.

Chick, Chick, Rabbit Circle Game

The children stand in a circle. One child is "it" and walks around the outside of the circle. The child who is "it" taps each child on the head and says, "Chick, chick, chick...rabbit." When the child says "chick," the tapped child squats down. When the child says "rabbit," however, the tapped child hops around the circle chasing the child who is "it," until they go around the circle one time. Then, the tapped child becomes "it" and repeats the game.

MUSIC

Peter Cottontail

Sing along with a record of "Here Comes Peter Cottontail."

Bunny Hop

Play the record and do the movements with the class. For added fun, do the bunny hop while wearing a Bunny Bracelet or Bunny Sock Puppet (see ART).

The class may also make headbands from 1 × 24 inch construction paper and staple on bunny ears. Use a loop of masking tape to attach a small construction paper or yarn ball for a bunny tail.

Easter Movements

Use recorded music. Children pretend to be waddling ducks, pecking chickens, hopping bunnies, etc., in rhythm with the music.

Egg Walk

Place cutouts of colored eggs on the floor in a large circle arrangement. The children walk around the circle as a record plays. They should stop on an egg whenever the music stops. With this age group, it is probably best if everyone gets to stop on an egg *every* time, rather than the more common game of eliminating an egg each time so that one child is "out" every time the music stops.

Egg Roll

Roll an egg to music. Start and stop rolling the egg as the music starts and stops.

Like an Easter Bunny

(Tune: "Mulberry Bush")

1. This is the way we dye the eggs, dye the eggs, dye the eggs.
    This is the way we dye the eggs,
    Like an Easter Bunny.
2. Hide the eggs
3. Hop to school
4. Eat our food
5. Go to sleep

ROLE PLAY

Hiding Easter Eggs in the Room

Provide a basket with a handle and six to eight plastic eggs. Let the children take turns being the one who hops around like a bunny to hide the eggs. Be sure all the eggs are found each time, before repeating the game.

Easter Parade

Encourage children to put on dress-up clothes, hats, jewelry, wigs, and shoes. Have them pretend to be in an Easter parade.

Some children may pretend to pose for pictures while a child role plays being a photographer.

SCIENCE

Eggs

1. Show pictures of animals that hatch from eggs.
2. Have children put in the correct sequence pictures of an egg, a baby chick, and a hen. "Which one happens first?" "Which happens second? last?"
3. Crack a fresh egg and a hard boiled egg. Talk about the differences. Spin a fresh egg and a hardboiled egg with your fingers. What happens to each one?

Hatch Baby Chickens or Ducks

Share a children's book that tells about hatching chickens or ducks. Get fertile eggs from a farmer or hatchery. Use a commercial incubator, build your own incubator, or rent one from a hatchery.

Chicken eggs take approximately twenty-one days to hatch. Make a chain of twenty-one eggs glued together. Number the eggs so that the first egg is number 20 and the last egg is 1. Glue a baby chick at the bottom. Each day, let the children tear off one egg to help them anticipate when the chicks will hatch.

Keep the baby chicks in the room for a day or two. Children may handle them gently, when supervision is available.

Make arrangements with a local farmer to raise the chickens. If possible, include a field trip to the farm to deliver the baby chickens as a class. The children will enjoy seeing the new home for their baby chickens and knowing that their chickens are safe and well cared for.

Natural Dyes

Spinach leaves—green
Cranberries—light red
Yellow onions—yellow
Beets—deep red
Blueberries or blackberries—blue

Show the children how natural dyes are made. Boil one of the above vegetables or fruits in a small amount of water. Discuss how the water gradually becomes colored from the fruit or vegetable. Put in a cool hard boiled egg. Leave it in for several minutes until it's dark enough. Discuss how the egg changes from white to lightly colored to deeply colored.

Color

CONCEPTS

- The primary colors are red, yellow, and blue.
- When two primary colors are mixed, they produce a new color.
- The nine colors that preschool children should become familiar with are: red, yellow, blue, green, orange, purple, white, brown, and black.
- Rainbows of color can be observed when the sun shines through water.
- Color helps our world to be attractive and more enjoyable.

ART

Colorful Experiences

1. Provide colored chalk to use inside on boards and outside on cement.
2. Make "Color Collages" by providing yarn, sequins, colored telephone wire pieces, glitter, construction paper, and buttons. Make a collage using items of just one color when it's that color's day.
3. To make color posters, provide large papers with one color word printed at the top of each. The children cut out pictures of the appropriate color for each poster.

Rainbow World

Coffee filters; food coloring; eye dropper; small cups.

Let the children drop a food coloring mixture of half water and half food coloring randomly on a coffee filter. Use several different colors and watch how the colors blend together to create a new color.

Allow each child to make three filters. Form a "rainbow world" by stapling the three together at the center sides to form a triangular shape. Add string and suspend from the ceiling.

Poke-a-Pic

Styrofoam trays; round toothpicks.

Provide a tray and a toothpick for each child. The children poke holes in the styrofoam to make a design or a picture. After they are finished, hold their creations up to the window so the light shines through.

Foiled Again

Squares of aluminum foil; tempera paint or permanent markers; cotton swabs.

Have each child use a cotton swab to paint a design on the aluminum foil. Each color or paint should have its own swab.

If desired, use markers instead of paint.

Sacks of Many Colors

Lunch sacks; tempera paint, markers, or crayons.

The children paint or color designs or pictures on the sacks. Let the sacks dry and save for use at circle time. Encourage the children to name and discuss each color used. (See Color Table in the LANGUAGE ARTS section.)

Jewels from Salt

Rock salt; rubbing alcohol; food coloring; light blue construction paper.

In a small jar, mix several drops of food coloring with a tablespoon of rubbing alcohol. Add several spoonfuls of rock salt. Tighten the lid and shake to color the salt pieces. Spread on a paper towel to dry. Do each color separately. When all the salt is colored and dry, let the children glue the "jewels" to construction paper to make a collage.

"Stained" Glass Windows

Soap flakes; tempera paint; glass classroom window(s); drop cloth; paintbrushes.

Add soap flakes to the tempera paint. This will not only thicken the paint but also make it easier to wash off later. Spread a drop cloth on the floor and/or tack it to the wall. Let the children paint on the windows.

"Color" Headbands

Manila paper; catalog pictures or construction paper cutouts; stapler; marker.

Precut a 2 inch manila strip for each child. Staple as a headband. Print each child's name on the headband. Provide precut objects of the color of the day for the children to glue on their headbands. For instance, for red day, use an apple, a truck, a ball, a balloon (complete with a piece of string), a T-shirt, a wagon, etc. Make the objects from construction paper or cut them from the catalog. If desired, repeat this activity throughout the study of colors. Try sponge painting one of the "Color" headbands. Add the name afterwards.

"Color" Necklace

Colored styrofoam egg cartons or construction paper cut in various shapes; a hole punch; colored plastic straws cut in 1 inch pieces; yarn; tape.

Cut yarn in lengths long enough to fit over the child's head. Put glue or tape around one end to facilitate the threading process. Tie the first piece to the bottom end of the yarn. Children punch a hole in each shape and then thread straw pieces and shapes in any pattern desired. When they're finished, tie the ends together and let the children wear them home.

Wallpaper Collage

Wallpaper sample books; manila paper; glue.

Choose wallpaper sheets appropriate for the color of the day. Give each child one fourth of a page. The children tear the wallpaper into smaller pieces. Put all the pieces in the center of the table to share. Each child may glue a collage of wallpaper scraps on manila paper. These will make a striking display on the wall. Print the color word in big letters on the wall and surround it with these pictures.

Squirt Art

Syringes (doctor's office or pharmacy; make sure needles are removed before children handle the syringes); tempera paint; manila paper.

This project will turn out best if done by just a few children at one time. Cover the table. Provide manila paper and a syringe for each color of paint available. Demonstrate drawing the paint into the syringe and squirting it *carefully* onto the paper. Let the children trade paint and syringes to enhance their creation. Children love this experience and the results are fascinating!

Finger Painting with Plastic Wrap

Roll of plastic wrap; finger paint or tempera paint; liquid soap; manila paper.

Tape a sheet of plastic wrap in front of each child. Put a dab of liquid soap and several drops of paint on the plastic wrap. Encourage the children to paint not only with their fingers but also with the sides and back and palm of one hand. Allow the creations to dry in place. Staple to a sheet of manila paper, or cut out black construction paper frames to frame the pictures before hanging them in the windows.

Tye Dye

White cotton T-shirts or muslin squares; fabric dye prepared as directed and put in 5 gallon plastic buckets; twisters from bread wrappers.

Ask the children to bring shirts from home or provide large squares of muslin to make bandanas. You will need a shirt or muslin square to demonstrate how to gather small sections of material and put twisters around them. Encourage the children to do several twists on the front and back, plus both sleeves. Secure each twist tightly. Demonstrate dipping the shirt or muslin into one or more of the dyes. Experiment with dipping only part of the fabric in one color and dipping the rest into a second color. Let the colors overlap to produce a new color!

The greatest fun is untwisting the ties to view the magical color creation! (Caution parents to wash the shirts in cold water.)

BLOCKS

Use the small table blocks as a change of pace for one day. Have the children pull a colored chip from a hat. The color they draw is the color of blocks they build with for a set time limit, perhaps three to five minutes. At the end of the limit, let them change colors of blocks with a friend and build a new creation.

BULLETIN BOARD

Post the caption "Colors, Colors" on the bulletin board. Use two large tagboard cutouts of children holding colored "flags," each with the color name printed on the flag. Tie a length of yarn, the same color if possible, to each flag. Cut out pictures and/or construction paper shapes of appropriate colors to display in color groups randomly about the bulletin board. Connect the flag to the group of pictures of the corresponding color with the length of yarn. As a variation, let the children match the color pictures to the corresponding flag by connecting the yarn in some manner.

COOKING

"Colorful" Snack Ideas

Blue: *Blueberry muffins; blue popcorn balls.*
Green: *Lime gelatin; green eggs and ham.*
Brown: *Refried beans with corn chips; peanut butter and honey; graham crackers.*
Purple: *Grape juice; plums; grape jelly.*
Orange: *Carrot sticks; cheese crackers; oranges.*
Yellow: *Bananas; pineapple juice; lemonade.*
Red: *Cherries; cherry or strawberry gelatin; strawberries; tomatoes.*
Any color: *Milk with two drops of food coloring added.*

Banana Coins

1 banana per child
Dry gelatin mix
Small sandwich bags
Plastic knives

Let each child cut a banana into slices for "coins." Then, put the Banana Coins into a small sandwich bag. Spoon 2-3 teaspoons of dry gelatin into the bag. Demonstrate how to gather the bag closed and shake to cover the Banana Coins.

Color Swirl Cake

Baked oblong cake
Whipped topping
Food coloring

Bring a baked oblong cake to class. Cut a piece for each child. Provide a plastic knife and whipped topping to frost their piece of cake. After spreading whipped topping, each child drops one or two drops each of red, blue, and yellow food coloring. Encourage them to gently swirl the colors with the plastic knife. Talk about the new colors made.

Red, White, and Blue Sundae

Vanilla yogurt
Cherries or cherry pie filling
Blueberries or blueberry pie filling
Coconut and/or peanuts

The children spoon yogurt into a small bowl. Spoon a layer of cherries on top, then add another layer of yogurt. Top the last layer with a few blueberries and coconut or peanuts, as each child desires.

LANGUAGE ARTS

Books

Allington, Richard. *Colors*. Raintree Children's Books, 1979.
Bradbury, Lynne. *Colors and Shapes*. Ladybird, 1981.
Burningham, John. *Colors*. Crown, 1985.
Carle, Eric. *My Very First Book of Colors*. Harper and Row, 1974.
Curry, Peter. *Colors*. Price-Stern, 1983.
DeBrunhoff, Laurent. *Babar's Book of Color*. Random House, 1984.
Duvoisin, Roger. *House of Four Seasons*. Lothrop, 1956.
Graham, Bill and Susan Hulme. *Let's Look for Colors*. Putnam, 1984.
Havard, Katherine. *Do You Know Colors?* Random House, 1979.
Hoban, Tana. *Is It Red? Is It Yellow? Is It Blue?* Greenwillow, 1978.
Hynard, Stephen. *Snowy, the Rabbit*. Children's Press, 1983.
Kirkpatrick, Rena K. *Look at Rainbow Colors*. Raintree Publishers, 1978.
Lionni, Leo. *Colors to Talk About*. Pantheon, 1985.
Lionni, Leo. *Little Blue and Little Yellow*. Obolensky Inc., 1979.
Miller, J.P. *Learn About Colors with Little Rabbit*. Random, 1984.
Muntean, Michael. *Getting Ready: Colors and Shapes*. Western, 1984.
Nye, Loyal. *What Color Am I?* Abington, 1977.
O'Neill, Mary. *Hailstones and Halibut Bones*. Doubleday, 1961. (Poems about color)
Poulet, Virginia. *Blue Bug Goes to the Library*. Regensteiner, 1979.
Savage, Dorothy. *The Black Peephole Book*. E.P. Dutton, 1986.
Savage, Dorothy. *The Green Peephole Book*. E.P. Dutton, 1986.
Savage, Dorothy. *The Red Peephole Book*. E.P. Dutton, 1986.
Savage, Dorothy. *The Yellow Peephole Book*. E.P. Dutton, 1986.
Zolotow, Charlotte. *Mr. Rabbit and the Lovely Present*. Harper and Row, 1962.

Fingerplays

What Colors Do I See?

Sit together in a circle. As you repeat the verse together, the children stretch out their arms to point to things of that color. Then, stop to name each thing before repeating the verse using a different color.

Looking for colors,
What colors do I see?
I see red things
Looking at me.

A Color a Day

Choose one color for the day. Emphasize that color as much as possible in various activities. Each day, everyone wears at least one item of clothing of that color. You should also participate. Have scarves, pins, and construction paper cutouts on hand for children who forget to wear the color of the day. Circle times would be a good time to point out what the children are wearing: "Chris has blue socks; Matthew wore a blue shirt today." Lunch is another good time: "The peas on the plate are green; the peaches are yellow." When the class is outside, look for the appropriate color of passing cars.

Color Table

Provide a table for objects that are the color of the day. Children may bring something from home (marked with name) or find something in the room. Children may put it on the table for all to see.

At circle time use these objects in a game. Have the children bring their Sacks of Many Colors to circle time. (See ART section.) After the children are seated, bring objects from the Color Table and put them on the floor in the center of the circle. You or designated children give directions to each child about what objects to choose for their sack: "Scott, choose something red for your sack. Don, find a blue object for your sack." Be sure to stress that everyone's treasures will be put back on the table and the children aren't going to keep another child's property.

Color Pick

Use a shoe box covered with different colors. You put several objects of different colors into the box. The children take turns picking an object, identifying the color, and returning the object to the box.

Color Bingo

Refer to the LANGUAGE ARTS section in the SHAPES AND SIZES unit (see November Curriculum guide) for the procedure of this game, plus a sample bingo card to duplicate. Children love to play bingo.

Color Line Up
(Transition Activities)

1. You name a color. The child or children wearing that color may line up.
2. You name a color and an article of clothing. The children wearing that piece of clothing in that color may line up or get a drink of water.
3. Call a child's name. The child names his/her favorite color and lines up or joins the group.

Fishing Colors

Provide precut "fish" of different colors with a paper clip for the mouth. Use a stick or piece of dowel rod and a length of string with a magnet tied to the end. A plastic kiddie pool will add to the fun of this fishing game. You name the color of fish and the child who should "catch" it. After catching the appropriate fish, the child names the next fisher and what color of fish he/she could catch. Encourage speaking in complete sentences.

Bubble Blast

Mix one cup of powdered soap in a quart of warm water. Add food coloring and mix well. Give each child a plastic straw and a paper cup with a small amount of soap mix in the bottom. Encourage younger children to *blow* on the straw, not suck on it. Children are intrigued with blowing colored bubbles!

Concentration

You should prepare the following: Cut tagboard into approximately 3 × 5 inch pieces. Glue a matching piece of fabric on two of the cards. Prepare at least twelve pairs. More cards allow two children to work independently at once. Laminate or cover each card with clear contact paper to keep the cards clean and little fingers from picking the corners of the fabric.

Two or more children may play Concentration by taking turns flipping over cards and trying to match pairs by remembering where the cards are. As a variation, one child may work independently by matching all the cards at the table.

Color, Color, What's the Color?

Pass out color cards (paint samples from a paint store work well) to each child. You hold up a color—the child or children with that color stand up and name the color, then sit down. Continue through as many colors as the class knows. Go faster and faster as they learn more and more colors.

Color Completion

Write simple sentences on tagboard strips that can be completed with a color word. You may make up these sentences or work with the children to develop the sentences as a class activity. "Ms. Jones drives a *blue* car. Susie is wearing a *green* dress." Make color cards, using the color word plus a construction paper circle of that color glued on the card at the beginning of the word. The children may use the color cards for flash cards as an independent activity as well as for completing the sentence strips. The children will be able to "read" the color words from the beginning with these cards. Laminate the cards for longer wear.

I Am a Color

You interview each child once throughout the week. Record the interview to play back during circle time. The children try to guess who is speaking.

The child pretends to be a color. You may ask questions, such as:
1. What color are you pretending to be?
2. Are you a holiday color? What holiday?
3. Do children like to wear you?
4. Are any children wearing you today?

Continue with questions as long as the interest continues.

MATH

NUMBER CONCEPTS

Stitch-a-Number

Write a numeral on a styrofoam meat tray. Let the children name their favorite color and stitch the numeral using that color of yarn and a blunt needle. Then, let each child add the correct number of small gummed stickers under the numeral. You may also print the number word on the tray.

Bead Draw

Place a shallow box containing wooden beads in the center of the table or tables. You instruct the children to choose "one red bead" or "two yellow beads" from the box. Expand on this game by naming a shape to choose or indicating large or small beads.

Shape Game

You should prepare the following: Make sets of all the basic shapes in different sizes and colors from construction paper. Laminate or encase in clear contact paper for use throughout the year. Shapes of about 3 × 3 inches would be good for the largest size. Sets of two sizes smaller would also be good to have. Endless games of counting, matching, or categorizing are possible with these simple-to-do shapes. Two examples follow.
1. Have the children count all of the red shapes, just the red circles, or just the large red circles.
2. A small group of children works with a set of all the shapes. One child holds up a triangle and the other children find and hold up triangles or any shape of the matching color.

COLOR

Counting

You say: "I'm thinking of three yellow things in this room" or "I'm thinking of two orange objects." The children tiptoe around the room to find the required number of objects in the required color. They then bring the objects back to the table and count them together.

Dot-to-Dot

Prepare a simple dot-to-dot page for the children. Use a triangle, square, or rectangle as the basic form.

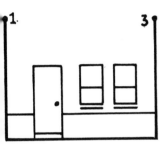

MATH VOCABULARY

Inch—Foot—Yard

Cut tagboard strips for each child to manipulate. Make twelve 1 inch pieces, three 1 foot lengths, and one strip a yard in length. Talk about small, bigger, biggest. Line up the like pieces end to end. Some children may discover that the 12 inch pieces are the same length as the 1 foot pieces or that the three 1 foot pieces are the same length as the yard piece. Be sure to use and reuse the terms "inch," "foot," and "yard." Most children probably will not grasp the concept, but will store the experience for future development.

MOVEMENT

Floor Squares

Tape several 3 × 3 foot squares on the floor using different colors of plastic tape. The children take turns tossing bean bags into the color designated by you.

Variation: 1. Play a record for the children to march, slide, walk backwards, or hop around the squares.
2. Direct children, one at a time, to stand in the yellow square, the blue square, etc. You may also substitute "beside" or "around" for the word "in."

Color Command Game

Make color cards by gluing swatches of different colors of construction paper on separate cards. These cards should be about 3 × 5 inches in size. Write an activity command on the back of each card, such as: Take two giant steps; hop four times; jump up and down six times; jog in place. Limit it to one command per card.

Pass out colored buttons or construction paper circles to each child. You or a child draws a color command card from the box. Any child with the matching color button must do what the command card indicates.

Twister

The game of "Twister" helps reinforce colors. Depending on the age of the children involved, you may decide whether or not to use the terms "right" and "left." It will prove to be just as much fun for the children if you do not use the terms.

Lollipop Game

Cut construction paper circles from several colors and glue each to the end of a popsicle stick. Place clay or play dough in the bottom of a shallow bowl. Stick the lollipops into the clay. Blindfold one child, turn the child around three times and point the child towards the lollipop bowl. The child may choose one lollipop. Remove the blindfold and name the color. The child chooses the next player. Repeat until all have had a turn.

Variation: Use the game with the color command cards. You read the command that corresponds to the color of the lollipop drawn. The child does as the card commands.

MUSIC

Color Parade

Using 9 × 12 inch construction paper, cut a triangular flag for each of the nine familiar colors (see CONCEPTS). Attach the flag to a straw. Give each child a flag and have a color parade complete with marching music.

Variation: Make enough to have pairs of flags. The children march around the room and find their partner with the same color flag. Two classes together will make this activity more fun.

Shaker Instruments

Color the outside of small boxes or toilet paper tubes with crayons or markers. Put in a small handful of dried beans and/or rice. Tape or staple closed. The children may use the instruments to keep rhythm while singing or listening to a record.

Red, Yellow, Blue

(Tune: "Three Blind Mice")

Red, yellow, blue,
Red, yellow, blue,
See how they mix.
See how they mix.
We make all the colors with just these three.
They make us feel happy and they look lovely.
Red, yellow, blue.
Red, yellow, blue.

Swing and Sway

Provide crepe paper streamers or scarves of various colors. You might provide streamers of only the color the class is studing that day.

Play soft, flowing music. Give each child one or more streamers. Have them swing the streamers about as they move in gentle rhythm to the music.

SCIENCE

Magic Colors

Put water into three baby food jars with the labels removed. Add 3-4 drops of red food coloring in one, yellow food coloring in another, and blue food coloring in the other. Have a piece of chart paper handy to record the children's observations and comments.

Next, add several drops of red food coloring to each jar. Observe and record what happens in each jar. Pour the water out and repeat all the steps, except add several drops of yellow coloring at the end. Pour water out and repeat using blue food coloring as the last addition.

As a culminating activity, make a poster based on the data gathered from these experiments. Using construction paper shapes of appropriate colors, glue the shapes on the posterboard to show red + red = red; red + yellow = orange; red + blue = purple; etc.

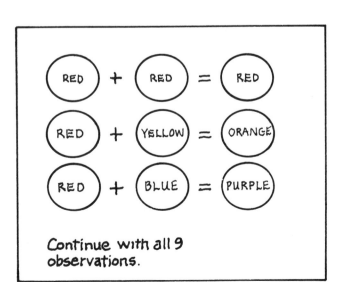

Growing Crystals

Use an aluminum foil pie pan as a container for this delightful project. Scatter broken pieces of charcoal in the pie pan. In a paper cup, mix 2 tablespoons salt, 2 tablespoons bluing, and 2 tablespoons ammonia. Sprinkle over the charcoal pieces. Drop food coloring of several different colors on the charcoal. The crystals will start to grow almost immediately. Children love to watch this experiment.

Add more salt solution every two days to keep the crystals growing. Caution: Be sure to keep the crystal garden out of reach of the children when you are not there to supervise!

Magic Telescope

Red, yellow, and blue cellophane (available at florist shops); paper towel tubes

Put a single color of cellophane over one end of the tube and secure with a rubber band. Have the children look through the other end. What color do objects or people appear to be? Repeat, using each color one at a time. Then, add another color over the top of the one on the tube. Do the objects again change color? See if the children can predict what the new color will be when you add the second color of cellophane. They may use the poster made during the food coloring experiment.

Colored Glasses

Use old empty frames from eyeglasses. Tape colors of cellophane over the openings. The children put on the colored glasses and look around to see how things may look different.

Rainbows with No Rain

1. Set a clear jar filled with water in the window as the sun is shining. The children should be able to see a rainbow.
2. Set a prism on white paper on a table or the floor. Choose an area that will catch the sun's rays. Have the children watch and talk about what they see.

COLOR

Spring and Growing Things

- Spring is the season that comes after winter and before summer.
- Nature's things begin to grow in spring: The grass turns green, leaves grow on trees and bushes, some flowers bloom.
- Some people plant seeds in a garden to grow fresh fruits and vegetables to eat.
- The weather in the spring is warmer and it rains more in some areas.
- Days become longer and nights become shorter.

ART

Spring Butterflies

Nonwoven interfacing; food coloring; eyedroppers; Butterfly Pattern at end of this section.

Cut butterflies from interfacing. (Different sizes will make an interesting display on a wall or tree branch.)

Wet each butterfly and fold in half. Drop different colors of food coloring on the wings, until they are covered with color. Unfold and allow to dry.

Flower Vase

Salad dressing bottle (clean and brought from home); variety of colors of art tissue paper cut in 2 inch squares; glue thinned slightly with water.

Each child dips the tissue into the glue and puts the squares on the bottle in a collage fashion. Encourage them to cover all of the bottle. (Continue work on the project at two or three different times, so the children don't become too tired.) Allow the bottle to dry completely. Use as a vase for real or dried flowers.

Nature Collage

Take the class on a Spring Walk to observe signs of spring (see SCIENCE section).

Provide glue and construction paper. Let each child make a collage of the items each collected on the walk.

Spring Vegetable Prints

Meat trays or paper plates for paint; tempera paint; vegetables; manila paper

Cut the vegetables into easily handled slices or pieces. (If you cut them and let them dry for a while, the paint will stick better.) The children gently dip each vegetable slice into a small amount of the paint and press it on a paper again and again until it will no longer print. Encourage them to use a variety of vegetables and colors. Green peppers, onions, radishes, carrots, potatoes, and squash make interesting shapes and prints.

Spring Chick

Outline of a baby chick; cotton balls; dry yellow tempera powder; plastic bags; glue; meat trays or paper plates.

Shake the cotton balls in a plastic bag with dry yellow tempera powder. Pour small amounts of glue on meat trays or paper plates.

The children gently touch a cotton ball to the glue and place it in the chick outline. Repeat the process until the chick is filled in or until each child is finished with his/her picture.

Cereal Blossoms

Puffed wheat cereal; glue; construction paper in pastel colors, with stems and leaves drawn on.

Let the children glue clusters of puffed wheat on the stems to make blossoms.

Leaf Prints

Several sizes and types of leaves; manila paper; thick tempera paint (add soap flakes or wheat paste to thicken); brushes.

Cover a work area with a newspaper for each child. Have each child paint a leaf with tempera paint. *Be sure they paint the leaf on the vein side.* Then, keep pressing the leaf on the paper until it no longer prints.

Encourage the children to use different colors and different sizes of leaves for a more interesting effect.

SPRING AND OTHER THINGS

Easy Kite

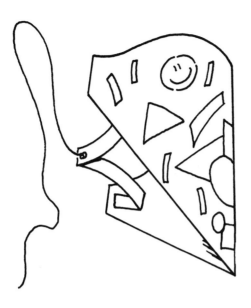

Easy Kite Pattern; construction paper scraps; tagboard; hole punch; string; glue; twig.

Trace the Easy Kite Pattern at the end of this section on a folded piece of construction paper. Trace the strip on a folded piece of tagboard. Punch a hole through the strip as shown.

The children decorate their kite by gluing on a collage of construction paper bits and pieces. Then, help them glue the strip to the kite as shown. Attach a long string, and the kite is ready to fly. Find a twig outside, tie the kite string to it, and wind up the string.

This kite will fly with only a slight run on the part of the child. Children are excited by how easily they can make their kite fly!

Pastel Colors

Manila paper; tempera paint.

Discuss how we find soft and light colors in spring. Let children help stir white paint into smaller amounts of red, blue, and yellow paint to make pastel shades.

Have the children paint designs with the pastels on manila paper.

Rice Collages

Rice; tempera paint; manila paper; glue.

Shake rice in a tightly covered jar with a very small amount of tempera paint.

The children make designs on the manila paper by squirting or brushing on glue. They then spoon the colored rice on the glue to complete the collage. Allow the collage to dry for several hours.

Bottle Cap Garden

Bottle caps; one piece of manila or construction paper per child; crayons or markers; thick tempera paint (add soap flakes or wheat paste to help the tempera paint stick to metal, plastic, and glass surfaces).

Ask children to bring from home a variety of throwaway bottle caps and lids. Have the children paint the caps and lids. When the lids are dry, children glue them to a piece of manila or construction paper to serve as the center of flowers. Then, they add stems, leaves, ground, and other details with crayons or markers.

Kites

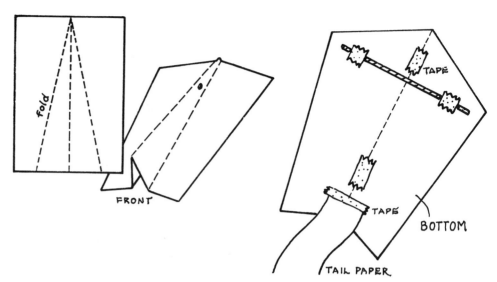

Kite Pattern at end of this section; crayons or markers; drinking straws; string or thread; paper.

Duplicate the Kite Pattern for each child. Encourage them to use crayons or markers to decorate the side with the dotted line any way they wish.

Show the children how to fold each pattern in half on the dotted line and punch a small hole as shown. Then, fold on the second dotted line.

Turn the kite over. Open the kite shape and tape the seam together. Tape on a straw for support as shown in the illustration.

Cut 2 × 18 inch strips of paper for the tail of the kite. Let the children decorate this tail with crayons or markers, or make decorative cuts in it, like a snowflake. Tape the tail to the back as shown. (Adding machine tape makes a perfect tail. Check with secretaries for used tape.)

Tie a long string on the front of the kite, at the punched hole, and it is ready to fly. Tie a twig or half of a straw to the other end of the string for holding and winding up the string when finished.

Pressed Flower Arrangements

Wild flowers; waxed paper; iron.

Let the children pick and arrange small bunches of wild flowers and weeds. Lay each arrangement between two equal-size pieces of waxed paper.

Lay something heavy on each arrangement to press it overnight. Then, you should use a warm iron to seal the edges.

Provide a precut paper frame for each child to glue over his/her arrangement. This also makes a great bookmark, if children make a narrow arrangement.

SPRING AND GROWING THINGS

Clothespin Butterflies

Wooden clothespins (non-pincher type); colored art tissue paper; construction paper scraps; pipe cleaners; glue; tempera paint in bright colors; string.

Each child paints one clothespin with tempera paint. When it's dry, the child makes wings for the butterfly by laying together two to four pieces of 3 × 5 inch tissue (in different colors), pinching them together in the middle, and gluing them up into the clothespin opening.

Make antennae with pipe cleaners. Add eyes and other details with construction paper.

Tie a string through the opening of the clothespin, so the butterfies may fly or hang from the ceiling as beautiful mobiles.

Wallpaper Flower Garden

Wallpaper samples; glue; manila paper.

Children cut many different flowers from the floral wallpaper samples. Glue the flowers to the manila paper. Add stems, leaves, ground, etc., to complete the garden.

3-D Flowers

Five to six 2 inch tissue paper circles per flower; green construction paper; paper or markers for stems and leaves; brads.

Gather five to six circles for each flower. Carefully poke a brad through the centers of the circles and fasten to green paper. Gently bend each layer out to form a flower. Add the stem and several leaves. Three such creations on each paper make an attractive display.

Ceramic Flowers

Ceramic dough (see Art Recipes); tempera paint.

Give each child an equal amount of the dough. Show them how to roll thin stems, press small balls with their thumb or fist to make petals and leaves, and vary the size and shape of the petals. Smooth pieces with a finger dipped in water.

When the children have had ample time to play with the dough, have each child make one or more flowers to keep. Flowers will dry in 36 hours at room temperature. Dry on a rack or a screen so the underside dries well. When the flowers are dry, let the children paint them with tempera paint.

BLOCKS

1. As the children build towers, fences, or other structures, provide a ruler and a yardstick and assist in measuring the buildings. The children probably cannot grasp that the tower is 15 inches tall, but they can understand that it is taller than the ruler but not as tall as the yardstick. Encourage the children

Spring Walk

Take the class on a walk to observe and listen to spring things. Point out interesting growing things as you walk. Talk about new leaves, green grass, sprouts, and blossoms.

Each child may carry a small paper sack to collect interesting things that are appropriate to pick up: small stone, blade of grass, wild flower, twig, etc.

Back in class, let the children look at their treasures with a magnifying glass. Have them count the things and make a Nature Collage (see ART).

Magnifying Glass

Provide one to three magnifying glasses. When plants are large enough, encourage the children to study growing roots and leaves under the glass.

Hairy Harry

Decorate a large styrofoam cup or coffee can, so it looks like a face. Fill it with potting soil and plant bird seed just under the surface. Water it gently. In just two to three days, you should have sprouts growing for Harry's hair. In a week, the sprouts should be 2-5 inches tall.

Have the children feel the sprouts. Let them run their fingers through the ''hairy'' growth.

Discuss how plants need soil, water, and light to grow.

If you wish, when you make Hairy Harry, plant another cup, which you *don't* water. Label it ''No Water.'' Contrast its growth with the growth of the cared for plant.

Also plant another cup, which you keep covered with a box but continue to water. Label it ''No Sunlight.'' Compare the growth to the other plant.

Greenhouse Bag

Large, clear plastic bag and tie; seeds planted in well-drained container.

Put seed container(s) in bottom of bag. Gather ends of bag together and blow in it, so it stands away from the sides of the container. Close the bag tightly with the tie.

Keep the greenhouse in a shaded spot. The seeds probably will not need watering again until sprouted.

Remove the sprouted plants from the greenhouse for continued growth in a sunny area.

Grow either one class plant or individual children's plants in the greenhouse.

to take turns being the tower inspector or the fence inspector and measuring the structures, with your assistance.

2. Demonstrate how two blocks of a certain size, laid end to end on top of a longer block, make the same length. Review the concepts of "half" and "whole." Let the children take turns manipulating the blocks to find the half and whole.

BULLETIN BOARD

Winter/Spring

Divide a bulletin board in half. Have a bare winter tree on the left side and a green-leafed spring tree on the right. Label the left side "Winter" and the right side "Spring."

Cut out pictures of winter and spring weather, clothes, and activities. Have the children use pushpins to classify the pictures by pinning each to the proper side of the board.

COOKING

Eggs in a Nest

1 slice bread per child
1 egg per child
Butter or oleo
Frying pan

Cut a 2 inch hole from the center of the bread slice. Melt butter in a frying pan. Brown the bread on both sides in the frying pan. Lower the heat. Carefully crack the egg into a small bowl. Slide the egg into the ring of bread. Put a lid on the pan and cook 3-5 minutes or until egg is done as desired.

Orange Julius

6-8 ice cubes
1 cup orange juice concentrate
1½ cups milk
1 raw egg
Blender

In the blender, crush ice cubes. Add remaining ingredients. Blend until frothy. Serve immediately. Delicious and nutritious too!

SPRING AND GROWING THINGS

Yogurt Fruit Dip

One 8 ounce fruit yogurt (blueberry or peach work well)
2 bananas
2 apples
2 oranges
Round toothpicks
Plastic knives

Have the children wash their hands. Give each child a portion of each fruit to slice. (Good for muscle development and independence skills.)

The children spear the fruit slices with a toothpick and take turns dipping the fruit in the yogurt before eating. Yum!

Flower Cupcakes

Baked, but unfrosted, cupcakes
Canned frosting
Small colored marshmallows
Plastic knives

Have the children wash their hands. Give the children a dab of frosting and let them frost their own cupcake. Show the children how to put marshmallows on top of the frosting in the shape of flower petals.

LANGUAGE ARTS

Books

Allington, Richard. *Spring*. Raintree Children's Books, 1981.
Baum, Arlene and Joseph. *One Bright Monday Morning*. Random House, 1962.
Brooks, Sandra. *What Happens in Spring*. Standard Publishers, 1982.
Brown, Marc. *Your First Garden Book*. Little, 1981.
Casey, Patricia. *Spring Days*. Putnam Publishing Group, 1984.
Cox, Rosamund Kidman. *Flowers*. Hayes Books, 1980.
Crowe, Robert L. *Tyler Toad and the Thunder*. Dutton, 1980.
Dowden, Anne Ophelia Todd. *From Flower to Fruit*. Crowell, 1984.
Duvoisin, Roger. *Two Lonely Ducks*. Alfred A. Knopf, 1955. (Counting book)
Ets, Marie Hall. *Gilberto and the Wind*. Viking Press, 1963.
Flack, Marjorie. *Tim Tadpole and the Great Bullfrog*. Doubleday, 1959.
Fujikawa, Gyo. *Let's Grow a Garden*. Putnam Publishing Group, 1978.
Galland, Sarah. *Peter Rabbit's Gardening Book*. Warne, 1984.
Glovack, Linda. *The Little Witch's Spring Holiday Book*. Prentice-Hall, 1983.
Kellogg, Steven. *The Mysterious Tadpole*. Dial Press, 1977.
Krauss, Ruth. *The Happy Day*. Harper and Row, 1949.
Kuskin, Karla. *The Bear Who Saw the Spring*. Harper and Row, 1961.
Lenski, Lois. *Spring Is Here*. Henry Z. Walck, 1945.
Lionni, Leo. *Inch by Inch*. Astor-Honor, 1962.
Lobel, Arnold. *The Rose in My Garden*. Greenwillow, 1984.
McCloskey, Robert. *Make Way for Ducklings*. Viking Press, 1969.
Moncure, Jane Belk. *What Will It Be?* Children's Press, 1976.

Moore, Inga. *The Vegetable Thieves*. Viking Press, 1984.
Podendorf, Illa. *Weeds and Wild Flowers*. Children's Press, 1981.
Selsam, Millicent. *A First Look at the World of Plants*. Walker, 1978.
Selsam, Millicent. *Seeds and More Seeds*. Harper and Row, 1959.

Teacher Resource Books

Cooke, Emogene. *Fun-Time Window Garden*. Children's Press, 1957.
Crowell, Robert L. *The Lore and Legends of Flowers*. Crowell, 1982.
Mandry, Kathy. *How to Grow a Jelly Glass Farm*. Pantheon Books, 1974.

Fingerplays

Plant a Seed

Plant a seed in the ground,	(Plant a pretend seed in palm of one hand. Close fist.)
Water and sunshine all around.	(Other hand becomes watering can to sprinkle water on the seed.)
Little seed, in the ground so still, Will you grow up? Yes I will!	(Index finger of one hand slowly pushes up through closed fist of other hand.)

Spring Flowers

We are a little garden.	(Wiggle fingers of one hand.)
We like the sun and showers.	("Shower" down on garden with fingers of other hand.)
When it doesn't rain on us, We wilt our pretty flowers.	(Fold down fingers of garden hand.)

Feel Spring

Talk about the way some things feel in spring: new leaf not completely opened; fully developed leaf; grass blade; pussy willows; flower stem and petals; etc.

1. *Game:*
   Blindfold child (or close eyes) and select one object you've been talking about for the child to identify by feeling it.
2. *Feel Box:*
   Cover or decorate a shoe box that has a lid. Cut a circle in one end large enough for a small hand to fit through it. Glue the top of a sock around the inside of the circle to serve as a sleeve and prevent children from seeing inside the circle.

   Lift the lid and put a spring-related object inside without the children seeing it. The children must put their hand gently through the sock "sleeve" and into the box to feel what is inside. They must then try to identify the object. Easy to make and a great favorite with children!

Smells of Spring

Talk about the way some things smell in spring: freshly cut grass; soil ready for planting; two or three different kinds of flowers.

Game: Blindfold the child (or close eyes) and you hold an object you've talked about for the child to identify by smelling it.

I Spy a Spring Thing

Outside or inside, let the children take turns finding and naming a sign of spring by saying each time, "I spy a spring thing. It's a _____ ." (new leaf, jackets instead of coats, short sleeves instead of long sleeves, warm sun, flowers, bug, green grass, etc.)

Vocabulary Development

Use these words in as many natural settings as possible: plant; soil or dirt; water; sun, sunlight, or sunshine; leaves; roots; primary roots (the first root growth); secondary roots (formed when the first root begins to branch—a cutting in water needs secondary roots before it should be planted in dirt); sprout; stem. Help children understand how these words relate to growing things.

Look, Listen, and Say Box

Two shoe boxes, covered or decorated as you wish.

Use a marker to divide the inside of each lid into four equal sections. Number each section 1-4, or code each section by putting a different-colored dot in each. Put five of the same spring objects into each box.

Two children sit back to back. Each has a Look, Listen, and Say Box. The children take turns describing one object and telling the other child in which section to place the object. For example, for a blade of grass, a child might say: "Get the long, skinny green thing and put it in number 3." The second child then describes an object to place.

After each child has had two turns, each numbered section should have an object in it and one object should be left in the box. The children then turn around to see if their Look, Listen, and Say Boxes match.

You may wish to vary the objects before a new pair of children play the game, to keep the thinking and fun fresh.

This activity moves quickly and adapts easily to objects of any theme. It encourages oral language, listening, and thinking.

Clothesline Classification

String a clothesline across a corner or in a nontraffic area. Let children cut out pictures of spring clothes from catalogs to hang on the line with pinch-type clothespins.
1. Discuss what is first, second, third, and last on the line.
2. Classify the clothing by types or by color. Put all the cutout clothes in a pile or small box. Ask a child: "Hang up all the clothes with pink in them"; "Hang up all the shirts"; etc.

Counting

1. Count leaves as they grow on classroom plants.
2. Count "treasures" found on Spring Walk (see SCIENCE).
3. *Buttons*
   Ask parents to donate unneeded buttons. Count the buttons each child brings in.
4. *Push and Count*
   On a large styrofoam meat tray, mark off four, six, or eight sections with a black marker. Print a numeral in each grid. Sit with children as they insert the appropriate number of pushpins into each grid. Children love to handle pushpins, but need to be supervised.

Classification

1. *Buttons*
   Classify the buttons by:
   a. whether they have one, two, or four holes
   b. color
   c. small, bigger, biggest
2. *Seeds*
   Save seeds from apples and oranges. Also use beans, acorns, and sunflower seeds. Put a mixture of these seeds into a small plastic bowl with a lid.
   Let children separate the seeds and put the like ones together.(A four-cup section of an egg carton helps.)
   If children are old enough, count how many seeds you have of each kind, before you put them back together in the bowl.

Number Bingo

Divide four 9 × 12 inch cards into fourths. Print a numeral in each grid. Make each card different. Cut out a die using the Die Pattern at the end of this section. Print a different numeral on each side and fold together. Have a supply of small construction paper circles to use as markers. Show children how to roll the die. If any player's card has the numeral showing on the die, he/she places a marker on that numeral. Play the game until all players fill their cards.

Perky Math Pots Game

Purchase five to ten flower pots from a discount store or plant nursery. Glue small circles on each pot for each number from 1-5. Make "flowers" by using straws (for stems) and simple construction paper petals.
   The children "plant" the flowers by putting the appropriate number in each pot. Store flowers in a pretzel can or saltine box.
   Variation: Increase the game to ten flower pots and flowers.
   Variation: Print numerals on the pots instead of using dots. Have the children match the appropriate number of flowers to each numeral.

Plant a Seed
(Gross Motor Variation of Fingerplay)

Plant a seed in the ground,

(Crouch down with arms folded over head.)

Water and sunshine all around,

(One arm becomes a watering can to sprinkle water on the seed)

Little seed, in the ground so still,
Will you grow up?
Yes I will!

(Stretch arms up slowly like a plant growing. Gradually stand all the way up with arms in the air.)

Bean Bag Walk

Each child has a bean bag to balance on head, shoulder, or outstretched arm while walking carefully around the room. Soft or slow-paced music playing in the background might add to the fun.

Bean Bag Relay

Divide children into two or three groups. Line up like a train. The front children start by passing the bean bags between their legs to the second child. That child passes the bean bag to the third child in the same manner. Continue to the end of the line.

Variation 1: Pass the bean bag over the head.
Variation 2: Pass the bean bag by alternating the above actions.

MUSIC

Old McDonald Had a Garden

(Tune: "Old McDonald Had a Farm")

Old McDonald had a garden, Ee-igh, Ee-igh, oh.
In his garden he had to plant, Ee-igh, Ee-igh, oh.
With plant-a-seed (bending and planting motion) here and plant a-seed there,
Here a seed (point here and there), there a seed, everywhere a garden seed.
Old McDonald had a garden, Ee-igh, Ee-igh, oh.

In his garden he had to water, Ee-igh, Ee-igh, oh.
Sprinkle, sprinkle here (use arm motions)...

In his garden he had to hoe, Ee-igh, Ee-igh, oh.
Chop, chop here (bending and hoeing motion)...

In his garden he had to pick, Ee-igh, Ee-igh, oh.
Pick-a-carrot here, pick-a-lettuce there,
Here a bean, there a corn, everywhere a garden plant.
Old McDonald had a garden, Ee-igh, Ee-igh, oh.

Circle Motions

(Tune: ''Ring Around a Rosy'')

Walking in a circle,
Walking in a circle,
Stop and clap, stop and clap,
All fall down.

1. Hopping in a circle
2. Marching in a circle
3. Jogging in a circle
4. Stretching in a circle

Farmer in the Dell

Sing and play ''Farmer in the Dell'' as a circle game. As a variation, children may put people and animals on the flannel board as the characters are mentioned in the song. Talk about the foods farmers grow.

ROLE PLAY

**Flower Arrangements/
Flower Delivery**

Provide artificial flowers (or wild flowers, if available). Have the children make bouquets to place in plastic vases to brighten the room.

Let the children pretend to call the florist and have an arrangement of flowers delivered to someone in the room.

The delivery person may wish to wear a hat (see WAYS WE TRAVEL unit).

Garden

Children stick the ends of artificial flowers or Child-Made Flowers into styrofoam pieces, so each will stand by itself. Then, they may arrange the flowers in a garden and pretend to weed it, water it, etc.

Child-Made Flowers
1. Cut out individual cups from egg cartons. Children may paint or decorate them. Add a pipe cleaner for the center and the stem of the flower.
2. Provide cupcake liners. Children add details to make a flower. Put a pipe cleaner through the center of the liner to make the flower center and stem.

Spring Cleaning

Provide old rags for dust rags. Also bring some aprons to tie on the children. Let children pretend to clean the home living center or the room.

Have the children use small amounts of spray window cleaner to clean a window or mirror.

Eggshell Garden

Fill eggshell halves with potting soil. Store them in the bottom half of an egg carton, so they will stand up.

Plant *several* seeds in each shell. Let each child water a plant lightly with a teaspoon. Stick a popsicle stick with a child's name on it in each shell so each child may keep track of how his/her plant is growing.

Plants will grow well in a greenhouse bag. Marigolds grow especially well with this method.

When seedlings have several leaves, transplant outside by gently crushing the eggshells as you place them in the ground.

Tadpoles

Read Steven Kellogg's *The Mysterious Tadpole*. Discuss how tadpoles grow. Bring tadpoles into the classroom. Take pictures of the sequence as the tadpoles change. On a chart, write the date by each picture to show the children how long the sequence takes.

Container Garden

Put stones in the bottom of a large plastic container or tub. Mix soil, some sand, and a little fertilizer. Pour over rocks. Plant carrots, radishes, lettuce, tomatoes, green peppers, strawberries, etc. Plant only one variety of vegetable or fruit in each container. Be sure to mark the container with the name of the contents; marker on a popsicle stick is perfect. Water, give tender loving care, and reap the harvest.

You may do this as a single class project, or the whole school can become involved with their own containers.

Visible Roots

Method 1

Line the inside of a clear glass with a paper towel. Stuff in more paper toweling or a sponge to hold the paper towel around the inside of the glass. Wet the toweling.

Gently place lima beans (which have been soaked in water overnight) between the toweling and the glass, so they are easy to see through the outside of the glass.

Keep the toweling moist. In a few days, the children will be able to see the roots growing. Watch for the first roots (primary roots) and the branchings (secondary roots).

Method 2

Bring in easy to root houseplants. Put cuttings in jars of water. Let the children watch as the "starts" take root. Talk about primary roots and secondary roots, how roots are important to the plants, etc. Then, plant in soil and watch them continue to grow. Spider plants, philodendron, ivy, and coleus all do well rooting in water. Save the plants to use as Mother's Day surprises in May, if children wish.

Butterfly Pattern

Die Pattern

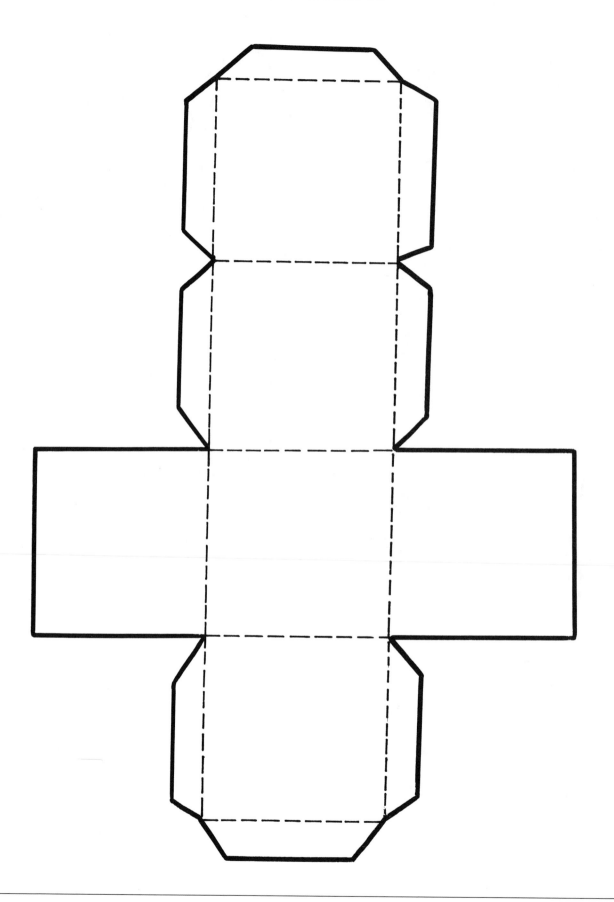

Easy Kite Pattern

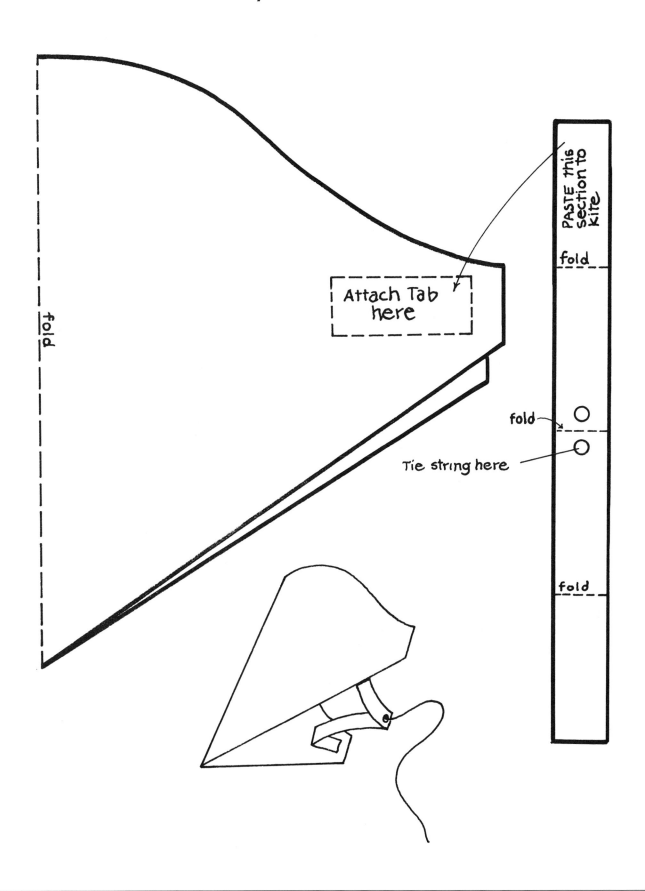

fold

Attach Tab here

PASTE this section to kite

fold

fold

Tie string here

fold

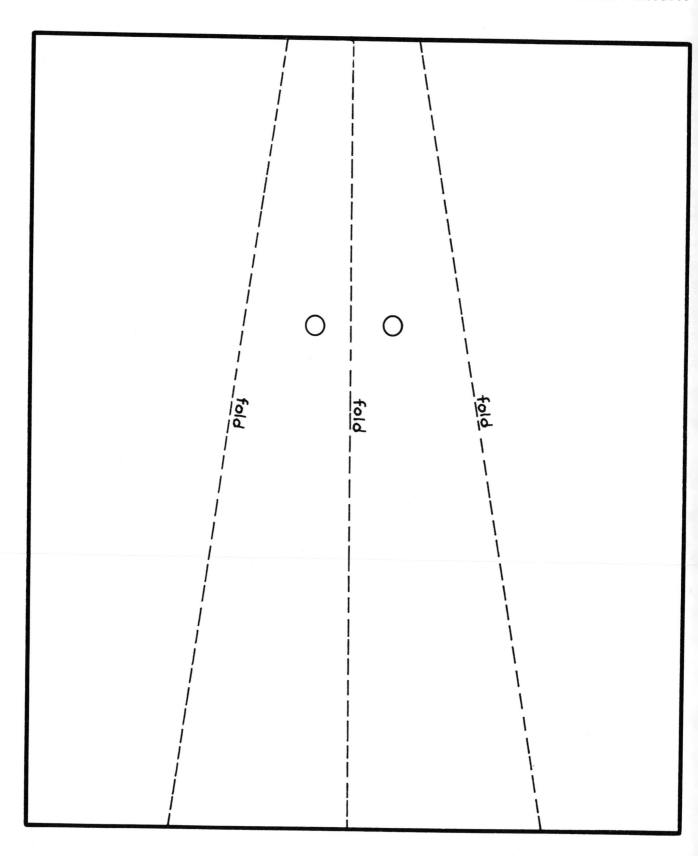

fold

fold

fold

SPRING AND GROWING THINGS

WILD WEST

CONCEPTS

- The "West" is a term that refers to the southwest region of the United States.
- Some people like to wear western clothes, such as jeans, boots, shirts, and cowboy hats.
- In earlier times, people lived, traveled, and dressed differently than most people do today.

ART

Cowboy Hat Mobile

Tagboard hats; dried peas, beans, and lentils; glue; paintbrushes; tempera paint or markers.

You or the children may cut cowboy hats from tagboard. The children paint or color the hat as desired. Then, use a marker to draw lines for the hat band. Using a paintbrush, spread glue, an inch or two at a time, between the lines. The children cover the area with peas, beans, or lentils of their choice. Continue gluing until the band is covered. Allow to dry flat, then dump off excess. Punch a hole in the hat, attach a string, and suspend from the ceiling.

Campfire Flame

Large posterboard or piece of cardboard; orange and red tempera paint; paint-brushes.

Each class needs to paint a campfire for use during lunch on Western Day. You may draw and cut out a large cardboard flame. Cover the table and let the children take turns painting until the flame is covered with paint. Allow one side to dry, then paint the other side. Store in a safe place until Western Day.

Western Crayon Rubs

Posterboard cutouts of simple western objects, such as a cowboy hat, steer, horse, lariat, and boots; old crayons; paper.

The children put one of the cutouts under a paper and rub the outside of the paper with crayons. (The rubbings work best if the crayons are peeled and used on their sides instead of on their points.) Put other cutouts under the paper and rub with a different color to overlap colors and shapes.

Galloping Horse

Posterboard horse pattern, as shown; yarn; glue; pincher-type clothespins; crayons or markers.

Make a simple horse pattern from posterboard, so the children or you can trace it and cut it out. Let the children color it as desired. Punch a hole at the end and tie on a piece of yarn for a tail. Glue some yarn on for a mane, if desired.

Attach two pincher-type clothespins for the horse's legs. By holding the legs and wiggling the front and back of the horse up and down, the children can make the horse appear to gallop. Use the horses during music time to move in rhythm when the class is singing.

Finger Paint with Shaving Cream

Shaving cream; dry tempera paint powder.

Use tabletops. Spray on *small* amounts of shaving cream. Let the children explore moving it around on the tabletop with their hand and fingers (less messy if you encourage children to paint with only one hand and keep one clean). Let them use fingers to "gallop" through the cream. Does it look like animal tracks? Use one finger to draw circles like a western lariat.

Informally discuss how the shaving cream feels and smells. What happens if we sprinkle tempera paint powder on the cream and rub it in?

Clean up by helping each child wipe his/her painting area with a sponge.

BONUS: After this activity, the tables are all clean, and the room will smell very fresh.

Cowboy Hats

9 × 12 inch manila paper; crayons; scissors; glue.

Let the children use crayons to color on the paper any way they wish. Then, cut a semicircle large enough for a head to fit through. Fold the semi-circle up to make the crown of the hat. Round off the corners of the edges.

Paste on a construction paper hat band. Add a real or cut out small feather, if desired.

Spirals

Record player; paper plates; colored markers.

Place the record player where children may safely use it without tripping over the cord. A low tabletop or the floor works best.

Punch a hole in the center of each paper plate. The child puts the plate on the record turntable, turns it on, and gently uses markers of different colors to make spiral designs on the plate. Let the children experiment with various record speeds. Discuss how the shape of their designs is like the pattern made by a whirling lariat.

Western Sponge Painting

Flat sponges cut into simple western shapes, such as boots, cowboy hat, horse, etc.; tempera paint; meat trays or paper plates; manila paper.

Put small amounts of tempera paint on the meat trays or plates. Children dip the sponge shapes into the paint and press them on their paper. To limit the messiness, pinch a clothespin on each sponge before using it. The children use the clothespin as a handle.

Western Scarves

Large triangle for each child, cut from unbleached muslin (very inepensive fabric); markers or fabric crayons.

Let the children decorate their triangle with markers or fabric crayons. Then, show children how to tie their scarves around their neck, western style. They may also tie the scarves on as a face mask. Discuss how cowboys used their scarves to tie over their faces for protection from wind and dust.

Cowboy Me

Butcher paper; markers or crayons; yarn; posterboard hat pattern.

Draw around the children as they take turns laying on a sheet of butcher paper. Let the children use markers and/or crayons to decorate their body shapes to look like a cowboy or cowgirl. Have yarn available for hair. Have the children draw around the hat shape and add the cowboy hat to their person.

Have a mirror available. ''Look in the mirror. What else do you see that you could add to your picture?'' Children will usually add many more details to their Cowboy Me if they are allowed to look in a mirror as they work!

Display idea: Tape the finished projects along one wall. Print a name card under each one to identify the child. Put a brown fence made from butcher paper across the front of all the cowboys and cowgirls to complete the western look.

Horse Finger Puppets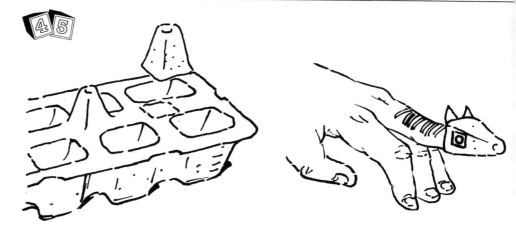

Egg cartons; looseleaf paper hole reinforcements; construction paper; markers or crayons; yarn (optional).

Cut the tall crowns from egg cartons. Have children glue on hole reinforcements for eyes. Add details with markers or crayons for mouth, nose, etc.

The children cut out construction paper ears. Fold up each ear at the bottom and glue it to the horse's head. If desired, glue on yarn strips for a mane.

Children use the horse puppet on the middle finger, so their other fingers can be the horse's "legs."

Patterned Cowboy

Cardboard or posterboard patterns for a shirt, hat, head, boots, jeans, and hands (use Cowboy Pattern at the end of this section); wallpaper sample books; scissors; glue; crayons or markers; construction paper.

Have the children trace around all of the patterns on wallpaper, except the head. Trace the head on construction paper. After they cut out the pieces, have the children glue them together. Add facial features as desired.

BLOCKS

1. Build a corral and a barn in which to keep the cows and horses. To add to the fun, provide animals and other equipment for the children to use in their play.
2. Build a ranch house for the cowboys.

BULLETIN BOARD

Draw several western symbols on tagboard. Paint them, cut them out, and laminate them. Possible symbols include: hat, boots, saddle, brands, lariat. Label the board "Western Ways." Pin the symbols on the board along with the word printed under each object. Use a rope as a border for the bulletin board.

Talk about each item. If possible, bring to class several actual items for the children to touch and handle.

No-Cook Candy Bars

> *Soda crackers*
> *Peanut butter (crunchy is best)*
> *Canned vanilla or chocolate frosting*

Wash hands. Let the children use spreading knives, plastic knives, or spoons to spread a layer of peanut butter and a top layer of frosting on the crackers. Simple to make! Simply delicious, and they do taste like candy bars!

Butter

> *1 pint heavy whipping cream*
> *Clean jar with good sealing lid*
> *¼ teaspoon salt (optional)*

Pour cream into jar and seal tightly. Sit on floor for added safety. Take turns shaking jar until butter forms. (Add a couple of ice cubes to speed up the process.) Perhaps count to ten as a group as each person takes a turn shaking the jar. Watch for and talk about changes inside the jar. Discuss how and why people used to have to make their own butter.

Pour off the residue. Talk about why this residue is called "buttermilk." Taste it. Scrape out the butter. Add salt for flavoring, if desired. Spread butter on soda crackers or baked refrigerator biscuits.

Wild West Baked Beans

> *1 pound dried beans*
> *1½ quarts water*
> *½ cup brown sugar*
> *3/4 teaspoon salt*
> *3/4 teaspoon dry mustard*
> *¼ cup ketchup*
> *Electric frying pan*

Day 1: Show the dried beans to the children. Talk about how cowboys often used beans for food, because dried beans can be stored almost anywhere. Cover the beans with water and let them soak overnight to soften.

Day 2: Examine the softened beans. Let the children help measure and mix together the last four ingredients. Stir the beans and mixture together. Add 2 cups of the water in which the beans soaked. Cook the beans in an electric frying pan at 325° for 4 hours.

LANGUAGE ARTS

Books

Bowman, James Cloyd. *Pecos Bill: The Greatest Cowboy of All Times*. Whitman, 1937.
Gorsline, Marie and Douglas. *Cowboys*. Random House, 1980.
Gorsline, Marie and Douglas. *The Pioneers*. Random House, 1982.
Gorsline, Marie and Douglas. *North American Indians*. Random House, 1978.

Gregory, O.B. *Cowboys*. Rourke Publications, 1982.
Helberg, Kristin. *Cowboys*. Troubador Press, 1982.
Martini, Teri. *Cowboys*. Children's Press, 1981.
Martini, Teri. *Indians*. Children's Press, 1982.
Nework, Peter. *Cowboys*. Bison Book, 1983.
Tinkelman, Murray. *Cowgirl*. Greenwillow, 1984.
Wildsmith, Brian. *Daisy*. Pantheon, 1984.

Teacher Resource Books

Dana, Bill. *Cowboy-English, English-Cowboy*. Ballantine, 1982.
Felton, Harold W. *Cowboy Jamboree: Western Songs and Lore*. Knopf, 1951.
Jeans Companies' Addresses:
    Jordache, 4987th Avenue, New York, NY 10018
    Lee, P.0. Box 2940, Shawnee Mission, KS 66201
    Levi Strauss, Two Embarcadero Center, San Francisco, CA 94106
    Oshkosh B'Gosh, 112 Otter, Oshkosh, WI 54901

Fingerplays

Little Cowpoke

I am a little cowpoke,	
With a horse so tall.	(Hold arm above head and look up.)
But my hat's too big,	(Pull pretend hat down over ears.)
And my boots are too small.	(Walk as if feet hurt.)
I want to rope some cattle,	(Make lasso motion above head.)
But I'm afraid I'll fall!	(Make a scared face, put hand out to catch self.)
So I'll just wait'll next year,	
To ride with y'all!!	(Hold reins and rock back and forth.)

Horses

Visit a ranch or a place with horses. Discuss how horses are saddled and cared for. Discuss what they eat.

Branding

1. Talk with the children about why cowboys used brands. Show them several examples of brands.
2. *Matching*. Draw brands on separate cards. Make a matching set of brands on cards. Mix up the sets and have the children match the brands.
3. The children may make up their own brands. Everyone tries to guess what the brands stand for and what they mean. Each class may make up a "class brand" for the week. Post it on the door. Send messages to office or other classes signed with the brand. Guess which brand belongs to which classroom. For example: Ms. Marshall's class might choose the Rocking M (𝓜) or the Lazy M (⋛).

People Mix-Up

Provide pictures of people dressed as a cowgirl, as a cowboy, and in two or three other dress styles or uniforms. Draw them by hand or cut them from magazines or coloring books. Cut each picture in thirds. Mix up the thirds and put together mixed-up people. Discuss "top," "middle," and "bottom."

Talk about what each person would really wear. For example, "Would a girl really wear a skirt along with her football jersey?"

Candy Bars

Make the No-Cook Candy Bars recipe (see COOKING). Let the class create a name for the candy bar ("Peanut Butter Yum-Yum," "Cracker Bar," etc.). Make a copy of the recipe for each child. Have the children draw a picture of themselves making and/or eating the bars and take the recipe home.

Old West—New West

Find six to eight pictures that show life in earlier days vs. life today. For example: man in Davy Crockett style buckskins, man in today's cowboy jeans and hat; log cabin, modern home; horse and buggy, car.

Discuss with the class that ways of living change. Hold up the pictures and let the children decide whether each picture is the old way or today's way. Most importantly, ask them to explain their ideas. For example, a child may say that buckskins are today's way of dress because he has a leather jacket with fringe on it!

Today's Cowboy

Discuss: "Why do some cowboys still ride horses?" "Why do cowboys dress the way they do?"

Write a Letter to a Jeans Manufacturer

As a class, make up a letter to send to a jeans company asking for free information about how jeans are made. Sign the letter, letting the children add their own names or personal touches as appropriate. Imagine the excitement when the answer arrives in the mail for your class!

After the information arrives, help the class write a story about how they wrote the letter and what materials they got back. Copy the class story for each child to take home and share with her/his parents.

Guest Speaker

Invite a senior citizen to come to class and talk to the children about earlier days and earlier ways. If possible, have some old photographs available to show styles of dress, life, buildings, etc.

This activity has a special plus. So few children live close to their grandparents. It is important to help them have opportunities to learn from older people.

Western Day (Culminating Activity)

Plan a whole day with a western theme. The entire school should be involved to maximize the fun. Everyone dresses western—teachers and administrators included!

Western Day Activities

1. *Steer Roping*
   Outside fun! Make a lariat. Let children practice throwing it at a post or a chair outside. Enjoy the physical coordination as they pretend to rope a steer! Talk about why cowboys and cowgirls have to know how to rope cattle.
2. *Pin the Rider on the Horse*
   Glue three or four magazine pictures of horses on a large posterboard. Cut a boy or girl picture from a catalog for each child in class to use as a rider. Write the child's name and attach a ring of tape to the cutout. Take turns blindfolding each child with a bandana. (Some children may prefer to just close their eyes.) Child turns around, then tries to put the rider on a horse.
3. *Brand the Steer*
   The object and method of play is the same as the above game. Draw a steer on a piece of posterboard. Put an ''X'' where the brand should go. Using a cutout of the class brand, the children try to stick their brand closest to the ''X.''
4. *Jeans Races*
   Have ''sack races'' with children using oversized old jeans to step into instead of sacks.
5. *Boot Mystery Game*
   Using the boot pattern at the front of the April Curriculum guide, cut out three or four construction paper boots. Staple to three upside down paper cups. Hide one ''cowboy critter'' (M&M candy) under one cup. Mix up cups and have the child guess where the ''critter'' is.
   For twos, start easy. Use different colors for boots. Use two cups and mix up only once. *Everyone wins*. Work up to three cups, same color of boots, and mix up several times.
   For three- through five-year-olds use your judgment. Everyone needs to win the first time.
6. *Tug-of-War*
   Play tug-of-war using a pair of oversized jeans. Make a line with masking tape on the floor. Two or three children on each side hold onto one leg of the jean. At a signal, the tugging begins!

WILD WEST

7. *Lunch or Snack Time*

For lunch, eat as the cowboys did on a trail drive. Cook beans. Make corn-bread or biscuits. Have beef jerky, if possible. Each class may contribute a dish to the best of their ability. Serve the meal on foil pie pans and sit around the "campfire," if desired.

To make a campfire, arrange three or four pieces of firewood (from home) in the center of the room. Wedge Campfire Flame (see ART) between the logs. Sit around it for snack and/or lunch.

After lunch, sit around the "fire" to visit and sing songs. This may also be a modeling time during which the children stand up and turn around to show their western clothes.

MATH

NUMBER CONCEPTS

Counting

1. *Pairs*
   Using the boot pattern at the front of the April Curriculum guide, cut several pairs of cowboy boots from wallpaper samples or fabric scraps. Laminate. Count the number of boots. Match the boots in pairs.
2. Count the number of cowboys and cowgirls in the classroom.
3. Count the number of points on a sheriff's badge.

Cowboys and Beans

Draw several simple cowboy figures. Print either numerals (1-5 or more) or dots in sets of 1-5 or more on each cowboy. Provide a bowl of dried beans. Tell the children that the number tells them how many beans the cowboys ate for dinner. Have them place the appropriate number of beans on each cowboy figure.

MATH VOCABULARY

Inch—Foot—Yard

Cut tagboard pieces of 1 inch, 1 foot, and 1 yard. Display the three lengths on the board and cover with a paper. Have the children hide their eyes as you remove one of the pieces. The children take turns guessing which one is missing. Encourage them to use the correct name of each piece. After the children guess the piece, let someone choose an object in the room to measure with the missing piece.

Shapes

1. Have posterboard cutouts of geometric shapes for the children to identify: square, circle, rectangle, triangle, star.
2. *Flag Shapes*
   Observe and discuss the shapes in the United States flag. Use the following terms as you talk with the class: "star," "rectangle," "square," "stripes." Ask the children to find each of those shapes in the flag.

MOVEMENT

Lariat Antics

You need a large lariat for the following activities.
1. The children jump through the loop while you hold it.
2. Lay the rope on the floor. The children jump in and out of the loop with both feet or on one foot.
3. Gallop around the outside of the loop while it is lying on the floor. Gallop to fast western music.
4. Children make a circle around the outside of the rope. All of the children pick up the rope with two hands. While holding onto the rope, do exercises, such as raising rope over heads, bending down to toes, jumping in place, climbing motion, swinging first one leg and then the other in and out of loop. Walk around in a circle while holding onto the rope. (Children may try trotting and faster movements, but you will risk a massive falling down of children.)
5. With the loop on the floor, part of the class steps inside the large loop and walks around in one direction. The rest of the class stays on outside of the loop and walks around in the opposite direction. After they understand the idea, the children may try trotting, skipping, sliding, etc. Use music, if desired.

Horses in the Corral

Mark off a corral area using the rug area, masking tape, or a large rope. Have the children pretend to be horses and stay in the corral while they do the following activities.
1. Gallop in place.
2. Walk on all fours (knees not touching the floor), shaking their pretend mane and tail.
3. Walk on all fours (knees touching the floor), raising the front part of the body and neighing.
4. Spread out and kick up their heels.

Horseshoes

Make a set of posterboard horseshoes.
1. Toss the horseshoes.
2. Follow the horseshoes around the room through an obstacle course.

MUSIC

Get on a Horse
(Circle Game)

(Tune: "She'll Be Coming Round the Mountain")

He'll be galloping through the West when he comes.
He'll be galloping through the West when he comes.
He'll be galloping through the West, he'll be galloping through the West,
He'll be galloping through the West when he comes—Ya hoo!
2. He'll be wearing boots and spurs when he comes—Jingle, jingle!
3. He'll be cooking at a campfire when he comes—Yum, Yum!
4. He'll be lassoing the cattle when he comes—Rope them dogies!

WILD WEST

(Tune: "London Bridge")

(Children all gallop around in a circle as they sing.)
Get on a horse and gallop around, gallop around, gallop around.
Get on a horse and gallop around in our corral.

(Children hold hands with a partner and gallop in a circle.)
Choose a friend and gallop around, gallop around, gallop around.
Choose a friend and gallop around in our corral.

(Children find place and sit down with head resting on arms.)
Gallop back home and lie right down, lie right down, lie right down.
Gallop back home and lie right down in our corral.

Make a Guitar

Bring a shoe box or cigar box. Stretch three to five rubber bands of varying thickness around the box. Gently pluck the bands to make sounds.

Compare this instrument to a guitar. How is it like a guitar? How is it different?

Play this new instrument on Western Day as everyone sits around the campfire to sing songs.

I'm a Cowboy, I'm a Cowgirl

(Tune: "Turkey in the Straw")

(Bend legs at knee, up and down, in rhythm to the song.)
I'm a cowboy, I'm a cowgirl.
I live way out west.
I can ride the wildest horses,   (Gallop.)
And I am the best.   (Put thumbs in armpits; hold chest out
                                        in pride.)

I can rope all of the cattle.   (Swing pretend lariat above head.)
I can brand them every one.   (Lean forward with arm outstretched
                                        as if branding.)

Come out west,   (Beckon with hand.)
And I'll show you how it's done!   (Point to self.)
Dum-diddaley-dum-dum; dum-dum,   (Pat knees in rhythm.)
Ya-hoo!   (Wave pretend hat over head.)

Davy Crockett

Listen to "The Ballad of Davy Crockett" on a record. The local library will probably have a copy. The children will learn the chorus very quickly.

Learn and sing other children's western songs.

WILD WEST

ROLE PLAY

Life in the West

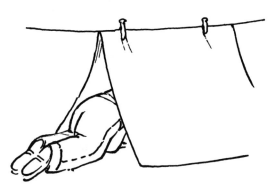

Drape a sheet or blanket over a table or a clothesline. Secure with clothespins and rocks, bricks, or large blocks.

Let two or more children at a time pretend to be camping outside.

Scenes from the West

1. Role play churning butter, building a barn, or saddling a horse.
2. Pretend to be horses or a rider on horseback. Gallop, buck, walk, drink water, neigh, eat hay.

SCIENCE

Cactus

Bring in several cacti to observe. Explain that cacti are a part of the West. Horses, cattle, and cacti live together in the pasture. Talk about how cacti store water in their stems and how the roots of cacti do not grow deep in the soil.

Wear gloves. Cut open one cactus, so the children may see what is inside.

Vibration

Make a ruler sing. Hold a thin ruler (wood, plastic, or metal) so half of it extends over the edge of a table. Bend it down and let it go. Listen as it "hums and sings."

When it moves up and down like that we call it *vibration*. It is moving the air around it, and that's why it makes the noise it does. You may demonstrate vibration further by holding a piece of paper next to a comb and blowing through the comb. Play your shoe box guitar (see MUSIC) and talk about vibration.

Listening for Horses

Have you ever seen a western movie in which the Indian puts an ear to the ground to find out if horses are coming? Sound carries through the ground and through other materials, such as tabletops. Have two children sit at opposite ends of a long table. Let them take turns scratching under the table while the other child puts an ear on the table. Talk about how much louder and clearer the sound becomes when you listen with an ear on the table.

Barbed Wire

Show some samples of barbed wire. Talk about why it is used. Compare different styles of barbed wire with the fence wire commonly used around houses.

May Curriculum

1. Mothers and
   Mother's Day

2. Farm Animals

3. Nursery Rhymes

Mothers and Mother's Day

CONCEPTS

- Mother's Day is a special day to honor mothers.
- Mothers are grown-up girls (women, parents) who have children.
- We have special feelings for mothers.

Caution: If you know that a child does not have a mother in the household, take the opportunity to talk privately with the child before beginning the unit. Depending on the needs of that child, you may elect to avoid a class unit that celebrates just mothers. Consider celebrating ''A Very Special Woman Friend'' day or week in your classroom. Gear activities toward an aunt, grandmother, sister, babysitter, or any significant woman identified by each child.

ART

Mother's Day Cards

9 × 12 inch construction paper; various art materials as indicated.

Fold the construction paper in fourths to make a card shape. Decorate the outside of the cards using one of the following methods.

Sponge or Q-Tip painting
Crayon or marker designs
Hand prints—repeated and overlapped to cover the entire sheet
String painting
Collage of tissue paper pieces

After the outside has dried, open the cards and complete the inside by including a photograph of the child, a poem about mothers, a simple greeting such as ''I love you'' with the child's name under it, or by printing a dictated sentence about mother from the child.

Wrapping Paper

Let the children design their own wrapping paper to add a special touch to a gift they have made. Use a large piece of newsprint. Let the children decorate it using one of the ways suggested for decorating the outside of the Mother's Day Cards (above).

Special Potted Plants

The plant cuttings started in the SPRING AND GROWING THINGS unit or a seedling for an inexpensive flowering plant; small clay pots; fabric scraps; glue; shellac; round toothpicks.

Each child decorates a flowerpot by dipping small fabric scraps in glue and applying to the pot in a collage fashion. Overlap the fabric to cover the entire clay pot. When it's completely dry, the children brush the pot with clear shellac.

Transplant the cuttings into the decorated pot (see SCIENCE section of this unit). To complete the gift, print a message from each child on a small strip of paper. Glue or tape one end of the message to a toothpick and stick it in the soil of the plant, so it stands up like a small flag.

Mother's Day Magnets

2 inch wood trim (8 inch lengths at home center store); gummed stickers; magnetic tape (craft store); clear varnish or shellac; miter box and saw; sandpaper; small paintbrushes.

Cut the wood to a size appropriate for the children to begin working—18 inches is a good length. Mark where the child is to saw, usually 2 inches is enough. Assist, but let the child saw the wood. Then, show the children how to sandpaper and dust off the edges. Next, let the children choose a sticker and apply it to the wood. Cover the table with newspapers and allow the children to varnish the sides and top of their creations. Dry overnight. Cut a ½ inch piece of magnetic tape for the children to apply to the back of the creations to complete the decorative magnets.

This activity is easily expandable to allow the children to make two or three magnets each.

Variations:
1. By choosing appropriate stickers, the children may make magnets for themselves as part of another unit.
2. Make extra magnets to use for counting during math activities.

Glass Picture Frames

Glass furniture coasters; photo of child or a small picture drawn by the child; felt scraps.

The children glue the picture face-up onto the bottom of the outside of the coaster. Then, they glue a felt circle to cover the outside bottom of the coaster, so the picture only shows from the inside.

Wooden Circle Coaster

3 inch wooden circles cut from ¼ inch plywood; light-colored or white latex paint; ric-rac.

Have the children paint one side of the circle. Let dry. Then, have the children paint the other side of the circle. Let dry. Next, glue the ric-rac around the outside edge of each circle.

Use permanent markers to write a message for each child on the coaster.

Table Placemat

Shavings from old crayons; waxed paper; construction paper; iron.

Let the children spread crayon shavings on a piece of waxed paper. Encourage them to spread out the shavings, so all of the colors don't melt together for a muddy effect.

Cover the design with a second piece of waxed paper. You can then press the design with a warm iron to seal the paper and melt the shavings. Glue the design on a piece of construction paper to complete a special placemat for Mother's Day.

Variation: Increase the special effect by placing a small card with a message on it with the crayon shavings before ironing. The note might be a thought from the child, printed by you, to that special person at Mother's Day.

Snowstorm Gift

Clean baby food jar with tight-fitting lid; moth flakes; white glue; small plastic flower or small laminated picture/figure drawn by each child.

The children glue the flower or the picture so it stands up on the inside of the lid. Let it dry overnight.

Then, the children put two to three tablespoons of the moth flakes in each jar and carefully fill it with water. Screw the lid on tightly. Run a bead of white glue around the outside seam of the lid to seal it tightly to the jar. Let it dry overnight.

Shake the jar and turn it upside down to enjoy the snowstorm effect.

Pressed Flower Art

Wild flowers and weeds; waxed paper; construction paper; iron.

Let the children arrange some flowers on a piece of waxed paper. Lay a second piece of waxed paper on top of the arrangement and press overnight under a book or heavy object. You should use a warm iron to seal the waxed paper.

Fold the construction paper in half. Cut a large opening of any shape on the front of the construction paper. Glue or tape the pressed flowers inside the folded paper, so that the opening on the front of the paper becomes a frame for the pressed flowers.

Hanging Hands

12 inch by 6 inch piece of burlap per child; construction paper; 9 inch long dowel rods; fabric glue; yarn.

Demonstrate how to fringe the burlap about ½ inch on all sides except the top. Let the children choose a piece of construction paper and trace around their hand. The children may then cut the handprint out and glue it on the burlap. Also glue on a small printed message: "A Helping Hand." Fold the top edge of the burlap down 1 inch and apply glue along the edge. Hold for a few seconds. When it's dry, put the dowel through the opening. Tie a length of yarn to both ends of the dowel for hanging on the wall or the refrigerator.

MOTHERS AND MOTHERS'S DAY

Trivet Gift

Provide for each child: ten popsicle sticks; six wooden beads; glue; tempera paint, if desired.

Cover a work area with newspapers. Paint the sticks, if desired. Glue five sticks at right angles to the other five sticks to form the lattice pattern shown in the illustration. Glue three beads to both ends of the trivet on the underneath side. The beads provide an air space between the hot item sitting on the trivet and the table surface.

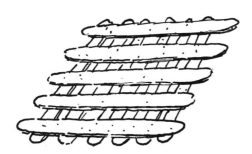

"Mother" Dolls

Toilet paper tubes; small paper cups; wallpaper samples; pipe cleaners; construction paper scraps; yarn; glue.

Let each child glue a paper cup upside down on the toilet paper tube as shown. Cut a piece of wallpaper to glue around the tube like a dress. Add pipe cleaner arms, yarn hair, and facial details as desired.

paper cup —

pipe cleaners —

wallpaper —

tube —

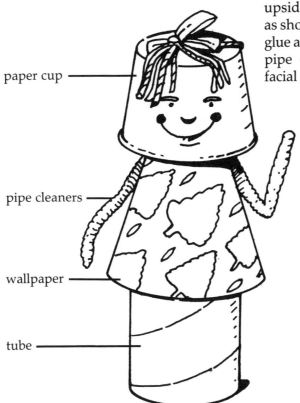

BLOCKS

1. Declare this week Bridge Construction Week. Divide the children into four or five groups. Each day a different group may construct a bridge. If possible, take a photo of each bridge. Display each bridge picture in or near the block area.
2. Encourage the children to construct building areas to represent home, work, and school. Have the children build roads between each building area, so mothers can drive from home to school to work and back again.

BULLETIN BOARD

Here's Mom

Put the caption ''Here's Mom'' on the bulletin board. Take a picture of each child's mother or ask the children to bring a picture of their mother. Display these pictures in the center of large construction paper flowers. Have the children bring a picture of themselves from home and display these along the bottom of the bulletin board. Let the children take turns matching each child with his/her mother by pinning the child's picture in the center of a small flower by the mother's flower.

Variation: Let each child dictate a message for Mom, which you print on another flower. Display these flowers as a border around the bulletin board. Examples: ''I love you''; ''You're special to me''; ''I'll help with the dishes.''

COOKING

Peanut Butter Rolls
(No Cooking)

1½ cups graham crackers—crushed
¼ cup sugar
½ teaspoon cinnamon
½ cup peanut butter
⅓ cup light corn syrup
Powdered sugar
Waxed paper

Stir together first three ingredients. Add peanut butter and syrup and mix well to form a stiff dough. (Mixing with a pastry cutter or hands works well.)

Have children wash hands. Give each child a piece of waxed paper. Place a spoonful of the dough and a teaspoonful of powdered sugar on each paper. Let the children roll the dough into any shape desired. Then, roll the completed shapes in the powdered sugar before eating.

Frozen Bananas

½ banana for each child
Popsicle sticks

Wash hands. Let children peel bananas and cut them in half. Gently push a stick in one end of each banana half.

Spread them on a cookie sheet and put in freezer for one hour or more. After they are frozen, the bananas will keep for a long time if stored in a plastic bag in the freezer.

LANGUAGE ARTS

Books

Alda, Arlene. *Sonya's Mommy Works*. Messner, 1982.
Alexander, Martha. *Nobody Asked Me If I Wanted a Baby Sister*. Dial Press, 1971.
Eastman, P.D. *Are You My Mother?* Random House, 1960.
Howe, James. *The Case of the Missing Mother: Starring Jim Henson's Muppets*. Random House, 1983.
Johnston, Tony. *The Quilt Story*. Putnam, 1985.
Kroll, Steven. *Happy Mother's Day*. Holiday House, 1985.
Lasker, Joe. *Mothers Can Do Anything*. A. Whitman, 1972.
Lewin, Hugh. *Jafta's Mother*. Carolrhoda Books, 1983.
Lorian, Nicole. *A Birthday Present for Mama*. Random House, 1984.
Mitchell, Joyce Slayton. *My Mommy Makes Money*. Little, Brown, 1984.
Mizumura, Kazue. *If I Were a Mother*. Thomas Y. Crowell, 1968.
Moncure, Jane Belk. *Our Mother's Day Book*. Children's Press, 1977.
Polushkin, Maria. *Mama's Secret*. Four Winds Press, 1984.
Schlein, Mirran. *The Way Mothers Are*. Albert Whitman, 1963.
Shannon, George. *Surprise*. Greenwillow Books, 1983.
Shecter, Ben. *The Discontented Mother*. Harcourt Brace Jovanovich, 1980.
Tobias, Tobi. *The Dawdlewalk*. Carolrhoda Books, 1983.
Zolotow, Charlotte. *Say It*. Greenwillow Books, 1980.

Fingerplays

Old Mother Hubbard

Recite ''Old Mother Hubbard'' rhyme with the children.

Mothers Are Special

Mothers are special,
They need a hug from you.
   (Cross arms and hug shoulders.)
They take the time to let us know
That we are special too!
   (Point to self and smile.)

My Mother and Your Mother

My mother and your mother,
  (Close fists with thumbs up.)
Were going on their way.
  (Make fists walk forward.)
"We have to work today."
"Ok!"
  (Fists rush behind back.)

Repeat as above, changing the last two lines as follows:
"Let's go shopping today."
"Ok!"
"Let's take the kids to the park today!"
"Ok!"

Here Are Mother's Knives and Forks

Here are Mother's knives and forks;
  (Interlock fingers, palms up.)
This is Father's table;
  (Interlock fingers, palms down.)
But baby has a special time,
Rocking in a cradle.
  (Interlock fingers and rock back and forth; thumbs and little fingers should be extended.)

This Is a Mom

Hold a group discussion about Mothers.
  Who has a mom who works away from home?
  What kinds of jobs can moms do at home? away from home?
  What do you like to do with your mom?
  What does your mom like to do to have fun?
  What makes your mom sad? angry? happy?

Dreaming of Presents

Prompt children by saying: "Let's have a dream. Dream of special things you would each like to do for your mother or to get for your mother." Talk about the children's dreams.

Mother-Baby Match

1. Match pictures of animal mothers with pictures of their babies.
2. Match pictures of human mothers with pictures of their babies.

My Mother Is...

Let each child talk about his/her mother while you write what is said. If the child is hesitant, ask him/her to finish an idea, such as "My mother is _____ ."
"My mother can _____ ." "My mother says _____ ."

What Do Moms Wear...?

Ask this question, then add several variations. For more involvement, let the children pretend to dress and go to the suggested places.

''What do moms wear when they go to work in an office?''
''What do moms wear when they take you to the park?''
''What do moms wear when they rake the leaves?''
''What do moms wear when they take you to the swimming pool?''
''What do moms wear when they work at home?''
''What do moms wear when they watch TV with you?''

Photographs of Feeling

Collect a set of photographs or pictures from magazines of mothers with and without children. Show the class a picture and have them try to identify the feelings from the facial expressions. ''How do this mother and child feel?'' ''Why does this boy have that look on his face?''

Pass a Face
(Transition Activity)

1. Have the children sit in a straight line or in a circle. The first child makes a face. The second child repeats the first child's face, then makes a different face. The third child repeats the last face, then makes a different face. Continue for all the children. (Encourages observation skills and memory.)
2. As an alternative game, every child repeats the same face as made by the first child. The last child then guesses and tells the feeling shown by the face.

Grandmother/ Grandfather

Invite a grandmother or grandfather to come to class to talk with the children. Perhaps she/he could read a story to the class.

Coupon Book for Mother

What do you do to help your mother?
Trace around each child's hand. Make three to six hands for each child. The children cut them out, punch a hole at the top, and tie them together with a piece of yarn. Write on each hand something the child says he/she can do for Mother or to help Mother. ''I can clear my dishes from the table.'' ''I can empty the trash.'' ''I can fold my own clean socks.''

Classification

Set of pictures of mothers, grandmothers, and children; three 18 inch pieces of thick yarn; 3 labels: ''mothers,'' ''grandmothers,'' ''children.''

The children make a large ring on a tabletop or floor with each of the yarn pieces. Put a label in or beside each ring. Then, let the children classify the set of pictures by placing them in the correct rings.

MOTHERS AND MOTHER'S DAY

"This Is My Mother!"
Booklet

Each child may draw pictures or cut them from a magazine. Pages may include showing a mother at home, at her workplace, or with her child and family. You may add captions dictated by the child.

Tell a Story

Provide pictures of mothers doing a variety of things with and without children. Show the class a picture and ask one child to make up a story by telling what is happening, what will happen next, or what happened just before the picture was taken.

For added interest, record each child's story on a tape recorder. Number the pictures and place them and the tape where children can listen by themselves. Encourage children to rewind the tape and put the pictures back in order.

Visit from a Mother

Invite a mother with a baby to visit the class and show the children how the baby should be held, fed, and perhaps bathed and diapered.

Have two or three jars of baby food for the children to taste. Discuss how it tastes to them.

Discuss what the baby can and cannot do: walk, talk, sit, crawl, cry, laugh, etc.

MATH

NUMBER CONCEPTS

Mom's Children

Laminate a picture of a mother figure. Glue a piece of felt or sandpaper on the back for flannel board usage. Have available pieces of paper with a numeral written on them. As you change the numeral that the mother is holding in her hand, the children may take turns putting that many pictures of children beside the mom on the flannel board.

Variation: The child who is counting the children may walk around the classroom touching the heads and counting the specified number of children. As they are counted, the children stand up.

How Many?

Set out a number of different objects: pencils, pictures, cars, crayons, paper clips, etc. Ask: "How many _____ are there?" Let the children take turns counting the items asked for. Vary the question to include size and color vocabulary. "How many little _____ ?" "How many tall _____ ?" "How many yellow _____ ?"

Let the children take turns asking another child "How many _____ ?"

Jewelry Math

Collect old, discarded pieces of jewelry. Make cards for numerals from 1-10 or more.

Children lay the numeral cards in order. Then, they put a piece of jewelry on each card according to the number of beads or parts on each piece of jewelry.

MATH VOCABULARY

First—Second—Third

Make and laminate one to three 12 × 18 inch poster(s) as shown.

Provide sets of pictures cut from magazines: foods, clothes, toys, etc.

Let the children look at each set and place their first, second, and third choices in each circle.

I would choose these things.

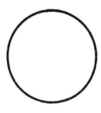  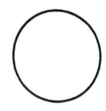

First   Second   Third

Centimeter—Meter

Compare the two measurements. Ask which is long and which is short. Measure several items that the children bring to you. Have children name things in the room that would be close in size to the centimeter or close in size to the meter. Be ready with clues and a meter stick!

MOVEMENT

Mother Says

Play this game just like "Simon Says." For example:

Mother says: make your bed; come to dinner; listen to a story; color a picture; eat a snack; etc. The children act out only the movements that are preceded with "Mother says...."

MOTHERS AND MOTHER'S DAY

Mommy, Mommy

You and the children stand together and do the movements suggested by the verse.

Mommy, Mommy, let's sweep the floor.	(Pretend to sweep.)
Mommy, Mommy, let's go to the store.	(Pretend to drive a car.)
Mommy, Mommy, let's bake a cake.	(Pretend to mix ingredients.)
Mommy, Mommy, let's take a break.	(Wipe brow and whisper, "whew."
Mommy, Mommy, loves me so.	(Draw heart shape in air with two index fingers.)
Mommy, Mommy, watch me grow.	(Stretch arms up high.)
Mommy, Mommy, turn out the light.	(Make "click" sound and turn pretend switch off.)
Mommy, Mommy, say good-night.	(Put hands together beside cheek and tilt head.)

MUSIC

Rock-a-Bye Baby

Have the children sit in a circle on the floor and pretend to cradle and rock a baby as they softly sing the song. Repeat the song and sing even softer as everyone pretends that baby is going to sleep.

What, Oh, What Does Mommy Do?

(Tune: First two lines of "Twinkle, Twinkle Little Star")

What, oh, what does Mommy do?
She holds me when I'm feeling blue.
What, oh, what does Mommy do?
She smiles when I say "I love you!"

ROLE PLAY

Moms

Provide lots of dress-up items so children can dress up as moms. Wigs, jewelry, hats, purses, high-heeled shoes, long skirts, and nightgowns make popular dress-up items.

Include a mirror, so children may observe themselves.

Babies

Have two or more dolls in the home-living area so children can role play taking care of children. Provide several sets of clothes for the dolls, because children *love* to change the dolls' outfits.

Diapers, a plastic baby bottle, and a baby stroller will add to the role play.

SCIENCE

**Cycles of Life/
Human Growth**

Six 3 × 5 inch tagboard cards; magazine pictures: 1) baby, 2) young child, 3) older child, 4) young adult, 5) older adult, 6) senior citizen.

Glue a picture on each card. Explain the life cycle to the class. Let the children sequence the cards and tell a story. More than one order is possible. For example, a child could order the cards to show baby to senior citizen. But a child could also start with the adult picture and tell a story such as ''First, there is a mommy. Then, she has a baby...''

Mother's Day Plants

Plant rootings from SPRING AND GROWING THINGS unit; potting soil; decorated and dried flower pots from ART (in this unit).

Demonstrate how to plant the root cuttings in the newly decorated flower pots. Allow the children to plant a rooted cutting in their pots to take home.

Farm Animals

CONCEPTS

- Farms are places away from cities where people live and raise animals and crops.
- The most common farm animals are horses, cows, chickens, pigs, sheep, dogs, cats, and goats.
- Farm animals make different sounds.
- Most farm animals are fenced in, so they stay in a certain area.
- Farms have special buildings for farm animals. Some of these buildings are barn, shed, coop, and stable.
- Farms produce many of the products we use each day.

ART

Clothespin Animals

2 spring-clip clothespins for each child; stencils of animal shapes for children to draw around or animal body shapes cut out from magazines; construction paper or tagboard.

Simple coloring books are a good source for patterns. For very young children, you may have to cut out the animals. Let children cut off the legs of their animal shapes. Then, glue the animal body shapes on construction paper or tagboard for backing to make it stiff. Children clip two clothespins on the shape to make the four legs of the animal. The animals will stand up by themselves. (Children may color the clothespins, if desired.)

Children love to clip the clothespins on and off numerous times. These creations are also effective for use in farm scenes and play in farm activities.

Grain and Seed Collages

Grains and seeds or wild bird seed; half sheets of construction paper; glue.

Provide an assortment of grains and seeds typical in your area. If necessary, you may purchase inexpensive wild bird seed.

Children glue the seeds on half-sheets of construction paper to make a collage. If desired, draw an outline of a farm animal on the construction paper and use the seeds to fill in the shape.

Corn Cob Painting

Corn cobs; tempera paint; meat trays; manila paper.

Put tempera paint in the meat trays. The children dip corn cobs in the tempera paint and paint designs on the manila paper. Encourage them to use the side of the cob and roll designs. Let the children dip the top of the cob in the paint and discover what designs they can make using only the top.

Dough-Ball Animals

Play dough (see Art Recipes).

Show children how to make an animal from play dough ball shapes.

Children roll play dough into balls of three different sizes. Then, they put an animal shape together by watching you use a large ball for the body, a medium-size ball for the head, and four small balls for the legs. Add small pieces for ears, eyes, nose, mouth, and tail.

Deodorant Bottle Roll-On Painting

Roll-on deodorant bottles; tempera paint; paper; manila paper cutouts of farm animals and buildings (optional).

Clean and save empty roll-on deodorant bottles. Gently pull off the plastic roll-on applicators and fill the bottles with different colors of tempera paint. Tightly replace the plastic applicators.

Let children explore with rolling the paint across large sheets of paper. Encourage them to mix the colors by rolling one color over part of another color on the paper. You may provide large manila paper cutouts of farm animals or buildings for the children to paint.

Textured Crayon Mural

Large piece of butcher paper (for added fun, cut the paper into a barn shape or a farm animal shape); unwrapped crayons; sandpaper; wire screening; nylon net; stencils; popsicle sticks.

Let the whole class take turns putting textures under the paper and rubbing over them with the sides of unwrapped crayons. Some suggestions for interesting textures include: sandpaper, wire screening, stiff nylon net, stencils, and popsicle sticks. Hang the finished mural for all to enjoy.

Pipe Cleaner Animals

Pipe cleaners; scrap construction paper.

To make imaginary animals, twist together colored pipe cleaners. Show children how to bend pipe cleaners into a head shape and how to twist pipe cleaners to make legs and other body parts. Add details with construction paper: eyes, spots, a tail, etc.

FARM ANIMALS

Buttermilk Chalk Picture

Buttermilk that the class made when making butter (see COOKING in WILD WEST unit); colored chalk; construction or manila paper for each child.

Cover the work area with newspapers. The children use cotton balls to dab the buttermilk over part of their paper. They then use chalk of different colors to draw on the buttermilk-moistened areas. (The buttermilk lets the chalk slide more easily over the paper.) Have children dab buttermilk on another part of their paper and continue drawing with the chalk until their picture is complete.

Animal Boxes (Class Project)

Large cardboard box; tempera paint, markers, or crayons.

Use a dark marker to draw a large animal shape on each side of a large cardboard box. Children use tempera paints, crayons, or markers to color in each animal shape. If desired, add a folded paper roof on top of the box, so it looks as if the completed animals are inside a barn or shed.

Display in a corner, out of the traffic area, or in a farm scene area.

Bean Bags

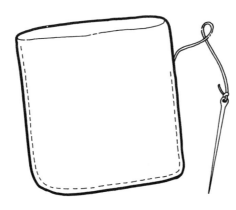

Light-colored fabric that doesn't ravel; crayons or markers; dry beans or rice; sewing machine or needles and thread.

For each child, cut two 3 × 5 inch pieces of the fabric. Sew three sides together as shown and leave the other side open. The children use crayons or markers to decorate their bean bag fabrics.

Pour dry beans or rice in a large plastic bowl. Let children take turns using a ¼ cup measuring cup or a ladle to fill their bag carefully with beans or rice. Sew the bag shut with a sewing machine or show children how to sew using a long running stitch. (Staple the opening to hold it closed while the children are sewing.) Children are surprisingly proud of the bean bag they made "all by themselves."

Bean Bag Animal Toss

2-4 shoe boxes; tempera paint.

In the lid of each box, cut a farm animal shape large enough for a bean bag to go through *easily*. Have the children paint each box and lid a bright color. Dry.

Place the boxes on the floor along a wall, so they won't slide around when bean bags hit them. This location also helps to control where the bean bags fall.

Let children take turns tossing their bean bags at the animal shapes. If desired, they can keep track of the points they make as the bags go in the boxes.

Vary the game by asking children to hit only the first box, hit only the middle box, toss overhanded, toss underhanded, step back two steps, etc. (This activity is great fun and is also good for motor development, eye-hand coordination, vocabulary development, and following directions!)

Farm Animal Sculptures
(Three Day Project)

Play dough (see Art Recipes); Art Bread Dough (see Art Recipes); tempera paint.

1. First day.
   Practice making animal forms. Provide balls of play dough. Show children how to put together different-sized balls of play dough to make an animal shape. (See Dough-Ball Animals in this unit.)
   Encourage the children to change their animal by changing the size of some of the balls or by rolling slightly different shapes to put together. "How many things can you add to your animal to make it different?" Use tiny balls for eyes, spots, tail, ears, stripes, etc.
2. Second day.
   Sculpt farm animals with Bread Dough Recipe (see Art Recipes).
   Let children mold Farm Animal Sculptures from dough they mix themselves. Encourage them to roll balls and put shapes together as they did with the play dough.
   Let the animals dry at room temperature for one or two days, depending on the size of the sculptures.
3. Third day.
   Use tempera paints to paint the Farm Animal Sculptures.

Farm Mural
(Whole Class Project)

Large piece of butcher paper; tempera paint; manila paper.

Spread out the butcher paper on a table or floor covered with a plastic dropcloth or newspapers. Let children paint a background on the paper, making it look like brown ground and blue sky. Let it dry.

Have the children draw and color or paint farm animals on 9 × 12 inch manila paper. Then, they may cut out the animals to glue or tape on the painted background. Add a barn, fence, and other farm buildings if desired.

FARM ANIMALS

Wooly Lambs

Cotton balls; construction paper, manila paper, or tagboard; markers; construction paper scraps; glue; scissors.

Help the children trace around one hand on a piece of construction paper, manila paper, or tagboard. Let them carefully cut out the hand. Then, have them glue cotton balls all over the back of the hand as shown. Add an eye and other details.

BLOCKS

Let the children build fences, farm buildings, etc. Supply farm animals and equipment to enhance the fun of "farming."

BULLETIN BOARD

Display the caption: "Where's My Mother?" on the board. Create a farm scene by adding a barn, silo, house, trees, fences, etc. Draw or trace farm animals on tagboard. Color, laminate, and cut out the figures. Display adult farm animals around the bulletin board. Provide baby animals pinned along the bottom edge of the board or spread out in the farm scene. Let the children take turns using pushpins to pin the baby animal next to the correct adult animal.

FARM ANIMALS

Old-Fashioned Farm Breakfast

Butter

(see recipe in COOKING section of WILD WEST unit)

Syrup

> **1 cup light corn syrup**
> **½ cup brown sugar**
> **½ cup water**
> **½ teaspoon maple flavoring**
> **½ teaspoon vanilla**
> **1 tablespoon butter**

Cook and stir syrup, sugar, and water until the sugar dissolves. Stir in the flavorings and butter. Serve warm.

Farm Pancakes

> **2½ cups sifted flour**
> **2 tablespoons baking powder**
> **1 teaspoon salt**
> **2 tablespoons sugar**
> **2 beaten eggs**
> **1/3 cup salad oil or melted shortening**
> **Griddle or electric frying pan**

Sift together the first four ingredients. Stir in the other ingredients. Stir by hand until moistened. The batter should be lumpy. Cook on a hot griddle or electric frying pan. Makes twenty-four dollar-size or sixteen 4 inch pancakes.

For added fun, carefully pour the batter into the shapes of letters for the initial of the first name of each child. Children love eating their own letter.

Chocolate Milk

> **3/4 cup milk per child**
> **Teaspoon for each child**
> **Chocolate drink mix**

Wash hands. Children sit at table with a spoon and their cup of milk. Pass around the mix and let each child carefully measure out and add to the milk the proper amount of mix for one glass.

Stir well. As children wait for all to finish: 1) Sing ''This Is the Way We Stir Our Milk'' (Tune: ''Mulberry Bush''); 2) Discuss where milk comes from: ''Does milk come from any animal besides a cow?''

Enjoy the drink together when all have finished mixing.

Pigs in a Blanket

Individual recipe:

> *1 refrigerator biscuit*
> *½ hot dog*
> *Waxed paper*

Wash hands. Each child pats out one biscuit on a piece of waxed paper. Then, the children shape their patted-out biscuit around a hot dog. Bake on cookie sheets for 10 minutes at 400°.

Corn on the Cob

> *Fresh corn on the cob, ½ cob per child*
> *Butter*
> *Salt and pepper*
> *Plastic knives*

Purchase corn on the cob at the store or farmers' market. Let the children help and watch as you husk the corn. (Husking corn outside will reduce the cleanup mess.) Cut the cobs in half. Cook in boiling water for five minutes and drain and cool slightly before the children handle it. Provide plastic knives, serve with butter, salt, and pepper to taste.

LANGUAGE ARTS

Books

Bonforte, Lisa, illus. *Farm Animals*. Random House, 1981.
Brown, Margaret. *Big Red Barn*. Addison-Wesley, 1956.
Campbell, Rod. *Baby Animals*. Scholastic, Inc., 1984.
Curran, Eileen. *Hello, Farm Animals*. Troll Associates, 1985.
Dragonwagon, Crescent. *Jemima Remembers*. Macmillan, 1984.
Freedman, Russell. *Farm Babies*. Holiday House, 1981.
Goldsborough, June. *Mother Goose on the Farm*. Western Publications, 1975.
Greeley, Valerie. *Farm Animals*. P. Bedrick Books, 1984.
Helweg, Hans. *Farm Animals*. Random House, 1980.
Hutchins, Pat. *Rosie's Walk*. Macmillan, 1968.
Jacobsen, Karen. *Farm Animals*. Children's Press, 1981.
Kitchen, Bert. *Animal Alphabet*. Dial Books Young, 1984.
Klimo, Kate, ed. *Animals in the Country*. Simon and Schuster, 1982.
Klimo, Kate, ed. *Animals on the Farm*. Simon and Schuster, 1982.
Kuchalla, Susan. *Baby Animals*. Troll Associates, 1982.
Lobel, Arnold. *The Book of Pigericks*. Harper and Row, 1983.
Low, Alice. *All Around the Farm*. Random House, 1984.
Miller, Jane. *The Farm Alphabet Book*. Prentice-Hall, 1983.
Miller, Jane. *Farm Counting Book*. Prentice-Hall, 1983.
Noguere, Suzanne. *Little Raccoon*. Holt, Rinehart and Winston, 1981.
Steele, Mary. *The Crow and Mrs. Gaddy*. Greenwillow Books, 1984.
Stiles, Norman. *Farmer Grover*. Western Publishing, 1977.
Whitehead, Patricia. *Let's Go to the Farm*. Troll Associates, 1985.

Wildsmith, Brian. *Daisy*. Pantheon, 1984.
Williams, Garth, illus. *Baby Farm Animals*. Western Publishing, 1983.

Fingerplays

This Little Pig (Traditional Rhyme)

This little pig went to market.
This little pig stayed home.
This little pig had roast beef.
This little pig had none.
This little pig cried, ''Wee, wee, wee,''
All the way home.

(Using forefinger of one hand, touch thumb and fingers of other hand in sequence.)

This Little Cow

This little cow eats grass.
This little cow chews hay.
This little cow drinks water.
This little cow walks away.
But this little cow says, ''Moo, moo, moo,''
And gives us milk each day.

(Point to or wiggle fingers in sequence.)

Film

''Pigs!'' 11 minutes; color and sound.

No narrative. Funny and fascinating scenes of real piglets exploring a barnyard, eating, and sleeping. Children find it delightful.

Discuss: colors of pigs seen; sounds heard—grunts, oinks, squeals; what does it mean to ''eat like a pig''?

Farmer Puppet

Adapt any puppet to look like a farmer. Have the farmer puppet appear with a bag or basket of animal pictures or plastic animals. Let the puppet tell the children that he/she wants to start his/her own farm. The children must help the farmer decide which animals should go on the farm and which ones should go in a zoo. When the children say an animal belongs on the farm, the farmer asks them what it does on the farm or where it lives.

Silhouette Match

Trace around farm animal cookie cutters on black construction paper. Cut them out to make animal silhouettes. Glue the silhouettes on a folder to make a folder game. Or, just leave them separate, so children can spread them out to work. Provide the original cookie cutters in a small box or bowl. Let the children match each cookie cutter to its silhouette.

Variation: If cookie cutters are not available, you may use tagboard cutouts or magazine pictures of the animals for making and matching the silhouettes.

FARM ANIMALS

Farm Products

Show pictures of eggs, cheese, milk, pork, butter, ice cream, beef, and chicken. Ask the children which animal gives us each of the products.

Farm Rhymes

I go oink, oink. I'm rather big.
I have a curly tail. I am a _____ . (pig)

I make milk. But you can't see how.
I chew green grass. I am a _____ . (cow)

I am fun to ride, of course.
But I also do work. I am a _____ . (horse)

I have some horns and a hairy coat.
When I'm little, I'm a kid. When I'm big, I'm a _____ . (goat)

There's a story about three of us losing our mittens.
When we're big, we're cats. When we're little, we're _____ . (kittens)

Nursery Rhymes

Repeat nursery rhymes that mention farm animals: "Hey Diddle Diddle," "Baa, Baa, Black Sheep," "Old Mother Hubbard," "Mary Had a Little Lamb," "Little Bo-Peep." This is a good circle time or transition time activity.

Vocabulary Development

Stress the names of mother and baby animals:
    chicken—chick
    pig—piglet
    cat—kitten
    goose—gosling
    horse—colt
    cow—calf
    sheep—lamb
    dog—puppy
    duck—duckling
Use pictures of animal adults and babies. Play various games using matching or memory skills, such as Concentration.

Feel Box Game

(See SPRING AND GROWING THINGS unit for directions for making a simple Feel Box.)

Provide a set of small, plastic farm animals, such as those sold in the novelty area of most discount stores. Secretly put one plastic animal inside the Feel Box. Let children take turns feeling and discovering which animal is inside. Repeat the game with a different animal.

---

420   FARM ANIMALS

Crazy Pictures

To encourage oral communication and visual discrimination skills, make a set of crazy farm animals pictures. Use tagboard or index cards. On each card, draw a simple farm animal with an error somewhere in the picture. For example, a horse with whiskers, a pig with a horse's tail, or a lamb with five legs.

Ask children to look at each picture and tell you what is crazy about that picture. Encourage the children to point to the error and to use the proper word for each error.

As an alternative, leave a small part of each animal incomplete. Children also enjoy telling what is missing on each picture.

Animal Memory Game

Provide a set of small, plastic farm animals. Place three animals on a tray. Ask children to look at the animals and try to remember them. Then, place a towel over the tray to remove the animals from view. Ask the children: "What animals do you remember?" After they discuss it, lift the towel to "check" if they were correct.

As the children are successful, gradually increase the number of animals on the tray to four or possibly five at a time. As an alternative, you can remove one or more animals and ask which are missing.

Farm Animal Questions (Transition Activity)

At snack time, or when there is just a minute left, discuss one or more of the following subjects with the children.

"What animals are usually found on a farm?"

"How does a farmer take care of his animals?"

Talk about the dairy products made from cows' milk. Repeat "Baa, Baa, Black Sheep" and talk about getting wool from sheep.

Farm Visit

Take a field trip to a nearby farm. Locate all the animals and name the special buildings found there. Encourage the children to touch animals, when it is safe to do so.

Model of a Farm

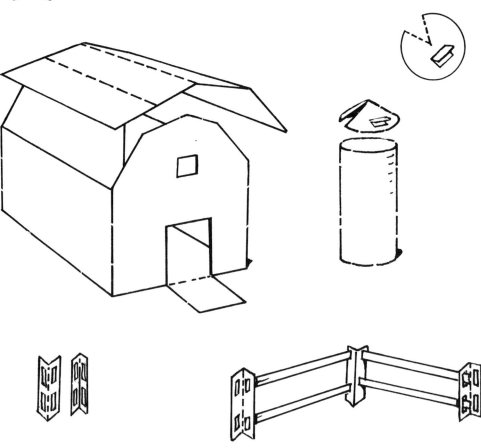

Cut a barn shape from a cardboard box. Cut and fold a rectangle for the roof. Cut out the main front door of the barn and fold it down for a ramp.

Use an oatmeal box for a silo. Cut a triangle wedge out of a circle and tape it together to make a cone-shaped roof for the silo.

Cut strips of cardboard into fence rails and posts as shown. Set up the fence by fitting the rails into the post slots.

Let children paint the farm with tempera paint.

Add hay, plastic farm animals or Slotted Farm Animals (see pattern at end of section), tractors, etc., for increased fun and conversation.

Slotted Farm Animals

Use the pattern at the end of the section to get you started on making some simple slotted animals to stand up in your Model of a Farm. You may also make many other animals in this manner. Slotted animals stand up best when made of posterboard or stiff paper.

FARM ANIMALS

Counting Ears of Corn

Provide precut corn stalks from green construction paper. Lay a large piece of butcher paper on the table. Have the children glue their corn stalk in the farmer's corn field. Tack butcher paper to the wall. Then, give the children small squares of yellow construction paper with corn shapes drawn on them. The children may cut them out.

Have one child glue one ear of corn on a stalk, the next, two ears on another stalk, and so forth according to the ability of the group. If necessary, have several stalks with just one or two ears of corn, so every child has a chance to glue an ear of corn. Print the numeral for the number of ears of corn under each corn stalk.

Eggs-in-a-Basket

Provide five or more plastic eggs in an egg carton and a basket with a handle for carrying. Let the children take turns putting a certain number of eggs in the basket. When they have counted all of the eggs into the basket, the children then count the eggs from the basket back into the carton. Repeat the activity as long as the children continue their interest.

Variation: Have two egg cartons spread apart in the room. Have the children count the correct number of eggs into the basket, then carry them over to place in the second egg carton. Some able learners may talk with you about adding and subtracting eggs from one carton to the other.

The Cows

Here is the barn so big as you see.

(Make a barn shape by extending arms and touching the fingers of both hands to make the pointed roof line.)

In walk the milking cows,
One two three.
Soon there'll be milk for you and me.

(Make a walking motion with two fingers, then hold up 1, 2, 3 fingers.)

Classification

Let the children classify pictures or models of farm animals.
1. Classify them by color.
2. Classify them by the number of legs.
3. Classify them by size.

Barn Match

Make a set of barns and several different farm animals. Print a numeral on each barn. Color dots on each animal. Laminate each, if desired. Store the game in a small box or zip-lock plastic bag. The children spread out the figures and match the animals to the appropriate barn. (Examples on facing page.)

MATH VOCABULARY

Centimeter/Meter

Cut masking tape in centimeter lengths and meter lengths. Stick the pieces of tape on the tabletop, door, wall, floor, or anywhere else where it will show well. Call the children's names, one at a time, and say either "centimeter" or "meter." That child is to stand by or point to the appropriate length of tape at any location available.

MOVEMENT

Farm Animal Music

Choose a farm animal and let the children move like that animal as a record is played. Horses, ducks, cows, and lambs work very well.
Stop the music. Repeat the activity using another farm animal.
For added fun, gallop to the music riding stick horses.

Old McDonald

As the children sing "Old McDonald," two or three children pretend to be an animal mentioned. Take turns and sing enough verses to allow all children to participate.

What Do You Do?

(Add movements as appropriate.)

Oh, what do you do Mr. Bird, Mr. Bird?
  I fly in the sky this way.
Oh, what do you do Mr. Horse, Mr. Horse?
  I run and I trot all the way.
Oh, what do you do Ms. Cow, Ms. Cow?
  I eat green grass all the day.
Oh, what do you do little child, little child?
  I skip and I hop as I play!

Button Drop

Use a muffin tin. Place felt circles in the bottom of each cup (to cushion the noise). Write numerals from 1-5 or more on squares and lay them on top of the felt. Provide buttons. Let the children stand over the muffin tin and try to drop the appropriate number of buttons into each cup.

Variation: Have the children stand back three steps from the muffin tin. Let them try to toss (underhanded) a button into a cup and name the numeral in that cup.

MUSIC

Farm Worker

(Tune: "Yankee Doodle")

I'm a worker on a farm,
Riding on a tractor.
Plowing, working all the day,
To make the crops grow the right way.

Cows and horses, pigs and ducks,
All need their food and water.
Which I gladly bring to them,
To help them grow up healthy.

Other Familiar Songs

"Farmer in the Dell"
"I Know an Old Lady Who Swallowed a Fly"
"Old McDonald Had a Farm"
"Bingo"

Working on the Farm

(Tune: "Mulberry Bush")

We are working on the farm,
On the farm, on the farm.
Oh, we are working on the farm,
So early in the morning.

1. This is the way we feed the cows... (Move as if scooping hay.)
2. This is the way we ride the horse... (Hold pretend reins, move up and down in place.)
3. This is the way we plant the corn... (Take pretend seed from hand, bend over, put in ground.)
4. This is the way we gather eggs... (Put pretend eggs in basket.)
5. This is the way we pet the cats... (Make petting motions.)

    Repeat the chorus to end the song.

ROLE PLAY

Farmer and Animals

Let children take turns being the farmer caring for the animals, feeding them, and putting them in their pens. Put chairs together to make imaginary pens for the animals.

Baby Chicks at Nap Time

At rest time pretend to be baby chicks. Let the children tuck their head under their arm as if it were a wing.

SCIENCE

Hatching Chicks

See SCIENCE section in the EASTER unit for suggestions about hatching fertile chicken eggs.

Dairy Products

Discuss how milk and cream from a cow can be made into so many important products for us to eat.

As you make butter (see COOKING), stop often to view the changes in the cream. Taste the buttermilk.

Share a book (or have someone visit) to explain how cheese is made.

Make a poster or mobile showing all the things made from milk.

Lamb's Wool

Show a piece of wool. Let the children feel and smell it. Ask them which animal gives us wool.

Slotted Farm Animals

Nursery Rhymes

CONCEPTS

- Hearing and/or reciting nursery rhymes enables children to enjoy the humor of the rhymes and expands their oral language.
- Nursery rhymes are an important part of the heritage shared by almost all English-speaking people.
- Rhymes let children play with language and learn that words are fun.

ART

Little Miss Muffet Spider

Small paper plates; black tempera paint; 8 black, ½ inch construction paper strips per child; glue; elastic or elastic thread (optional).

To make the spider's body, each child paints both sides of a paper plate with black tempera paint. Allow to dry. Glue on half an oval piece of paper plate for the head and eight black legs, either flat or accordion-folded strips. For special fun, attach a 6-8 inch piece of narrow elastic or elastic thread so the spider can dangle and dance.

Humpty Dumptys

Large piece of butcher paper; red tempera paint; construction paper; sewing notions and scraps; black marker; newspapers; dropcloth.

Cover a section of the wall with butcher paper—lay papers, old shower curtains, or a dropcloth on floor. Children paint the paper red all over—this may take a while! When it's dry, mark lines with a pencil so a child can follow your lines with a black marker to make a brick effect. Decorate large egg shapes of construction paper with markers, material scraps, etc. Set all eggs on "top" of the "wall."

Clothespin Sheep

Clip-style clothespins; black spray paint; tiny google eyes or sequins; 3 × 4 inch fleece lining; popsicle sticks.

Clip a clothespin at each end of a popsicle stick. Spray paint black. Dry thoroughly. Attach tiny google eyes or sequins on each side of the stick at one end. Cut a piece of fleece lining to cover all but the last half inch of legs, head, and tail. Fold over the stick and glue to make the body.

Old Woman's Shoe

Construction paper; yarn; hair pins; hole punch; magazine or catalog.

Give each child two construction paper shoe patterns with hole-punched edges. Thread the yarn through a hair pin for the children to use as a needle. Demonstrate how to lace the shoe together. Each child may cut out pictures of children from magazines or catalogs to ''live'' inside the shoe.

Baa, Baa, Black Sheep/ Mary Had a Little Lamb/ Little Bo-Peep Sheep

Cotton balls; sheep cutout; markers or crayons; glue; dry black tempera paint powder (optional).

Provide each child with cotton balls and a sheep cutout. The child glues the cotton balls on the sheep. Encourage the children to cover the entire body area. Draw an eye and mouth with a marker or crayon.

Variation: Make a black sheep. Before doing the art activity above, put the cotton balls in a baggie with a spoonful of dry black tempera paint powder and shake well.

Old King Cole Crown

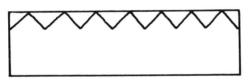

18 × 3 inch construction paper strips; sequins; glue; stapler.

Give each child a strip of paper. Draw lines on each strip as shown, so children will know where to cut.

Each child uses crayons to decorate a crown. Glue sequins on for ''jewels.'' Fit each child's crown to his head size. Staple the ends together.

Mother Hubbard's Cupboard

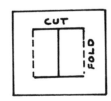

Construction paper; women's magazines; glue.

Cut a piece of construction paper as shown. The paper now has ''cupboard doors'' which will open.

Children make a collage of food items from magazines. Then, glue the cupboard door paper on the collage so children can open the doors to show the food inside.

Mother Hubbard's cupboard will never be bare again!

Blind Mice

Pine cones; pipe cleaners; black string or yarn; construction paper scraps.

   Provide a pine cone for each child. Lay it on its side. Cut one pipe cleaner in fourths. Wedge or twist the pipe cleaner pieces into the pine cone for legs. Glue or tie on a length of yarn for the tail. Add scraps of construction paper for eyes, nose, and mouth. Curl the ends of another pipe cleaner to the center to resemble eyeglasses. Wedge on the pine cones in front of the eyes.

Humpty Dumptys

Eggs; markers; sewing notions.

   Boil eggs in class. When the eggs are cool, have children use markers to make Humpty Dumpty a face and other details. Yarn and material scraps can be added for hair, clothes, and hats.

Jack and Jill

Manila paper; green tissue paper pieces; nut cups; pipe cleaners.

   Each child draws a big hill on manila paper. Cut out the hill and draw a picture of Jack and Jill on it. Glue green tissue paper to cover the remainder of the hill. Bend and poke a half of a pipe cleaner through each side of the nut cup to resemble a pail. Glue the "pail" on its side to the bottom edge of the hill cutout.

Wee Willie Winkie Nightcaps

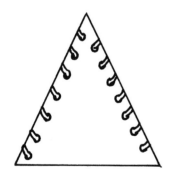

Construction paper; yarn, with bobby pins for needles; hole punch; markers or construction paper scraps.

   Give each child two construction paper triangles. The triangle should be large enough to fit on a child's head like a hat. Children hole-punch the edges and use yarn to lace the triangles together. Decorate the hats using crayons, markers, or construction paper scraps.
   The caps could be made from fabric scraps for a longer lasting nightcap.

Unfinished Rhymes

Construction paper; markers, crayons, or chalk.

   Write an unfinished nursery rhyme at the top of each child's paper. Children then draw pictures to finish the rhyme.

    Hickory dickory dock,   Little Bo-Peep
    The mouse ran up the _____ .   Has lost her _____ .

NURSERY RHYMES

BLOCKS

1. Encourage the children to build the castle that Old King Cole lived in.
2. Little Bo-Peep lost her sheep. Build a pen to keep them safely in. Provide plastic, wooden, or stand-up paper cutouts of sheep to add to the play.
3. Bring stuffed bears and a doll. Build a house for Goldilocks and the Three Bears.
4. During cleanup time, recite "One, Two, Buckle My Shoe." Count the blocks and "lay them straight" as the children put the blocks away.

BULLETIN BOARD

Twinkle, Twinkle, Little Star

Print the nursery rhyme on a large paper to put in the center of the board under the caption "Twinkle, Twinkle, Little Star." Cut the paper to look like a cloud.

Ask children to bring pictures of themselves to school, or take a snapshot of each child. Put each picture on a foil or construction paper cutout of a star. Place the "stars" all around the copy of the nursery rhyme on the bulletin board.

Hey, Diddle, Diddle— A Moving Picture

Print the nursery rhyme on a large paper to put in the center of the board under the caption "Hey, Diddle, Diddle." Make large cutouts of a moon, a cat with a fiddle, a cow, a dog, and a dish and a spoon. Position them appropriately on the bulletin board. Then, staple a piece of yarn or elastic from the moon down to the cow. Tape a 1 × ½ inch paper strip into a loop on the back of the cow and through the yarn piece, so the cow may slide up and down the yarn to "jump over the moon." For more movement, attach additional paper loops and yarn pieces to make the fiddle bow move and to make the dish and spoon move along a pathway.

COOKING

**Humpty Dumpty
Scrambled Eggs**

*Paper cup and a spoon or fork for each child
1 egg for each child
1 tablespoon milk
Pinch of salt*

Have each child crack one egg and pour it into paper cup. Add milk and salt. Stir together. Cook individually or all together.

For extra fun, save the pieces of eggshell. Each child tries to put "Humpty Dumpty" together again.

**Miss Muffet Curds
and Whey**

(Children never know what curds and whey are when they recite "Little Miss Muffet." Make some together and give them a try.)

*2 cups **whole** milk
1 tablespoon vinegar*

Stir milk over medium heat until it starts to bubble. Remove from heat. Add vinegar and continue stirring until curds form. Strain off the whey, squeezing out all of the extra with a spoon. Add a touch of salt. Serve on plain crackers.

**Little Boy Blue
Haystacks**

*One 3 ounce can chow mein noodles
One 6 ounce package butterscotch morsels
2 tablespoons peanut butter
Electric skillet*

Melt the butterscotch morsels and peanut butter together in an electric skillet on a low heat setting. Stir in noodles. Mix until well coated. Drop by teaspoons on waxed paper. Set in a cool place to harden. Makes twenty to thirty small haystacks.

Banana Rolls

*Chocolate syrup
½ banana per child
Peanuts*

Wash hands. Let the children help chop the nuts. Then, let each child use a table knife to slice a half banana. Let them dip the banana slices in chocolate and roll each slice in the chopped nuts.

LANGUAGE ARTS

Books

Aragon, Hilda. *My First Nursery Rhyme Book*. Pueblo Acoma Press, 1981.
Cauley, Lorinda Bryan. *The Three Little Kittens*. Putnam, 1982.

Chorao, Kay. *The Baby Lap Book*. Dutton, 1977.

De Paola, Tomie. *The Comic Adventure of Old Mother Hubbard and Her Dog*. Harcourt Brace Jovanovich, 1981.

Howard, Nina. *Barber, Barber, Shave a Pig*. Children Learn Cr., 1981.

Ireson, Barbara. *The Faber Book of Nursery Verse*. Faber & Faber, 1982.

Marshak, Samuel & David Harms. *The Merry Starlings*. Harper and Row, 1983.

Moorat, Joseph. *Thirty Old-Time Nursery Songs*. Metropolitan Museum of Art, 1980.

Mother Goose. *Mother Goose*. Random House, 1984.

Mother Goose. *Mother Goose: A Collection of Classic Nursery Rhymes*. Holt, Rinehart and Winston, 1984.

Patience, John. *The Land of Nursery Rhymes*. Derrydale, 1984.

Potter, Beatrix. *Beatrix Potter's Nursery Rhyme Book*. Warne, 1984.

Scott, Louise B. *Rhymes for Learning Times*. Denison, 1984.

Smollin, Michael J. *The Sesame Street Players Present Mother Goose*. Random House, 1982.

Stevens, Janet. *The House That Jack Built*. Holiday House, 1985.

Stobbs, William. *One, Two, Buckle My Shoe*. Bodley Head, 1984.

Wolff, Ashley. *The Bells of London*. Dodd, Mead, 1985.

Fingerplays

Nursery Rhymes

Let the children help you decide fingerplay actions to add to nursery rhymes as you recite them together.

Vocabulary Concepts

Nursery rhymes offer valuable opportunities to reinforce children's understanding of words that denote position and placement. These are especially important words, because they are frequently used when adults are giving directions for children to follow. Some of the position words you may reinforce through nursery rhymes are listed below. Adding gestures and actions to these words as children recite the rhyme will provide fun and increase understanding.

"Little Miss Muffet": on; beside; away
"Peter, Peter Pumpkin Eater": in
"Hey Diddle, Diddle": over; away
"Jack and Jill": up; down; after
"Wee Willie Winkie": through; upstairs; downstairs
"Little Boy Blue": in; under
"Little Bo-Peep": alone; behind
"Hickory Dickory Dock": up; down

Name That Rhyme

You name an animal or object from a familiar rhyme. Examples include: sheep, haystack, spider, candlestick. The children try to guess the rhyme and recite it. You may prompt, if necessary.

Nap Time Version of Wee Willie Winkie

Wee Willie Winkie runs through the town,
Upstairs and downstairs in his lunch-gown;
Rapping at the window, crying through the lock,
"Are the children ready to rest?
It's after twelve o'clock."

(If more appropriate, change last lines to:

"Are the children ready to rest?
It's almost twelve o'clock.")

Humpty Dumpty Double-Sided Stick Puppet

5 × 7 inch plain index card; popsicle stick; markers; eggshells.

Draw a wall on each side of the card. On one side draw Humpty Dumpty sitting on the wall. On the other side, glue eggshells along the bottom of the card. Glue or staple on the stick.

Show the Humpty Dumpty side as you begin to recite the rhyme. Flip the card around to show the other side as you recite the end of the rhyme.

Hickory Dickory Dock

Make the mouse run up the clock! Give each child a copy of the pattern at the end of this section. Color it, if desired. Cut off the bottom of the handout as marked. Cut out (or around) the mouse. Use a pencil point or a hole punch to punch a hole in the black circle at the top of the clock and on the mouse's nose.

Put one end of a 6-8 inch piece of string or yarn through the mouse's nose and tape it to the back of its face. Put the other end of the string through the hole in the clock. Leave it loose. Gently, slowly pull the string to make the mouse move up the clock as you all recite the rhyme.

Rhyming Words

Recite rhymes most familiar to the children. After a rhyme is well known, leave off the last rhyming word of the verse for the children to say.

Picture the Nursery Rhyme

Duplicate the pattern at the end of this section so that there is a copy for each child. Cut the four pictures apart. Glue each picture on a posterboard piece, if desired.
1. *Picture Matching*
   Hold up one picture. Each child holds up the copy of the same scene.
2. *Reciting*
   Recite a verse. Each child holds up the picture that goes with that verse.
3. *Rhyme Ring*
   Provide a metal or plastic reclosable ring for each child. Hole punch the top left corner of one set of pictures. Put the pictures on the ring for the child to carry around and say each verse.

NURSERY RHYMES

Hickory Dickory Clock

Use a working alarm clock or kitchen timer that ticks. Set the alarm to go off in 2-4 minutes. While the children turn their backs or put their heads down, hide the clock. The children then get to be silent "mice" trying to find the clock by its ticking before the alarm sounds.

Bo-Peep Rhymes

Recite "Little Bo-Peep." Use the verse to encourage other rhyming combinations. The following examples are starters.

Little Bo-Porse has lost her _____ . (horse)
Little Bo-Pen has lost her _____ . (hen)
Little Bo-Pow has lost her _____ . (cow)
Little Bo-Pat has lost her _____ . (cat)

Cookie-Sheet Magnetic Rhymes

Use coloring books and magazines to find pictures for the characters in several nursery rhymes. For example:

Little girl + sheep = "Little Bo-Peep" or "Mary Had a Little Lamb";
Woman + shoe + children = "Old Woman Who Lived in a Shoe";
Horn + hay + cow + sheep = "Little Boy Blue."

Attach a paper clip to each character. Lay them on a metal cookie sheet. Moving a magnet under the cookie sheet makes the character "move." Let children take turns making the characters move as the rhyme is recited.

Mother Hubbard's Cupboard Game

Discuss "cupboard." What do we usually call it?

The children sit in a circle. Take turns going around the circle, letting children say things to put in Mother Hubbard's cupboard. Encourage them to think about things that really belong in a cupboard: "Would milk go in a cupboard?" Children's examples during the game might be as follows:

"I will put in cereal"; "I will put in cans of beans"; etc.

Later, change the game, so it stresses oral sequence memory. Every child must repeat what has been put in the cupboard before he/she adds another thing.

1st: "I will put in potatoes."
2nd: "I will put in potatoes and canned fruit."
3rd: "I will put in potatoes, canned fruit, and chips," etc.

Blind Mice

Discuss: What does it mean to be "blind"?
What would be hard/easy to do if you were blind?
How would it feel?

Use scarves or long scraps of fabric scraps to blindfold half the class. Have seeing children lead blinded children gently around the room. Encourage them to move slowly and help each other.

Change roles. The seeing children put on the blindfolds and are led around by their partners.

Discuss how the children felt when they could not see where they were going.

Choral Speaking

Arrange a rhyme, so the children can try choral speaking. It's great practice at recitation and taking turns! You can divide any rhyme in many ways. Here are two examples. (Help the children to add some actions to the verse.)

Two Groups
#1: Hey, Diddle, Diddle, the cat and the fiddle,
#2: The cow jumped over the moon.
#1: The little dog laughed to see such sport,
#2: And the dish ran away with the spoon.

Three Groups
#1: Humpty Dumpty sat on a wall.
#2: Humpty Dumpty had a great fall.
#3: All the king's horses and all the king's men
All: Couldn't put Humpty Dumpty together again!

Choral speaking "sounds" neat. Have the class perform for another class. Serve snacks together for a party flair. (Also great for parent night!) You might want to record the choral speaking on a tape recorder, so the children may play it back later to hear themselves.

Doggie Bone Game

Recite "Old Mother Hubbard" and play this game. Children love it and it is very effective in calming down activity levels.

Bring a real bone or pick something to designate as the "bone." One child is the doggie. She/he sits alone with her/his back to the rest of the class. The rest of the class sits in a line behind her/him a few feet. Place the bone right behind the "doggie."

You silently point to one child in the line, who then tries to sneak up and steal the bone without the doggie hearing. If the doggie hears, she/he barks and the child must sit down. If the child is successful in stealing the bone, the group says: "Doggie, doggie, where's your bone?" The doggie then tries to guess who is hiding the bone. Pick a new doggie and repeat the game.

MATH
NUMBER CONCEPTS

Flannel Board Shoe

Make a large shoe shape from flannel or felt. Make children from felt. Or, simply use pictures cut from magazines with a piece of felt, velcro, or sandpaper glued on the back of each, so it will "stick" to the flannel board. Then, let the class count the number of children as you place them in or on the shoe.

Flannel Board "Bo-Peep"

Use sheep cut from nonwoven interfacing or white flannel. Put one sheep at a time on a flannel board. The children count as the sheep are put on the board. Children may take turns counting the sheep over and over.

Children in a Shoe

    Provide a collection of old shoes and a set of small toy children. Tape a numeral on each shoe. Have the children put the correct number of toy children inside each shoe.

Eggs in a Dozen

    Provide an egg carton and a set of plastic eggs. Let the children determine how many eggs will fit in the carton by filling it with the plastic eggs. Use the word ''dozen.''

Clocks

    Together, touch and count the numerals on a real clock. Provide a clock puzzle. Have the children put the clock together, so the numerals are in the correct order. Ask them to check the puzzle by comparing it with the real clock.

MATH VOCABULARY

Long—Short

    Provide old shoes and boots to lace. Have both *long* and *short* shoelaces. Talk about which are long and which are short. Let the children decide which length to use in each shoe or boot.

Measurement: Centimeter/Meter

1. Measure the castle made during block time.
2. Measure a real fiddle and bow.
3. Provide real bones to measure for Old Mother Hubbard.

MOVEMENT

Blind Mice Walk the Line

    Blindfold the children, or have them cover their eyes if they do not want to be blindfolded. Lay a rope on the floor in a straight or zigzag pattern, depending on the abilities of the children.

    For added fun, make mouse ears headbands during craft time. Cut 1 × 18 inch strips of paper. Cut black or gray mouse ears from construction paper. Staple the ears to the headband. Staple each headband to fit each child. Mouse tails can be made of 18 inch construction paper strips ½ inch wide, taped to clothes.

Jack Be Nimble

    Children jump over a rope or a block on the floor. Cut a cardboard candle out and tape it to a block, so the candle stands up. Let ''Jacks'' jump over. Vary difficulty according to age of group. Discuss why it would not be smart to jump over a real burning candle!

Winkie Jog

Jog in place while reciting "Wee Willie Winkie." Bend forward as you jog to pretend to go downstairs. Bend back as you jog to pretend to go upstairs.

Humpty Dumpty Rock

Have the children sit on the floor. Show them how to make themselves into an egg shape by tucking their heads down, putting their knees up, and putting their arms around their knees. Rock back and forth in place.

MUSIC

Nursery Rhyme

You may sing the words to "Old King Cole," "Little Boy Blue," "Baa, Baa Black Sheep," or "Humpty Dumpty" to the tune "Skip to My Lou" by repeating some lines. One example follows:

Old King Cole was a merry old soul,
Old King Cole was a merry old soul,
Old King Cole was a merry old soul,
    And a merry old soul was he.

He called for his pipe and he called for his bowl,
He called for his pipe and he called for his bowl,
He called for his pipe and he called for his bowl,
    And he called for his fiddlers three!

Singing Familiar Songs

Sing some of the children's favorite songs that mention nursery rhyme characters, such as "Three Blind Mice."

ROLE PLAY

Nursery Rhyme Theater

Choose character parts and act out nursery rhymes. Discuss what to do to act like a certain character. Show them how to walk in place, etc.

Nursery Rhyme Box

Provide a large cardboard box. The children paint a big pumpkin on one side and a large boot or shoe on the opposite side.

Turn the box so the pumpkin shows for "Peter, Peter Pumpkin Eater." Let a child get into the box at the appropriate time in the verse. Turn the box so the shoe side shows for "Old Woman Who Lived in a Shoe." Let two or three children get in the box at the appropriate time in the verse.

NURSERY RHYMES

Three Little Pigs

Provide straw, sticks, and a brick for props. Add hats to be worn by the three pigs and by the people who sell the straw, sticks, and bricks. Encourage the children to decide how the pigs can pay for each purchase.

Old King Cole

Provide crowns, capes, pipes, bowls, and an old fiddle (if possible) to enable children to dress up as kings and act out the Old King Cole nursery rhyme.

SCIENCE

Hard Boiled Eggs

"What happened to Humpty Dumpty when he fell?" "What would happen to a real egg if you dropped it?" Discuss and demonstrate how to make hard boiled eggs.

"What would happen if you dropped a hard boiled egg?" Try to spin a fresh egg and a hard boiled egg on one end. "Which one spins?" Cut a hard boiled egg in half. Talk about the white and the yolk. Talk about their shapes.

Insects and Spiders

Ask children to bring in pictures from magazines of insects and spiders. (*National Geographic* has fantastic pictures for this purpose.) Discuss how they are alike and how they are different. Count the number of legs on several insects and spiders. Have the class dictate a story about what they discover.

Jack and Jill's Well

Show pictures of wells. Discuss how people got water before we had faucets and running water in our homes.

Demonstrate the principle of how a well worked.

Deep bowl or bucket; paper cup; 12 inch string or yarn; dowel rod or stick (long enough to rest across top rims of bowl).

1. Punch a hole in the top of the cup. Tie one end of the string to the cup through the hole. Tie the other end of the string to the dowel rod.
2. Put some water in the bottom of the bowl.
3. Rest the rod across the top rim of the bowl.
4. Lower the cup into the water and raise the cup with water by turning the rod, thus winding or unwinding the string on the rod.

Fur

Provide some samples of synthetic fur and real animal fur. Provide a magnifying glass. Have the children feel, smell, and visually examine the furs. Discuss how they are alike and how they are different. Later, let children classify the furs: animal fur; not animal fur. List together all the animals that have fur mentioned in nursery rhymes.

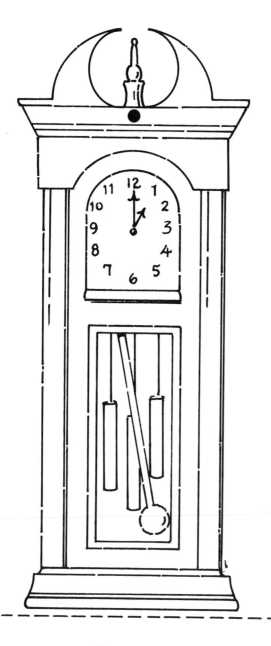

HICKORY DICKORY DOCK

HICKORY DICKORY DOCK.
THE MOUSE RAN UP THE CLOCK,
THE CLOCK STRUCK ONE,
THE MOUSE RAN DOWN!
HICKORY DICKORY DOCK.

CUT HERE

NURSERY RHYMES

Picture the Nursery Rhyme

Nursery Rhymes

Humpty Dumpty
Humpty Dumpty sat on a wall.
Humpty Dumpty had a great fall.
All the king's horses and all the king's men
Couldn't put Humpty Dumpty together again!

Peter, Peter Pumpkin Eater
Peter, Peter Pumpkin Eater,
Had a wife and couldn't keep her.
He put her in a pumpkin shell,
And there he kept her very well.

Little Miss Muffet
Little Miss Muffet
Sat on a tuffet
Eating her curds and whey.
Along came a spider
Who sat down beside her
And frightened Miss Muffet away!

Hey, Diddle, Diddle
Hey, Diddle, Diddle,
The cat and the fiddle,
The cow jumped over the moon.
The little dog laughed
To see such sport,
And the dish ran away with the spoon.

Jack and Jill
Jack and Jill
Went up the hill
To fetch a pail of water.
Jack fell down
And broke his crown
And Jill came tumbling after.

Wee Willie Winkie
Wee Willie Winkie runs through the town,
Upstairs and downstairs in his nightgown;
Rapping at the window, crying through the lock,
''Are the children all in bed, for now it's eight o'clock?''

From *We Care*, Copyright © 1988 Scott, Foresman and Company.

Baa, Baa, Black Sheep
Baa, baa, black sheep,
Have you any wool?
Yes, sir, yes, sir,
Three bags full.
One for my master,
And one for my dame,
And one for the little boy
Who lives down the lane.

Old Mother Hubbard
Old Mother Hubbard
Went to the cupboard
To fetch her poor dog a bone.
But when she got there,
The cupboard was bare.
And so the poor dog had none.

The Old Woman Who Lived in a Shoe
There was an old woman who lived in a shoe.
She had so many children she didn't know what to do.
She gave them some broth without any bread.
She whipped them all soundly and put them to bed.

Little Boy Blue
Little Boy Blue, come blow your horn.
The sheep's in the meadow; the cow's in the corn.
Where is the boy who looks after the sheep?
He's under the haystack fast asleep.
Will you wake him? No, not I!
For if I do, he's sure to cry.

Three Blind Mice
Three blind mice, three blind mice,
See how they run, see how they run!
They all ran after the farmer's wife,
Who cut off their tails with a carving knife.
Did you ever see such a sight in your life,
As three blind mice?

Mary Had a Little Lamb
Mary had a little lamb; its fleece was white as snow.
And everywhere that Mary went, the lamb was sure to go.
It followed her to school one day: That was against the rule.
It made the children laugh and play to see a lamb at school!

NURSERY RHYMES

From *We Care*, Copyright © 1988 Scott, Foresman and Company.

Little Bo-Peep
Little Bo-Peep has lost her sheep
And doesn't know where to find them.
Leave them alone and they'll come home
Wagging their tails behind them.

Old King Cole
Old King Cole
Was a merry old soul,
And a merry old soul was he.
He called for his pipe,
And he called for his bowl,
And he called for his fiddlers three!

Twinkle, Twinkle, Little Star
Twinkle, twinkle, little star;
How I wonder what you are!
Up above the world so high,
Like a diamond in the sky.

Hickory Dickory Dock
Hickory dickory dock.
The mouse ran up the clock.
The clock struck one;
The mouse ran down!
Hickory dickory dock.